lonely planet

Madagascar

Northern
Madagascar
p122

Western
Madagascar
p100

Eastern
Madagascar
p158

Antananarivo
p28

Central
Madagascar
p48

Southern
Madagascar
p73

D0064423

THIS EDITION WRITTEN AND RESEARCHED BY

Emilie Filou, Anthony Ham, Helen Ranger

Contents

NOSY BE P123

PARC NATIONAL DES
TSINGY DE BEMARAHA P111

Contents

UNDERSTAND

SURVIVAL GUIDE

SPECIAL FEATURES

Welcome to Madagascar

Lemurs, baobabs, rainforest, desert, hiking and diving: Madagascar is a dream destination for outdoors lovers – and half the fun is getting to all these incredible attractions.

Wild World

Madagascar is unique: 5% of all known animal and plant species can be found here, and here alone. The island's signature animal is the lemur of course, but there are many more weird and wonderful creatures: the eerie-looking fossa (a cat-like predator), colourful and camouflaged chameleons, oddly shaped insects, vivid frogs, graceful rays and turtles, several species of sharks, and humpback whales during the winter months. Trees and plants are just as impressive, be they the distinctively shaped baobabs, the fanning *ravinala* (travellers' palm), the hundreds of orchids or the spiny forests of the desert south.

Epic Landscapes

The remarkable fauna and flora is matched by epic landscapes of an incredible diversity: you can go from rainforest to desert in just 300km. Few places on earth offer such an intense kaleidoscope of nature. There are sandstone canyons, limestone karsts, mountains, fertile hills cascading with terraced rice paddies, forests of every kind – rain, dry, spiny – and a laterite-rich soil that gave the country its nickname of 'Red Island'. With 5000km of coastline, the sea is never very far away, turquoise and idyllic in some places, dangerous in others.

Island Adventures

Making the best of Madagascar can be challenging (and expensive): it is the world's fourth-largest island and its roads are dismal. For those who relish an adventure, however, this is a one-of-a-kind destination: the off-road driving is phenomenal, and there are national parks that only see a few hundred visitors a year, regions that live in autarky during the rainy season and resorts so remote you'll need a private plane or boat to get there. There are also more activities than you'll have time for: hiking, diving, mountain biking, kitesurfing, rock-climbing, you name it. Oh, and there are plenty of natural pools, beaches and hammocks on which to recover, too.

Cultural Insights

Madagascar has been populated by successive waves of migrants from various corners of the Indian Ocean. This cultural melting pot has evolved into an intricate set of beliefs and rituals that revere ancestors' spirits. For travellers, attending a *famadihana* (traditional exhumation and reburial when relatives can communicate with their forebears) can be the highlight of a trip. There is much history to discover, too, from Antananarivo's sacred hills to the pirate history of Île Sainte Marie.

Why I Love Madagascar

By Emilie Filou, Writer

Madagascar is unlike anywhere else I have been to – fantastically beautiful, amazingly diverse for its size (similar to France) and still so unspoilt. Vast tracts of the country are virtually uninhabited and seldom explored, and nothing comes easy. But that's what makes it so unique and rewarding. Plus the fact that after a day of bumping around in a dusty 4WD, or fighting off leeches on muddy trails, you can be served a meal worthy of a fine European restaurant, capped with exquisite rum – that's definitely my kind of travel!

For more about our writers, see page 288

Above: Allée des Baobabs (p119)

Madagascar

Parc National de Marojejy
Hike in pristine rainforest (p155)

Travel the infamous RN5
Classic 4WD adventure (p177)

Nosy Be
Dive, snorkel, sail and explore (p123)

Tsingy de Bemaraha
Scale surreal limestone

MOZAMBIQUE

COMOROS

Grande Comore
Mohéli
Anjouan
Mayotte

Mozambique Channel

15°S

45°E

50°E

15°S

200 km
100 miles

Cap d'Ambre

Diego Suarez (Antsiranana)

Parc National Montagne d'Ambre

Réserve Spéciale Ankarana

Ambilobe

Vohémar (Iharana)

Ambodibonara
Hell-Ville Nosy Be
Ankify
Ambanja
RN6

Tsaratanana Massif

Maromokotro (2876m)

Béalanana

Marojejy Massif

Parc National de Marojejy

Sambava

Andapa

Antalaha

Cap Est

Masoala Peninsula

Parc National de Masoala

Maroantsetra

Nosy Mangabe

Antsohihy

Mandritsara

RN6

Borizny (Port Bergé)

Parc National d'Ankarafantsika

Ambondromamy

Soanierana-Ivongo

RN5

Mananara

Parc National de Mananare-Nord

Île Sainte Marie (Nosy Boraha)
Ambodifotatra

Mahambo

Tamatave

Mahajamba River

Softa River

Katsepy
Soalala
Majunga (Mahajanga)

Marovoay

RN4

Lac Kinkony

Besalampy

Parc National des Tsingy de Namoroka

Maevatanana

Betsiboka River

Mahavavy River

Lac Alaotra

Maningory River

Ambatondrazaka

Vohidiala

RN4

Tambohorano

Maintirano

Mahambo

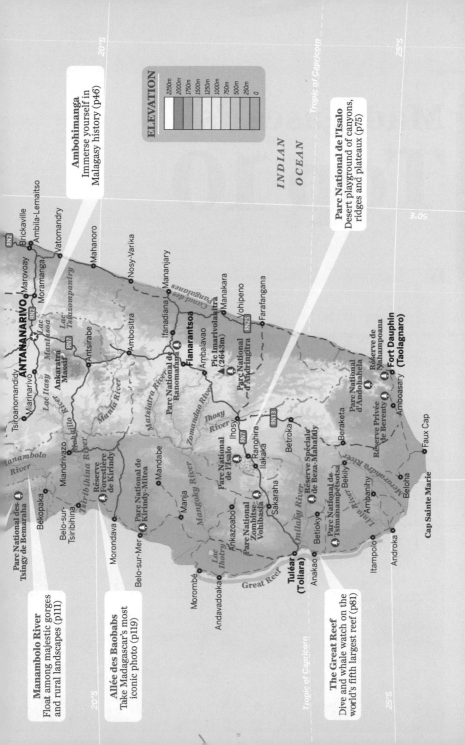

Manambolo River
Float among majestic gorges and rural landscapes (p111)

Allée des Baobabs
Take Madagascar's most iconic photo (p119)

The Great Reef
Dive and whale watch on the world's fifth largest reef (p81)

Ambohimanga
Immerse yourself in Malagasy history (p46)

Parc National de l'Isalo
Desert playground of canyons, ridges and plateaux (p75)

ELEVATION

2250m
2000m
1750m
1500m
1250m
1000m
750m
500m
250m
0

INDIAN OCEAN

Tropic of Capricorn

Pare National des Tsingy de Bemaraha

Bekopaka
Belo-sur-Tsiribihina
Miandrivazo
Morondava
Belo-sur-Mer
Andavadoaka
Morombé
Réserve Forestière de Kirindy
Pare National de Kirindy-Mitea
Ankazoabo
Mandabe
Manja
Betioky
Anakao
Toliara (Tuléar)
Itampolo
Androka
Beloha
Cap Sainte Marie

Tsiroanomandidy
Miarinarivo
ANTANANARIVO
Ankaratra Massif
Antsirabe
Ambositra
Fianarantsoa
Pic Imarivolanitra (2643m)
Ambalavao
Ihosy
Ranohira
Ilakaka
Sakaraha
Réserve Spéciale de Beza-Mahafaly
Pare National Zombitse-Vohibasia
Pare National de Tsimanampetsotsa
Ampanihy
Bekily
Bereketa
Beraketa
Betroka
Faux Cap

Tsroanomandidy
Marovoay
Brickaville
Ambila-Lemaitso
Vatomandry
Moramanga
Mahanoro
Nosy-Varika
Mananjary
Manakara
Manakara
Vohipeno
Farafangana
Ifanadiana
Pare National de Ranomafana
Pare National d'Andringitra
Réserve de Nahampoana
Fort Dauphin (Taolagnaro)
Pare National d'Andohahela
Amboasary
Réserve Privée de Berenty

Lac Tsihaokanampaniry
Lac Itasy
Lac Mantasoa
Lac Tsihaokanampaniry
Lac Tsohy

Manambolo River
Tsiribihina River
Mahajilo River
Mania River
Matsiatra River
Zomandao River
Mangoky River
Onilahy River
Linta River
Menarandra River

Canal des Pangalanes
Great Reef
INDIAN OCEAN

Madagascar's
Top 10

Parc National de l'Isalo

1 It's not just because of its epic desert landscapes – canyons, ravines, gorges, savannah-like plains and their numerous ochre hues – that Isalo (p75) is so popular, it's also because there is so much to do here: hiking, via ferratas (fixed-cable routes), horse riding, mountain biking, 4WD circuits and swimming in natural pools. Let's not forget lemur- and bird-watching, nor admiring the technicolour sunsets and exquisite clarity of the night skies.

Nosy Be

2 The 'big island' (p123) is a dream destination: you could spend two weeks here and on the surrounding islands and still feel like you haven't had enough. There's world-class diving and snorkelling, turquoise sea, exquisitely soft light and arresting views, and you can also visit spice plantations, explore kilometres of inland trails, see fabulous wildlife in the marine and nature reserves, feast on an abundance of seafood and sail to small islands nearby.

JORDIEASY/GETTY IMAGES ©

LKPRO/GETTY IMAGES ©

ALASTAIR MACEWEN/GETTY IMAGES ©

Tackle the Infamous RN5

3 If you revel in the idea of a road challenge, this is it. It may be a *route nationale,* but make no mistake: the 240km stretch of the RN5 (p177) between Maroantsetra and Soanierana-Ivongo is no road. It is a track, a quagmire, an obstacle course, a river in places, a mountain in others, but not a road. Semantics aside, travellers who complete the journey will have anecdotes to last them a lifetime. Mananara, halfway through the trip, is also one of the few places in Madagascar where you're likely to see an aye-aye.

Parc National de Marojejy

4 With pristine mountainous rainforest, thick root-filled jungle and waterfalls, Marojejy (p155) is a primordial place, where the 'angel of the forest' (the endemic silky *sifaka,* pictured) inhabits mountains, and spectacular views of the Marojejy Massif open up through the canopy. A superb trail romps through the landscape, climaxing with a climb to the 2132m summit. Permits also provide entry to the remote and beautiful Réserve Spéciale d'Anjanaharibe-Sud, where travellers will be rewarded with the wail of the *indri.*

Sunset at Allée des Baobabs

5 Few things say Madagascar more than this small stretch of the RN8 (p119) between Morondava and Belo-sur-Tsiribihina. Lined with majestic baobabs, it comes into its own at sunset and sunrise when the trees cast their long shadows on the red sand and the sky lights up with orange and purple hues. In addition to the Allée, you'll find plenty more baobabs across southern and western Madagascar. Some live for up to 1000 years and reach epic proportions: Majunga's sacred baobab measures 21m around its trunk!

Tropical Haute Cuisine

6 The freshest of ingredients combined with traditional and colonial influences have produced a divine strand of fusion cuisine. Zebu meat (pictured) rivals beef in succulence and tenderness, spices add piquancy to sauces, and the tropical sun-ripened fruit finds its way into anything from sorbets to macerated rum. Antananarivo (p38) has the best selection of restaurants, but Mad Zebu (p111) in Belo-sur-Tsiribihina, La Table d'Alexandre (p134) in Nosy Be and Piment Banane (p172) in Tamatave are other establishments worth seeking out.

MTCURADO/GETTY IMAGES ©

MILOSK50/SHUTTERSTOCK ©

Ambohimanga

7 This is Madagascar's only cultural site on Unesco's World Heritage list, and with good reason: Ambohimanga (p46) was the seat of King Andrianampoinimerina, the Merina sovereign who decided to unify the warring tribes of the island so that his kingdom would have no frontier but the sea. The cultural significance of the site goes beyond history: Ambohimanga is revered as a sacred site by the Malagasy, who come here to invoke royal spirits and request their protection and good fortune.

Diving & Snorkelling the Great Reef

8 Madagascar boasts the world's fifth-largest coral reef – 450km of fringing, patch and barrier reefs from Morombé in the north to Itampolo in the south. Work involving local communities and marine conservation groups have maintained the reef's health despite increasing pressure. Anakao (p91; pictured) has some of the best infrastructure on the reef, with the added bonus of whale watching in winter. Other spots that will blow you away are the 'cathedrals' at Ifaty and Mangily and the serene village of Ambola.

Tsingy de Bemaraha

9 There is nothing else on earth quite like the jagged limestone pinnacles of Parc National des Tsingy de Bemaraha (p111). A Unesco World Heritage Site, the serrated, surreal-looking peaks and boulders are a geological work of art, the result of millennia of water and wind erosion. Just as remarkable is the infrastructure the national park has put in place to explore this natural wonder: via ferratas (fixed-cable routes), rope bridges and ladders, with circuits combining forests, caves, pirogue trips and even abseiling.

Manambolo River

10 Taking a trip down the Manambolo (p110) means disconnecting completely from everything: for three days there are no cars, no roads and precious little mobile-phone coverage. It's just you, your guide and the pirogue. It is an experience of utter relaxation, with little more to do than admire the landscape, gawp at the spectacular gorges, take in local life, sing by the campfire and marvel at the night sky. Make sure you pick a reliable operator.

DENNISVDW/GETTY IMAGES ©

Need to Know

For more information, see Survival Guide (p249)

Currency
Ariary (Ar)

Language
Malagasy and French

Visas
Required for all visitors:
Ar60,000/100,000/
140,000 (for 30/60/90
days). A *vignette* (tourist
tax) of €10 is also now
charged upon arrival at
the airport.

Money
ATMs (Visa and Master-
Card) widely available in
large towns and cities.
In more rural areas,
cash rules. Euros are the
easiest foreign currency
to exchange.

Mobile Phones
Local SIM cards can be
used in European and
Australian phones; other
phones will have to be
set on roaming.

Time
East Africa Time (GMT/
UTC plus three hours)

When to Go

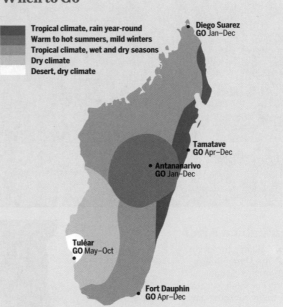

Tropical climate, rain year-round
Warm to hot summers, mild winters
Tropical climate, wet and dry seasons
Dry climate
Desert, dry climate

Diego Suarez
GO Jan–Dec

Tamatave
GO Apr–Dec

Antananarivo
GO Jan–Dec

Tuléar
GO May–Oct

Fort Dauphin
GO Apr–Dec

High Season
(Jul & Aug)

➡ Especially busy
because of European
school holidays.

➡ It's winter – balmy
temperatures by day
and cool nights (cold
in the highlands).

➡ There's also
a spike of high-
season activity at
Christmas/New Year.

Shoulder
Season (Apr–
Jun, Sep–Dec)

➡ The best time
to go: warm
temperatures and
fewer visitors.

➡ Because of
the rain, some
attractions close
early (November),
others reopen late
(June).

Low Season
(Jan–Mar)

➡ Cyclone season:
the east coast
is particularly
vulnerable, but all
coastal areas are
susceptible.

➡ Rainy season
everywhere – many
areas inaccessible.

➡ Discounts
available in most
hotels.

Useful Websites

Lonely Planet (lonelyplanet.com/madagascar) Destination info, traveller forum.

Madagascar Tourisme (www.madagascar-tourisme.com) National tourist office site, with lots of info and great photographs.

Wild Madagascar (www.wildmadagascar.org) Background information, conservation news.

David Attenborough's Madagascar (www.bbc.co.uk/nature/collections/p00db3n8) BBC site with inspirational videos and images.

Travel Madagascar (www.travelmadagascar.org) Practical information about planning a trip to Madagascar.

Madagascar National Parks (www.parcs-madagascar.com) Detailed background and practical information about Madagascar's national parks.

Important Numbers

Country code	ℐ261
Landline prefix	ℐ020
Mobile prefix	ℐ032, 033 or 034
Police	ℐ117
Fire	ℐ118

Exchange Rates

Australia	A$1	Ar2200
Canada	C$	Ar2200
Europe	€1	Ar3500
Japan	¥100	Ar2700
New Zealand	NZ$	Ar2000
South Africa	R10	Ar1900
UK	£1	Ar4500
US	US$1	Ar3200

For current exchange rates, see www.xe.com.

Daily Costs

Budget:
Less than €60

➡ Basic double (shared facilities) €7–12

➡ Food from *hotelys* (roadside stalls) for breakfast and lunch; dinner at a restaurant

➡ Travel between cities by *taxi-brousse*; chartered taxi for day trips

Midrange:
€60–150

➡ Double room (mostly en suite) €12–25

➡ A good meal costs around €10

➡ At the upper end, hire a car and driver

Top End:
More than €150

➡ Accommodation varies wildly: €25 in a guesthouse to €500 in a full-board resort

➡ Travel by private 4WD with driver; internal flights to save time

Opening Hours

Shops geared towards tourists tend to open longer at the weekend.

Banks (Antananarivo) 8am to 4pm Monday to Friday.

Banks (rest of the country) 7.30am to 11.30am and 2pm to 4.30pm Monday to Friday.

Bars 5pm to 11pm.

Restaurants 11.30am to 2.30pm and 6.30pm to 9.30pm.

Shops 9am to noon and 2.30pm to 6pm Monday to Friday, 9am to noon Saturday.

Arriving in Madagascar

Aéroport d'Ivato, Antananarivo (p44) Taxis cost Ar40,000 during the day, Ar50,000 at night. It's 45 minutes to 90 minutes to the city, depending on traffic. A number of hotels in Ivato offer complimentary airport transfer. The Navette Adema shuttle bus (Ar10,000, one hour) picks up and drops off passengers at selected hotels from 5am to 10pm.

Getting Around

Madagascar is a huge place, the roads are bad and travel times long (it takes 24 hours to drive from Antananarivo to Diego Suarez, 18 hours to Tuléar etc), so be realistic about how much ground you want to cover or you'll spend every other day in the confines of a vehicle.

Private vehicle If you can afford it, this is the best way to explore Madagascar. You'll be able to go anywhere, whenever suits you. The off-road driving can be great fun, too.

Taxi-brousse (bush taxi) They are slow, uncomfortable and not always safe, but they are cheap, go (almost) everywhere and you can't get more local than that.

Plane Can be huge time savers, but they can be expensive and subject to frequent delays and cancellations.

For much more on **getting around**, see p259

If You Like...

Beaches

With two oceans, 5000km of coastline and dozens of islands, Madagascar's beaches are one of the country's top attractions. Many rival the beauty of traditional beach destinations, with the added bonus of fewer visitors.

Anakao A perfect arc of white sand, turquoise water and laid-back atmosphere; the pearl of the Great Reef. (p91)

Anjajavy Only accessible by private plane or boat, the beaches on Anjajavy Peninsula bring a whole new meaning to the word remote. (p106)

Île aux Nattes (Nosy Nato) A classic tropical island, with curving white-sand beaches, reclining palms and the most inviting sea. (p174)

Salary Just one resort for 7km of beach; this is what exclusivity feels like. (p89)

Nosy Iranja This postcard-perfect duo of islands becomes one at low tide, when a slim sandbank emerges. Tour companies in Nosy Be arrange day trips. (p137)

Wildlife

Famed for its wildlife, Madagascar is to nature lovers what France is to foodies. But you'll have to be patient, time your visit right and have Lady Luck on your side to see the best it has to offer.

Indri Madagascar's largest lemur is easily seen – and heard! – at Parc National Andasibe Mantadia. (p162)

Aye-aye Famed for its elongated 'magic digit', this highly endangered, curious-looking lemur is now a rare sight. (p187)

Iconic baobabs Most commonly found in the southern half of the country, the collection on Allée des Baobabs has become one of Madagascar's signature views. (p119)

Humpback whales Every year from July to September, hundreds of whales make the long journey from Antarctica to mate and give birth in the warmer waters of the Indian Ocean and the Mozambique Channel. (p174)

Turtles Beloved of divers and snorkellers, turtles thrive all along the Malagasy coast, including Parc National de Masoala. (p181)

Hiking

With such an alluring shoreline, it's easy to forget that about 70% of Madagascar's land surface sits at a lofty 1000m to 1500m above sea level. Cue superb mountains, extinct volcanoes, dramatic peaks and, ergo, fabulous hiking.

Massif de l'Andringitra World-class hiking, a hardly visited national park and wonderful accommodation options. (p69)

Parc National de Marojejy A trek through the primordial rainforest of the Massif de Marojejy progresses from scenic walk to full-on climbing expedition – turning back is possible! (p155)

Parc National des Tsingy de Bemaraha Scale the weird and wonderful *tsingy* (limestone pinnacle fomrations) along the park's sensational via ferrata (fixed-cable route; p111).

Parc National de l'Isalo Southern Madagascar's hiking destination par excellence, with stunning canyons and gorges. (p75)

Parc National de Masoala There are short and long-distance trails through this pristine primary rainforest. They are hard work, but worth it for the exceptional wildlife. (p191)

Food & Drink

Madagascar is a culinary delight. Thanks to a mix of cuisines and prime fresh ingredients (plentiful seafood, succulent zebu meat and fruit and vegetables

bursting with flavour), you're certain to eat well wherever you go.

Camarons Try the Malagasy prawn (there are saltwater and freshwater varieties) for a fraction of what you'd pay back home. (pp63, 105 & 118)

La Varangue Antananarivo's culinary gem. Make sure you treat yourself to outstanding Franco-Malagasy gastronomy. (p39)

Société de Rhum Arrangé Flavoured rum is the red island's signature drink. There are dozens to try (and take back home), from vanilla to lychee, chocolate or ginger, at this shop in Nosy Be. (p131)

Vanilla Madagascar's flagship plant grows in abundance on the northeast 'vanilla coast'. Visit plantations in Sambava. (p153)

Millot Plantations Discover how spices, cocoa and aromatic plants are grown and processed at this beautiful plantation, sampling them as you go. (p137)

Top: Nosy Iranja Be (p137)
Bottom: Giraffe-necked weevil (p248)

PLAN YOUR TRIP IF YOU LIKE...

Diving & Snorkelling

Madagascar is home to the world's fifth-largest coral reef, which partly explains why diving here is so good. The fauna is exceptional, with sharks, turtles, whales and rays.

Nosy Be Dozens of dive sites within half an hour's boat ride, with a huge variety of seascapes, from shipwrecks to reefs and spectacular drops. (p123)

Nosy Tanikely Now a protected marine reserve, Nosy Tanikely is one of the best and most accessible snorkelling spots in Madagascar (turtles guaranteed; p136).

Ifaty & Mangily A great range of dives, including the famous

'Cathedral', a network of stunning rocky arches. (p87)

Anakao The best spot on Madagascar's southern reef, with good snorkelling, even better diving and great accommodation to boot. (p91)

History & Culture

Although many come to Madagascar for its incredible nature, the island has a rich and diverse culture, influenced by the waves of migrants who gradually populated the island and the colonial powers who hoped to control it.

Ambohimanga The most sacred of Antananarivo's 12 sacred hills and the long-standing home of Malagasy royalty. (p46)

Rova It may be a shadow of its former self, but the queen's palace in Antananarivo's Haute-Ville is steeped in history. (p30)

Famadihana Visitors are often welcome at traditional exhumation ceremonies – an opportunity to reassess our own beliefs about life and death. (p205)

Île Sainte Marie's pirate cemetery Overlooking the Baie des Forbans, where many pirates lived, this cemetery is a fascinating reminder of the island's lawless past. (p182)

Shopping

Finding souvenirs is no hardship in Madagascar: there are woven baskets, gemstones, spices, clothes, rum, silk, leather goods and much more.

Lisy Art Gallery This Antananarivo boutique is like a shopping kaleidoscope of Madagascar. Pretty much everything you have seen in the country is available here at reasonable (fixed) prices. (p41)

Soalandy Finding silk at such low prices back home is unthinkable, so make the best of the local production in Ambalavao (and watch the production process, too; p69).

Le Jardin des Sens Essential oils, spices and beauty products in lovely premises in Nosy Be. (p131)

Kudeta Etnik Shop A gorgeous boutique with high-end Malagasy clothes and accessories in Antananarivo. (p41)

Creature Comforts

If you've had enough of hiking, diving, wildlife seeking and bumping around in a 4WD, put your bags down for a few days at one of these wonderful retreats.

Eden Lodge Remote, serene and ecofriendly, Eden Lodge, near Nosy Be, is the place to go to be at one with nature. (p137)

Princesse Bora Lodge & Spa Pirogue tubs in the spa, suspended beds in the bungalows and a dizzying wine list...this is as close to perfection as you can get. (p183)

Le Soleil des Tsingy Understated elegance, stellar service and views to die for, especially from the pool. (p114)

Isalo Rock Lodge A triumph of contemporary design in age-old landscapes, with fabulous service, pool and spa. (p78)

Epic 4WD Journeys

If this were a TV program, it would open with 'don't try this at home'. Far from putting travellers off, though, the challenge that is Madagascar's roads is something many revel in, so here are our favourite bone-shaking, tyre-bursting, vehicle-bashing road trips.

RN5 from Maroantsetra to Soanierana-Ivongo Depending on how you look at it, this is either the country's worst road or its best 4WD adventure. (p167)

Coastal road from Morondava to Tuléar The highlights of this journey are the northern end of the Great Reef and an overnight stay at the serene village of Belo-sur-Mer, ensconced in the dunes. (p120)

Coastal road from Tuléar to Fort Dauphin This road is practically a walk in the park between Tuléar and Itampolo – until it disintegrates and virtually disappears. The sealed sections sport craters worthy of the moon. (p75)

Month by Month

January

This is the beginning of cyclone season, which runs until March. Cyclones affect mostly the east coast, but they can strike the west coast, too. Most areas have received some rains by now, turning arid landscapes into numerous shades of green.

⭐ New Year Celebrations

Like the rest of the world, the Malagasies welcome the new year with much partying on New Year's Eve and New Year's Day.

February

The weather may be sweltering and humid, but for those who do make it at this time, the wildlife rewards are unique. Summer is also cruise-ship season from Tamatave to Nosy Be.

👁 Reptiles & Amphibians

After many months of hibernation or reduced activity, snakes and frogs come out in force in the hot and humid summer climate. This is the best time of year to admire their colourful displays and incredible variety.

👁 Orchids

Madagascar has more than 1000 species of this delicate plant, 90% of which are endemic. Many are endangered, however, so being able to see these floral works of art in the wild is an increasingly rare experience.

April

Many areas that were inaccessible during the rainy season are starting to reopen. Be prepared for slower travel times, however, and copious amounts of mud.

⭐ Easter

The main festival of the Christian calendar is fervently celebrated in Madagascar. Extended families gather, wear their best clothes, attend Mass together (sometimes twice on Sunday) and share a meal.

May

In the north, the wind has picked up and will blow until the end of the year. Tourism starts picking up again.

🏄 Kitesurfing

A combination of fantastic wind and good surf has turned Baie de Sakalava and Mer d'Emeraude (northern Madagascar) into the Malagasy capital of this extreme sport. Tuition and equipment are available and a couple of hotels offer special kitesurfing packages.

⭐ Zegny'Zo Festival

For a shot of artistic zing, head to Zegny'Zo, an international street-arts festival with a carnival-like atmosphere in Diego Suarez. (p140)

⭐ Donia

Held at the end of May or the beginning of June, the week-long Donia (www.festival-donia.com) in Nosy Be is Madagascar's most high-profile arts festival. It is primarily a music event, although the fringe also involves a carnival and various sporting events. (p129)

June

The last few inaccessible roads in the east start opening up. Humpback whales begin arriving along the western and eastern coasts to give birth and mate. Tourism season is well on its way.

🎊 Fête de l'Indépendance

Madagascar's independence day is a big deal. The official celebrations in Antananarivo feature military parades, speeches, shows and much flag waving. Elsewhere, there are street celebrations, themed parties in nightclubs and a profusion of red, green and white decorations.

July

It's winter and temperatures regularly drop below zero in the highlands at night. Bring a very warm sleeping bag if you're camping and plenty of layers for hotels without heating (surprisingly numerous!).

🎊 Famadihana

The 'turning of the dead', or exhumation, ceremonies to commemorate ancestors take place in the highlands from July to September. The practice is common from Antananarivo to Fianarantsoa and is an important celebration. Foreigners are sometimes invited.

⊙ Vanilla Season

The country's flagship plant is harvested between July and October. It is a labour-intensive process, as vanilla pods mature at different times. Flights are full to the vanilla-growing northeast region at this time of year, so book ahead.

August

With school summer holidays in full swing in Europe, August is peak tourism season in Madagascar. Book ahead for the most popular trips and in areas with limited accommodation, such as Parc National des Tsingy de Bemaraha.

🏃 Whale Watching

Humpback whales migrate annually from their feeding grounds in Antarctica to the warm waters of the Indian Ocean and Mozambique Channel to mate and give birth. Famed for their spectacular breaching (jumping), they can be observed all along the coast from July to September.

☆ Hira Gasy

Enjoy an afternoon of *hira gasy* – traditional storytelling narrated through dancing, singing and oratory jousting. Shows take place year-round but are especially popular in winter, when it's not too hot.

September

With spring under way, this is the perfect time of year to come to Madagascar. Temperatures are pleasant, there is little rain and the kids have gone back to school.

🏃 Birdwatching

Dry, deciduous forests are at their barest at this time of year – a godsend for birdwatchers. Deprived of their usual camouflage, Madagascar's 280 bird species, a third of them endemic, are easier to observe. Don't forget your binoculars.

October

As with spring all over the world, there is stunning blossom, birth and mating – a great time of year to admire wildlife. Temperatures are also at their best – warm but not stifling.

🍴 Mango Season

The delectable mango bursts onto the scene, inundating market stalls and roadsides and making its way into every dessert and fruit salad. The green fruit is picked in August and September to make *achards* (a pickled condiment) and savoury salads.

⊙ Jacaranda Blossom

The exquisite purple blossom of the jacaranda tree is a sight to behold: its delicate colour contrasts beautifully with urban greys and country greens, while petals carpet the ground like a Technicolor version of snow.

⊙ Fossa Mating Season

The normally elusive fossa, Madagascar's biggest predator (and the baddie in *Madagascar* the cartoon movie), makes quite a show of its loud nuptials. It's best observed in the Réserve Forestière de Kirindy in western Madagascar. (p114)

✨ Madajazzcar

Going strong for more than 25 years, this annual jazz festival in Antananarivo taps into Madagascar's rich musical tradition and brings together local and foreign jazz performers. Many of the events are free.

November

Rains come early in parts of western Madagascar, making some roads inaccessible. Elsewhere, however, this is a lovely time of year, with visitor numbers petering out and the weather warming up.

⊙ Baby Lemurs

If you thought lemurs were cute, wait until you see the babies, clinging to their mother's fur or being carried by the scruff of the neck. The entire troop generally looks after the young.

✕ Lychee Season

Madagascar provides around 70% of the lychees consumed in Europe, but fear not, there are plenty left in the country to gorge on. The season lasts until January and lychees are a favourite Christmas food.

December

Christmas is a low-key event for Malagasies: families go to Mass and share a meal. Tourism peaks briefly around festive celebrations, with many Europeans enjoying the warm weather and tropical showers.

Top: *Hira gasy* performance (p40)
Bottom: Whale watching (p184), Île Sainte Marie

Itineraries

2 WEEKS Essential Madagascar

A combination of the classic RN7 with some island R&R in glorious Nosy Be.

On day one, head from Antananarivo down to the highland town of **Antsirabe**, with its wide colonial streets and colourful rickshaws. On day two, wind your way to **Parc National de Ranomafana** through the highland's scenic landscapes, stopping en route at the arts-and-crafts capital, **Ambositra**. Spend day three hiking and searching for lemurs in Ranomafana's rainforest.

On day four, drive to the superb **Parc National de l'Isalo**, stopping in **Réserve d'Anja** on your way to see the oh-so-cute ring-tailed lemurs. Spend the next two days exploring Isalo's stunning desert plains and canyons.

On day seven, head to **Tuléar**, making sure to stop at **Arboretum d'Antsokay** on your way. On day eight, fly to Antananarivo (Tana) and then on to **Nosy Be** the next day. Enjoy some beach R&R on day 10. The next day, take a day trip to **Nosy Komba** and **Nosy Tanikely** for unrivalled snorkelling. On day 12, visit **Réserve Naturelle Intégrale de Lokobe**. Fly back to Tana on day 13. Take a day trip to Ambohimanga for your last day, or shop for souvenirs.

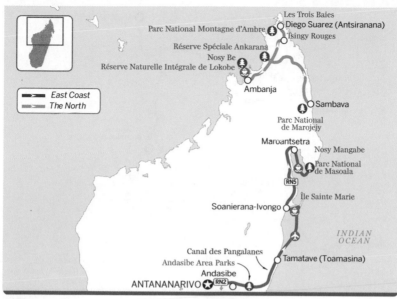

 2 WEEKS The North

Northern Madagascar offers rainforest hikes, spectacular rock formations and tantalising white beaches.

Fly to **Sambava** and head out early to **Parc National de Marojejy** the next day, spending a couple of days trekking on this sensational massif. It's a day's drive from Sambava to the beautiful **Réserve Spéciale Ankarana**, a wilderness of caves, pinnacles and dry forests. Spend a day here and continue on to the northern belle of **Diego Suarez**, with a stop at the terracotta-coloured **Tsingy Rouges** on the way.

Take a day to discover Diego's heritage and explore the wild coastline of **Les Trois Baies**. Take another day trip to the mountainous **Parc National Montagne d'Ambre**.

From Diego, it's a half-day drive to **Ambanja** – visit the cocoa and spice plantations before boarding a boat at Ankify for **Nosy Be**. Spend three or four days enjoying its coral reefs and beaches, putting a day aside for the fabulous **Réserve Naturelle Intégrale de Lokobe**. Fly back to Tana from Nosy Be.

 2½ WEEKS East Coast

Exploring this coast is challenging but by no means impossible, though budget travellers will balk at the cost of heading beyond Île Sainte Marie, since Maroantsetra is hard and expensive to get to.

Head east along the RN2 from Antananarivo to charming **Andasibe**, jumping-off point for the luxuriant, misty rainforests of **Andasibe Area Parks**. Spend a couple of days waking to the cries of the legendary *indri* (Madagascar's largest lemur), hiking and birdwatching before winding down the RN2 to **Tamatave**, gateway to the waterways and lakes of the **Canal des Pangalanes**. Allow three or four days for this aquatic wonderland.

Back in Tamatave, fly to gorgeous **Île Sainte Marie**. Tour the island by quad- or motorbike and take a whale-watching trip (July to September).

If you relish a challenge, take a boat to **Soanierana-Ivongo** and drive the infamous **RN5** (4WD only) to **Maroantsetra** (two days). Spend a night at **Nosy Mangabe** and a couple of nights in the pristine **Parc National de Masoala**. Fly to Tana from Maroantsetra.

PLAN YOUR TRIP ITINERARIES

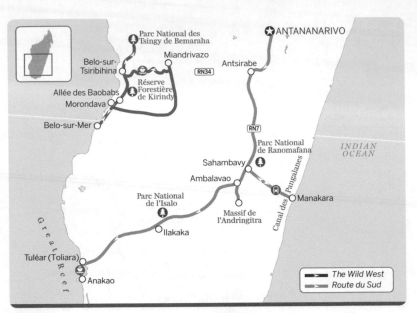

The Wild West
Route du Sud

Route du Sud
3 WEEKS

This classic route will whisk you from Antananarivo down to Tuléar along the famed RN7.

First stop is **Antsirabe**, where you should visit some of the town's famed artisans. Drive to **Sahambavy** and its glorious tea-plantation landscapes. The next day, hop on the scenic FCE train to **Manakara**, where you can tour the Canal des Pangalanes.

Drive to **Parc National de Ranomafana** and hike in the park's rainforest. Time your visit to the highland town of **Ambalavao** to coincide with Madagascar's largest zebu market, then allow three or four days to explore the spectacular **Massif de l'Andringitra** with its granite peaks, phenomenal hikes and wonderful lodges.

Further south is the fantastic **Parc National de l'Isalo**, with jagged sandstone massifs, cool canyons and delightful natural pools. Two days will do it justice.

Stop at the sapphire boom town of **Ilakaka** on your way to the perfect beaches of **Anakao** and the Great Reef. From **Tuléar**, fly back to Antananarivo.

The Wild West
2 WEEKS

This itinerary requires some planning ahead, but once you've got your boat and your 4WD booked, you'll be off in a flash.

Book a descent of the Tsiribihina River. Trips start from **Miandrivazo**, a day's drive from Antananarivo. From there, it takes 2½ days to drift down to **Belo-sur-Tsiribihina**.

Arrange for a 4WD and driver to meet you at the boat landing in Belo and continue north to **Parc National des Tsingy de Bemaraha**. You'll need at least two days to explore the Grands and Petits Tsingy. It's then a day's drive through scorched landscape down to **Réserve Forestière de Kirindy**, home to the elusive fossa and the giant jumping rat. Make sure to go on a night walk. On your way to Morondava, stop at the iconic **Allée des Baobabs**.

After a day recuperating in the laid-back seaside town of **Morondava**, head down to the fishing village of **Belo-sur-Mer** for a couple of days. You can then drive on to Tuléar (during the dry season only), or go back to Morondava and fly or drive back to Antananarivo.

Regions at a Glance

Madagascar is the world's fourth-largest island, and with its big size comes a huge amount of diversity.

Central Madagascar is the most popular part of the country, and the most accessible. The coastal regions are the realm of the 4WD and can be challenging to travel (the northwest being the exception).

Southern Madagascar will appeal to divers and snorkellers, while beach bums will be better off in Île Sainte Marie in the east or Nosy Be in the north.

Western Madagascar will delight those in search of something a little different, while activities enthusiasts will be at home in northern Madagascar.

Eastern Madagascar is the most remote region, but those who make it there will be rewarded with pristine environments.

Antananarivo

History
Food
Shopping

History & Culture

The development of a Malagasy identity is intimately linked to the emergence of Antananarivo (Tana) as a capital: this is the home of the kings who brought together the island's tribes.

Gastronomy

Foodies of the world, rejoice: Tana's got fusion cuisine down to a T. Imagine French gastronomy, prepared with the freshest Malagasy ingredients, add a *soupçon* of Creole, a smidgen of Indian and voila!

Retail Therapy

Tana is a potpourri of arts, crafts, clothes and deli shops. Hard-nosed bargain hunters head for the markets, while more conventional shoppers love the well-stocked boutiques.

p28

Central Madagascar

Culture
Hiking
Artisans

Malagasy Life

Travellers often start their trip in Madagascar with the highlands, and what an introduction to Malagasy life: accessible homestays, colourful markets (including the country's biggest zebu market) and colonial architecture.

Amazing Hikes

Massif d'Andringitra is in a hiking league of its own. The trails are challenging, the views breathtaking and there's good infrastructure.

Arts & Crafts

Much of Madagascar's signature arts and crafts – raffia work, woodcarvings, miniatures, silk weaving – originate from the highlands and visiting artisans' workshops and purchasing unique souvenirs is part and parcel of the destination.

p48

Southern Madagascar

Diving
Beaches
Hiking

....

Great Reef
It is the world's fifth-largest coral reef, ergo one of the world's finest diving destinations. There are multiple dive sites all along the reef and many professional outfits to choose from.

Remote Beaches
Malagasy beaches rarely suffer from overcrowding, but many southern beaches are so off the radar that the likelihood of your having the beach to yourself is actually quite high.

Scenic Hikes
Madagascar's southern hinterland is a paradise for hikers. Parc National de l'Isalo offers numerous circuits, including via ferratas (fixed-cable routes), in its scenic desert canyons. For more of the same, but with even fewer crowds, head to Massif du Makay.

p73

Western Madagascar

Baobabs
Seafood
Scenery

....

Magnificent Giants
The Malagasies call baobabs 'roots of the sky', after their crooked branches, and in western Madagascar they come in all guises: in majestic avenues, intertwined, straight or bottle-shaped.

Fabulous Seafood
Foodies will rate the region for its cheap and outstanding seafood, including lobster and crayfish as well as fish, often prepared with a divine blend of local spices.

Photogenic Landscapes
From meandering rivers to immense beaches, arid plains to deciduous forests, serrated peaks to undulating sand dunes, western Madagascar is easy on the eye.

p100

Northern Madagascar

Activities
Islands
Plantations

....

Diving & Hiking
Adrenalin junkies, look no further. Here, you can trek in mist-shrouded rainforest, scale rock cliffs on deserted islands, kitesurf along unspoilt beaches and dive with whale sharks and rays. Oh, and beachcombing counts, too.

Paradisiacal Islands
It's a cliché but the islands around Nosy Be more than live up to it. Sadly, paradise doesn't come cheap.

Vanilla & Spice
If you've ever wondered where the delectable vanilla comes from, what a pepper plant looks like, or how fruity cocoa beans become chocolate, visit one of the country's beautiful plantations to find out.

p122

Eastern Madagascar

Whale Watching
Rainforest
Islands

....

Humpback Migration
Île Sainte Marie (Nosy Boraha) and Baie d'Antongil have been the nursing and mating grounds of humpback whales since time immemorial. Take to the water to admire these endangered giants in all their breaching glory.

Unspoilt Rainforest
Eastern Madagascar is one of the last areas in the country where huge tracts of rainforest remain. Explore it on foot or by boat on the Masoala Peninsula.

Tropical Islands
For sheer escapism, you can't do better than idyllic Île Sainte Marie and Île aux Nattes. Both cater admirably to those in need of R&R, but Sainte Marie also holds the promise of adventure in the north.

p158

On the Road

Antananarivo

POP 1.37 MILLION

Best Places to Eat

➡ Le Saka (p39)
➡ La Varangue (p39)
➡ Saka Express (p38)
➡ La Ferme d'Ivato (p46)
➡ Villa Isoraka (p39)

Best Places to Stay

➡ Hôtel Sakamanga (p36)
➡ Lokanga (p38)
➡ Hôtel Niaouly (p34)
➡ Le Manoir Rouge (p46)
➡ Résidence Lapasoa (p38)

Why Go?

Tana, as the capital is universally known, is all about eating, shopping, history and day trips. The town centre itself, with its pollution and dreadful traffic, puts off many travellers from staying, but bypassing the capital altogether would be a mistake: Tana has been the home of Malagasy power for three centuries and there is a huge amount of history and culture to discover, as well as some unexpected wildlife options.

In the city itself, the Haute-Ville, with its beautiful colonial buildings, steep streets and cool climate (average altitude in Tana is 1400m), is a great place to wander about. There are also some excellent markets and shops that stock products and crafts from across the country at very competitive prices. Finally, Tana is *the* place in Madagascar to treat yourself to a fine meal: some establishments rival Europe's Michelin-starred restaurants, but without the price tag.

When to Go
Antananarivo

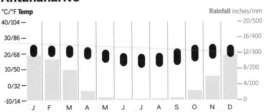

Jun–Aug Winter season in Tana, when night temperatures drop below 10°C.

Jul–Sep *Famadihana* season, when families exhume their ancestors' bones to celebrate.

Oct The purple blossoms of jacaranda trees line the shores of Lac Anosy.

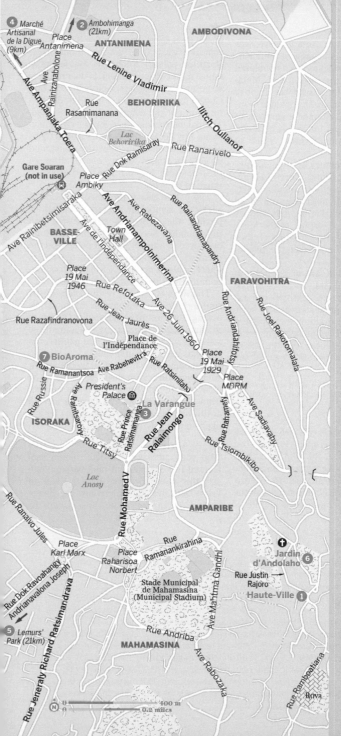

Antananarivo Highlights

1 Follow our walking tour through Antananarivo's lovely **Haute-Ville** (p35)

2 Spend an afternoon in the spiritual home of Malagasy identity, the royal hill of **Ambohimanga** (p46)

3 Splurge on dinner at **La Varangue** (p39)

4 Shop till you drop (and haggle all you can) at **Marché Artisanal de la Digue** (p42)

5 Get your lemur fix at wildlife sanctuary **Lemurs' Park** (p44)

6 Attend an afternoon of *hira gasy* – music, dancing and storytelling spectacles – in Tana, perhaps at **Jardin d'Andolaho** (p40), or in one of the surrounding villages

7 Treat yourself to a massage with Madagascan essential oils at **BioAroma** (p41)

History

The area that is now Antananarivo was originally known as Analamanga (Blue Forest), and is believed to have been populated by the Vazimba, ancestors of today's Malagasy, about whom little is known. In 1610 a Merina king named Andrianjaka conquered the region, stationed a garrison of 1000 troops to defend his new settlement, and renamed it Antananarivo, 'Place of 1000 Warriors'.

In the late 18th century Andrianampoinimerina, the unifying king, moved his capital from Ambohimanga to Antananarivo, where it became the most powerful of all the Merina kingdoms. For the next century Antananarivo was the capital of the Merina monarchs and the base from which they carried out their conquest of the rest of Madagascar.

Tana remained the seat of government during the colonial era, and it was the French who gave the city centre its present form, building two great staircases to scale the city's hills, and draining swamps and paddy fields to create present-day Analakely. In May 1929 the city was the site of the first major demonstration against the colonialists.

Today the greater Antananarivo area is Madagascar's political and economic centre.

◉ Sights

Central Antananarivo is relatively compact, which means that it is easily explored on foot. The catch is that it's hilly, with plenty of stairs. Haute-Ville, with its numerous old buildings, is a great place to explore. Don't linger on Ave de l'Indépendance in the Basse-Ville; however, pickpockets are rife.

★ Rova   HISTORIC BUILDING

(Palais de la Reine; Map p32; Rue Ramboatiana; admission Ar10,000; ◷9am-5pm) Tana's *rova* (fortified palace), known as Manjakamiadana (A Fine Place to Rule), is the imposing structure that crowns the city's highest hill. Gutted by a fire in 1995, it is still under restoration but the compound can be visited. The palace was designed for Queen Ranavalona I by Scottish missionary James Cameron. The outer stone structure was added in 1867 for Queen Ranavalona II, although the roof and interior remained wooden, much to everyone's regret in 1995...

The palace gate is protected by a carved eagle, the symbol of military force, and a phallus, the symbol of circumcision and thus nobility. Succeeding rulers built (and destroyed) a number of other palaces on the premises; there are ruins scattered about. There is also a replica of King Andrianampoinimerina's palace at Ambohimanga.

The Rova is also the resting place of the country's greatest monarchs; the most imposing stone tombs are located to the left of the main gate. The plain grey ones are those of kings, while the queens' are painted red (red was the colour of nobility).

Remember that it is *fady* (taboo) to point your finger directly at the royal tombs or the palace itself. The Rova, which can be seen from almost anywhere in Tana, is located at the very top of Haute-Ville. A taxi here is likely to cost around Ar10,000.

Musée Andafivaratra   MUSEUM

(Map p32; admission Ar10,000; ◷9am-5pm) Housed in a magnificent pink baroque palace, this museum is the former home of Prime Minister Rainilaiarivony, the power behind the throne of the three queens he

---

LA MICHELINE

In 1929 French engineer André Michelin, of tyre fame, patented the use of pneumatics on rail vehicles in a bid to improve passenger comfort. Trials were hugely successful and 'Micheline' wagons were soon zooming up and down the world's rail tracks.

Madagascar didn't escape the craze and got its first Micheline in 1932. By 1953, there were seven in regular service, but lack of maintenance and investment slowly caused the Madagascan railway system to fall into disrepair – Michelines included.

It wasn't until the revival of the rail system in the early 2000s that plans to restore the pneumatic wagons were hatched. Following restoration by the Michelin Museum in France, one Micheline (Map p36; ☏034 00 503 57; www.madarail.mg; Gare Soarano), which seats 19 passengers in old-world class, resumed service in 2011, chugging its way between Tana and Andasibe (Périnet) or Antsirabe at weekends. But the wagon had been out of action for eight months at the time of writing, with the authorities unable to say whether and when it would get back on the rails.

married in succession (Rasoherina, Ranavalona II and Ranavalona III) between 1864 and 1895. The museum's collection is a dusty assortment of memorabilia from Merina kings and queens, but it illuminates some of the colourful characters of that era. The museum was closed in 2015 due to leaks, but is planned to reopen in 2016.

The Merina crown jewels were stolen in 2013 and are yet to be recovered. Of the remaining artefacts, among the most interesting is a portrait of mad Queen Ranavalona I, dumpy in a coral silk crinoline and scowling out from her oil painting, while Jean Laborde, the French adventurer presumed to be her lover, glowers from beneath his beard in a black-and-white photograph.

There's also a huge gilt throne, originals of important trade treaties between Madagascar and the US, the UK and France, coats of chain mail, and a random selection of presents from foreign crowns through the ages. Explanations of the exhibits are in English as well as French.

Presidential Palace
HISTORIC BUILDING

(Map p36) This beautiful 19th-century manor was an official French residence for many years. It became the Madagascan presidential palace in 1975 and remained so until president Didier Ratsiraka decided to build a more modern complex about 15km south of the capital in 1991. The mansion remains an official residence but is generally quiet.

In a bid to balance the colonial architectural influence, Andry Rajoelina, president of the high transitional authority between 2009 and 2013, ordered that a replica of the King's palace at Ambohimanga be built right next to it.

Parc de Tsarasaotra
WILDLIFE RESERVE

(www.boogiepilgrim-madagascar.com/tourisamedurables/tsarasaotra-parc; Lac Alarobia; admission Mon-Fri Ar12,000, Sat & Sun Ar14,000; ⊙6am-6pm) Lake Alarobia may be located at the heart of Antananarivo's industrial area, but it is a vital refuge and nesting site for 14 threatened endemic bird species such as the Madagascar pond heron, Meller's duck and Madagascar little grebe. The site is classified Ramsar (International Convention on Wetlands), a treaty highlighting the importance and fragility of wetlands and protecting key sites, and the reserve is privately managed by tour operator Boogie Pilgrim (p263).

Accessing the site is, sadly, a bit of a mission as tickets can only be obtained from Boogie Pilgrim's office in Tana Water Front

during office hours. This is particularly disappointing for keen birdwatchers who will want to get there first thing in the morning, which means getting your tickets the day before. A taxi from Tana Water Front to the park will cost you around Ar5000 to Ar8000.

Gare Soarano
NOTABLE BUILDING

(Map p36) Tana's old train station doesn't see much passenger traffic these days, so the lovely building has been converted into a small, upmarket shopping centre. There are regular art shows of works by Malagasy artists, as well as chichi boutiques and a couple of more prosaic shops (airlines, telecoms etc).

Lac Anosy
LAKE

(Map p32) Antananarivo's heart-shape lake lies in the southern part of town. It is particularly lovely in October, when the jacaranda trees lining its shores are covered in purple blossoms. On an island connected to the shore by a causeway stands a large golden angel on a plinth, the Monument aux Morts (Monument to the Dead; Map p32; Lac Anosy), a WWI memorial erected by the French. It is currently not advised to walk in this area so the best way to appreciate Anosy is from the viewpoints in the Haute-Ville.

Analakely Market
MARKET

(Map p36) Antananarivo's main market is a shadow of the former *zoma* (market), for which the capital was legendary, but it's still a packed, teeming place, selling clothes, household items, dodgy DVDs and every food product you could imagine, plus a few you probably couldn't. Don't bring any valuables with you.

Musée d'Art et d'Archéologie
MUSEUM

(Map p36; Rue Dok Villette; ⊙9am-4pm Mon-Sat) **FREE** This small museum in Isoraka gives an overview of archaeological digs around the island, including displays of grave decorations from the south (known as *aloalo*), rotating exhibits on Madagascan life (cooking, music etc), and a few talismans and objects used in traditional ceremonies. A tip for the guide (if there is one) is customary.

Tours

Tany Mena Tours
TOUR

(Map p36; ☎020 22 326 27; www.tanymenatours.com; Ave 26 Juin 1960) This agency specialises in sustainable tourism and offers highly original tours around Antananarivo. Tours combine historical highlights with cultural

Antananarivo

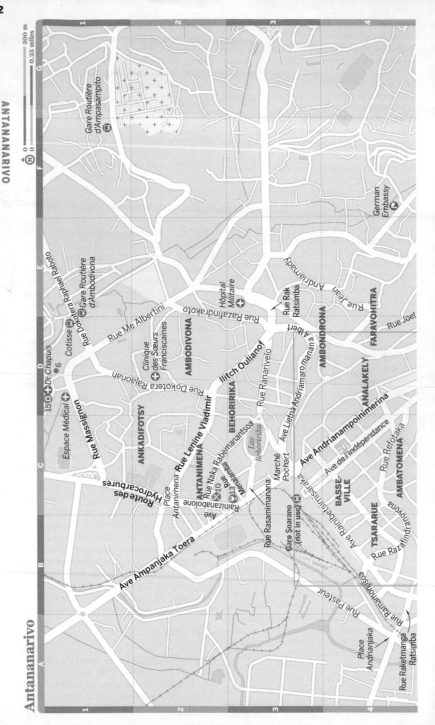

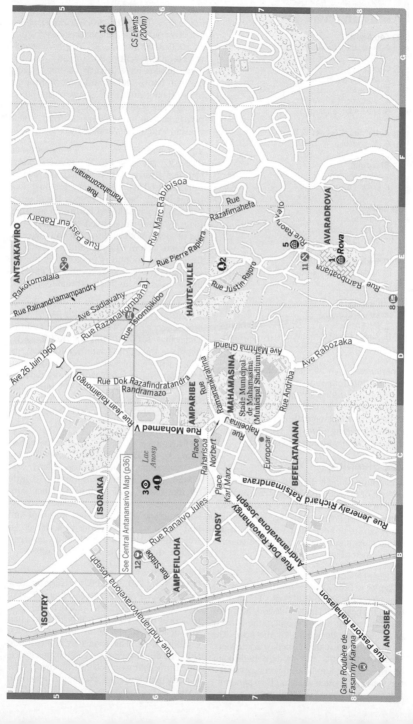

CS Events
(200m)

14

ANTSAKAVIRO

Rue Ramahazomanana

Rue Marc Rabibisoa

Rue Pasteur Rabary

Rakotomalala

6

Rue Rainandriamampandry

Rue Sadiavahy

Ave Sadiavahy

Rue Razanakombana

Rue Tsiombikibo

Rue Pierre Rajera

HAUTE-VILLE

Rue Razafimahefa

Rue

2

Rue Justin Rajoro

5

Rue Raonivo

AVARADROVA

Rova

1

11

Rue Ramboatiana

8

Ave 26 Juin 1960

Rue Dok Razafindratandra
Randramazo

Rue Jean Ralaimongo

AMPARIBE

Rue Mohamed V

Rue Ramankralina

MAHAMASINA

Ave Mahtma Ghandi

Rue Andriba

Rue Rajoelina J

Stade Municipal
de Mahamasina
(Municipal Stadium)

BEFELATANANA

Ave Rabozaka

See Central Antananarivo Map (p36)

ISORAKA

Lac
Anosy

3

4

12

Rue Stibbe

AMPEFILOHA

Rue Ranaivo Jules

Place
Raharisoa
Norbert

Place
Karl Marx

ANOSY

Europcar

Rue Jeneraly Richard Ratsimandrava

Rue Dok Ravoahangy
Andrianavalona Joseph

ISOTRY

Rue Andrianaikarivelona Joseph

Rue Pastora Rahajason

ANOSIBE

Gare Routière de
Fasan'ny Karana

8

Antananarivo

experiences, such as visits to local villages or traditional artisan workshops, attending *famadihana* ceremonies etc (from €40 per person per day). Most tours are led by trained historians or anthropologists (some English-speaking). Two-day trips in the surrounding highlands are also offered.

🛏 Sleeping

Accommodation in Tana is pricier than in the rest of the country; budget travellers will have to push to Ar40,000 for a double room. A number of hotels offer 'day rates', which allow guests to keep their room until early evening, as many flights out of the country leave late at night.

★ **Hôtel Niaouly**   HOTEL €
(Map p32; ☑ 020 22 627 65; www.niaouly.com; Rue Tsiombikibo; r Ar30,000-45,000; ☎) Located between the beautiful Haute-Ville and the trendy bars and restaurants of Isoraka, the Niaouly punches above its weight for the price. The rooms are pretty with polished wooden floors, Madagascan crafts and modern bathrooms (cheaper rooms are dark however). And as if this were not enough, there is also a panoramic terrace and a good restaurant.

Hôtel Moonlight   HOTEL €
(Map p36; ☑ 034 06 265 15, 020 22 268 70; hasina herizo@yahoo.fr; Rue Rainandriamapandry; s/d/tr Ar25,000/32,000/42,000; ☎) This budget stalwart is an excellent option in a lively part of town. Rooms have brightly coloured walls, parquet floors and brand-new bathrooms (most rooms now have showers but share toilets). The staff are friendly, and there are two large communal terraces from where you can watch the world go by.

Villa Isoraka   GUESTHOUSE €€
(Map p36; ☑ 020 24 220 52; www.villa-isoraka. net; Rue Raveloary; d80,000-100,000, without bathroom Ar60,000; ☎) There are just five rooms in this beautiful French townhouse. The rooms with shared bathroom are particularly good value given the standard of the decor: a modern design, with beige and chocolate colour themes and comfortable furnishings. Room 5 is the top pick but eschew Room 2 as it lacks a window. The garden is an exquisite place to breakfast.

Hôtel Tana-Jacaranda   GUESTHOUSE €€
(Map p36; ☑ 034 22 562 39, 020 22 694 63; www. tana-jacaranda.com; 24 Rue Rainitsarovy; s without bathroom Ar30,000, d Ar55,000-78,000; @☎) Rooms at this super-friendly, family-run hotel are simple, quiet and clean. There is also a tip-top dining room with fabulous views of the Rova and the Haute-Ville, piping hot water in the showers, good wi-fi, a guest computer and multilingual, wonderfully helpful staff.

Le Karthala   PENSION €€
(Map p36; ☑ 033 11 971 56, 020 22 248 95; www. le-karthala.com; 48 Rue Andriandahifotsy; s/d €18/20; ☎) The Karthala's motto is 'a little bit like home', and Arianne and her family certainly have a way of making guests feel welcome. The rooms are well kept and homely, there is a gorgeous roof terrace on which to relax or sip a drink, and guests can use the kitchen. Rates include breakfast.

Chez Francis   HOTEL €€
(Map p36; ☑ 020 22 613 65; hotelchezfrancis@ yahoo.fr; Rue Rainandriamapandry; d Ar35,000-50,000; ☎) New owners Sébastien and Gina took over Chez Francis in July 2015 and had lots of ideas to spruce up this great-value establishment. The rooms were clean and tidy but due a revamp, so watch this space. One thing that won't change however is the superb panorama, so ask for a room with a view.

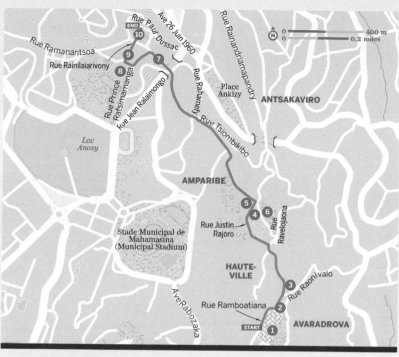

🏃 City Walk
Antananarivo Walking Tour

START POINT DE VUE DU ROVA
END PLACE DE L'INDÉPENDANCE
LENGTH 2.2KM; ONE HOUR

The views from the lookout below the **1 Rova** make it clear why the city's rulers decided to build their palace here: the Madagascan landscape unfolds for miles in every direction.

A few hundred metres downhill, on your right-hand side, you'll find a **2 bas-relief** (1940) by Malagasy artist Charles Rabemanantsoa that tells the history of Madagascar. Rabemanantsoa trained at the school of fine arts, which used to be in what is now **3 Musée Andafivaratra**, the magnificent pink baroque palace of Prime Minister Rainilaiarivony (r 1864–1895). From here, wend your way down to the reconstruction of **4 Jean Laborde's house**, a beautiful wooden building that served as Madagascar's first French consulate.

At the end of the street is **5 Cathédrale de l'Immaculée Conception**, which was built on the spot where Queen Ranavalona I ordered Christian martyrs to be thrown from the cliffs. To your right is the **6 Jardin d'Andolaho**, where *hira gasy* (traditional shows) are held on Sunday afternoons in winter.

From here, amble down through the Haute-Ville's quiet lanes to **7 Rue Ratsimilaho**, famous for its jewellers. Turn left on Rue Prince Ratsimamanga to have a look at the old **8 Presidential Palace**, with its white, green and red sentry boxes that match the Madagascan flag colours; at night, the fountains at the front are lit with multicoloured spotlights, adding a trendy touch to the classic facade.

Head up Rue Rainilaiarivony, where you'll see a **9 memorial** to the victims of the 7 February 2009 riots, which eventually led to Andry Rajoelina overthrowing president Marc Ravalomanana. Finish your walk on the shady **10 Place de l'Indépendance** – the friendly Buffet du Jardin is the perfect place to relax with a THB (Madagascar's signature beer).

Central Antananarivo

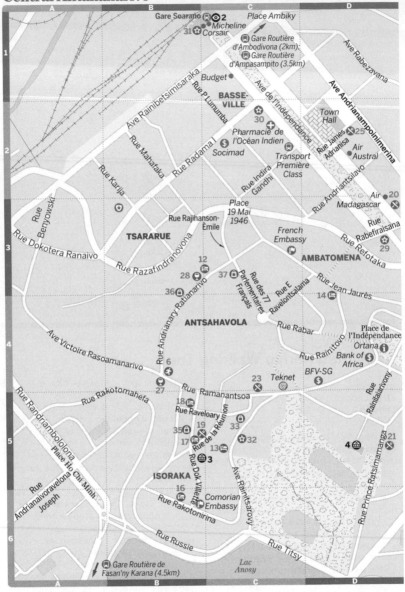

Hôtel-Restaurant Shangaï HOTEL €€
(Map p36; ☎ 020 22 314 72; www.shangai-hotel.com; 4 Rue Rainitovo; d Ar55,000-60,000, tr Ar70,000; ☎) The rooms at this family-run hotel in the embassy quarter are impeccable if rather plain Jane. Ask for a room on the 2nd or 3rd floor to make the best of the light and city views.

★**Hôtel Sakamanga** BOUTIQUE HOTEL €€€
(Map p36; ☎ 020 22 358 09; www.sakamanga.com; Rue Andrianary Ratianarivo; d €20-80; ❀ @ ☎ ☎)

A perennial favourite, the Sakamanga offers fantastic accommodation for both midrange and top-end travellers who set store by a friendly atmosphere, varied rooms, characterful decor and beyond comprehensive services. The intriguingly mazy layout (with enough artefacts in the corridors to stock a museum) leads to an unexpected pool with bar and terrace. Reserve well in advance, as it is almost always full.

★Lokanga
BOUTIQUE HOTEL €€€

(Map p32; ✆020 22 235 49; www.lokanga-hotel. mg; Haute-Ville; r €140; 🕾) This superb 1930s house, a stone's throw from the Rova, has been lovingly renovated by owner Fabiola Deprez and furnished with exquisite taste (many of the antiques belonged to her family). There are just five rooms, each with a theme and sweeping views of the city. The excellent restaurant serves brunch, afternoon tea and sundowners (to make the best of the west-facing terrace).

★Résidence Lapasoa
BOUTIQUE HOTEL €€€

(Map p36; ✆020 22 611 40; www.lapasoa.com; 15 Rue Réunion; d/ste Ar135,000/210,000; ❋@🕾) The exquisite Lapasoa is a modern twist on colonial decor: there are polished wood floors, beautiful wooden furniture (including stunning four-poster beds), colourful fabrics, and light flooding in from skylights and big windows. The top-floor rooms, with their high, sloped ceilings, are the loveliest. The same owners run the superb Kudéta (opposite) restaurant next door.

Le Pavillon de l'Emyrne
BOUTIQUE HOTEL €€€

(Map p36; ✆020 22 259 45; www.pavillon delemyrne.com; 12 Rue Rakotonirina; s/d/ste from €65/75/105; ❋@🕾) In a beautiful 1920s house, the Emyrne has a handful of rooms with an exclusive feel. Each has been individually decorated with a refined mix of vintage and modern. Some rooms have their own garden or verandah. Those on the lower ground floor are a little dark, however. Rates include breakfast and complimentary massages.

Eating

Tana excels at eating: you'll find some of the country's best restaurants in the capital, and although they're slightly more expensive than in the rest of the country, they're often great value for the quality.

★Saka Express
CAFE €

(Map p36; www.sakamanga.com; Rue Andrianary Ratianarivo; mains Ar6500-12,000; ⊘11am-9pm; 🕾🍴) The Hôtel Sakamanga's snack cafeteria and takeaway outlet is the best place in town for lunch on the go. There are pizzas, kebabs and sandwiches, all bursting at the seams with fillings. There are a few tables inside, which fill quickly at lunchtime. Delivery to neighbouring hotels (including in Isoraka) is possible.

Mad'Délices
MADAGASCAN €

(Map p36; Rue Ramanantsoa; mains Ar5000-7000; ⊘6.30am-9.30pm Mon-Sat; 🍴) This cheerful little restaurant in the heart of Isoraka serves hearty Madagascan meals such as pork with greens, zebu stew and omelettes. It's also a good place for breakfast: the pastries are excellent and there is an espresso machine.

Leader Price
SANDWICHES €

(Route des Hydrocarbures; cakes/sandwiches from Ar2500/5000; ⊘9am-7pm Mon-Sat; 🍴) This supermarket chain churns out excellent (and great-value) sandwiches, quiches, tarts and cakes; take away for a picnic or eat in the cafe upstairs.

TANA'S CAFE CULTURE

Whether it's a remnant of French influence or a sign that Tananarivians have a sweet tooth, the Madagascan capital has a number of cafes, some in a league of their own when it comes to cakes and pastries.

Pâtisserie Colbert (Map p36; Hôtel Colbert, Rue Prince Ratsimamanga; pastries Ar1500-3000, sandwiches & quiches Ar5000-8000; ⊘6.30am-7pm; 🕾) This excellent patisserie is a popular meeting place for local businesspeople and a great place for breakfast, a quick lunch or an afternoon treat – the cake selection is mouth-watering, and the ice creams are very popular too. It also sells gourmet chocolates, which make for fantastic presents.

Cookie Shop (Map p32; Ave Rainizanabolone; snacks Ar1900-5000; ⊘8am-6pm Mon-Sat; 🕾) This bright, sparky cafe used to be a favourite of American expats before the embassy moved out of town. It's still popular with foreigners but has also acquired a growing young and trendy Madagascan clientele, who love the bagels, cookies and muffins on offer.

La Potinière (Map p36; Ave de l'Indépendance; cakes from Ar1000; ⊘6.30am-6pm Mon-Sat, to noon Sun) This Chinese-run bakery heaves at weekends, when locals come for a treat. As well as pastries, it has a range of quiches and sandwiches for a light lunch.

Shoprite SUPERMARKET €
(Map p36; Ave Andrianampoinimerina; 8.30am-7.30pm Mon-Sat, to 3pm Sun) Well-stocked supermarket.

★**Le Saka** FUSION €€
(Map p36; 020 22 358 09; www.sakamanga.com; Hôtel Sakamanga, Rue Andrianary Ratianarivo; mains Ar11,000-24,000) Striking the perfect balance between gastro French and straightforward local cooking, Le Saka is a Tana institution. The restaurant is housed in a gorgeous wooden house full of old black-and-white photos and local artwork. The chef whips up some mighty desserts using Madagascan chocolate. Make sure you finish your meal with a house rum or coconut punch. Booking essential.

★**Villa Isoraka** FUSION €€
(Map p36; Rue Raveloary; mains Ar11,000-22,000; 🌐) In a gorgeous private mansion reminiscent of those found in wealthy Parisian suburbs, Villa Isoraka has opened an original restaurant. By day, it serves mostly the local business clientele in the garden or in the lovely dining rooms, but at night it becomes a trendy restaurant-cum-wine bar. The fusion food is fabulous and the portions are huge.

Le Petit Verdot FRENCH €€
(Map p36; 27 Rue Rahamefy; mains Ar12,000-20,000; noon-2pm & 6.30-10pm Mon-Fri, 6.30-10pm Sat) This tiny red-brick bistro, spread over three floors from cellar to mezzanine, scores high on homey atmosphere and hearty French food. The foie gras is terrific, there is a fantastic selection of meat and fish dishes, and the wine selection is the best in Madagascar (261 references from around the world, including some local vintages).

Grill du Rova INTERNATIONAL €€
(Map p32; 020 22 627 24; Rue Ramboatiana; mains Ar11,000-18,000, Sun menu Ar35,000; 10am-5pm; 🅿) Not content with having one of the loveliest locations in town (just 100m from the Rova, with great views), the Grill du Rova also serves up delicious food (including fresh, homemade pasta). It is especially popular on Sundays when it has live music and dancing (set menu only).

★**La Varangue** INTERNATIONAL €€€
(Map p36; 020 22 273 97; www.hotel-restaurant-lavarangue-tananarive.com; 17 Rue Prince Ratsimamanga; mains Ar34,000-37,000, 2-course lunch menu Ar50,000; 🌐) One of the best address-

es in the city for real gourmet cuisine, La Varangue serves an elaborate melange of French gastronomy and Madagascan flavours. Meals are served either in the beautiful dining room, with its low lighting and fabulous antique collection, or on the terrace, which overlooks a charming garden. Booking advised.

Chez Mariette MADAGASCAN €€€
(Map p32; 020 22 216 02; Rue Rakotomalala; menu Ar60,000; 7-10pm) Superchef Mariette Andrianjaka has cooked for notables as diverse as Paloma Picasso and Prince Albert of Monaco during her long career. These days she entertains guests in her 19th-century villa, preparing elaborate multicourse set meals based on *haifi* cuisine – traditional royal banquets. Advance reservation is mandatory. Chez Mariette is up in the Haute-Ville – taxis know where to find it.

The service and the atmosphere are stuffy, but the food is good and the portions gargantuan; drinks are extra.

Kudéta FUSION €€€
(Map p36; 020 22 611 40; www.kudeta.mg; 16 Rue Réunion; mains Ar15,000-25,000, 2-course lunch menu Ar20,000; 🌐) Playing on the region's reputation for political instability may not be very PC, but it really would take a coup d'état to unseat this stylish bar-restaurant from its position at the pinnacle of Tana's fashionable eating scene. The menu makes imaginative use of local ingredients, creating a sophisticated fusion cuisine that suits the chic ethnic decor perfectly. Bookings are advisable.

🍸 Drinking & Nightlife

As well as the town's dedicated bars and clubs, you could try the (often busy) bars

HIRA GASY

Traditional Madagascan performances of acrobatics, music and speeches, *hira gasy* events are held most Sunday afternoons in the villages around Antananarivo. Check newspapers for details: entry is generally very cheap (Ar500 to Ar1000), and the experience is great fun.

Tana's regional tourist office Ortana (p43) also organises a *hira gasy* (2pm to 4pm Sunday, August and September) at **Jardin d'Andolaho** (Map p32) in the Haute-Ville in an effort to revive the tradition. It is free to attend, although spectators normally throw small notes (Ar100 or Ar200 for instance) to show their appreciation.

of the restaurants Le Saka (p39) and Villa Isoraka (p39). The Café de la Gare is another good place for a drink.

Outcool Web Bar BAR
(Map p36; Rue Andrianary Ratianarivo; ⊙10am-12.30am; 🕏) This sociable bar is one of the nicest hang-outs in Tana: it's laid-back, cheerful and very popular with young and cool Malagasies, many of whom come here partly for the free wi-fi. Draft beer (Ar2500) is the most popular tipple; light meals are available.

Buffet du Jardin BAR
(Map p36; www.lebuffetdujardin-antananarivo. com; Place de l'Indépendance; ⊙7am-11pm Sun-Thu, 24hr Fri & Sat; 🕏) This long-standing bar received a facelift in 2013 and has now become a firm favourite amongst locals, expats and tourists alike for anything from a morning coffee to evening drinks or a night out (it serves good food). There is live music on Thursdays, Fridays and Saturdays.

Manson BAR
(Map p36; Rue Ramanantsoa; ⊙8.30pm-late) The clientele in this trendy bar can be a little seedy. It's a shame because the graffiti decor is fun, and the music pretty good.

Kudéta Urban Club LOUNGE
(Map p32; www.kudeta.mg; Hôtel Carlton, Anosy; ⊙10am-late Mon-Sat) Tana's most exclusive (and expensive) bar turns from bar/lounge during the day to nightclub/DJ platform as the night draws in; there are regular parties and events.

Le Club CLUB
(Map p32; Ave Rainizanabolone; admission Ar5000; ⊙10pm-5am Fri & Sat) Tana's biggest, flashiest club space, designed in a modern style, has DJs spinning recent tunes from their lofty winged booth above the dance floor.

☆ Entertainment

To find out what's going on and where, buy any of the three national daily newspapers (*Midi Madagasikara, Madagascar Tribune* and *L'Express de Madagascar*), all of which have advertisements for upcoming events, particularly in the Friday issue. Posters around town also give plenty of notice of forthcoming concerts. Other good resources include the free listings magazines **Sortir à Tana** (www.sortiratana.com), **No Comment** (www.nocomment.mg) and **Tana Planète**, which you will find in every hotel and restaurant in town.

Most nightclubs in Tana are packed with prostitutes, so unaccompanied guys can expect a bit of unsolicited attention.

Le Café de la Gare LIVE PERFORMANCE
(Gare Soarano; Map p36; Gare Soarano; ⊙9am-11pm; 🕏) The stylish Café de la Gare holds regular live music sessions and runs a cinema on Sundays (cartoons at 2pm, and a film at 4pm and 6pm, either in French or in English with French subtitles). Events are free, just get yourself a drink.

Hôtel Le Glacier LIVE MUSIC
(Map p36; Ave 26 Juin 1960; admission Ar5000; ⊙6pm-2am) This slightly disreputable bar has cabaret, bands and traditional music performances every night of the week; it's always full and the atmosphere is good.

Institut Français
Madagascar PERFORMING ARTS
(Map p36; 📞020 22 213 75; www.institut francais-madagascar.com; 14 Ave de l'Indépendance) Antananarivo's foremost cultural venue hosts excellent concerts, theatre events, dance performances, art exhibitions and film screenings almost daily. Pop in to pick up the bimonthly schedule or check it online. Booking is recommended for most of the shows.

Théâtre de Verdure CONCERT VENUE
(Map p36; Ave Rainitsarovy) This amphitheatre has occasional shows featuring artists from the Madagascan charts, as well as regular gospel-music or church-choir concerts that

set the crowd on fire. Tickets are generally very cheap.

Shopping

The shopping in Tana is top-notch, with an excellent range of souvenirs from across the country as well as original boutiques. The city has a couple of shopping malls, including **Tana Water Front** (Map p32; www. centre-commercial-tanawaterfront.com; Ambodivona; ☺9am-7pm Mon-Sat, to 3pm Sun), 2km north of the centre, with a food court, a supermarket and the usual amenities. English books are hard to come by: your best bet are hotel libraries/swap shelves.

Lisy Art Gallery   SOUVENIRS
(Map p32; Route du Mausolée, ☺8am-6pm Mon-Sat) This huge shop stocks anything and everything you could possibly want to bring back from Madagascar, from bottles of *rhum arrangé* (rum with macerated fruit) to leather goods, raffia baskets, hats and spices. The only thing you won't find are gemstones. Prices are fixed but reasonable. It's a short taxi ride from the centre (Ar5000 one way). Card payments accepted.

**Épicerie Fine La Ferme
de Morarano**   FOOD & DRINK
(Map p36; www.ladistilleriedumaido.com/ madagascar.html; Rue Raveloary; ☺9am-6pm Mon-Sat) This shop sells the products of an organic farm in the highlands. It specialises in essential oils, which are used in a range of natural lotions and potions (moisturiser, shampoo, soap etc). You can also buy the oils themselves in small bottles, along with artisan jams, chutneys and spices.

Kudeta Etnik Shop   ACCESSORIES
(Map p36; Rue Isoraka; ☺9.30am-12.30pm & 1.30-5.30pm Mon-Sat) A gorgeous boutique stocking high-end, well-finished Madagascan products such as raffia baskets and purses, silk scarves, jewellery, framed photographs and original clothes by Malagasy designers.

La Teeshirterie   CLOTHING
(Map p36; Rue Andrianary Ratianarivo; ☺8am-6pm Mon-Sat, 9am-4pm Sun) By far the best place to come for Madagascar's funky T-shirts. You'll find all the main brands here (Baobab, Carambole, Maki etc), and a large choice of models and sizes. Credit cards accepted.

Pili Pili Dock   FOOD & DRINK
(Map p32; Tana Water Front; ☺9am-6pm Mon-Sat, to noon Sun) If you'd like a gourmet souvenir from Madagascar, look no further than Pili Pili Dock. The boutique is stunning and everything is beautifully packaged – spices

---

CAPITAL PAMPERING

Spas, massages and treatments are good value in Tana, and there are plenty of options to choose from.

Balnéoforme Colbert (Map p36; ☎020 22 625 71; www.hotel-luxe-madagascar.com; Hôtel Colbert, 29 Rue Prince Ratsimamanga; admission Ar50,000; ☺6.30am-8.30pm Mon-Sat, 10am-8.30pm Sun) For a truly indulgent experience, try this fantastic spa with a mosaic swimming pool, Finnish sauna and Turkish bath. The entrance fee also gives you access to the gym. For additional pampering, there is a treatment list an arm long. It's not cheap (Ar50,000 to Ar100,000), but worth it if you've just arrived back in Tana after some hard hiking.

BioAroma (Map p36; ☎020 22 326 30; www.bioaromamada.com; 54 Rue Ramanantsoa; ☺8am-6pm Mon-Sat, 8.30am-12.30pm Sun) As well as selling local oils and bath, spa and spice products, BioAroma offers a comprehensive range of massages (from Ar30,000 for 30 minutes) as well as facials, scrubs, reiki, manicures and pedicures.

Homeopharma (Map p36; ☎034 49 150 58; www.madagascar-homeopharma.com; 47 Rue Ratsimilaho; ☺8am-6pm Mon-Fri, 9am-4pm Sat) The state-approved natural-health chain Homeopharma has outlets all over Tana and throughout the country; many, such as this branch, offer massages and other treatments (Ar20,000).

Le Royal Palissandre Spa (Map p36; ☎020 22 605 60; www.hotel-restaurant-palissandre. com; 13 Rue Andriandahifotsy; ☺9am-9pm) A gorgeous spa, with a beautiful heated outdoor pool and a hammam (Turkish bath); a number of treatments such as massages, scrubs and facials are available (from Ar90,000).

in grinders, flavoured rum in tall bottles, salad spoons in zebu horns etc. Prices are obviously higher than in a market, but you pay for the presentation and the convenience.

Marché Artisanal de La Digue SOUVENIRS
(La Digue; ☉9am-5.30pm) A popular place to pick up souvenirs is this market located about 12km out of town on a bend in the Ivato airport road. There are products from all over the country, including embroidered tablecloths, raffia products, woodcarvings, spices, vanilla, gemstones etc. Bargaining is essential – divide the initial price by three or four and work from there.

A taxi (around Ar20,000 return) is the easiest way to get here and back with your purchases. Otherwise, if you're going to the airport with a taxi, leave an hour early and stop on your way there. Cash only.

Roses & Baobab ARTS, CRAFTS
(Map p36; www.rosesetbaobab.com; Rue des 77 Parlementaires Français; ☉9am-7pm Mon-Sat) A collective of local artists showcasing sculptures, wood carvings, paintings, metalwork and more.

CS Events OUTDOOR EQUIPMENT
(www.csevents-madagascar.com; Route du Mausolée, Andrainarivo; ☉8.30am-12.30pm & 1.30-6pm Mon-Fri, 8am-1pm Sat) For hiking and camping gear and the like; there is a wide but expensive selection of international branded products.

Espace Loisirs BOOKS
(Map p36; Rue Ratsimilaho; ☉8am-noon & 2-5.30pm Mon-Fri, 8.30am-noon & 2-5pm Sat) The best selection of newspapers, magazines and books in town (all in French), as well as maps.

ⓘ Information

DANGERS & ANNOYANCES
➜ Insecurity has increased in Tana since the political events of 2009. It is not safe to walk after dark; you should always travel by taxi at night.

➜ Pickpocketing is rife around Ave de l'Indépendance and Analakely, so be very careful with your belongings.

➜ Touts posing as official guides prey on travellers who haven't arranged to be met at the airport; stick to the official taxi rank or book one through your hotel.

EMERGENCY
Ambulance (☑020 22 625 66)
Fire (☑118)

Police (Map p36; ☑117)

INTERNET ACCESS
Every hotel in Tana now offers free wi-fi (even if only in the reception area), as do an increasing number of bars and restaurants. The quality of the connection varies; it is usually good enough for emails/social media, but not necessarily for Skype or data-hungry downloads.

Teknet (Map p36; Rue Ramanantsoa; per 45min Ar2000; ☉8am-6pm Mon-Sat, 2-6pm Sun; ☎) Internet cafe with good computers with large screens and a fast connection; printers and scanners available.

MEDICAL SERVICES
Clinique des Sœurs Franciscaines (Map p32; ☑020 22 235 54; Rue Dokotera Rajaonah, Ankadifotsy) Has X-ray equipment and is well run.

Dr Chapuis (Map p32; ☑020 23 208 88; Tana Water Front) A reliable dentist.

Espace Médical (Map p32; ☑020 22 625 66; Ambodivona) A private clinic with 24-hour A&E, with laboratory and X-ray equipment; it organises medical repatriations.

Hôpital Militaire (Map p32; ☑020 23 397 51; Rue Moss, Soavinandriana) The best-equipped hospital in the country.

Pharmacie de l'Océan Indien (Map p36; ☑020 22 224 70; 118 Ave de l'Indépendance) Centrally located and well-stocked.

Pharmacie Métropole (Map p36; ☑020 22 200 25; www.pharmacie-metropole.com; Rue Ratsimilaho; ☉8am-12.30pm & 2-6.30pm Mon-Fri, to noon Sat) One of Tana's best and most convenient pharmacies.

MONEY
All banks change foreign currencies, and most will change travellers cheques and offer cash advances on credit cards (both Visa and MasterCard). Virtually all now have reliable ATMs although some aren't accessible outside banking hours.

Bank of Africa (BOA; Map p36; Place de l'Indépendance; ☉8am-3.30pm) Has a Visa-only ATM.

BFV-SG (Map p36; Rue Ramanantsoa; ☉8am-4pm Mon-Fri) Has an ATM.

BNI Madagascar (Map p36; Ave 26 Juin 1960; ☉8am-4pm) Has an ATM (Visa and MasterCard).

Socimad (Map p36; Rue Radama I; ☉8am-5pm Mon-Fri) Changes cash and travellers cheques. Also has a 24-hour office at the airport.

POST
Tana's two main post offices are in **Basse-Ville** (Map p36; Ave 26 Juin 1960; ☉8am-4pm Mon-Fri, 8.30-11am Sat) and **Haute-Ville** (Map

p36; Rue Ratsimilaho; ⊙8am-4pm Mon-Fri, 8.30-11am Sat).

TOURIST INFORMATION

Ortana (Map p36; ✆034 20 270 51; www.tourisme-antananarivo.com; Place de l'Indépendance; ⊙9am-5pm) This is the place to go to if you would like a guide to visit historical sites around Tana such as the Rova and Musée Andafivaratra, Ambohimanga, Ilafy etc. Most guides are knowledgeable and many speak English and/or Italian as well as French. Staff can also advise on other sights around the capital.

The office also organises one- to three-hour group walks around the Haute-Ville on Mondays, Wednesdays and Saturdays (Ar5000 to Ar20,000 per person depending on the circuit and the number of people).

❶ Getting There & Away

AIR

You can get domestic and international flights to and from Ivato airport. The following airlines have offices in Tana:

Air Austral (Map p36; ✆020 22 303 31; www.air-austral.com; 23 Ave de l'Indépendance)

Air France (✆020 23 230 23; www.airfrance.com; Tour Zital, Route des Hydrocarbures, Ankorondrano)

Air Madagascar (Map p36; ✆020 22 222 22; www.airmadagascar.com; 31 Ave de l'Indépendance)

Corsair (Map p36; ✆020 22 633 36; www.corsair.fr; Gare Soarano, 1 Ave de l'Indépendance)

Madagasikara Airways (✆034 05 970 07, 032 05 970 07; www.madagasikara airways.com; La City, Ivandry)

BUS

Cotisse (Map p32; ✆032 11 027 33; www.facebook.com/cotisse.transport; Ambodivona) Nice 16- or 19-seater Mercedes minibuses that link Antananarivo with Tamatave (Ar24,000, seven hours, hourly departures on the hour between 7am and noon, then 7pm and 8.30pm) and Majunga (Ar38,000, 11 hours, departures at 7am and 4pm). Cotisse has its own terminal, with a modern waiting room (power sockets, wi-fi, cafeteria and TV). Departures are punctual.

Transport Première Class (Map p36; ✆033 15 488 88, 032 40 134 76; www.malagasycar.com; Hôtel Le Grand Mellis, 3 Rue Indira Gandhi) Runs comfortable, air-con vehicles only between Tana and Majunga (Ar78,000, 10 hours, daily). It sits just two people to a row and includes a packed lunch. Departure is at 7am; drop-off is on the corniche in Majunga. Booking essential. Sometimes runs services to Nosy Be too.

Transpost (Map p36; ✆020 22 302 27; Post Office, Rue Ratsimilaho; ⊙7.30am-5pm Mon-Fri, to noon Sat) More punctual than normal *taxis-brousses*, but similar in comfort and price, Transpost is run by Madagascar's postal service. It has minibuses between Majunga and Tana only (Ar25,000, 12 hours; Tuesday, Thursday and Saturday); pick-up and drop-off is at the central post office in both cities. Departure is at 6am sharp. Booking required.

CAR

The best place to arrange a car and driver is from one of the reputable tour agencies (p263) operating in the country. Big international car-rental agencies are also present in Tana, but they often come with a driver too. Prices quoted are for short journeys.

Budget (Map p36; ✆020 22 611 11; www.budget.mg; 4 Ave de l'Indépendance) A compact car/4WD with driver costs per day Ar198,000/342,000, plus fuel, for a short journey.

Europcar (Map p32; ✆020 23 336 47; www.europcar.com; Enceinte Rayim Rond) From Ar129,000 a day for a short trip in a small city car (with driver); fuel is extra.

TAXI-BROUSSE

For morning departures, turn up early (6am); for afternoon departures, come around 2pm. It may take up to four hours for some vehicles to fill.

Gare Routière d'Ambodivona (Northern Taxi-Brousse Station; Map p32; Ambodivona) About 2km northeast of the city centre. A taxi to/from the centre costs Ar4000.

Gare Routière d'Ampasampito (Eastern Taxi-Brousse Station; Map p32; Ampasampito) About 3.5km northeast of the centre. A taxi to/from the centre will cost Ar6000.

Gare Routière de Fasan'ny Karana (Southern Taxi-Brousse Station; Map p32; Anosibe) About

---

❶ IVATO AIRPORT

➡ The bureaux de change at Ivato airport offers similar rates to the banks in Tana; it also exchanges travellers cheques.

➡ BNI Madagascar at the terminal has an ATM that accepts both Visa and MasterCard.

➡ All three phone networks have booths in the arrivals area where you can buy a SIM card and credit.

➡ Ariary are not accepted in the departure area, even at the cafe (euros or US dollars only).

TAXIS-BROUSSES FROM ANTANANARIVO

DESTINATION	STATION	FARE (AR)	TIME (HR)	APPROX DEPARTURE TIME
Antsirabe	Fasan'ny Karana	10,000	3	All day
Ambanja	Ambodivona	60,000	18	Afternoon
Diego Suarez (Antsiranana)	Ambodivona	70,000	24	Afternoon
Fianarantsoa	Fasan'ny Karana	26,000	8	Morning & afternoon
Fort Dauphin (Taolagnaro)	Fasan'ny Karana	100,000	60	Afternoon Tue & Thu, morning Sat
Majunga	Ambodivona	30,000	12	Morning & afternoon
Manakara	Fasan'ny Karana	41,000	13	Afternoon
Miandrivazo	Fasan'ny Karana	24,000	9	Afternoon
Moramanga	Ampasampito	5000	2	All day
Morondava	Fasan'ny Karana	44,000	16	Afternoon
Tamatave (Toamasina)	Ambodivona/ Ampasampito	20,000	7	Morning & afternoon
Tuléar (Toliara)	Fasan'ny Karana	52,000	18	Afternoon

4km southwest of Lac Anosy. A taxi to/from the centre costs Ar10,000.

ℹ Getting Around

TO/FROM THE AIRPORT

Ivato airport is 12km from the city centre. A taxi to/from the city centre costs Ar40,000 during the day, Ar50,000 at night. A much cheaper but slower alternative is **Navette Adema** (☑ 034 05 565 48, 034 05 565 47; ☺ 5am-10pm), a shuttle service running between the airport and selected hotels in the town centre, with a terminus at Gare Soarana (Ar10,000, one hour). To go to the airport, ask your hotel to book the shuttle (that way they can chase it if it's running late), and make sure you leave plenty of time as it's not possible to know how many pick-ups the shuttle will have to do before setting off.

TAXI

Tana's cream-colour taxis are plentiful and cheap, even at night. Fares are negotiable: a journey in town should cost Ar4000 to Ar8000 during the day, or Ar5000 to Ar10,000 at night. Always agree on a price before leaving. You may pay a different rate for the same route depending on whether you are going downhill or uphill!

TAXI-BE

Large minibuses called taxi-be meander around Antananarivo and the outlying suburbs; the standard fare is Ar400. They are of limited use to travellers because of the difficulty to work out a) the route and b) where bus stops are. If you do take a taxi-be for a straightforward journey (to Ivato or Ambohimanga for instance), be very careful with your belongings as pickpockets are a real problem.

AROUND ANTANANARIVO

The highlands around Antananarivo are often ignored by travellers pushing on to other regions, but the whole area is perfect day-trip country. Two of Antananarivo's 12 sacred hills are easily accessible, offering great insight into the history and culture of the Merina people. If you don't have your own transport, the best way to see the sites around Tana is to charter a taxi for the day; a lovely day trip would be to combine Ilafy, Ambohimanga and Ivato (expect to pay Ar120,000 to Ar150,000).

Lemurs' Park

You will find nine species of lemur at **Lemurs' Park** (☑ 020 22 234 36; www.lemurs park.com; RN1; admission Ar25,000; ☺ 9am-5pm), a private reserve located 22km west of the capital on the RN1. It's a good place to visit if you haven't had the chance to see lemurs elsewhere, or if you need one final lemur fix before you go! The lemurs are free-ranging (except for the two nocturnal species, which are confined to rather small cages) and well habituated, so you'll see them up close. There are about 50 individual lemurs including Coquerel *sifakas*, ring-tail lemurs and black-and-white ruffed lemurs.

Most of the animals are former pets or individuals that were threatened in their natural habitat, and the reserve has a breeding program together with other private sanctuaries.

Nestled on a bend of the River Katsaoka, the 5-hectare park is a beautiful and tranquil spot. The park can arrange transfers from Tana if you don't have your own vehicle: it costs Ar60,000/70,000 return for one/two people, including admission. Call ahead to arrange.

Ivato

About 13km from Antananarivo is the village-suburb of Ivato, where the international airport is located. If you just have one night or day to spend between flights, spend it here: you'll save yourself time (traffic between Tana and Ivato is perennially bad) and money, and there is plenty to see and do in Ivato itself.

◉ Sights

Le Village   WORKSHOP
(☑ 020 22 451 97; www.maquettesdebateaux. com; Route de l'Aéroport, Talatamaty; ⊗ 8am-4.30pm Mon-Sat) Around 30 highly skilled artisans work here producing scale models of historic ships, fishing boats and famous vessels. Everything is made by hand – from miniature cannons to the ships' sails. One model takes about six months to complete. You can view the artisans at work from Monday to Friday. The showroom (models start at €200) also opens on Saturday.

The workshop is located about 6km south of the airport in the direction of Tana.

Croc Farm   FARM
(Ivato; admission Ar15,000; ⊗ 9am-5pm) This is an unusual place: a commercial crocodile farm that breeds crocs and sells their meat and skin, as well as a zoo where you can see the reptilian giants in all their basking glory, along with lemurs, chameleons and even the rare fossa (striped civet).

The park's about 3km from the airport. A taxi will cost around Ar15,000 return from Ivato, including an hour's wait.

The displays on crocodiles are highly informative: many of the biggest specimens (well over 6m) have been brought here

ANTANANARIVO IVATO

Around Antananarivo

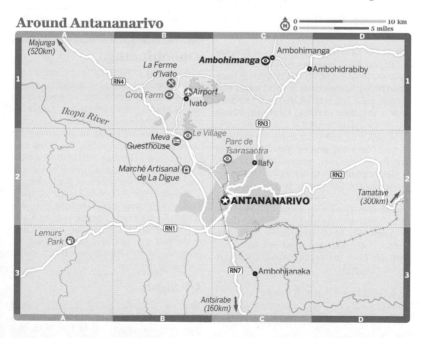

because they were becoming a danger to humans in their natural habitat. You can eat crocodile in the park's restaurant (mains Ar20,000).

🛏 Sleeping & Eating

★ **Le Manoir Rouge**   GUESTHOUSE €
(☎ 032 05 260 97; manoirrouge@gmail.com; Ivato; €20/25 dm/s/d/f without bathroom, €8/12/14/19, d/f with bathroom; ☎) Under new and dynamic ownership since 2015, this backpacker-friendly guesthouse is a mere 900m from the airport. It has real charm, with creaky floorboards and a lovely big garden. The varied rooms (most with shared bathroom) sleep up to four people. There is a good on-site restaurant too (mains Ar10,000 to Ar12,000) offering fresh market cuisine, and regular evening entertainment. Airport transfer included.

Meva Guesthouse   GUESTHOUSE €€
(☎ 032 42 896 62; www.mevaguesthouse.com; Talatamaty; s/d/f Ar50,000/65,000/95,000; ☎) Located about 6km south of Ivato, on the road to Tana, this gorgeous guesthouse is a warm and authentic place to stay. The Dutch-Malagasy owners have thought about everything: the rooms are homely and spacious, guests have access to the kitchen, the garden is beautiful, and rooms on the upper floors have nice views of the neighbouring paddy fields.

★ **La Ferme d'Ivato**   INTERNATIONAL €€€
(☎ 032 11 584 95; www.lafermedivato.com; Ivato; 2-/3-course menus Ar27,000/35,000; ☺ 11am-3pm) If you fancy a long, languid lunch surrounded by fragrant plants and greenery, this is the place to come. La Ferme d'Ivato is, as its name suggests, a working farm (animals, fruit and vegetables). It's certified organic and the on-site restaurant serves the farm's delicious products, cooked with a Madagascan twist of spices and flavours.

Guests get the chance to visit the farm after lunch. The only downsides are the rather dear fixed-price menu and the location, about 6km beyond the airport, down a rough dirt road. You'll need your own vehicle; otherwise the farm can arrange a transfer from the airport (Ar60,000 for up to four people).

ℹ Getting There & Away

➡ A taxi between the airport and Ivato village will cost Ar5000.

➡ A taxi from Ivato village to Antananarivo costs Ar30,000.
➡ Taxi-be route D (Ar500, one hour) links the *taxi-brousse* stand behind Gare Soarana in Tana to Ivato bus station, near the market.

Ilafy

Originally called Ambohitrahanga, Ilafy was founded around the turn of the 17th century on a sacred hilltop and was used as a country residence by the Merina royal family. The wooden residence was redesigned in the 1830s by Ranavalona I and used as a hunting lodge by Radama II, whose body was initially buried in a modest tomb on the grounds before being transferred to the *rova*.

The hunting lodge was reconstructed in 1957, after the original had fallen into disrepair; it now houses the **Ethnographic Museum** (Ilafy; admission Ar3000; ☺ 9am-noon & 2-5pm Tue-Sun), which illustrates tribal life around Madagascar with exhibits including model tombs, hunting and fishing tools, modern wooden carvings, and information about magic and religious rituals. A knowledgeable guide will show you around; a tip of Ar2000 to Ar5000 is appropriate.

Ilafy lies 12km from Antananarivo, just east of the road leading to Ambohimanga. You'll need your own transport to get here.

Ambohimanga

Ambohimanga ('blue hill' or 'beautiful hill') was the original capital of the Merina royal family. Even after the seat of government was shifted to Antananarivo for political reasons, Ambohimanga remained a sacred site, and was off-limits to foreigners for many years. The entire hill was listed as a Unesco World Heritage Site in 2001 for being 'the most significant symbol of the cultural identity of the people of Madagascar'.

The entrance to Ambohimanga village is marked by a large traditional gateway, one of the seven gateways to the eyrie-like hilltop. To one side is a large, flat, round stone. At the first sign of threat to the village, the stone would be rolled by up to 40 slaves, sealing off the gate.

◉ Sights

★ **Rova**   PALACE
(admission Ar10,000; ☺ 9am-5pm) Poised atop Ambohimanga hill is the Rova, the

THE MERINA

The region surrounding Antananarivo is known as Imerina (Land of the Merina Tribe). Historically, the Merina have been Madagascar's dominant tribe, reigning over the country for several centuries.

Merina hierarchy was based on a three-tier caste system, largely dependent on skin colour. The *andriana* (nobles; generally fairer-skinned and with pronounced Asiatic rather than African features, reflecting their Indonesian ancestry) comprised the upper echelon, while the *hova* (commoners) made up the middle class. The remainder – descendants of former slaves – were known as the *andevo* (workers).

The first Merina kingdoms were established around the 16th century, and by the late 19th century they were the dominant tribe in Madagascar. Ordinary Merina citizens customarily worked as administrators, shopkeepers, teachers and traders. Their position was enhanced by the choice of Antananarivo as the seat of the French colonial government, and by the establishment of an education system there.

Today, the Merina are still among the best-educated Malagasies and many remain at the forefront of public life: former president Marc Ravalomanana, coup leader Andry Rajoelina and the current president Hery Rajaonarimampianina are all Merina.

fortress-palace. The walls of the compounds were constructed using cement made from sand, shells and egg whites – 16 million eggs were required to build the outer wall alone. Inside, there are two palaces: the traditional palace (1788) of the all-powerful Merina king Andrianampoinimerina, and the European-styled summer palace of Queen Ranavalona I (r 1828–1861), constructed by French engineer Jean Laborde in 1870 (he was thought to be Ranavalona's lover).

The word 'palace' seems over the top to describe King Andrianampoinimerina's simple wooden hut (1788), but palace it was. The original was thatched, but Jean Laborde replaced the grass roof with more durable wooden tiles in the 19th century.

The central pole of the hut is made from a single trunk of sacred palisander (rosewood), which was reportedly carried from the east coast by 2000 slaves, 100 of whom died in the process. The top of the pole is carved to show a pair of women's breasts, a symbol of the king's polygamy. The king supposedly hid in the rafters when visitors arrived, signalling whether the guest was welcome by dropping pebbles onto his wife's head.

The royal bed is in the sacred northeast corner of the hut and is elevated to indicate the king's superior status. The simple furniture is aligned according to astrological rules.

Behind the hut are the open-air baths where the king performed his royal ablutions once a year, in the company of his 12 wives and diverse honoured guests. After-

wards his bathwater was considered sacred and was delivered to waiting supplicants.

Next door to King Andrianampoinimerina's hut, in a striking style contrast, is Queen Ranavalona I's elegant summer palace. It's been beautifully restored and has original European-style furniture inside. The dining room was lined with mirrors, which allowed the queen to check that no one was sneakily poisoning her food.

Ambohimanga is still revered by many Malagasies as a sacred site, and you will see offerings (zebu horns, blood, sweets and honey, as well as small change) at various shrines around the compound where individuals or families have come to invoke royal spirits for luck and fertility. Don't disturb these sacred locations and never point at them with your finger outstretched.

There are sensational views of the surrounding countryside from around the compound.

Make sure you take a guide to go round the Rova to learn about the site's historical and cultural significance. Guides (French- and English-speaking) trained by Oscar, the local tourist office, are available by the entrance where you pay your admission.

❶ Getting There & Away

Ambohimanga is 21km north of Antananarivo and easily visited as a day trip in combination with Ilafy. Taxis-bes (route H) leave throughout the day from Ambodivona (Ar700, 1½ hours). From the village, you'll need to walk 1km up the hill to the Rova.

Central Madagascar

Best Places to Eat

➡ La Rizière (p67)

➡ Chez Jenny (p55)

➡ Café Mirana (p54)

➡ Sharon (p63)

➡ Le Rendez-Vous des
Pêcheurs (p50)

Best Places to Stay

➡ Lac Hôtel (p63)

➡ Camp Catta (p72)

➡ Chambres des Voyageurs
(p53)

➡ Chez Billy (p53)

➡ Hôtel Anjara (p56)

Why Go?

The classic tourist route from Antananarivo (Tana) takes you south along the RN7 through central Madagascar, a high plateau stretching all the way to Fianarantsoa. You'll twist and turn through these highlands, a region of scenic hills and rice paddies that resists generalisation.

Here you'll find a potpourri of travellers' delights: bustling market towns clogged with colourful pousse-pousse (rickshaws), a famous railway line, a distinctive architecture of two-storey mud-brick homes, a mountain stronghold of lemurs, the legacy of French colonialism, national parks with landscapes ranging from thick jungle to wide-open grandeur, and some of the best hiking Madagascar has to offer.

For many people this is their introduction to the country, and it's a good one, with almost all attractions accessible by paved road.

When to Go
Antsirabe

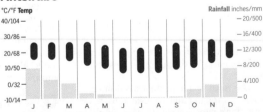

Jul–Sep *Famadihana* (exhumation and reburial) ceremonies take place across the region.

Apr & May The countryside is at its greenest following the end of the rainy season.

Sep & Oct Best weather of the year; animals are active, and lemurs have babies.

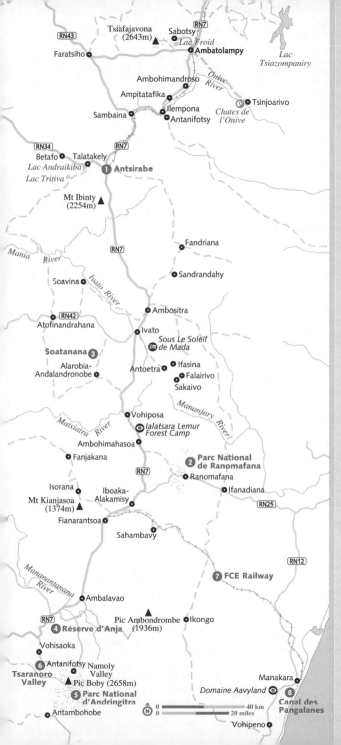

Central Madagascar Highlights

1 Hit the trails around **Antsirabe** (p52), by foot or mountain bike

2 See how many species of lemurs you can tot up during your time in **Parc National de Ranomafana** (p58)

3 Watch Madagascan wild silk being made in **Soatanana** (p54)

4 Commune with ring-tailed lemurs in **Réserve d'Anja** (p68)

5 Scale Madagascar's second-highest mountain, Pic Boby, in spectacular **Parc National d'Andringitra** (p70)

6 Sit by the village well in the paradisiacal **Tsaranoro Valley** (p71)

7 Ride the colourful **FCE railway** (p66) from Fianarantsoa to Manakara

8 Paddle a pirogue down the **Canal des Pangalanes** (p61)

ℹ️ Getting There & Around

Perhaps the most common itinerary in Madagascar is to head down the RN7 from Tana to Tuléar (Toliara), sampling everything along the way, then fly back to Tana. Nearly all of central Madagascar's towns and attractions lie near this two-lane highway, one of the few reasonably well-maintained sealed roads in the country. Many people take a detour on the colourful FCE railway, continue on to the coast via Isalo, worship sun and reef a bit, then fly back to Tana.

This makes central Madagascar an easy destination for budget travellers, who will be able to go everywhere by *taxi-brousse*. For attractions that do require a private vehicle, enquire with local tour operators, ask your hotel, or charter a taxi.

Ambatolampy

A charming and very typical plateau town, Ambatolampy lies 68km south of Antananarivo on the RN7, among the picturesque forests and hills of the Ankaratra Massif. The town is best-known for its aluminium artisans, who make the ubiquitous *marmites* (aluminium pots) that you can see in every household and hotel up and down the country.

◎ Sights

Aluminium Pot Workshop   WORKSHOP
Travellers can visit local workshops and watch the artisans at work. The metal used to manufacture pots here is scavenged from car parts etc. It is melted in furnaces and then poured in handmade moulds of very fine laterite and coal powder. The workers are incredibly dexterous and fast: one team of two can produce up to 50 pots a day. A donation will be expected – Ar5000 is appropriate.

🛏️ Sleeping & Eating

La Pineta   GUESTHOUSE €€
(☑ 020 42 493 02, 034 74 265 40; lapinetasarl@ yahoo.com; Route d'Antsirabe; d/tr Ar35,000/48,000, without bathroom Ar32,000/44,000; 🛜) With its vaguely Mexican-sounding name and vaguely Swiss-chalet feel, La Pineta is an unusual but lovely option in Ambatolampy. The five pretty rooms have creaky, shiny wooden floors and bright colours. Meals (menu Ar20,000) are served either in the homely dining room or in the garden.

⭐ **Le Rendez-Vous**
des Pêcheurs   INTERNATIONAL €€
(☑ 032 05 098 43; www.madarun.com; mains Ar10,000-16,000) Going strong since 1951, the Rendez-Vous is a local institution. Every tour travelling between Tana and Antsirabe or enjoying a day trip in the highlands seems to stop here for lunch. The dining room has the feel of an old-fashioned canteen (with log fire in winter) and the food is excellent: hearty and great value.

There are spacious rooms (double Ar41,000, without bathroom Ar31,000) on the 1st floor; just like in the dining room, the furniture hasn't changed since the 1950s, but it's immaculate and the manager is a mine of information on the area. He can also organise tours between here, Antsirabe and Ambositra.

ℹ️ Getting There & Away

All *taxis-brousses* heading south towards Antsirabe pass through Ambatolampy (Ar10,000, one hour).

Antsirabe

POP 251,560

Antsirabe is best-known for its thermal springs. The city emerged as a spa town in the late 1800s when Norwegian missionaries built a health retreat here (still in use to this day). French colonists then turned it into a chic getaway from nearby Tana, hence the numerous turn-of-the-century villas and the broad tree-lined avenues so typical of French cities.

Much of this colonial heritage is fading now, nowhere more so than at the famous **Hôtel des Thermes** (☎ 020 44 487 62), whose magnificent facade hides a seriously ageing interior. But the city itself is full of life: it is a beacon of industry in Madagascar (the town has large textile, food and drink factories); many Tananriviens would move here at the drop of a hat if they could. Travellers will no doubt find the city's energy infectious, and its wealth of sightseeing, activity and eating options appealing.

◎ Sights & Activities

Antsirabe is famed for its skilled artisans and a popular activity is to visit a few workshops over the course of a morning or afternoon. Some people charter a pousse-pousse for the occasion and let the driver take charge of the itinerary (make sure you discuss the number of stops, length and price beforehand; allow Ar20,000 to Ar40,000 for a circuit), but you could simply take a different pousse-pousse between each stop, if you know where you want to go.

Antsirabe

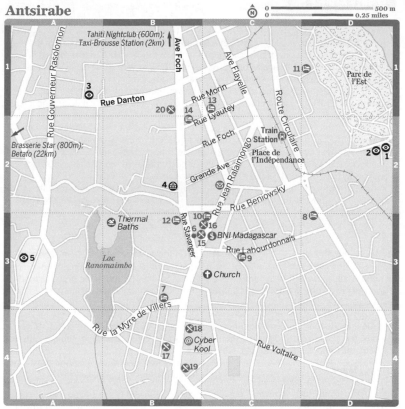

Antsirabe

Chez Mamy Miniatures WORKSHOP
(Parc de l'Est; ⏰9am-5pm) This family work-shop specialises in the creation of minia-ture objects (cars, rickshaws, bicycles etc) made from recycled materials – anything from aluminium cans to (unused) intrave-nous tubes, textile and old cables. They'll demonstrate how to make parts of their models; it's an incredibly fiddly and inven-tive process.

WORTH A TRIP

A TRIP TO THE LAKES

There are two attractive lakes outside of Antsirabe that are popular day trips from the city. **Lac Andraikiba**, the closest and largest of the two, is 7km west off the road to Betafo. Frequented by Malagasy tourists, it has craft booths with some annoying hawkers, but it's also easy to get away for a nice quiet walk or picnic.

The turquoise **Lac Tritriva**, a further 12km away, also has a hawker problem, and there is a Ar5000 entry fee, but this crater lake is even prettier, and the path around it makes for an easy circumnavigation.

You'll find the lovely **Case à Tritriva** (☑ 034 67 159 56; Lac Tritriva; 2-/3-course menus Ar10,000/12,000) nearby, ideal if you fancy a hot meal rather than a sandwich. Run by a Franco-Malagasy couple, they serve simple, wholesome cuisine in the courtyard of their home, complete with panoramic views. There is also basic accommodation if you fancy a night away from the bustle of town (half board per person Ar25,000).

A great way to get to the lakes is to cycle – Rando Raid Madagascar rents mountain bikes and provides an excellent map guaranteed to get you there and back; it also organises guided mountain biking and canoeing trips to the lakes. Green Park also rents bikes (Ar25,000 per day).

Atelier Corne de Zébu WORKSHOP
(Parc de l'Est; ⊙9am-5pm) Zebu horn is a versatile – and beautiful – material, which artisans at this workshop turn into numerous objects, from jewellery to salad spoons, sculpted animals and accessories. You'll see the whole production process, from how to separate the bone from its keratin shell to polishing the final products with old denim.

Sabotsy Market MARKET
(⊙7am-4pm Sat) A Madagascan version of a Moroccan souk, this sprawling open-air market, with distinct areas of jewellery, clothing, food and more, will keep you occupied for hours either shopping or simply absorbing the spectacle. Located in a vast walled compound, it is a Pandora's box of unusual sights and sounds, not to mention things for sale, with all of local society seemingly on display.

Chez Marcel WORKSHOP
(Rue Danton; admission incl 8 packets sweets Ar10,000; ⊙7.30am-5.30pm Mon-Sat) The technique used to make traditional sweets here hasn't changed in decades: a syrup is prepared, then rapidly cooled down and kneaded on a granite slab. Ingredients such as vanilla, orange peel, ground coffee or crystallised ginger are added to the mix for flavour; the preparation is then cut into individual sweets. Voila – done and dusted in 15 minutes!

Brasserie Star BREWERY
(☑020 44 481 71; n.razafindralova@star.mg; Rue Danton; ⊙tours 9am & 2pm Tue, Wed & Thu) FREE Wondering where all that Three Horses Beer comes from? Look no further. Madagascar's dominant and unmissable brand is made in this, the country's biggest brewery. Starting at the THB billboard on the corner of Ave Foch and Rue Danton, head west on Danton (towards Morondava) for 800m. If you've seen breweries elsewhere, though, this will be familiar.

Bookings required. Visitors must wear long trousers and closed shoes.

★**Rando Raid Madagascar** MOUNTAIN BIKING
(☑032 04 900 21; www.randoraidmadagascar.com; Rue Stavanger; half-/full-day mountain biking excursion Ar50,000/90,000; ⊙8.30am-noon & 3-6pm Mon-Sat) The area around Antsirabe is a paradise for outdoor sports, and Bazoly and Jean-Marc have devised a plethora of activities (mountain biking, hiking, horse riding, canoeing, quads and motorbikes, often in combination) and excursions (lakes, mountains, Betafo, anything from half a day to several days) to make the best of this amazing playground.

As well as organised excursions, they rent bikes (half/full day Ar20,000/25,000) and motorbikes (half/full day Ar50,000/65,000.)

⏰ Tours

Antsirabe is a popular place to organise a tour down the Tsiribihina River in western Madagascar. These floating trips are often combined with a visit to Parc National des Tsingy de Bemaraha and last around seven days.

AGAVE TOUR
(Association des Guides Agréés Volontaires de l'Environnement; ☎ 020 44 484 88; chezbilly@moov. mg; Chez Billy, Antsirabe) This local guides' association was created to encourage greater professionalism, collaboration and sustainable practice among guides. This is the most reliable organisation to contact to organise a guide, whatever your plans; it is based out of Chez Billy.

🎊 Festivals & Events

Just when you thought you'd seen it all: June to September is the time for *famadihana* (literally, the 'turning of the bones'), the ritual exhumation and celebration of ancestors' bones by the Betsileo and Merina people. *Famadihana* are joyous and intense occasions, which occur in each family roughly every seven years.

Famadihana ceremonies take place in the *hauts plateaux* (highlands) region from Tana to Ambalavao every year. Hotels or guides can help you find one and arrange an invitation. If you receive an invite, it's polite to bring a bottle of rum or a monetary contribution as a gift for the host family, and to ask before taking pictures. Foreigners are generally warmly welcomed, and most people find that the experience, far from being morbid, is moving and fascinating.

🛏 Sleeping

Antsirabe offers a vast array of sleeping options and caters particularly well to budget travellers. Do ask for extra blankets on winter nights.

⭐ **Chez Billy** GUESTHOUSE €
(☎ 020 44 484 88; chezbilly@moov.mg; Antsenakely; d/tr/q without bathroom Ar27,000/32,000/42,000; 🛜) This eclectic melange of guesthouse, bar and restaurant, awash in loud art, inspires a hostel-like conviviality among the staff, backpackers, guides and in-the-know *vazaha* (foreigners) who form its crossroads clientele. The rooms are simple but well-kept, the showers hot and powerful, and the jovial owner Billy, a former guide, is a mine of information. It's always full so book ahead.

Lovasoa GUESTHOUSE €
(☎ 020 44 486 85; www.lovasoa.mg; Rue Stavanger; dm/d Ar15,000/80,000, d without bathroom Ar40,000; 🛜) Run by the Lutheran Church and a Norwegian aid agency, this guesthouse in the centre of town is a little gem. The grounds are large and feel like a little oasis. Inside, the dorms (which sleep eight) are immaculate and cheerful, with separate bathrooms for men and women. There are gorgeous double rooms too, which are surprisingly high-end, and therefore more expensive.

Green Park BUNGALOW €€
(☎ 020 44 051 90; greenparktsara@yahoo.fr; Rue Labourdonnais; campsites per tent Ar7000, d/f Ar40,000/50,000; 🛜) The bungalows are simple but pretty at Green Park (do check a couple as some are a little damp), but it's the beautiful garden and pond that seal the deal (and the proximity to Chez Jenny, the town's best restaurant). Camping is also available.

Trianon GUESTHOUSE €€
(☎ 020 44 051 40; www.hotel-letrianon-antsirabe. com; Ave Foch; s/d/tr Ar60,500/79,500/91,500; 🛜) This charming throwback to the colonial era, a nicely renovated French chateau with grand embracing stairways, is just oozing with atmosphere, from its old airline posters to its uniformed staff. The classy restaurant and terrace strike just the right note, as do the chequered tablecloths in the breakfast room. The downside is the location, off a busy road.

Antsirabe Hôtel HOTEL €€
(☎ 034 07 762 02; salama_deo@yahoo.com; Mahazoarivo Nord; d/tr/f Ar55,000/65,000/90,000) Located north of the centre, in a residential neighbourhood, this family-run hotel is a friendly and welcoming option. The two-storey villa is modern and homely, and the rooms, although simply furnished, are huge, light and comfortable.

Hôtel Hasina HOTEL €€
(☎ 020 44 485 56; www.hotelhasina.com; Rue Ralaimongo; d/tr Ar39,500/47,000, d without bathroom Ar35,500; 🛜) Right in the town centre, Hôtel Hasina is good value, if uninspiring. The rooms overlooking the street are lighter and come with balconies, but those at the back are quieter.

⭐ **Les Chambres du Voyageurs** GUESTHOUSE €€€
(☎ 032 83 083 61; www.chambres-voyageur.mg; d/t/f bungalows Ar100,00/125,000/200,000; 🛜) 🍃 This ecolodge is a rarity in Antsirabe, an island of nature on the edge of the city. The owner's passion is gardening and you'll find some 800 species of plant in its themed gardens (Majorelle, Alhambra, Japanese etc), as well as 14 species of birds, tortoises

WORTH A TRIP

SOATANANA

Borocera Madagascariensis, an endemic silkworm that feeds on tapia trees, is Madagascar's answer to *Bombyx Mori*, the originally Chinese silkworm that feeds on mulberry trees. They both produce silk in their cocoons, and although the fibres look slightly different (Madagascan silk, also called wild silk, is darker, coarser and less shiny), they have the same properties: incredibly insulating, light and soft.

Wild silk has been woven in Madagascar for centuries. Cocoons are harvested in the wild (there is no sericulture of *Borocera Madagascariensis*), then prepared in artisanal workshops – they need to be boiled for several days before drying. The fibre then needs to be threaded, dyed and woven.

The village of Soatanana is famed for its silk weaving, and you can come and visit the artisans (mostly women) at work. Cocoons are bought from villagers who live near the tapia forests; they are then prepared and woven into scarves here.

Most women work on their loom at home so the visits are an intimate experience. You can of course buy scarves here: prices are low (Ar15,000 to Ar70,000 depending on the size) and the choice is bewildering. Some scarves are made exclusively of wild silk; others use a mix of wild and farmed silk *(Bombyx Mori)*.

Simple accommodation (rooms Ar12,000) is available if you would like to spend the night in the village. Meals cost Ar8000.

The village of Soatanana is located about 40km southwest of Ambositra: 13km south on the RN7, then 15km west on the RN35 to the village of Anjoman' Akona, before taking a dirt road for the last 10km. The trip from Ambositra takes about 1¼ hours; if you don't have your own vehicle, you could charter a taxi, or contact GGAM (p56) or ORTAM (p56) in Ambositra.

and chameleons. The brick bungalows are pretty, spacious and very comfortable. Meals (Ar30,000 for three courses) can be provided on request.

Couleur Café
BOUTIQUE HOTEL €€€

(☑020 44 485 26; www.couleurcafeantsirabe. com; Route d'Ambositra; d/tr/f Ar125,000/153,000/ 175,000; ☜) If you're after a romantic night, this exquisite boutique hotel is the place for you. The brick 'pavilions' are an elegant blend of modern decor and Madagascan crafts (lampshades, rugs, coffee tables etc), and each has its own fireplace. There is an excellent restaurant (menu Ar32,000). Rates include breakfast.

Résidence Camélia
GUESTHOUSE €€€

(☑020 44 488 44; www.laresidencecamelia.com; Ave de l'Indépendance; d Ar70,000-126,000) A genteel guesthouse with a tranquil shady garden and fresh, uplifting rooms in various shapes, sizes and prices. The charming restaurant (mains from Ar12,000), with its vaulted ceiling and winter fireplace, is a noteworthy bargain. Start with a drink in the piano bar.

✗ Eating

Food is excellent and inexpensive in Antsirabe, even at top-end hotels. Among the latter,

Résidence Camélia and Couleur Café are the best. Chez Billy (p53) also serves delicious and cheap meals.

★ Café Mirana
MADAGASCAN, BAKERY €

(Rue Ralaimongo; mains Ar4000-7000; ☺7am-6.30pm) This cafeteria is one of the busiest in town, with reason: its bakery is the best for miles (the croissants get top marks, as does the bread), and the restaurant out back churns out tasty, great-value Madagascan staples such as *vary' aminana* (rice soup served for breakfast), *mi sao* (noodle stir-fry), zebu stews etc. The terraces at the front are perfect for people-watching.

Croustipain
BAKERY €

(Rue Ralaimongo; pastries Ar2000, light meals Ar5000-7000; ☺6am-7.30pm) The local branch of this national chain is a good option for breakfast: the *viennoiseries* are excellent and the spacious dining room stocks the local papers. The savoury pastries, samosas and quiches make for a cheap takeaway lunch.

Restaurant Razafiramamonjy
CHINESE €

(Ave de l'Indépendance; mains Ar5000-11,000) This locally recommended place, frequented by Malagasy families, has an extended menu: it's mostly Chinese, with the odd

Madagascan dish thrown in for good measure. The satellite TV broadcasts European and American sporting events (football, basketball etc).

Shoprite　　　　　　　　SUPERMARKET €
(Antsenakely; ☺8am-7pm Mon-Sat, 8.30am-1.30pm Sun) Large supermarket with a bakery counter.

★**Chez Jenny**　　　　　INTERNATIONAL €€
(Rue Labourdonnais; mains Ar10,000-15,000; ☺noon-2pm & 6-10pm Tue-Sun; 🕸) Hands down the best restaurant in town, Chez Jenny is a winning combination of colourful decor, delicious food, warm service and atmosphere, complete with a well-stocked bar and a cosy fireplace for cold winter nights. Try the duck in three pepper sauce or opt for one of the lovely pizzas.

Le Pousse-Pousse　　　　　FUSION €€
(Antsenakely; mains Ar11,000-15,000; ☺11am-10pm Mon-Sat) This charming place, where you eat inside a pousse-pousse, is known for its cheeseburgers – rare hereabouts – and delicious fusion cuisine (such as stir-fried pork in pineapple, or duck in peppercorn and honey sauce). There is occasional live music.

Zandina　　　　　　　　　　PIZZA €€
(5 Ave Foch; mains Ar10,000-15,000; ☺11.30am-10pm; 🕸) Zandina has become something of an institution thanks to its all-day service, good wi-fi connection, satellite TV, and generally warm and relaxed atmosphere. The food is good too, a mixture of salads, grills and pizzas. Portions are huge.

🍸 Drinking & Nightlife

Nightlife in Antsirabe doesn't match the array of hotels and restaurants. The **Tahiti nightclub** (Route de Tananarive; ☺10pm-3am Fri & Sat) at the Hotel Diamant is the long-standing choice for dancing. Otherwise, people tend to congregate in hotel and restaurant bars, such as those at Chez Billy (p53), Zandina or Restaurant Razafiramamonjy.

ⓘ Information

There are several banks in town: the **BNI Madagascar** (Rue Ralaimongo) has a 24-hour ATM. For internet, if your hotel connection isn't good enough, you can try Zandina.
Cyber Kool (Ave de l'Indépendance; per hour Ar1000; ☺8.30am-9.30pm; 🕸) Busy internet cafe; the connection can be slow. Wi-fi available.

ⓘ Getting There & Away

Antsirabe is 170km south of Antananarivo. The *gare routière* (*taxi-brousse* station) is located about 2.5km north of town, behind the Jovenna petrol station. *Taxi-brousse* services from Antsirabe:

TO	FARE (AR)	TIME (HR)
Ambositra	7000	3
Antananarivo	10,000	4
Fianarantsoa	15,000	6
Miandrivazo	15,000	7
Morondava	35,000	15
Tamatave	32,000	10

ⓘ Getting Around

Antsirabe can be easily negotiated on foot, but for longer trips, you'll have a wealth of options: pousse-pousse, *cyclo-pousse* or tuk-tuk. A trip around town should cost around Ar2000 with the first two (Ar5000 between the *taxi-brousse* station and the centre); for tuk-tuks, it's a fixed Ar1000 per trip, but the route often is more circuitous because of other passengers on board.

Ambositra

Ambositra (am-boo-str) is located in the centre of a picturesque valley lined with rice paddies and ringed by verdant peaks. The town is famous for the quality of its woodcarvings and marquetry (objects inlaid with coloured woods), which you'll find in dozens of shops, along with raffia products and other souvenirs.

It's a lot quieter and smaller than Antsirabe, so many people simply skip Ambositra and just stop in a couple of shops en route. If you're looking to explore the Zafimaniry villages however, Ambositra is the best place to organise a trip.

⊙ Sights

Many of the arts and crafts shops in town are located on the western half of the ring road at the heart of town. They all sell pretty much the same things, so take a stroll and have a look.

Benedictine Monastery　　　MONASTERY
(☺6.30am-noon & 2-5pm Mon-Sat, from 7.30am Sun) At the western edge of town is a Benedictine monastery, where the nuns sell delicious cheese, honey, jam and postcards. The church warrants a look if it's open; there is singing every day between 11.50am and noon.

☞ Tours

There are good walks from Ambositra to nearby villages, where you can see the artisans at work in their homes, carving wood with homemade tools or spreading brightly dyed raffia out in the sun to dry.

GGAM
TOUR

(Groupement des Guides Amoron'i Mania; ☑ 033 19 912 26) A local guides' association that is keen to promote sustainable tourism in Ambositra and the Zafimaniry villages.

ORTAM
TOUR

(Office Régional de Tourisme d'Amoron'i Mania; ☑ 020 47 710 21; Hôtel Mania) Loosely based out of Hôtel Mania (the hotel manager is the tourist office's president), ORTAM is a good place to organise tours of local workshops or walks in the surrounding hills. It can also recommend guides for trips to the Zafimaniry villages.

🛏 Sleeping

★Hôtel Anjara
GUESTHOUSE €€

(☑ 032 55 931 91; http://hotelanjara.blogvie.com; Vohidahy; d/f Ar35,000/45,000) You could spend days in this lovely guesthouse, a beautiful three-storey traditional Madagascan house set in a rambling garden, with panoramic views in every direction. To find it, take the stairs heading downhill from the western part of the ring road; cross the plain of paddy fields, and the hotel will be signposted to your right.

The rooms are huge and pretty, and although the bathroom arrangement is rather quirky (they're on the balcony), they're clean and well-maintained. Home-cooked meals are available (mains Ar3000 to Ar12,000), and the guesthouse rents bikes and organises excursions.

Hotel du Centre
HOTEL €€

(☑ 034 47 710 36, 032 86 658 39; hoteldu centre.mada@yahoo.fr; Rue du Commerce; d/ tr Ar30,000/45,000; 🖥) This concrete hotel right on the ring road is nothing to write home about, but it's clean, centrally located and well-priced.

L'Artisan Hotel
BUNGALOW €€

(☑ 034 04 642 53; artisan_hotel@yahoo.fr; Manarintsoa; d/f Ar50,000/70,000, bungalow Ar50,000-90,000; 🖥) Thanks to its excellent customer service and attention to detail, L'Artisan has gradually become top of its class. The Zafimaniry bungalows, which feature traditional woodcarvings and construction methods, are works of art (although they are a bit cramped – rooms and brick bungalows are more spacious). There are folk bands at meal times, and the owners can arrange excursions in the area.

Hôtel Mania
HOTEL €€

(☑ 034 97 478 90, 020 47 710 21; toursmania@ moov.mg; Rue du Commerce; d/f Ar37,000/60,000; 🖥) Tucked away in a leafy, gated courtyard in the centre of town, the well-run Mania has big, clean rooms and spotless bathrooms. The old building has more charm, but views are better from the new building (especially

Ambositra

ZAFIMANIRY VILLAGES

The cluster of villages southeast of Ambositra are famous for their woodcarving, and are a Unesco World Heritage Site. They're a popular homestay destination, where visitors stay with a family and experience life in this rural and remote part of the world.

Accommodation generally includes a bucket shower and composting toilet, a straw mattress, and traditional rice-based meals. There may be little or no English spoken. You may also get the chance to participate in traditional crafts, and to explore the region. The best villages to visit are **Sakaivo**, **Falairivo** and **Antetezandotra**.

GGAM and ORTAM in Ambositra organise three- or four-day circuits in the area, including transfers from Ambositra and stays in two or three villages. Allow about Ar100,000 per person per day.

Another alternative is to stay at the delightful **Sous Le Soleil de Mada** (☑034 07 344 14; souslesoleildemada@gmail.com; half board per person €25, 2-course lunch menus Ar15,000) and explore the region from here. Run with flair by a French couple, this scenic lodge has 15 Zafimaniry bungalows, all built and carved locally. They are a thing of beauty, and Jean-Marc and Brigitte's sense of hospitality is legendary. Evening meals are served on one large table and are joyous occasions (thanks in part to the great collection of *rhum arrangé*). There is a massage room and a small book exchange.

Sous Le Soleil de Mada is located 12km down the dirt road leading to Antoetra, the biggest (but least interesting) Zafimaniry village. If you don't have your own vehicle, Sous Le Soleil can organise transfers from Ambositra.

from the 3rd floor). The hotel can organise *taxi-brousse* bookings for you: you're then picked up on the doorstep on the day.

Motel Violette　　　　HOTEL €€
(☑020 47 710 84; motel-violette@wanadoo. mg; Route d'Antsirabe; r Ar32,000, bungalow Ar50,000; 🐾) The cottage-style bungalows, across the street from reception, are spacious and clean, with plenty of blankets, but eschew the rooms in the main building, which haven't been well-maintained, are flea-ridden and sit directly above a very loud karaoke bar.

✗ Eating

You won't remember Ambositra for its cuisine, but at least eating out won't break the bank.

Hotely Tanamasoandro　　MADAGASCAN €
(Rue du Commerce; mains Ar3000-9000; ☺11.30am-2pm & 6-9.30pm; 🐾) An unpretentious local favourite popular for both its decor (it doubles up as a woodcarving shop), and the huge portions of cheap Madagascan food.

Oasis　　　　CHINESE €
(RN7; mains Ar3000-9000; ☺11am-9pm; 🐾) This place near the southern *taxi-brousse* station has an inexpensive and tasty menu with lots of vegie and Chinese options, and a popular outside terrace.

Motel Violette　　PIZZA, MADAGASCAN €€
(Route d'Antsirabe; mains Ar8000-15,000; ☺noon-2pm & 6.30-10pm; 🐾) This restaurant has the best views in town, with Ambositra rising above the rice paddies; sadly the quality of the food is no match for the panorama. Pizzas are your best option. The restaurant often puts on traditional entertainment in the evening.

ℹ Information

There are a couple of banks and ATMs, including a BNI Madagascar.

ℹ Getting There & Away

➜ Transport to points north, including Antsirabe (Ar7000, two hours) and Antananarivo (Ar15,000, five hours), departs from the far northern end of town, about 600m north of the fork and down a small staircase from Rue du Commerce.

➜ Departures for Fianarantsoa (Ar9000, four hours) and other points south are from the southern *taxi-brousse* station.

Ialatsara Lemur Forest Camp

Created in 2002, this 10-sq-km **private reserve** (☑033 11 671 69; www.madagascar-lemuriens.com; admission Ar20,000) lies 83km south of Ambositra on the RN7, making it a convenient stop, and a logical one if you're not going to visit Ranomafana. It's also a nice way to break up the long drive. The reserve is home to six species of lemur and seven species of chameleon. A guide costs Ar25,000 for up to four people. Overall it's mildly pricey, but if this is your only chance to wander the jungle in search of wildlife, you should take it.

There are a number of simple bungalows (Ar35,000) with balconies and bucket showers in a camp setting, and family-style meals (Ar25,000), but travellers have complained that the welcome is frosty.

Parc National de Ranomafana

Ranomafana appears after a fantastic entrance through a dry rocky valley spotted with two-storey highlands houses. After a long day's travel, it feels like you have reached a mysterious island. The air is fresh and cool, and the nearby presence of the forest, with all of its strange sounds, alluring.

Created in 1991 largely to protect two rare species of lemur – the golden bamboo lemur and the greater bamboo lemur (the former discovered only in 1986) – **Parc National de Ranomafana** (entry permits per day Ar55,000)

contains 400 sq km of oddly shaped rolling hills carpeted in jungle and fed by rushing streams.

The park is known for its diverse wildlife, although some of it is quite elusive. There are 29 mammal species, including 12 species of lemur. On a typical day's walk, you are likely to see between three and five species, including the famed golden bamboo lemur (Ranomafana is one of its two known habitats – a handful of individuals are now well-accustomed to the presence of visitors).

The forest abounds with reptiles and amphibians, and the birdlife is exceptional, with more than 100 species, of which 68 are endemic to Madagascar. Although most visitors come for the animals, the plant life is just as impressive, with orchids, tree ferns, palms, mosses and stands of giant bamboo.

The gateway town for the park is Ranomafana, which is 6km east of the park entrance on the RN25.

🏃 Activities

Wildlife Watching

Seasons matter when it comes to wildlife in Ranomafana. Lemurs can be spotted pretty much year-round, but the best season for birdwatching is spring, from September through to December, when migratory species return to the park.

Parc National de Ranomafana

Reptiles and amphibians are at their most active in summer, from December to March; this is also the best time of year to admire the park's beautiful flora, including many orchids.

Hiking

The park is divided into three parcels of land containing both primary and secondary forest. The former is more impressive, with enormous trees, but takes more hiking to reach.

The names of the trails are confusing in Ranomafana because the park changed them but the signs and documentation haven't quite caught up.

The best thing to do is to discuss your options with your guide depending on how much you want to walk and what you want to get out of the walk.

The **Talatakely Trail** system in Parcel III (secondary forest) is the most visited and also one of the best for spotting lemurs (walks will vary from three to four hours). There is a nice lookout (where striped mongoose are regular visitors) and a pretty waterfall popular for picnics.

In Parcel I, a patch of degraded primary forest, the three- to four-hour **Vohipara Circuit** doesn't get the crowds of Talatakely but is still good for lemurs. Its USP (unique selling point) however is its birdlife.

For day trips, opt for **Vatoharanana**: it starts with Talatakely before venturing further into primary forest. The last part of the walk is technically out of the park and allows you to see the difference between protected and unprotected land. The circuit finishes in the village of Ranomafana.

If you want the full-on experience, the multiday treks **Valohoaka** and **Soarano** are for you. They take you even deeper into the park and you get to spend the night in the forest. Few people actually take these options, so the experience is unique.

🛏 Sleeping & Eating

Although technically not part of the park, there are several very handy options right by the park entrance.

Rianala Gîte　　　　　　　HOSTEL **€**
(☑034 14 360 36, 033 14 905 69; rianalagite@gmail.com; Ranomafana National Park entrance; dm/camping Ar12,000/5000) This is a great budget option, right by the park entrance, which will save you toing and froing between the village and the park. The rooms

---

ⓘ PARC NATIONAL DE RANOMAFANA

Best time to visit Between September and December, when the weather is warm and dry.

Key highlight Spotting a bamboo lemur.

Wildlife Lemurs, birds, frogs, chameleons.

Habitat Primary and secondary rainforest.

Gateway town Ranomafana.

Transport options *Taxi-brousse* from Fianarantsoa (Ar7000).

Things you should know Be prepared for rain and temperature swings, particularly in winter, when a 25°C day becomes a 10°C night.

---

are clean and come with blankets and hot water, and there is a nice porch to sit on. There are some great campsites a short walk away, too, with pitched thatched roofs.

There is also an on-site restaurant, and the friendly owners will reserve a seat for you on *taxis-brousses* heading to Fianarantsoa so that you can be picked up at the hotel.

Varibolo　　　　　　MADAGASCAN **€**
(Ranomafana National Park entrance; mains Ar5000-10,000; ⊗7am-9pm) Perched on a hill overlooking the national park, Varibolo scores equally high on location and taste. The food is simple – grilled chicken, *romazava* (beef and vegetable stew), sandwiches – but always good. It's right by the start of the trails so come for a prewalk breakfast (crêpes, yum!) or a postwalk lunch. Alternatively, they'll prepare picnic baskets.

ⓘ Information

The **MNP Office** (⊗7am-4.30pm) is located right at the entrance of the park. Park visitors pay the entry fee here, part of which goes to the community, and a guide fee (half-day Ar40,000, full-day Ar75,000, multiday Ar90,000 per day). Several guides speak good English.

ⓘ Getting There & Away

If you don't have a private car, travelling between Ranomafana and the park will be tricky. *Taxis-brousses* heading in/out of the village may be happy to take you (Ar2000); some hotels arrange transfer for about Ar10,000. Alternatively, hitch a ride with other travellers. See p260 for more on hitching.

Ranomafana

Like Antsirabe, the village of Ranomafana ('hot water') first evolved as a thermal bath centre popular with French colonials. The creation of Parc National de Ranomafana in 1991 and its growing popularity have caused the town to expand; it is now a busy place, especially on Sunday (market day) when street stalls, football games and children's rides give the town a festive atmosphere.

◉ Sights & Activities

Centre ValBio   RESEARCH CENTRE
(🗓 034 13 581 71; www.centrevalbio.org; admission Ar10,000) This international training centre for the study of biodiversity is housed in attractive buildings on the edge of the national park. If you have any interest in the scientific research going on in and around Ranomafana, you should make time to either visit the centre or to attend one of the regular evening lectures given by resident researchers (Ar60,000, including dinner).

One of ValBio's main activities is outreach within the communities living on the park's borders. The centre has therefore developed good relationships with local associations and is able to organise activities such as basket making and silk weaving, or visits to artisan workshops. All activities and tours must be booked in advance.

Ranomafana Arboretum   GARDENS
(RN25; admission Ar5000; ⊘ 8am-noon & 2-4pm) Located about 2km east of Ranomafana, this stunning arboretum is worth visiting for its scenic location alone. There are hundreds of species of tree here, many of which are extremely rare. There's a self-guided walking trail in English, with lots of explanations.

Thermal Baths   SWIMMING
(admission Ar5000; ⊘ 8am-noon & 1-6pm Wed-Mon) The hot springs after which Ranomafana is named are located across the Namorona River. The setting is pretty, and the swimming pool that is fed by the springs is very popular with locals. Best to swim here on Wednesday, as the pool is cleaned and refilled on Tuesday.

🛏 Sleeping & Eating

Ranomafana has a varied hotel offering for its size. Hotels are spread along an 8km

stretch of the RN25 heading west from town to the park entrance. If you don't have your own vehicle, pick one in Ranomafana itself to make life easier – all you'll have to sort out is a ride to the park.

Chez Gaspard   BUNGALOW €€
(🗓 033 01 155 05, 032 87 115 15; chezgaspard. ranomafana@gmail.com; Ranomafana; bungalow Ar45,000-90,000) This line of pretty bungalows, in a scenic tropical setting stretching along the river, is great value. Those furthest upstream are best; No 14 is a great family room that holds five. No on-site restaurant.

Hôtel Manja   HOTEL €€
(🗓 033 09 010 22; www.hotelmanja.com; Ranomafana; bungalow Ar55,000-70,000, r Ar55,000; 🗐) There are two types of accommodation here: bedrooms, which are on the dingy side, and bungalows, which are bigger and lighter. Bungalows at the top of the hill offer majestic views – to those who don't mind the stairs. It's currently the only place in Ranomafana accepting payment by card (5% surcharge).

Le Grenat   BUNGALOW €€
(🗓 034 12 780 84; legrenatran@gmail.com; Ranomafana; d/tr Ar60,000/90,000; 🗐) Le Grenat's tidy little bungalows have a nice location by the banks of the river, but the decor is rather kitsch. No matter, this is a well-run place with friendly management, and a great restaurant.

Cristo   LODGE €€€
(🗓 034 12 353 97; http://cristohotel.cabanova. fr; RN25; r Ar90,000) This lodge on the outskirts of town, perched on a gorgeous bend in the Namorona River, has idyllic views of the rainforest and hills. The upper-floor rooms in the main building bask in the glorious panorama, while the riverside bungalows are more secluded. The attractive lounge-restaurant with open fire is another draw, particularly on a rainy day, as are the amiable owners.

Wi-fi was soon to be installed at the time of our visit.

Karibotel   BUNGALOW €€€
(🗓 033 79 893 46; resa.karibotelranomafana@ gmail.com; RN25; d/f Ar105,000/125,000; 🗐🗩) Opened in 2014, the Karibotel is making a splash with its colourful bungalows, lovely bathrooms, stupendous views of Ranomafana and panoramic pool. It's located about halfway between the park and the village. Rates include breakfast.

Centrest Sejour LODGE €€€
(☑034 16 524 33; centrestsejour@gmail.com; Ranomafana; d/f Ar145,000/175,000; ☎) This is a very calm, peaceful and tidy hotel, with a lush tropical garden filled with local flowers and trees. The best rooms are the hillside bungalows with terraces and views. The restaurant, which has a mostly French menu, is excellent but pricey (mains Ar18,000). There is a pool room and guests can visit the hotel's private reserve at Mahakajy, 9km away.

Manja MADAGASCAN €
(Ranomafana; mains Ar6000-10,000; ☎) A long-standing favourite, Manja serves big portions of traditional Madagascan food such as *romazava, ravitoto* (pork stew with manioc greens) and *hen'omby ritra* (zebu in tomato sauce). Its flambé bananas are the best around. Sit in the big, wooden dining room or grab one of the prized tables on the porch.

Le Grenat INTERNATIONAL €€
(Ranomafana; mains Ar8000-16,000; ☎noon-2pm & 6-9pm) Everything from the soups and pastas to the zebu kebabs or the *poulet coco* (chicken in coconut sauce) is cooked just right at the convivial Le Grenat. It also serves local crayfish in season (spring).

ℹ Information
Be forewarned: there are currently no banks or ATMs in Ranomafana. The nearest banks are two hours away in Fianarantsoa. Credit cards are only accepted by Hôtel Manja.

ℹ Getting There & Away
Taxis-brousses go daily from Ranomafana to Fianarantsoa (Ar7000, two hours), Manakara (Ar15,000, five hours), and Mananjary (Ar10,000, three hours). When arriving, let the *taxi-brousse* driver know if you want to get off in the village, at the park entrance, or at a hotel in between.

Manakara
While Manakara is geographically on the east coast, virtually all travellers visit on a round-trip from Fianarantsoa, often by the famous FCE railway, making Manakara an important part of many a highlands itinerary. It is also a highly underrated destination that should not be overlooked. For those not planning on visiting the Canal des Pangalanes elsewhere, this is your chance. It can

make a welcome beach break from the highlands, particularly after hiking in the parks.

The town is innately interesting, as it is divided into two parts by the canal. The warm inland side, known as Tanambao, has a dynamic Caribbean vibe, with sandy streets, tin-roofed shacks and a buoyant daily market, while on the other side of the bridge lies the breezy seaside district of Manakara-Be. The bridge linking both sides partially collapsed in 2012 and a temporary bridge was erected in the old port instead; there is talk of the old bridge being fixed in 2016.

◉ Sights & Activities
You could easily combine a half-day trip to the Canal des Pangalanes in the morning with a visit to Domaine Aavyland in the afternoon.

★Domaine Aavyland PLANTATION
(☑032 44 653 25; RN12; guided tours Ar10,000; ☺9am-noon & 2.30-5pm) Some 18km south of Manakara on the road to Vohipeno, you'll find Domaine Aavyland, a 31-hectare organic plantation and distillery producing medicinal and fragrant essential oils such as *ravintsara, niaouly*, clove, cinnamon and ylang-ylang. Manager Jean offers fascinating two-hour guided tours of the plantation and distillery, explaining the virtues and production process of every essential oil.

Visitors get the chance to scrunch leaves as they go, and to try the essential oils at the end of the visit. Small bottles of essential oils are available for sale (Ar5000 to Ar10,000), as is the plantation's honey (Ar6000). Tours can be in English. Jean can also organise transfers from Manakara for those without a vehicle (Ar5000 per person). Visits (and transfers) must be booked at least the day before.

Canal des Pangalanes BOAT TOUR
The most popular excursion in Manakara is a pirogue day trip along the Canal des Pangalanes, which was dug out by the French in the 1890s to circumvent the capricious Indian Ocean. Tours usually make a couple of stops on the way (eg cultural monuments, a village, an artisanal distillery) and include a sumptuous lunch on the beach. Half-day tours are also possible.

A highly recommended guide is **José Francis Andriamitantsoa** (☑033 06 144 24, 034 69 072 31; josfrancis25@yahoo.fr; half/full day per person for 2 people Ar40,000/45,000), who not only speaks excellent English but also

Manakara

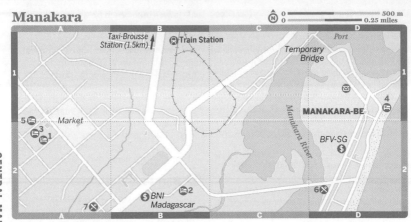

sings beautifully (helped along by his crew's backing vocals and the captain's handmade ukulele).

Mada Trekking Immersion
HIKING

(☑034 65 578 31; madatrekkingimmersion@hotmail.com) This dynamic outfit run by young Frenchman Manu runs multiday hikes, including a six-day route from Manakara to Ambalavao (allow Ar100,000 per day with a mix of camping and homestays). It also rents mountain bikes (Ar20,000 per day) and motorbikes (Ar55,000 per day) for excursions around Manakara, with or without a guide.

🛏 Sleeping

Tanambao has a number of serviceable concrete hotels with little to differentiate them except air-conditioning. In general it is much better to pay up a bit and stay on the beach, particularly in summer, when inland can be sweltering.

Délices d'Orient
HOTEL €

(☑020 72 217 34, 032 41 747 95; delicehotel@orange.mg; Tanambao; r Ar25,000-35,000; ☎) The rooms at the Délices aren't exactly delightful but you get a lot for your money: a bed with a mosquito net, a private bathroom with hot water and a decent wi-fi connection. A bargain all things considered.

Les Flamboyants
HOTEL €

(☑020 72 216 77; lionelmanakara@dts.mg; Tanambao; d Ar20,000-30,000; ☎) This is a good-value hotel in the centre of Tanambao, with a shady patio, fans and a good restaurant. The attentive owner has been living in

Manakara for more than a decade and is a mine of information.

Lac Vert
BUNGALOW €€

(☑034 19 918 75; http://lacvert.e-monsite.com; Tanambao; d/tr/f Ar60,000/70,000/90,000; ☎) Jean-Michel, the friendly owner, runs a tight ship at Lac Vert: the pretty bungalows with their green shutters and doors are immaculate, as are the leafy grounds. The verandah is a convivial place to gather round for a drink and a chat in the evening.

Club Vanille
BUNGALOW €€

(☑020 72 210 23, 034 17 209 68; hotellavanille manakara@yahoo.fr; Manakara-Be; bungalow Ar60,000) Located 8km south of Manakara, this is a satellite operation for the Hôtel Vanille in downtown Tanambao. Here you'll find some canal-side bungalows, and a restaurant offering catches of the day and cold beer. Best of all, you are caught between the absolute roar of the surf on one side, and the placid canal on the other. Shuttle service (Ar5000) available.

Sidi Hotel
HOTEL €€

(☑033 02 803 90; sidihotel@moov.mg; Tanambao; d Ar50,000-65,000; ❄☎) Big, kitsch and concrete pretty much sums up the appearance of this U-shape monster with drive-in courtyard in Tanambao. Rooms are very spacious and the facilities are good for the price.

Parthenay Club
BUNGALOW €€€

(☑020 72 216 63, 034 29 803 14; http://parthenay club-manakara.com; Manakara-Be; bungalow Ar70,000-100,000; ☎) These tiki-hut bungalows, set in a well-landscaped compound on the beach, are a great way to enjoy the

Manakara

unique feeling of straddling both canal and sea. Each bungalow has been individually decorated, with special attention given to the bathrooms (a rarity in Madagascar). The restaurant is excellent too (mains Ar12,000 to Ar18,000).

🍴 Eating

★ Sharon   MADAGASCAN €
(Tanambao; mains Ar2000-4000; ⊗11am-9pm Tue-Sun) This cheap and cheerful eatery heaves with young locals every night of the week. It serves the best *brochettes* (kebabs) in town, cooked on a street-side BBQ (don't miss the peanut dipping sauce). The huge *mi sao* are the house's other signature dish.

La Guinguette   MADAGASCAN €
(Manakara-Be; mains Ar8000-10,000; ⊗7am-10pm Wed-Mon) You can't miss this place, located at the base of the collapsed bridge in Manakara-Be. It's a great spot to sit and have a drink overlooking the canal, while the local fishers cast their nets. Or stay and enjoy the fresh seafood.

Les Délices d'Orient   INTERNATIONAL €€
(Tanambao; mains Ar8000-18,000; ⊗11.30am-2pm & 6-9pm) Les Délices is well-known in Manakara for its excellent cuisine, its seafood especially – grilled fish, prawns in coconut sauce, garlic *camarons* (a kind of king prawn). It's all delicious and great value, with friendly and efficient service to boot.

ℹ Information

Manakara has several banks and ATMs to choose from.

ℹ Getting There & Away

Taxi-Brousse There are usually two *taxis-brousses* per day between Manakara and Ranomafana (Ar13,000, five hours), continuing to Fianarantsoa (Ar13,000, seven hours). These

leave at 9am and 3pm or 4pm. There is one service a day to Tana (Ar30,000, 15 hours). The *taxi-brousse* station is 2km north of town.

Train Most travellers prefer to travel at least one way by train from Fianarantsoa. The train leaves on Wednesday and Sunday at 7am and takes anywhere between 12 and 24 hours to reach Fianarantsoa. Tickets cost Ar40,000/16,000 in 1st/2nd class.

ℹ Getting Around

Take a pousse-pousse or tuk-tuk in town. Fares to Tanambao/Manakara-Be from the railway station are Ar1500/2000. These double at night.

Sahambavy

Beautiful Sahambavy (sam-bav) is an idyllic place to put your bags down for a couple of days. The tender green of the tea bushes stretches for miles, there is a beautiful lake, a fantastic hotel-restaurant and a generally laid-back vibe.

Sahambavy is the second stop after Fianarantsoa on the FCE railway line (p66), so it's an ideal place to get on or off the train: the stretch between here and Fianar isn't very interesting, and more importantly it means you save an hour's sleep in the morning on the way to Manakara (or arrive an hour earlier in the evening coming from Manakara).

◉ Sights

Sahambavy Tea Estate   FARM
(admission Ar7000; ⊗7am-4pm Mon-Fri, to 9.30am Sat) This is Madagascar's only tea plantation. Visits take you from the fields to the processing plant and finish with a tasting. Tea is picked every day from October to April, and three days a week the rest of the year (visits cost Ar5000 when there is no picking as there is less to see). Tours are available in English.

Note that you should only pay for your visit at the processing plant where you will be issued with a ticket, and not at the estate gate (visitors have been ripped off).

🛌 Sleeping & Eating

★ Lac Hôtel   BOUTIQUE HOTEL €€€
(☑020 75 959 06; www.lachotel.com; Sahambavy; standard bungalow Ar80,000, stilt bungalow Ar130,000-170,000) Beautifully located on the shores of Lake Sahambavy, this exquisite boutique hotel offers a variety of accommodation, including show-stopping bungalows

on stilts. The local carvings and fabrics form a refined Madagascan style, and there are gorgeous views of the lake. Honeymooners and/or rail enthusiasts should plump for the vintage FCE wagon (Ar250,000), which has been lovingly renovated.

Hotel guests get free use of the pedalos, games and tennis table. There is also a fantastic restaurant that cooks with the hotel's own vegetable-garden products (three-course menu Ar35,000, mains from Ar7000).

❶ Getting There & Away

Sahambavy is located about 23km east of Fianarantsoa; the turn-off from the RN7 is clearly signposted, about 10km northeast of Fianar. The track is in pretty bad condition. There are daily *taxis-brousses* (Ar3000), or you could take the train.

Fianarantsoa

POP 200,760

Fianarantsoa (fi-a-nar-ant-*soo*), or Fianar for short, is like a mild version of Tana. Surrounded by hills, it is both a regional commercial, administrative and religious centre, and a major transit point. Tourists typically come here to spend the night on their way to Ranomafana or Isalo, or to take the train to Manakara.

But visitors can enjoy a historic old town, a great local market, some interesting places to stay, and a more laid-back ambience than that of the capital.

The city is divided into three parts. Basse-Ville (Lower Town), to the north, is a busy, chaotic area with the main post office, and the train and *taxi-brousse* stations. Up from Basse-Ville is Nouvelle Ville (New Town), the business area, with banks and several hotels. Further southwest and uphill is Haute-Ville (Upper Town), which has cobbled streets, a more peaceful atmosphere, numerous church spires and wide views.

◎ Sights

⭐ **Haute-Ville**   NEIGHBOURHOOD
The oldest and most attractive part of town is the pedestrian Haute-Ville (known as Tanana Ambony in Malagasy). It's famed for its architecture – two-storey brick houses with steep roofs, balconies and tumbling plants – which dates back to the late 19th and early 20th centuries. A stroll (or climb) around the cobbled streets here offers great views of the town and surrounding countryside. There are

six churches on this small hill alone, including the imposing **Ambozontany Cathedral**.

Many of the buildings in the Haute-Ville are in a bad state of repair – local association **Fondation Heritsialonina** is working to restore and promote the area's heritage. You'll see an information board about its mission on the main staircase.

Zoma   MARKET
(☺ daily) Fianar is a market town, with at least one small market open every day. The largest is the Zoma, where you'll find everything under the sun. It's held every day along Ave de l'Indépendance and Rue de Verdun, although Tuesday and Friday are best.

Maromby   MONASTERY
(www.maromby.org; Maromby; ☺ 9.30-11.30am & 3-4.30pm) The monks at this monastery continue to do what they have for centuries: make wine (red and white, and flavoured aperitifs) and honey (which you can buy in the shop). The modern church, with its striking stained-glass windows, vaulted wooden ceiling and carved doors, is particularly interesting as it reflects the integration of Christianity and Madagascan culture.

The monastery is located 7km northeast of Fianarantsoa. To get here without a private vehicle, take taxi-be 34 from Place Zoma towards Andriamboasary and ask the driver to drop you off at the junction where the monastery is signposted – you'll have to walk the last 300m.

☞ Tours

Most outfits propose day treks in the surrounding Betsileo villages (sometimes with overnight stays). A popular option is a day trip combining a pirogue river trip with a visit to the Sahambavy Tea Estate, handy for those without a vehicle. Fianarantsoa is also a good place to organise trips to Parc National d'Andringitra.

Mad Trekking   TREKKING
(☑ 034 14 221 73, 020 75 503 73; mad.trekking@moov.mg; Rue Philibert Tsiranana; ☺ 8.30am-noon & 2-5.30pm Mon-Fri) A reliable operator specialising in multiday excursions around Fianarantsoa, and hiking packages in hard-to-reach places such as Andringitra or the Makay (north of Isalo National Park). For two people, allow around €30 per person per day for local excursions, €60 to €70 for more adventurous hikes (prices include transport).

Fianarantsoa

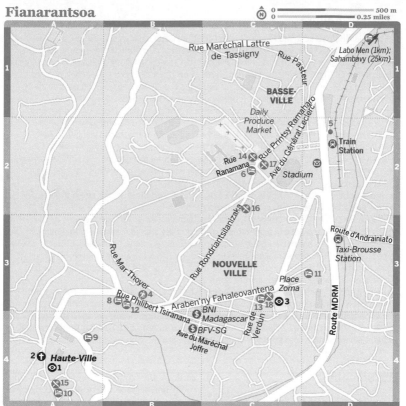

Fianarantsoa

Maison des Guides　　　　　　HIKING
(🗷 034 03 123 01, 032 02 728 97; coeurmalgache@
hotmail.com; Route MDRM; ☺ 8am-5.30pm Mon-
Sat, by reservation only Sun) Smartly located
in an old railway car in front of the train
station, this cooperative of local guides offer
a variety of tours in the area. It specialises
in hikes to the picturesque Betsileo villages nearby (half/full day for two people, per
person Ar25,000/30,000), as well as multiday hikes in Parc National d'Andringitra
and other areas. English-speaking guides
available.

THE FCE RAILWAY

A popular thing to do in Madagascar is to take the FCE (Fianarantsoa–Côte Est) railway between Fianarantsoa and Manakara on the east coast. The train leaves around 7am (theoretically – in practice it is almost always late) and chugs along at 20km/h on tracks built in the 1930s, reaching its destination between 12 and 24 hours later (yes, it's that variable). It all depends on the loading/unloading times along the way, the conditions of the tracks and the train, derailings (commonplace) and how heavy the train is.

Along the way you pass plantations, waterfalls and green hills, cross 67 bridges and four spectacular viaducts, and go through 48 tunnels. Despite its antiquity and unreliability, the train is still an economic lifeline for the people of the inland villages (where there are no roads), who use it to transport their cargoes of bananas and lychees to be sold and exported. Stopping at each tiny station is a colourful experience, with Malagasy passengers leaning out of the windows to haggle with hordes of vendors balancing baskets of bananas, crayfish or fresh bread on their heads.

For the best views of the cliffs, misty valleys and waterfalls en route, sit on the left side when going from Fianarantsoa to Manakara (and vice versa).

Because of the FCE's increasingly erratic schedule, taking the train requires a little planning and a good dose of pragmatism and flexibility should it all go wrong. The most scenic landscapes are between Sahambavy and Fenomby, so it is generally better to take the train from Fianar to Manakara to make sure you travel through this stretch in daylight (it's also downhill). However, the delays are often more severe from Fianar because this is where maintenance and repairs are done.

Bring enough water and food for 24 hours (street food is available along the way but comes with the usual precautionary warnings), and some warm clothes in winter.

For a more detailed history of the railway and the regions through which it passes, pick up a booklet called *Le Dernier Train du Corridor* by Maggie L Formentin (Ar5000) at Fianar's train station or in souvenir shops.

🛏 Sleeping

Raza-ôtel GUESTHOUSE €
(📲 020 75 519 15; d Ar40,000, d without bathroom Ar30,000; @🛜) At the end of a rough side road from Place Zoma, this is a charming family-run guesthouse. There are just four simple rooms with shared facilities (and one with private bathroom). Meals (mains Ar8000 to Ar10,000) are served in the cosy lounge. The owners also run Mad Trekking (p65) and are a mine of information on the area.

Peniela GUESTHOUSE €
(📲 032 40 486 56; peniela.house@yahoo.fr; Haute-Ville; d Ar32,000) One of the few buildings in the Haute-Ville to have been entirely renovated, the beautiful Peniela is a boon for travellers keen to stay in a traditional Madagascan highland house in relative comfort. The rooms are homely and clean, and the Haute-Ville is quiet and a joy to explore. There is no vehicle access for the last 200m.

La Case Madrigal GUESTHOUSE €€
(📲 032 60 316 40; http://lacasemadrigal.word press.com; d/f Ar75,000/100,000; 🛜) A lovely guesthouse on the edge of town, with just three simple but cosy rooms. The trump card is the convivial lounge-cum-dining-room and terrace where guests congregate in the evenings. Meals can be arranged (three-course menu Ar25,000). Rates include breakfast.

La Petite Bouffe GUESTHOUSE €€
(📲 032 02 481 65; lpetitebouffe@yahoo.fr; d/f Ar55,000/70,000; 🛜) This family-run guesthouse is great-value: the rooms are huge and tastefully furnished, the bathrooms are well-maintained, and the location at the foot of the Haute-Ville is excellent. Rates include breakfast.

Hôtel Cotsoyannis HOTEL €€
(📲 020 75 514 72; www.hotel.cotsoyannis.mg; 4 Rue Printsy Ramaharo; d Ar51,500-85,500; 🛜) The garden courtyard is the trump card of this town-centre establishment. The main difference between the rooms is the standard of the bathroom, but we don't feel it justifies the price hike so opt for one of the cheaper ones. All rooms are immaculate and most overlook the courtyard.

Tsara Guest House GUESTHOUSE €€€
(📲 032 05 516 12, 020 75 502 06; www.tsaraguest. com; Rue Philibert Tsiranana; d Ar98,000-175,000,

d without bathroom Ar48,000; 🛜) This classy plantation-style guesthouse is perennially popular. The public spaces are excellent: the reception area, with a roaring fire; a glass-walled restaurant serving delicious (if pricey) food (mains Ar13,000 to Ar22,000); and a beautiful outdoor terrace with great views. There are four categories of room, all slightly overpriced, but you're here for the amenities.

La Rizière　　　　　　　BOUTIQUE HOTEL €€€
(📧 020 75 502 15; www.lariziere.org; Haute-Ville; d Ar95,000-110,000; 🛜) This gorgeous hotel is the training ground of hospitality school La Rizière. Students here learn how to work in and run a hotel, and they're doing a pretty good job. The rooms are impeccable, with lovely wooden floors and bright green feature walls, and the atmosphere is warm and relaxed. There are sensational views of Fianarantsoa from the gardens.

Zomatel　　　　　　　　　HOTEL €€€
(📧 020 75 507 97; www.zomatel-madagascar.com; Place Zoma; d Ar60,000-120,000; ❄@🛜🏊) This surprisingly stylish hotel is particularly popular with groups. Rooms come with every comfort (hospitality tray, TV, hot water, wi-fi) and are tastefully decked out (bathroom included). Those in the old building are smaller and a little darker, but those in the new extension are huge and airy. There's a nice indoor pool, too. English spoken.

🍴 Eating

Chez Ninie　　　　　　　MADAGASCAN €
(Rue Rondriantsilanizaka; mains Ar4500-7000; ⊗8am-8.30pm) Don't be fooled by the facade: lurking out back is a rather chic open-porch dining area with an extensive, inexpensive and very tasty Madagascan menu that keeps this place very popular. Dirt cheap beer (Ar2000), too.

Chez Imanoela　　　　　　　　CAFE €
(Vieille Ville; sandwiches & cakes Ar2000-8000; ⊗9am-6.30pm Mon-Sat) What a great idea this was: a cafe in the picturesque and atmospheric Haute-Ville. The flower-decked terrace is a lovely spot to while away an hour or two, be it with a beer, coffee or light meal. Lunch options include freshly made soups or sandwiches. The cafe also bakes its own cakes.

Zomagrill　　　　　　　　CAFETERIA €
(Place Zoma; mains Ar10,000; ⊗6am-10pm; 🛜) The Zomagrill has filled a nice niche in Fi-

anar: somewhere cheap, reliably good and relaxed that appeals to young locals as much as to passing travellers. The morning pastries are among the best you'll have in Madagascar and the sandwiches, pizzas and ice creams are all equally good. Add the pool table and free wi-fi, and you can see why it's always busy.

Chez Dom　　　　　　　　FAST FOOD €
(Rue Ranamana; mains Ar6000-10,000; ⊗11am-2pm & 5-9.30pm Mon-Sat; 🛜) A small, colourful cafe offering local rum and a quick menu (burgers, omelettes, salads etc). It's frequented by backpackers, French expats and tourists. Some guides are based here; they offer the usual circuits around Fianar.

Supermarché 3000　　　　SUPERMARKET €
(Rue Printsy Ramaharo; ⊗8am-noon & 3-6.30pm Mon-Sat, 9am-noon Sun) The best-stocked place for self-caterers, particularly handy in preparation for long hikes in Andringitra, Isalo or Makay.

★La Rizière　　　　　　INTERNATIONAL €€
(📧 020 75 502 15; mains Ar12,000; ⊗noon-2.30pm & 6.30-9.30pm, closed Feb–mid-Mar) For gastronomic fare at average prices, make sure you book a table at La Rizière. The restaurant is a working culinary school and the chefs and waiters are all perfecting their trade. Service is charming (the chefs come and introduce themselves at the end of the meal) and the dining room phenomenal: a glasshouse with panoramic views of Fianarantsoa.

🛍 Shopping

Labo Men　　　　　　　　　　ARTS
(www.pierrotmen.com; ⊗8am-noon & 2-6pm Mon-Sat, 9am-noon Sun) Madagascar's most famous photographer, Pierrot Men, is a native of Fianarantsoa, where he still lives and works. His shop is stocked full of his beautiful images in various formats: postcards (Ar900), posters and framed photographs (Ar25,000 to Ar70,000) and coffee-table books.

ℹ Information

Fianar has many banks with ATMs that also change currency and do Visa card cash advances.

ℹ Getting There & Away

AIR
There is an airport in Fianar, but no regularly scheduled flights.

THE BETSILEO

The Betsileo, Madagascar's third-largest tribe, inhabit the *hauts plateaux* area around Fianarantsoa and Ambalavao. They only began viewing themselves as a nation after being invaded and conquered by the Merina in the early 19th century.

The Betsileo are renowned throughout Madagascar for their rice-cultivation techniques – they manage up to three harvests a year instead of the usual one or two, and their lands are marked by beautiful terracing and vivid shades of green in the rice paddy fields. Betsileo herders are famous for their trilby hats and the blankets they wear slung in a debonair fashion around their shoulders. Betsileo houses are distinctively tall and square, constructed from bricks as red as the earth of the roads.

As well as the *famadihana*, which was adopted from the Merina after the unification of Madagascar, an important Betsileo belief centres on *hasina*, a force that is believed to flow from the land through the ancestors into the society of the living. Skilled traditional practitioners are thought to be able to manipulate *hasina* to achieve cures and other positive effects. The reverse of *hasina* is *hera*, which can result in illness and misfortune.

TAXI-BROUSSE

Frequent *taxis-brousses* connect Fianarantsoa with Ambositra (Ar10,000, five hours), Antsirabe (Ar15,000, seven hours) and Antananarivo (Ar26,000, 10 hours).

Minibuses also go daily to Ambalavao (Ar3000, two hours), Ranohira (Ar25,000, seven hours) and on to Tuléar (Ar30,000, 12 hours). Departures from Fianarantsoa to Tuléar are at around 5pm. Heading east there are multiple vehicles daily between Fianarantsoa and Ranomafana (Ar7000, two hours) and Manakara (Ar13,000, eight hours).

TRAIN

➡ Fianarantsoa is connected to Manakara on the eastern coast by the famous FCE railway (p66). Departures from Fianarantsoa are scheduled for Tuesday and Saturday at 7am, and from Manakara on Sunday and Wednesday at 7am.

➡ There are frequent delays and cancellations, making it wise to visit the station the day before to confirm.

➡ The trip can take anywhere from 12 to 24 hours so you should pack enough food to keep you going (as well as warm clothes for the night).

➡ Tickets cost Ar40,000/16,000 in 1st/2nd class; there is a big difference in comfort, so much so that ticket masters are often reluctant to sell foreigners 2nd-class tickets.

❶ Getting Around

➡ Taxis operate day and night. The daytime price anywhere in the city is usually Ar3000, and Ar5000 at night (note that taxis can be hard to find after 9pm).

➡ Villages and destinations in the surrounding area are served by taxi-be (minivans), which have route numbers marked in their front window. The fare to all destinations is Ar500; departures are from the taxi-brousse station.

Ambalavao

Set amid beautiful mountainous countryside with numerous boulderlike peaks, Ambalavao is like a charming French village reduced through years of neglect to a Wild West outpost. The Gothic cathedral looks as if it's been parachuted in from the Loire Valley, although the surrounding landscape is signature Madagascan highlands.

There are no banks in Ambalavao.

◉ Sights

Réserve d'Anja   WILDLIFE RESERVE
(admission Ar10,000) This nifty little 370,000-sq-metre reserve encompasses three mountain-size boulders ('the three sisters') ringed at the base by a narrow forest full of ring-tailed lemurs. Anja's lemurs are famous for sunning themselves on the boulders (generally early in the morning); there are around 400 individuals in the reserve and they have grown accustomed to visitors so you'll get the chance to get relatively close. The reserve is a completely community-run initiative and has been extremely successful, generating revenues and jobs for the village.

Anja sees around 14,000 tourists a year, so you are unlikely to be alone, particularly from April to November. Guiding fees cost a hefty Ar24,000/36,000/48,000 for 30 minutes/one hour/two hours. Some guides speak basic English (they know their script well but struggle with questions).

Anja is located about 12km south of Ambalavao on the RN7. There are regular *taxis-brousses* (Ar1000) from Ambalavao.

Zebu Market
MARKET

(RN7; ☺ Wed) Ambalavao hosts the largest zebu market in the country. Tough, wizened herders walk from as far away as Tuléar and Fort Dauphin to sell their cattle. It is quite a spectacle, especially as the animals make their way up the bluff where the huge enclosure is located. The market reaches fever pitch around 10am or 11am. It's located about 1km south of Ambalavao.

Soalandy
WORKSHOP

(📞 033 14 987 45; RN7; ☺ 7.30am-5.30pm Mon-Sat, 9am-noon Sun) Madagascar is home to an endemic species of silkworm, which feeds on tapia trees in the wild and whose cocoons are threaded and woven like 'conventional' silk. The fascinating production process of this 'wild silk' is laid out in this workshop. You can buy beautiful scarves (Ar50,000 to Ar70,000) in the adjoining shop.

Fabrique de Papier Antaimoro
WORKSHOP

(📞 020 75 340 01; ☺ 7.30-11.30am & 1-5pm Mon-Sat, 8.30am-noon Sun) This workshop showcases the production of a unique kind of paper, made from the bark of a local bush, which has flowers pressed into it. Antaimoro cards, envelopes and picture frames are all for sale.

🏃 Activities

Foudia
HIKING

(📞 033 04 570 28, 034 03 794 28; www.pa-trek-mada.com; Ambalavao) This small tour operator organises circuits in Parc National d'Andringitra and the Tsaranoro Valley, as well as overland hikes between Ambalavao and Manakara. It also rents out camping equipment.

🛏 Sleeping & Eating

Résidence du Betsileo
HOTEL €€

(📞 032 28 259 80, 033 83 725 54; residencedubetsileo @gmail.com; s/d Ar35,000/45,000; 🐾) This charming bargain is the best place to stay – and eat – in town. New owners Holly and Jean-Marie are slowly renovating the building (the rooms do need updating), but the atmosphere is already great and Jean-Marie is a mean cook. Choose the off-street rooms.

Aux Bougainvillées
HOTEL €€

(📞 032 43 680 69; auxbougainvilleesambalavao@ gmail.com; d/tr/q Ar61,000/81,000/121,000; 🐾)

Draped in its colourful namesake plant, this hotel has a bit of character. Rooms are spread across several buildings in a quiet compound; all are comfortable, clean and rather colourful. There's a decent but expensive restaurant (mains Ar14,000 to Ar16,000), which is popular with tour groups at lunch.

Espace Zongo
LODGE €€

(📞 033 83 724 59; espacezongo@gmail.com; RN7; d/bungalow Ar40,000/65,000; 🐾) In a scenic spot 2km north of Ambalavao, Espace Zongo offers eight simple but impeccable rooms and a smattering of overpriced bungalows. It's all brand new but lacks a little spirit, even the spacious restaurant and terrace. The grounds are well kept, however, perhaps it just needs a little time to grow into its ambitions.

La Varangue du Betsileo
GUESTHOUSE €€€

(📞 032 63 376 48; www.varangue-betsileo.com; RN7; d/bungalow/f Ar80,000/140,000/150,000; 🐾) Located 8km south of Ambalavao on the RN7, the Varangue basks among glorious landscapes and enormous skies. The pretty rooms and bungalows (all newly built) are incredibly homely, and the friendly owners will bend over backwards to help their guests. The pool is a lovely bonus. Dinner is a set menu (Ar30,000).

Tsienimparihy
BAKERY, MADAGASCAN €

(Ambalavao; pastries from Ar1000, mains Ar7000-10,000; ☺ 7am-9pm) This bakery-cum-restaurant has a name for itself for the quality of its cakes and bread. The meals are good too: expect plenty of chicken/zebu in sauces, omelettes and noodles.

ⓘ Getting There & Away

Ambalavao lies 56km south of Fianarantsoa. The town has direct *taxi-brousse* connections with Fianarantsoa (Ar3000, 1½ hours), Ihosy (Ar8000, three hours) and Ranohira (Ar14,000, six hours). For destinations further north, you'll have to go to Fianarantsoa first.

Massif de l'Andringitra

Andringitra (an-*drintch*) is a majestic central mountain range with two gorgeous valleys on either side, the Namoly and the Tsaranoro (sometimes called the Sahanambo, for the river that runs through it), forming a paradise for walkers and climbers.

CENTRAL MADAGASCAR MASSIF DE L'ANDRINGITRA

One could easily spend a week hiking in this area. There are spectacular views in all directions, well-developed hiking trails, excellent accommodation, interesting villages, plus three extraordinary peaks: Pic Boby (Imarivolanitra), at 2658m the second-highest peak in the country; the Tsaranoro Massif, which reaches 1910m, including an 800m vertical column considered to be one of the most challenging climbs in the world; and the great stump of Pic Dondy (2195m). The latter two form the Portes du Sud (Gates of the South) and separate the Betsileo and Bara regions.

Now here's the most amazing part of all: there are less than 3000 visitors a year! This is mostly due to the difficulty of accessing the area (which is both time-consuming and costly). But imagine having Yosemite to yourself, and you're not far off the mark.

Technically most of the Tsaranoro Valley lies outside the park boundaries, but when people speak of Parc National d'Andringitra, they tend to mean this entire region.

Parc National d'Andringitra

Parc National d'Andringitra is the pièce de résistance of the wider Massif de l'Andringitra. It encompasses high-altitude plateaux of epic beauty, small tracts of primary rainforest, scenic trails along mountain streams and waterfalls, and Pic Boby, the highest accessible mountain in Madagascar. The best season to visit the **national park** (entry permits per day Ar45,000) is from June to November, when the rains aren't relentless (the park is officially closed from January to March, when heavy rains make access difficult). Afternoon mists are common in these high altitudes, and you should be prepared for bad weather at any time of year. If you are climbing Pic Boby, you will need a flashlight with several hours of battery life.

Parc National d'Andringitra & the Tsaranoro Valley

🏃 Activities

Wildlife Watching

Andringitra is mainly about hiking in spectacular scenery; it is not primarily a wildlife destination. Thirteen lemur species have been identified here, but sightings by visitors are rare since most of their habitat is outside the tourism zone. Ring-tails are the most commonly seen. The park's rich flora includes more than 30 species of orchid, which bloom mainly in October and November.

Hiking

The national park proper offers 100km of trails that traverse a variety of habitats and offer fantastic hiking. There are five main circuits catering to various abilities, but if you are going to come here, and are in good shape, take the Imarivolanitra Trail (p72) to the summit of Pic Boby to get the full Andringitra experience.

Other circuits include the easy **Asaramanitra** (6km, about four hours), which includes waterfalls and a cave, and the scenic **Diavolana** (12km, 10 hours), which is the next best choice after Imarivolanitra, as it takes in much of the plateau beneath the mountains. The best route for lemur-spotting is **Imaitso** (9km, four hours), which goes through the eastern primary forest. Details of the various routes are available at the park office.

🛏️ Sleeping & Eating

In the winter, temperatures fall into the cold-as-hell zone, reaching as low as -7°C at night. You will definitely need extra-warm clothing and a good sleeping bag. If you don't have your own camping equipment, Foudia (p69) in Ambalavao will see you right. As for food, you'll need to stock up in Ambalavao or, preferably, in Fianarantsoa, where groceries are cheaper and more varied (try Supermarché 3000; p67). Don't bring any pork as it is *fady* (taboo) in the park.

If you'd rather not have to worry about all the logistics, Foudia, Mad Trekking (p65) and Malagasy Tours (p263) all organise packages.

The park has five wilderness **MNP camping grounds** (per tent Ar6000) with roof-only sites, a cooking hut, running water and long-drop toilets.

Tranogasy   LODGE €€
(☑ 033 14 306 78; www.tranogasy.com; bungalow Ar69,000, without bathroom Ar48,000) These

---

ℹ️ PARC NATIONAL D'ANDRINGITRA

Best time to visit October to November during orchid bloom.

Key highlight Sunrise from the summit of Pic Boby.

Wildlife Ring-tailed lemurs, multi-coloured grasshoppers.

Habitat High plateau, meadows, rocky peaks, some primary rainforest (Imaitso).

Gateway town Ambalavao.

Transport options Private car.

Things you should know Water freezes at night during winter.

---

chalets near the Namoly park entrance are a great place to stay if you want to arrive in the afternoon, arrange your trek, and start off the next morning. The mountain valley setting is incredible.

ℹ️ Information

➡ The **MNP office** (☑ 020 75 340 81; www.parcs-madagascar.com; ☻ 6.30am-3.30pm) in Namoly has all you need to trek into the park, including entry permits. Here you can hire guides, porters and cooking utensils (but not camping equipment – you'll need to organise this in Ambalavao).

➡ Guide fees cost Ar20,000/35,000/50,000/70,000 for one/two/three/four days; porters (who will also cook for you) cost Ar10,000 per day and can carry up to 20kg. Note that only a couple of guides speak basic English.

ℹ️ Getting There & Away

The Namoly Valley is a nearly three-hour drive from Ambalavao, with some iffy bridges, but it is also a scenic trip through rocky hill country full of small villages, rice paddies and smiling children. The track is very rough and requires a 4WD.

Tsaranoro Valley

The Tsaranoro may be only one mountain chain away from the Namoly but it might as well be a separate country. It is much hotter and drier here than in the Namoly and it shows: the valley is dotted with mango trees, and zebu pastures dominate rather than lush paddy fields.

THE BEST OF ANDRINGITRA

The best way to see Andringitra is on the Imarivolanitra Trail. Enter through the Namoly Valley, summit Pic Boby and then descend into the Tsaranoro. The circuit usually takes three days but you could do it in two if you don't mind a long Day 2 (12 hours).

On Day 1, you'll hike from the Namoly park entrance to the Pic Boby base camp. This entails hiking up 600m or so until you reach a high plateau that hugs the rocky skyline for miles. It's a generally gentle climb, with a few steep 50m ascents, that takes four hours. The camp is by a stream, so you can fall asleep while listening to a waterfall beneath the stars.

On Day 2, awake early, and depart by flashlight at 4am for a two-hour hike to the summit, which is not where you think. When you reach the top of the skyline, with the sky beginning to lighten, you finally see what looks like Gibraltar sitting on top. This strenuous last leg takes you to the (second) roof of Madagascar, just in time for sunrise. Here you stand astride the entire island, a sea of clouds on one side, and an unbroken vista on the other. Beneath a cairn lies a metal box with a guestbook.

Now it's back to the camp for breakfast, and onwards to new territory. You walk along the flat plateau for hours, breathing in the finest scenery. The sky is huge, the ridgeline dramatic. After crossing over the mountains through a deep pass, the Tsaranoro Valley comes into view, a grand vista. You pass through an alluring desert landscape, with the unforgettable sight of the great Massif's vertical drop ahead.

About a third of the way down to the Tsaranoro is the second MNP campsite where you can break off. If you're carrying on, it's another three hours of down, down, down until you reach the first few villages, and another hour to Morarano and your hotel for the night, with the Gates of the South towering above. The next day you can hike more of the valley, or head back to the RN7. Unforgettable.

🏃 Activities

There are numerous walks to enjoy in Tsaranoro. Some tackle the Tsaranoro Massif, others simply take you to local villages, natural swimming pools and waterfalls. All hotels will be able to provide you with a guide.

🛏 Sleeping & Eating

★ **Camp Catta**   LODGE €€
(☑ 033 15 347 18; www.campcatta.com; Tsaranoro Valley; camping per site Ar7000, equipped tent Ar40,000, bungalow Ar90,000; 🛜🏊) This is the place to stay in the Tsaranoro Valley, with a breathtaking location at the foot of the Massif, quality accommodation and food, ring-tailed lemurs roaming through the camp and a gorgeous eco swimming pool (the water is cleaned by a reed bed). It's not cheap, but is worth it. Transfers available from Fianarantsoa (Ar175,000) and Ambalavao (Ar125,000).

Tsarasoa   LODGE €€
(☑ 032 02 216 15; marlixadventurepark@gmail. com; Tsaranoro Valley; camping per tent Ar15,000, hut/bungalow Ar40,000/125,000) 🌿 The beauty of Tsarasoa is that it has something for every budget: penny pinchers can camp; budget travellers will opt for the simple huts; whilst those who like their creature comforts will love the original bungalows (bathrooms with mosaics and coloured glass, suspended beds, panoramic views etc). All share the same beautiful setting and owner Gilles' inimitable welcome.

Tsarasoa is working hard to minimise its environmental footprint: it serves free filtered water to guests and has planted thousands of trees over the past decade.

Tsara Camp   LODGE €€€
(☑ 033 12 441 27, 020 22 248 47; www.boogie pilgrim-madagascar.com/hotels/tsara-camp/; Tsaranoro Valley; d Ar132,000) 🌿 In an awesome location in the centre of the Tsaranoro Valley, Tsara Camp features comfortable, well-equipped tents complete with private bathrooms (the open-topped shower is a nice touch). The camp lacks atmosphere and facilities however, and is rather overpriced.

ℹ Getting There & Away

The Tsaranoro Valley is 60km from Ambalavao but the 20km dirt road from the RN7 is in good condition so it takes a couple of hours. There is one toll of Ar2000.

Southern Madagascar

Best Places to Eat

➡ Auberge Peter Pan (p91)

➡ L'Estérel (p84)

➡ Isalo Rock Lodge (p78)

➡ Le Relais de la Reine (p78)

➡ Corto Maltese (p84)

Best Places to Stay

➡ Bakuba (p84)

➡ Anakao Ocean Lodge (p92)

➡ Talinjoo (p97)

➡ Isalo Rock Lodge (p78)

➡ Auberge Peter Pan (p91)

Why Go?

Southern Madagascar is a wide-open adventure among some of nature's most dramatic forms. The stark desert canyons of Parc National de l'Isalo rival those of Arizona. The west coast offers gorgeous coastal settlements that serve as gateways to the fifth-largest coral reef in the world. The cape is the last stop before Antarctica, and vast kilometres of spiny forest contain the strangest and most formidable plants on earth.

There are also two scruffy cities, Tuléar (Toliara) and Fort Dauphin (Taolagnaro), but that is not why you come. The question is how to tackle a region of this size. For many, a lodge in Isalo and a slice of beach are enough. But for others, the south is the perfect recipe for off-road exploration. After all, away from the RN7 it's strictly 4WD country.

When to Go
Tuléar

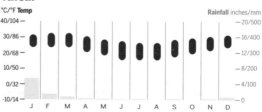

| **Jul–Sep** Whale-watching season on the Great Reef. | **Sep–Nov** Ideal 4WDing season. | **Dec–Mar** Rainy season makes travel difficult away from the RN7. Many roads are impassable. |

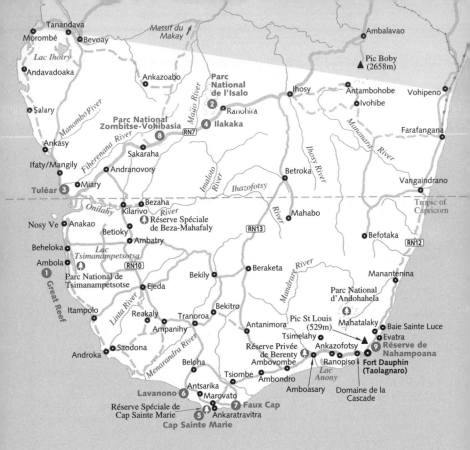

Massif du Makay

Tanandava
Morombé · Bevoay
Lac Ihotry
Andavadoaka
Ankazoabo
Massif du Makay
Ambalavao
Pic Boby (2658m)
Parc National de l'Isalo
Ihosy
Antambohobe
Vohipeno
Ivohibe
❷ Ranohira
Salary
Parc National Zombitse-Vohibasia
❹ Ilakaka
Farafangana
Ankasy
❽ RN7
Ifaty/Mangily
Sakaraha
Betroka
Andranovory
Vangaindrano
Tuléar ❸ · Miary
Onilahy River
Bezaha
Tropic of Capricorn
Kilarivo
Mahabo
Nosy Ve · Anakao
Réserve Spéciale de Beza-Mahafaly
RN13
Befotaka
Betioky
RN12
Beheloka
Ambatry
Lac Tsimanampetsotsa
Ambola ❶
RN10
Beraketa
Manantenina
Parc National de Tsimanampetsotse
Bekily
Parc National d'Andohahela
Ejeda
Itampolo
Bekitro
Pic St Louis (529m)
Mahataláky · Baie Sainte Luce
Reakaly · Tranoroa
Antanimora
Evatra
Ampanihy
Tsimelahy
Ankazofotsy
❾ Réserve de Nahampoana
Androka · Saodona
Réserve Privée de Berenty
Ranopiso · Fort Dauphin (Taolagnaro)
Beloha
Ambovombe
Lac Anony
Tsiombe
Ambondro
Antsarika
Amboasary
Domaine de la Cascade
Lavanono ❻ · Marovato
❼ Faux Cap
Réserve Spéciale de Cap Sainte Marie
❺ Ankaratravitra
Cap Sainte Marie

Great Reef

Manombo River
Mania River
Fiherenana River
Imaloto River
Ihazofotsy
Ihosy River
Mananara River
Mandrare River
Menarandra River
Linta River

INDIAN OCEAN

N 0 ————— 100 km
   0 ————— 60 miles

Southern Madagascar Highlights

❶ Dive the **Great Reef** (p81), then go whale watching from Anakao.

❷ Take a dip in the Piscine Naturelle, spot lemurs and walk the canyons at **Parc National de l'Isalo** (p75).

❸ Drive the sand track past a turquoise sea and to the spiny forest north of **Tuléar** (p82).

❹ Visit the sapphire mines of **Ilakaka** (p80): that ring will never look the same.

❺ Stand at the tip of the 'eighth continent' at **Cap Sainte Marie** (p94).

❻ Hang out with the surfers and marvel at the isolation at **Lavanono** (p94).

❼ Do like Sir David Attenborough and see elephant bird eggshell fragments in **Faux Cap** (p94).

❽ Track down rare birds and nocturnal lemurs at **Parc National Zombitse-Vohibasia** (p80).

❾ Say hi to the lemurs at **Réserve de Nahampoana** (p99).

❶ Getting There & Away

Fort Dauphin and Tuléar are the two hubs of the south, both served by Air Madagascar. Tuléar is the gateway to the Great Reef and is easily reached from Antananarivo (Tana) by *taxi-brousse* (bush taxi) or private car along the sealed, but deteriorating RN7. Fort Dauphin and the cape can only be reached by 4WD or by air from Tana.

THE DESERT

Two fine national parks and a sapphire boom town provide many reasons to linger in southern Madagascar's cauterised interior. Parc National de l'Isalo is one of Madagascar's best, with good wildlife and even better landscapes. Parc National de Zombitse-Vohibasia is a little-known jewel for birdwatchers. In between the two, Ilakaka feels like Madagascar's Wild West.

Parc National de l'Isalo

Parc National de l'Isalo (www.parcs-madagascar.com; adult/child per day Ar65,000/25,000) is like a museum dedicated to the art of the desert canyon. Gorges here are filled with yellow savannah grasses, sculpted buttes, vertical rock walls and, best of all, deep canyon floors shot through with streams, lush vegetation and pools for swimming. All of this changes with the light, culminating in extraordinary sunsets beneath a big sky. Add all this to easy access off the RN7 and you understand why this is Madagascar's most visited park.

At more than 800 sq km, there's plenty of room for exploration, with everything from two-hour to week-long hikes. The park is served by the small town of Ranohira, which contains the park office and most of the cheap hotels and restaurants, while fabulous resorts extend all along the park's southern border.

◉ Sights

Maison de l'Isalo MUSEUM
(⊕8am-5pm) FREE The buttons don't work at this once-interactive little museum, but it's still a good introduction to the history, culture and geology of the park. If you're staying in town, combine it with a trip to La Fenêtre, or pause on your onward journey towards Tuléar.

La Fenêtre de l'Isalo VIEWPOINT
La Fenêtre de l'Isalo is a popular natural rock window that frames the setting sun, although we actually prefer it for the surrounding views of sweeping plains and weird-and-wonderful rock formations turned golden at sunset. At the time of writing, visitors were encouraged not to visit alone due to the threat of robbery – if there are other vehicles in attendance, take the 800m track off the RN7; the turn-off is around 1.5km south of La Relais de la Reine (p78).

GETTING AROUND SOUTHERN MADAGASCAR

If you wish to go by road anywhere off the RN7 you'll need either a 4WD or, if there is public transport, a very strong stomach. *Taxis-brousses* can be brutal in the south.

At the time of research the state of some major routes was as follows (many of these routes are impassable in the rainy season):

RN7 to Tuléar Excellent sealed surface, showing signs of deterioration; no 4WD necessary.

Tuléar to Ifaty/Mangily Firm dirt road, 4WD in rain.

Ifaty to Andavadoaka via coast road Sand track with some rutted deep sand, requires 4WD.

Ifaty to Andavadoaka via RN9 More direct and quicker but potholed in patches; 4WD needed.

Tuléar to Anakao via Betioky Terrible road but better closer to Anakao; 4WD required.

Itampolo to Ampanihy via Androka Very bad, often rocky road, confusing tracks, maps not accurate. Use a local guide.

Ampanihy to Ambovombe Improved dirt road, particularly good on first half, but 4WD still needed.

Ambovombe to Ihosy Terrible road rutted by *camions-brousses* (large trucks) and not safe at time of writing, especially after dark.

Ambovombe to Fort Dauphin Terrible road, a deteriorated sealed surface with craters worthy of the moon; 4WD required.

La Reine de l'Isalo MOUNTAIN

(Queen of Isalo) If you like finding figures in stone, La Reine de l'Isalo sits about 3km south of the museum, on the left side of the road. It's cool once you spot it, but you'll probably need someone to point it out.

🏃 Activities

Wildlife Watching

Although animal life isn't the park's most prominent feature, there's a good chance you'll spot the park's three diurnal lemur species: ring-tailed lemur, red-browed brown lemur and Verreaux's sifaka. Your best chance of spotting them is between 11am and 3pm from March to October at the campsite close to the start of the Namaza trail; it's an 800m walk in from the car park. These three species can also be seen at **Canyon des Makis** (Canyon des Singes) and **Canyon des Rats**.

The park is also home to three nocturnal lemur species: grey mouse lemur, red-tailed sportive lemur and Coquerel's giant mouse lemur, but as night walks inside the park are no longer allowed, your only chance of seeing these is to camp overnight at Namaza or Canyon des Makis campsites. Even then, chances are slim. More than 50 bird species also inhabit the park, and birders get particularly excited here if they track down the Benson's rock thrush, Madagascar sand grouse, Madagascar partridge or the hooded vanga.

Near streams and in the lush pockets of forest in the deeper canyons, there are ferns, pandanus and feathery palm trees. At ground level in drier areas, look for the yellow flowering *Pachypodium rosulatum* (especially beautiful in September and October), which resembles a miniature baobab tree and is often called 'elephant's foot'.

Hiking

The length of time the various circuits require depends on whether you take a car to the trailhead (which we strongly recommend). Otherwise you must walk in from Ranohira, which is a long way across hot, open country in most cases. Bring sunscreen, a hat and enough water for your visit. Picnic lunches can be arranged – ask your guide or hotel.

➡ **Piscine Naturelle** Short hike to a beautiful natural pool. One of the easiest and most popular trails, although there is some steep walking. Start early as much of the trail leads across open country with no shade. It's 3km by car and 3km on foot.

➡ **Namaza** A variety of possibilities but one of the more rewarding heads through deep gorges, taking in (at its lengthiest) the lemur-rich Namaza campsite, the pretty Cascade des Nymphs, a ridgetop lookout and two deep natural pools. The full trail runs 6km and takes three to four hours.

➡ **Circuit Crête (Crest Circuit)** Begins at the Piscine Naturelle (combine the two hikes for a fine day walk) and then climbs up to follow the ridgeline with fine views en route. The hike covers 4km in 2½ hours and is of medium difficulty.

➡ **Canyons** Takes in the Canyon des Makis (aka Canyon des Singes), with chances of seeing lemurs, and the Canyon des Rats burial area. A 17km drive and easy 2km hike, taking around 2½ hours.

➡ **Falls of Anjofo** Hike by the river's edge to two waterfalls. It's 29km by car, and a somewhat difficult 3km hike that should take around five hours, including the drive.

➡ **Moyen Circuit** This title is used by guides as a catch-all for a variety of longer hikes that can be full day or even two to three days.

➡ **Grand Tour** An 80km, six- to seven-day hike that takes in as much as the park can offer, including the Portuguese Grotto, a picturesque, 30m-long cave in the park's north. The way to get away from it all.

Four-Wheel Driving

The **Malaso** 4WD circuit is primarily intended to provide a window on the park for those of impaired mobility. It leaves the RN7 south of town, although you'll still need to pick up

---

> ### ❶ PARC NATIONAL DE L'ISALO
>
> **Best time to visit** May to October.
>
> **Key highlight** Piscine Naturelle.
>
> **Wildlife** Three lemur species, more than 50 bird species, *Pachypodium*.
>
> **Habitat** Dry desert rock, spring-fed oases.
>
> **Gateway town** Ranohira.
>
> **Transport options** *Taxi-brousse* or car (4WD in park).
>
> **Things you should know** While the luxury resorts are expensive for Madagascar, they're a bargain compared to other parts of the world.

a guide from the park office in Ranohira. The route takes you across the plains and broad valleys and to the edge of some canyons, with stops at some short trails. It's a 42km, four-hour drive with some optional walking.

Via Ferrata

At two places, climbing aids have been bolted into the rock, scaling to the top for fine views. In both cases, you're provided with all of the equipment. The climbs are considered suitable for people who have never climbed before and those with basic fitness.

➡ **Via Ferrata** A 750m circuit around 27km northwest of Ranohira. The starting point is the same as for the Falls of Anjofo hike.

➡ **Le Relais de la Reine** (p78) This hotel offers a 1½-hour circuit up to the canyon summit for fine views. The climbing portion only lasts around 10 minutes, making it suitable for all fitness levels. It's open to nonguests and costs €20 per person.

Horse Riding

Le Relais de la Reine has a small equestrian centre that is open to nonguests and is a fine option for exploring the canyons beyond the park. One-hour/half-day rides cost €15/50 per person, while children's pony rides cost €5/8 per 30/60 minutes. Longer expeditions into the park are also possible.

Mountain Biking

The park's MNP office (p79) rents out OK mountain bikes for Ar20,000/30,000 per half/full day.

🛏 Sleeping

Accommodation options extend westward from Ranohira, along the southern border of the park. You can't go wrong with any of the premier properties here. Dining is done exclusively in hotels, but the quality is high everywhere.

In addition to the official campsites inside the park, camping elsewhere in the park is possible if you are going on a longer hike, but you'll need to obtain permission from the MNP office.

★ **Chez Alice**   BUNGALOW **€**
(☎033 07 134 44, 032 02 055 68; chezalice@ yahoo.fr; off RN7; camping for 2 people Ar20,000, paillotte without bathroom Ar22,000, d/tr/f bungalow Ar38,000/50,000/60,000) It's a rough drive in and somewhat bare surrounds hides this convivial backpacker's hang-out and budget

Parc National de l'Isalo

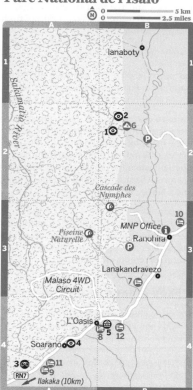

Parc National de l'Isalo

gem not far from the centre of Ranohira. Run by the irrepressible Alice, who would otherwise be running an Old West saloon, there are bungalows of various types and prices, all of which are colourfully painted and excellent value.

The restaurant is a super place to hang out, and the food (mains Ar8500 to Ar14,000, set menu Ar22,000) ranges from Malagasy to burgers.

Piscine Naturelle Campsite
CAMPGROUND €

(per person Ar5000) The campsite at Piscine Naturelle is equipped with showers, toilets, sheltered dining and a large cooking area.

Namaza Campsite
CAMPGROUND €

(per person Ar10,000) This excellent campsite is the best place in the park to spot lemurs, but you'd want to be all packed up by late morning when the crowds arrive. Watch for nocturnal lemurs at night. There's a toilet and a barbecue area.

Canyon des Makis Campsite
CAMPGROUND €

(per person Ar5000) Picturesque campsite inside the park – if you're lucky you'll spot nocturnal lemurs after dark.

PARK GUIDES

Parc National de l'Isalo's MNP office (p79) has a list of the 72 accredited guides, along with the languages they speak and their phone numbers.

If you take your own vehicle to the trailheads, guides usually cost Ar20,000 per person per circuit. Example combinations include Piscine Naturelle and Crest Circuit (Ar36,000), Piscine Naturelle, Namaza campsite and Cascade des Nymphs (Ar45,000) and Piscine Naturelle, Crest Circuit, Namaza campsite, natural pools and Cascade des Nymphs (Ar113,000).

Toussaint (📱033 71 029 66) Recommended guide speaking English, French, Spanish, Italian and German.

Charles (📱034 41 786 51) Recommended guide who speaks English, French and Italian.

Rolland (📱033 08 437 94) Speaks French and English.

Parson (📱034 12 241 84) French- and English-speaking guide.

Momo Trek (📱032 44 187 90; www.isalo-trek.com) Experienced Ranohira operator with all-inclusive hiking packages, including multiday expeditions to Massif du Makay.

Le Orchidée d'Isalo
HOTEL €€

(📱033 06 918 75, 032 44 676 89; www.orchidee-isalo.com; RN7; d Ar41,000-130,000, f Ar97,000) In the centre of town, just before the RN7 doglegs south if you're coming from the north, Le Orchidée d'Isalo has simple, tidy rooms with tiled floors, mosquito nets and hot water. Its top-of-the-range newer rooms, built in 2014, are the best in Ranohira itself. Management is friendly and hopes to fill the pool one day.

Hotel Berny
HOTEL €€

(Chez Berny; 📱032 05 257 69; off RN7; camping per vehicle Ar10,000, d Ar42,000-50,000, f Ar72,000) Ageing, and not doing so particularly gracefully, Hotel Berny is an eclectic local institution owned by the former mayor of Ranohira. Ignore the junkyard-style garden and you'll find surprisingly good rooms in a large stone building. Highlights include mosquito nets and zebu-horn toilet-paper holders. Berny also has some out-of-town campsites.

★ Isalo Rock Lodge
LODGE €€€

(📱020 22 328 60; www.isalorocklodge.com; off RN7; s/d incl breakfast €100/120; ❄️🛜🏊) This stylish hotel has a beautiful terrace overlooking sandstone formations, a spa and fitness room and a fluorescent pool with ever-changing colours. The restaurant (set menu Ar60,000) serves works of art, while the rooms, bathed in soothing earth tones, are triumphs of contemporary design. A sharp manager ensures perfection.

There's a walking trail with a natural pool and a steep ascent to a viewpoint at the summit of a nearby formation.

★ Le Relais de la Reine
BOUTIQUE HOTEL €€€

(📱020 22 336 23, 034 02 123 29; www.lerelaisdelareine.com; off RN7; d €85-98; 🅿️❄️🛜🏊) Beautifully designed, this lovely property sits among canyons with elegant stone-built cottages. Service is impeccable (it's the sort of place where you come back from dinner to find your bed prepared), the restaurant outstanding (three-course set menu Ar45,000) and there's a real attention to detail that you just don't find in many places in Madagascar's south.

The outstanding rooms (tiled floors, four-poster beds, exposed stone walls and soft lighting), refurbished in 2012, are merely the start. There's also a fine swimming pool, clay tennis court, a stunning garden with frangipani and bougainvillea, a stylish bar, a spa and massage centre, a via ferrata (p77) in the neighbouring can-

MASSIF DU MAKAY

North of Parc National de l'Isalo, the Massif du Makay is a destination that could just be Madagascar's next big thing. Qualifying as Madagascar's last lost world, and stretching almost 150km from southwest to northeast, and 50km across, this otherworldly sandstone massif is riven with verdant canyons, dramatic ridges and high plateaus. The rounded tongues of rock weave in intricate patterns like lava fingers with deep gashes of green in the shadows – it's like the best of Parc National de l'Isalo, but without the crowds and covering a much larger area.

At this stage, there's very little tourist infrastructure and only a few operators run bivouac expeditions here. Expect that to change. One Ranohira company that already offers week-long expeditions to the Massif du Makay is Momo Trek (p78), while further afield Malagasy Tours (p263), Mad Trekking (p65) and several international operators are offering trips here. Otherwise, your best bet is to discuss the options with Isalo park guides.

The Massif du Makay is a rough eight- to 10-hour 4WD journey north of Ranohira, with a ferry crossing (Ar10,000 per vehicle) across the Mangoky River at Beroroha.

yons and an equestrian centre (p77) for sunset gallops across the savannah.

It's 14km beyond Ranohira, on the left if coming from Tana.

Satrana Lodge　　　　　　LODGE €€€
(☑020 22 632 53, 034 14 260 87; www.satrana lodge-madagascar.com; d €73-102; P⬛🛜❄) This wonderful lodge, beautifully situated beneath a range of sandstone outcrops, has a majestic pool with endless desert views, a classy restaurant and atmospheric wood-floored safari-tent rooms with writing desks and open-air showers. There's even an outdoor astronomy bar – with drink in hand, you zoom in on a computer chart of the galaxy, the adjacent telescope whirs...and there you are.

Jardin du Roy　　　　BOUTIQUE HOTEL €€€
(☑033 07 123 07, 034 02 351 66; www.lejardindu roy.com; off RN7; bungalow €85-120; P⬛🛜❄) This stunning property shares amenities and owners with the adjacent Relais de la Reine. On offer are unique stone bungalows, including custom hand-crafted furniture, and all rooms are air-conditioned. Like its sister property, it's situated among sandstone formations.

Isalo Ranch　　　　　　BUNGALOW €€€
(☑020 24 319 02, 034 20 319 02; www.isalo-ranch. com; RN7; camping per person Ar15,000, d/f bungalow from Ar128,000/144,000; ❄) 🍃 The sand pathways of this lodge tie its bungalows together into a welcoming little village, aided by a shady and cosy restaurant with an international menu. It's solar energy only here and the rooms are as pleasing as the surroundings.

🍴 Eating

The top-end Isalo Rock Lodge, Le Relais de la Reine, Satrana Lodge and Jardin du Roy hotels all have stellar restaurants that are open to nonguests – book ahead if you're not staying overnight.

**Restaurant Le
Zébu Grillé**　　　MADAGASCAN, INTERNATIONAL €€
(☑032 44 676 89; www.orchidee-isalo.com; RN7; mains Ar7000-13,000) The best restaurant in Ranohira itself serves a good mix of Malagasy specials (such as pork with beans) and international dishes such as roast chicken, all in a pleasant setting in the heart of town. It's attached to Le Orchidée d'Isalo.

ⓘ Information

There are no internet cafes and only the top-end hotels have free wi-fi for guests.

There are no banks or ATMs in Ranohira. The nearest bank is in Ihosy, 91km away.

MNP Office (☑033 49 402 36, 033 13 172 58; off RN7; ⊙6.30am-4.30pm) The park office has a list of guides and official guiding fees posted outside its door.

ⓘ Getting There & Away

For points north, you may be lucky enough to find a *taxi-brousse* travelling between Tuléar and Antananarivo with an empty seat. Each morning one or two *taxis-brousses* connect Ranohira directly with Ihosy (Ar25,000, two hours), 91km to the east, from where there are more options.

Public transport from Tuléar generally arrives in Ranohira between 10am and 1pm, while vehicles from the north usually arrive before 10am.

SOUTHERN MADAGASCAR PARC NATIONAL DE L'ISALO

MINING THE OLD-FASHIONED WAY

The sapphire mining process begins with a borehole large enough to lower a person 30m into the earth. If round stones – the signs of an ancient riverbed – are found, sapphires might be found as well. This leads to the digging of a second hole by the mining equivalent of a bucket brigade, with one person shovelling to the next, and so on, for a very, very long time. If it rains, walls collapse and the digging begins anew. Some mines are dug by individual owners, while others are financed by groups of investors. Some yield valuable sapphires, others produce nothing. There have been enough of the former to create a sapphire rush in Ilakaka involving tens of thousands of people. In fact, Ilakaka sits on top of the biggest sapphire deposit in the world, all 40 sq km of it, even though you will not see a single piece of mining machinery beyond a spade. Just be careful what you are offered in the street. As the saying goes, 'the closer you get to the mine, the more synthetic you find'.

Ilakaka

Ilakaka is the perfect setting for a James Bond movie. Driving through the middle of nowhere about half an hour west of Ranohira, you come upon a sapphire boom town that has spontaneously erupted astride the RN7. The main street is lined with ramshackle structures selling provisions for the miners, from shovels to mobile phones. Side streets are lined with gem buyers in shaded huts and women with painted faces squatting on the footpath organising piles of stones by quality. The highlight is the nearby mining area, where hand-dug mines pockmark the earth. One can imagine 007 running across this landscape pursued by the henchmen of some evil gem lord.

In any case, you have to see this. By accident it has become one of the more fascinating sights in Madagascar, all the more so because it appears completely unconscious of the fact.

Ilakaka has long had a reputation for being dangerous, a reputation that was warranted in the past when the boom was hot, but has waned as it has tapered off into some kind of thin normality. You don't have anything to worry about here during the day, particularly during a tour, but we can't vouch for 3am, when the party ends.

Tours

Color Line TOUR
(033 17 720 17, 033 20 123 08; colorline.mada@gmail.com; ⊙8-10am & 1-3pm, showroom 7am-7pm) The gem dealer Color Line, at the southern end of the main street, on the left as you come from Ranohira, offers tours of the sapphire mines. Far from destroying the authenticity, it's fully part of it, taking you out to the rough-cut mines and explaining the whole process

and intrigue. The guide, Mohammed, speaks only French. Tours last 45 minutes to an hour.

Color Line also owns a gem and fossil shop on the main street.

Drinking

Al2O3 BAR
(⊙1-3am Fri) To enter the local scene in all its shadiness, attend the gem dealers' party starting at 1am every Friday night at Color Line's adjacent bar, known as Al2O3 (the formula for sapphire, naturally). This is only for a particular kind of traveller and is a long way from respectability – think the bar scene in the first *Star Wars* film, without the aliens.

We suggest you check earlier in the day with Color Line to make sure it's going ahead. Park nearby or get someone to pick you up.

Getting There & Away

If you're in Isalo and want to take the tour, call Color Line to arrange transport, or any *taxi-brousse* heading west on the RN7 will get you here. Otherwise we recommend visiting from Ranohira or en route elsewhere along the RN7.

From Ilakaka, *taxis-brousses* leave every morning and afternoon for Tuléar and Ambalavao (Ar25,000, six hours), sometimes continuing to Fianarantsoa (Ar25,000, seven hours).

Parc National Zombitse-Vohibasia

One of Madagascar's least-known yet most accessible parks, **Parc National Zombitse-Vohibasia** (www.parcs-madagascar.com; adult/child per day Ar45,000/25,000, guide Ar10,000) is a surprise packet; most visitors just drive on by and don't realise what they're missing. The park's dense dry forest is how all of Madagascar's arid south must once have appeared, and the park's 363 sq km are all that remain – a forested island in what has become a denuded semi-desert landscape. There are some real highlights here, including strangler figs and the occasional baobab.

The park's relict forest shelters an astounding 85 recorded bird species. Commonly sighted here are the grand and Coquerel's coua, white-browed owl, black parrot and blue vanga. But the real prize is the Appert's greenbul – sometimes, quantifying the science of extinction is all too easy because if this forest were to disappear, so too would this species as it survives nowhere else on the planet.

Lemurs are also an attraction here with eight recorded species. Most are nocturnal, but you're pretty likely to come across skittish bands of Verreaux's sifaka and the oh-so-cute (and endangered) Hubbard's sportive lemur. The latter is nocturnal but is commonly seen resting in tree hollows by day.

Pay your fees at the barely functioning park office, just set back from the RN7, and let a guide lead you along any of the circuits that range from 15 minutes to two hours in length. The optimum time for birdwatching is 6am to 9am.

🛏 Sleeping & Eating

Most visitors stop to visit en route between Isalo and Tuléar.

Zombitse Ecolodge   BUNGALOW €€
(☎ 033 80 651 63, 033 12 325 64; www.zombitse.de; RN7; s/d bungalow €30/35) Around 7km west of the park entrance, the only accommodation close to the park is a rather forlorn site – the grounds and all facilities could do with some sprucing up. The bungalows have poor mattresses but are otherwise OK. There's a simple restaurant. The real reason to stay here is to enable you to get to the park at dawn.

ℹ Getting There & Away

The park straddles the RN7, 90km west of Isalo and 147km northeast of Tuléar. Any *taxi-brousse* between the two can stop here. Trails start right by the roadside.

THE GREAT REEF

A reef stretches over 450km along the southwestern coast of Madagascar, making it the fifth-largest coral reef in the world. Running from Andavadoaka in the north to Itampolo in the south, it's the main attraction in the region, with its own changing personality.

The Great Reef

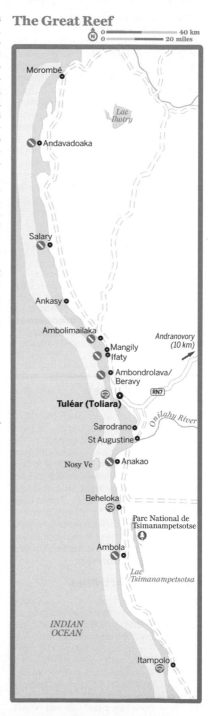

The Great Reef comes in three potential forms: a fringing reef close in, a patch reef of coral heads and an outer barrier reef. The last creates very broad and shallow inshore lagoons and makes for dramatic scenery, with large waves crashing in the distance, forming a vibrant line of white. The beaches range from broken coral to spectacular white powder. There are many activities to pursue here: sunbathing, snorkelling, diving, fishing, whale watching (mid-June or early July to September), surfing and sailing among them. Although the diving can't really compare with other spots in the West Indian Ocean such as Pemba, Mayotte or northern Mozambique, it remains a wonderful experience and the most remote sites, particularly those further offshore, are in the best shape.

❶ Getting There & Away

Tuléar is the hub of the Great Reef. North of Tuléar, there is little or no public transport after Mangily. With the exception of private planes, the northern hotels are all reached by private 4WD. Transfers can be arranged, but are expensive.

South of Tuléar, there are boat transfers to Anakao, which is a quick and wonderful way to arrive, but south of Anakao you need a private 4WD again, or *lots* of time.

Tuléar (Toliara)

POP 165,300

Tuléar is where the sealed road (the RN7) ends and many adventures begin – its main appeal is as most travellers' gateway to the Great Reef north and south of the city. Your most enduring memory here is likely to be a sea of pousse-pousse bouncing down dusty lanes and the city itself has little to detain you beyond an outstanding out-of-town arboretum and some fine hotels and restaurants. Add a somewhat raffish tropical ambience fuelled by local French and Italian expats and you have the setting for your first novel. Do take taxis after dark.

◎ Sights & Activities

★ Arboretum d'Antsokay   GARDENS
(☑ 032 02 600 15; www.antsokayarboretum.org; off RN7; adult/child Ar15,000/5000; ☉ 7.30am-5.30pm, closed Feb) This is the one must-see attraction in Tuléar. Essentially a 400,000-sq-metre distillation of the entire spiny forest in one place, it's a fantastic collection of 900 species of plants. Established by a Swiss botanist and conservationist in 1980, it's also a model for how much larger parks should be run.

There's a classy interpretation centre, a small museum, shop, self-guided tours in English, a stylish restaurant and some excellent, inexpensive bungalows with pool. MNP take note: clone this place.

The arboretum lies about 12km southeast of town, just a few hundred metres from the RN7, so it's a good stop as you arrive by car. Otherwise take a taxi, or ask any *taxi-brousse* heading towards Befety to drop you off at the junction (you'll have to walk in). Transfers to Tuléar or the airport cost Ar10,000.

La Table   MOUNTAIN
This table mountain is unmissable as you approach Tuléar down the RN7, about 10km from town. There's a relatively easy trail to the top, which takes about 15 minutes to climb, and it's a great place to watch the sunset. Go early or late in summer. For Ar30,000 you can hire a taxi in town to take you here and the nearby arboretum.

Musée Cedratom   MUSEUM
(admission Ar2500; ☉ 8-11.30am & 2.30-5.30pm Mon-Fri) Features exhibits on local culture, an elephant bird egg and other oddities, including a mask with real human teeth. Interesting place if you're ever lucky enough to find it open – the official opening hours mean little and the guardian of the door couldn't really give a toss whether you go in or not.

🛏 Sleeping

Chez Lala   HOTEL €
(☑ 020 94 434 17; Ave de France; d 25,000, without bathroom Ar20,000; ☎) This laid-back and genial guesthouse is your best budget option; most nights there are more Malagasy guests than foreigners. The simple rooms in the tropical courtyard are smaller than those in the parquet-tiled main block, but they're all decent value. A TV lounge, great espresso, loads of info and free wi-fi help clinch the deal.

Chez Alain   GUESTHOUSE, BUNGALOW €
(☑ 020 94 415 27; www.hotelchezalain-tulear.com; d Ar50,000-80,000, without bathroom Ar30,000; ℗❄☎) It may be close to the *taxi brousse* station, but Chez Alain has a quiet garden area sheltered from the surrounding clamour. The simplest rooms are basic but well kept, while any of the rooms with private bathrooms are well priced. The most expensive are spacious and have air-con.

★ Auberge de la Table   BUNGALOW €€
(☑ 032 02 600 15; www.antsokayarboretum.org; off RN7; d bungalow Ar60,000-95,000, tr Ar75,000-

Tuléar (Toliara)

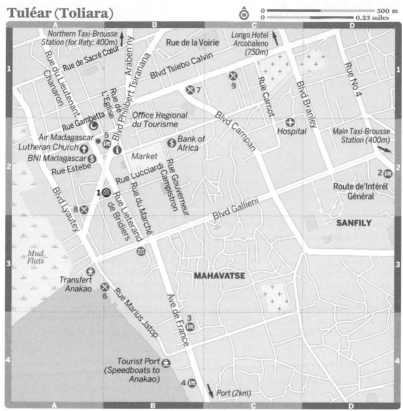

Northern Taxi-Brousse Station (for Ifaty; 400m)

Longo Hotel Arcobaleno (750m)

Rue de la Voirie

Rue de Sacré Cœur

Rue du Lieutenant Chanaron

Blvd Tsiebo Calvin

Araben'ny

Blvd Philibert Tsiranana

Rue de l'Eglise

Rue Gambetta

Rue Carrot

Blvd Branley

Rue No 4

7

9

Office Regional du Tourisme

Blvd Campan

Air Madagascar
Lutheran Church
BNI Madagascar
Rue Estebe

5

Bank of Africa

Hospital

Main Taxi-Brousse Station (400m)

Market

Rue Lucciardi

Rue Gouverneur Campistron

Rue du Marché

Rue Lieterand de Bridiers

Blvd Lyautey

1

8

Blvd Gallieni

Route de l'Intérêl Général

2

SANFILY

Mud Flats

Transfert Anakao

6

Rue Marius Jatop

MAHAVATSE

Ave de France

3

Tourist Port (Speedboats to Anakao)

4

Port (2km)

SOUTHERN MADAGASCAR TULÉAR (TOLIARA)

110,000; P 🛜 🏊) The bungalows at the Arboretum d'Antsokay, 12km east of the city, represent fabulous value as long as you don't need to be in town. They're beautifully appointed with some original stone furnishings, and they're lovely and quiet. The on-site restaurant is similarly excellent.

Longo Hotel Arcobaleno　　BUNGALOW €€
(📞032 82 614 75; www.longohotelarcobaleno. com; off Blvd Branley; d without/with air-con Ar50,000/70,000; P ❄ 🛜) This terrific Italian-run place feels like a small oasis of calm at the north end of town. Rooms are outstanding value for the price and those with air-con are a little larger. The bathrooms really sparkle and come with, wait for it, bidets. It's definitely the best midrange choice in the town itself.

Serena Hôtel　　HOTEL €€
(📞032 45 377 55, 020 94 411 73; www.serena tulear.com; Blvd Isiranana; d Ar70,000-95,000, ste

Tuléar (Toliara)

Ar200,000; ❄ 🛜) The rooms here are attractive and wonderfully central – the newer, more expensive doubles on the 2nd floor are worth the extra price and most have views over the centre of town. It's not quite the design hotel it once was, but for this price it's a steal.

> **ⓘ WARNING: BATTERIE BEACH**
>
> Tuléar is considered to be safe (although you should always take a taxi after dark), but there is one place to avoid: Batterie Beach. North of the city centre, Batterie Beach has been the scene of violent attacks on foreigners in recent years, and most foreign travel advisories and travel-insurance companies warn strongly against visiting. It lies beyond the city limits and there's little chance of wandering here by accident, but it's still worth knowing the name and steering clear of it.

★ **Bakuba**　　　　　　GUESTHOUSE €€€

(☑ 032 51 528 97; www.bakubaconcept.com; r/ste €80/120) It would be more accurate to describe this place as a work of art that you stay in rather than an arty guesthouse. The work of Bruno Decorte, a Frenchman who has spent much of his life in Africa, Bakuba has three unique rooms, with features such as a wall of water, a dugout-canoe-turned-bathtub and lamps made of gourds.

The house is anchored by large towers reminiscent of baobab trees. One serves as a hidden water tower, another as a hammam and conversation room. The interior contains a vast hall inspired by Mauritanian temples. Doorways are lined with real palm trunks, and the decor includes a fetching statue of a West African chief – Bakuba himself. If any of this sounds kitsch, think again. Decorte has managed to integrate everything with a strong sense of naturalism, in the manner of Gaudí. The hotel also has some more run-of-the-mill benefits, such as 100m of beachfront, catamarans and canoes, and quads for hire.

It's located 14km southeast of the centre, on the shore, on the way to the airport.

Famata Lodge　　　　　　LODGE €€€

(☑ 020 94 937 83, 032 02 108 48; www.famatalodge-tulear.com; d bungalow €26-36, f bungalow €38-48; ☀) Down the coast, 16km from town and 11km from the airport, lies this interesting ecolodge. Located in the mangroves, it has five bungalows and three safari tents, all with private bathroom, hot water and a large terrace. There's a restaurant and a great pool. The family bungalow is a steal, with an open wall facing the sea. A bit garish in spots, but otherwise well done.

Hotel Hyppocampo　　　　　　HOTEL €€€

(☑ 020 94 410 21, 032 42 866 83; www.hyppocampo-tulear.com; Ave de France; d/ste Ar163,000/243,000; ✲ @ ☀) With its great oceanfront setting, pool, good restaurant and well-appointed rooms, the Hyppocampo is the high end of in-town accommodation, although we reckon it's a touch overpriced. The suites have huge tubs and queen beds tucked away from a sitting room.

✖ Eating

Food Stalls　　　　　　BARBECUE €

(Blvd Tsiranana; brochette from Ar500; ☺ from 8pm) Grab a stool – this is where you down brochette and beer for the cheapest dinner in town and a real slice of local life. Popular into the wee hours, but take a taxi to and from here after dark.

Gelateria　　　　　　ICE CREAM €

(Rue Gambetta; sundaes Ar8000; ☺ 11am-11pm Tue-Sun; ☎) Have confidence in this place: it's owned by an Italian and he hasn't forgotten the motherland. Great ice cream, decent pizza and sandwiches, along with a patisserie for the early hours. Throw in free wi-fi and you have the perfect snack stop.

★ **L'Estérel**　　　　　　ITALIAN €€

(☑ 032 40 026 20, 032 40 618 66; Rue de la Voirie; pizza Ar9000-12,000, mains Ar11,000-14,000; ☺ noon-2pm & 7-10pm Mon-Sat) Our pick of the restaurants in Tuléar, Italian-run L'Estérel has a tranquil garden setting and a menu that includes some of the best Italian cooking in southern Madagascar – pasta, pizzas, salads you can trust – as well as the occasional French dish. Service is attentive without being in your face.

★ **Corto Maltese**　　　　　　INTERNATIONAL €€

(☑ 032 04 009 13; cnr Rue Gambetta & Blvd Campan; mains Ar10,000-18,000; ☺ noon-2.30pm & 7-10pm Mon-Fri) One of the best restaurants in Tuléar, yet moderately priced, this creative bistro offers an eclectic menu, including steaks that look and taste the part. Nice outdoor seating, too. Shame it doesn't open weekends.

Blu Bar　　　　　　INTERNATIONAL €€

(Blvd Lyautey; breakfast Ar7500-13,000, mains Ar12,500-22,000; ☺ 7.30am-late; ☎) This beautifully designed bar and expat hang-out with its own private beach is *the* place to come for breezy waterfront dining, with burgers, pizzas and kebabs to displace the memory of all that rice you've been eating. Quality can be patchy. We like it best for a sundowner, or for breakfast while you wait for the Transfert Anakao speedboat (its office is here).

Chez Alain   FRENCH €€
(Sans Fil; mains Ar12,000-17,000; set menu Ar25,000; ⊘11am-9pm) The restaurant here is best known for its extensive French menu, with serious zebu steaks topped with various sauces, all served in a pleasant garden setting.

ⓘ Information

There are plenty of banks and ATMs in Tuléar. We found **BNI Madagascar** (cnr Rue Estebe & Rue Lieutenant Chenaron; ⊘8-11.30am & 2-4.30pm Mon-Fri) much more efficient for changing money, but **Bank of Africa** (cnr Rue Campistron & Rue Raseta; ⊘8am-4pm Mon-Fri, 8.30am-noon Sat) opens longer hours. There's also an **Office Regional du Tourisme** (📱020 94 446 05; Blvd Tsiranana) to answer questions and it hands out a few brochures, but that's about it.

ⓘ Getting There & Away

AIR

Air Madagascar (📱034 11 222 01, 020 94 415 85) has an office in town, but not at the airport. It flies from Tuléar to Antananarivo (€192), Fort Dauphin (€50 to €150) and Morondava (€192). The schedule is a moving target.

BOAT

Transfert Anakao (📱034 91 468 36; www.transfert-anakao.com; per person one way/return Ar50,000/100,000) Transfert Anakao, an enjoyable speedboat, connects Tuléar with Anakao, leaving the former every day at 9am. It leaves Anakao at 7.30am (or earlier to connect with Air Madagascar's unpredictable timetable).

Anakao Express (📱034 60 072 61, 034 76 406 70; www.anakaoexpress.com; per person one way/return Ar50,000/100,000) This speedboat company leaves Tuléar around 9.30am and arrives in Anakao an hour later. It leaves Anakao at 7.30am, unless Air Madagascar decides to push its Tana departure earlier, in which case the speedboats adjust.

CAMION-BROUSSE

The mother of all *taxis-brousses*, the *camion-brousse* is a troop transport that plies the god-awful roads between Tuléar and Fort Dauphin (Ar40,000), with stops in Betioky (Ar15,000), Ampanihy (Ar24,000) and Ambovombe (Ar32,000). This takes a whopping 30 to 60 hours, depending on breakdowns and road conditions. But beware: these amusement-park rides are packed beyond capacity. Passengers bounce around and are frequently ill. There are a limited number of breaks. You'll need a scarf and pullover for the dust and wind. And if you do the trip in stages, you could spend a lot of time waiting for a seat, as the vehicles that pass the towns en route are often full. Finally, provisions are sparse along the way, so you need to stock up ahead of time. All things considered, we challenge you to find a rougher form of public transport.

TAXI-BROUSSE

Taxis-brousses leave the main station early every day for Antananarivo, arriving a day later. Vehicles to Antananarivo may fill up quickly, so get to the station early or book a seat the afternoon before. Destinations and fares along the way are listed below:

DESTINATION	FARE (AR)
Ambalavao	29,000
Ambositra	41,000
Antananarivo	52,000
Antsirabe	45,000
Fianarantsoa	32,000
Isalo/Ranohira	24,000

Transport along the sand road north to Ifaty/Mangily (Ar8000, three hours) departs from the northern *taxi-brousse* station on Rte de Manombo. There are a few trucks daily, generally departing between 6am and early afternoon.

A *taxi-brousse* leaves for Morondava a few times weekly (Ar60,000, two to three days). The road is very rough and you'll need to overnight in Manja (Ar33,000) on the way.

Taxis-brousses also connect Tuléar with St Augustine (Ar2500, two hours) along a good sealed road once a day, Tuesday to Saturday. Departures are at noon from Tuléar and 2am from St Augustine.

There's a *taxi-brousse* every Thursday to Beheloka and Itampolo (Ar35,000, 12 hours).

It's relatively easy to hitch a lift from Tuléar to Antananarivo as many tourist vehicles and supply trucks from Antananarivo return to the capital empty. Expect to pay a bit more than the *taxi-brousse* fare to cover fuel costs, but not much more. The best places to ask are the major hotels, particularly Chez Alain (p82). See p260 for more on hitching.

ⓘ Getting Around

TO/FROM THE AIRPORT

A taxi between the airport and the city centre costs between Ar15,000 and Ar20,000. Many hotels in Tuléar and Ifaty do airport transfers.

SNORKELLING THE GREAT REEF

The Great Reef is a prime snorkelling ground. However, human proximity has taken its toll, so some sections of the reef are in better shape than others. Using information on coral health and fish populations supplied by local marine conservation NGO Blue Ventures, we've graded the quality of the reef from one (low) to 10 (high).

Andavadoaka (grade 7) Some nice small bommies (shallow, isolated patches of reef) can be reached from shore. Slightly deeper reefs are a short pirogue (dugout canoe) trip from the village. Longer pirogue trips reach shallow sites off the island of Nosy Hao.

Salary (grade 6) Good sites are too deep to snorkel, but there are small bommies inshore.

Ifaty/Mangily (grade 6) Snorkelling can be done by pirogue in the Rose Garden Marine Reserve (for a fee).

Tuléar (grade 4) Reef can be shallow, but requires a short pirogue/boat trip.

Anakao/Nosy Ve (grade 5) Snorkelling in the marine reserve off the northern tip of the island (for a fee).

Beheloka (grade 6) Good sites are further offshore and need to be reached by a pirogue trip from the village.

Ambola (grade 6) Most sites can be reached by a pirogue trip from the village.

Itampolo (grade 8) One great site for snorkelling straight off the beach in the north, great coral cover, diverse fish and shallow depth.

CAR
Numerous companies hire 4WD vehicles. Your best bet is to ask for a recommendation from your hotel.

POUSSE-POUSSE
Standard rates for pousse-pousse rides start at about Ar500.

TAXI
For rides within town, taxis charge a standard rate of Ar2500 per person, but can climb as high as Ar15,000 at night. Don't be afraid to bargain.

Northern Reef

The reef north of Tuléar is a gentle curve punctuated by a number of villages and resorts all the way to Andavadoaka, some 207km distant. We're not huge fans of Ifaty and Mangily, but they have a few worthwhile spots to pause as you continue north. Once you get past Mangily you'll find yourself slithering down a sandy track through a spiny forest full of huge baobab trees and wandering tribespeople. From Ankasy north, the ocean is a shade of turquoise that looks for all the world like paradise.

Ambondrolava & Beravy

A 20-minute drive north of Tuléar, and before the quiet beauty of this beguiling coast really takes hold, the twinned and barely separated villages of Ambondrolava and Beravy have an appealing Mangrove Information Center. There's also a place to stay that avoids both the clamour of Tuléar and the resort scene of Ifaty and Mangily to the north.

☉ Sights

Mangrove Information Center   NATURE RESERVE
(☏ 032 54 042 76, 032 70 465 04; www.honko.org; guided tour per person Ar10,000-20,000) On the left, 15km north of Tuléar, you'll come upon a sign for the Mangrove Information Center, a 200-hectare wetland complex created by Honko, a Belgian NGO. The main attraction is a 1.5km wooden boardwalk. It's a nice place to stretch your legs on the way north, with a trail through the mangroves, educational placards and a tower overlooking a river. Guided tours of between 2km and 4km, and one to three hours in duration, are excellent.

🛏 Sleeping & Eating

Le Jardin de Beravy   GUESTHOUSE €€
(☏ 032 40 397 19; www.hotel-jardindeberavy-tulear.com; s €20-24, d €24-30, f €36, breakfast/set menu €4/13) Two kilometres beyond the Mangrove Information Center is Le Jardin de Beravy, a hotel and restaurant on the sea. There's a nice beach here with a view of the waves crashing on the outer reef. The rooms are a bit claustrophobic, except those with a

verandah, which includes the excellent corner room. There's also a dive centre.

Ifaty & Mangily

Ifaty and Mangily, 27km north of Tuléar, are two separate villages 3km apart that share the same beach, confusingly known as Ifaty Beach (the Dunes d'Ifaty, for example, is in Mangily). Ifaty is by far the smaller tourist destination, even while its name continues to usurp the latter. The popularity of this area is largely due to its location close to Tuléar and the decent dirt road that connects them. The beaches are really quite poor relative to other options: rocky at times, very shallow for much of the day and with seagrass beds rather than sandy bottoms. The unkempt villages, saturated by tourism, are not very attractive, either. Nevertheless, the snorkelling is good, the whales come past here and there are a lot of resorts to choose from, including some good ones.

◉ Sights

If you visit Ifaty village around 1pm to 2pm you can enjoy watching the local fishermen beach around 50 pirogues full of catch.

Reniala Nature Reserve   WILDLIFE RESERVE
(☏ 034 03 790 40, 032 02 513 49; http://reniala-eco tourisme.jimdo.com; admission from Ar15,000; ☺ 8am-6pm) This is a 60-hectare spiny forest full of baobab trees and some birds. There are two circuits, one of 45 minutes to an hour and the other of 1½ to two hours. If you have been to the arboretum in Tuléar, which is better, you don't need to repeat that experience here, unless you have a strong interest. You can also stay in simple **accommodation** (double bungalow with shared bathroom Ar20,000, room Ar30,000 to Ar40,000, breakfast Ar7000) here.

Village des Tortues   WILDLIFE RESERVE
(☏ 032 02 072 75; ☺ 9am-7pm) FREE Near Reniala, this 70,000-sq-metre park protects over 1000 radiated and spider tortoises. A guided tour of the grounds in English tells you the full story of these endangered animals and how they are being conserved. It takes less than an hour, so it's a worthy break from the beach. Guides will take you here and to the Reniala Nature Reserve for Ar15,000.

☆ Activities

Most hotels in this area organise activities for guests, including diving, snorkelling (around Ar25,000 per person), whale watching (July to September, around €50 per person) and pirogue trips.

Diving possibilities include everything from shallow inshore 5m to 10m dives up to 26m dives on the edge of the barrier reef. The latter focuses on two passes, north and south, with the former containing a famous network of rocky arches called the Cathedral. While most sections of the reef are damaged, there is a variety of fish.

Hotel de la Plage   ADVENTURE SPORTS
(☏ 032 04 362 76, 032 04 346 63; www.hotel plage-tulear.com) This Ifaty hotel organises fishing, scuba diving, kitesurfing, windsurfing and whale watching.

Atimoo   DIVING
(☏ 034 02 529 17; www.atimoo.com) This outfit takes a more adventurous approach than other operators, which tend to stick to their local section of the reef. Instead, Atimoo ranges from one end of the reef to the other in small dive parties that sometimes rough it ashore. Prices vary from €100 to €900, depending on the destination.

Nautilus Deep Sea Club   DIVING
(☏ 032 04 848 81, 032 07 418 74; www.nautilus mada.mg) Respected dive club catering to all levels of expertise and with its own bungalows and restaurant.

⛏ Sleeping & Eating

There are only three hotels in Ifaty, and around 20 in Mangily. A sound strategy here, at least in the low season, is to shop around by walking the Mangily beachfront before making a decision.

Bamboo Club   BUNGALOW €€
(☏ 020 94 902 13, 032 66 552 31; www.bamboo-club. com; thatched d bungalow Ar42,900-132,000, 1-/2-bed apt Ar105,600/188,100; ☎ ▓) This place caters mostly to divers, but offers neat grounds, comfortable bungalows on the beach, a small swimming pool and an excellent terrace restaurant serving Indian Ocean specialities (breakfast/set menu Ar9900/36,600). If you can, opt for one of the new solid bungalows over the older thatched versions.

Auberge'In   BUNGALOW €€
(☏ 034 18 218 01; s/d Ar30,000/60,000) Auberge'In is located 100m from the beach, but manages to be the best budget option in Mangily anyway. The dirt-cheap country bungalows with thatched roofs and small porches in a carefully groomed yard are quaint and attractive, and management is cheery.

VELONDRIAKE MARINE PROTECTED AREA

The Vezo people, who inhabit the southwest coast, depend on the sea for their livelihood and cultural identity. To achieve sustainable use of their natural resources, locals created Madagascar's first community-managed protected area, Velondriake, in 2006. The protected area spans more than 640 sq km, making it the largest locally managed marine reserve in the Indian Ocean, and is managed by 25 communities using *dina*, a traditional law recognised by the Malagasy government. Velondriake contains areas where traditional fishing activities continue, and others where it is temporarily or permanently forbidden. Conservation efforts even extend to aquaculture and family planning, in order to reduce dependency on natural resources. The program has been a great success and is being replicated elsewhere along the reef and in other parts of Madagascar by Blue Ventures and partner conservation groups.

Dunes d'Ifaty LODGE €€€
(☏020 22 376 69, 034 07 109 16, 032 07 109 16; www.lesdunesdifaty.com; d bungalow incl breakfast €125; P🖥🛜🏊) This high-end property has a magnificent thatched-roof lodge for eating and super bungalows made of locally quarried stone offer large porches to take advantage of prime views and breezes. Elegant interiors have brightly painted walls, Italian baths and thoughtful amenities. Beach security keeps away hawkers and ensures privacy, which is a problem further north.

Hôtel Le Paradisier LODGE €€€
(☏032 07 660 09; www.paradisier.net; d €71-110; 🛜🏊) 🍴 This luxury, but attractively priced Ifaty property has a tropical-jungle lobby that opens onto a sea-facing courtyard dining room and a shimmering infinity pool. The waterfront bungalows are nicely integrated into the beach rather than manicured, and everything runs on solar. Be careful of pricey extensions.

Chez Cecile SEAFOOD €
(☏034 94 907 00; www.surlaplagechezcecile.com; mains from Ar7500) There are some decent rooms in this bungalow village, but they are still outshone by its sand-floor restaurant.

This is Mangily's best informal dining option, with huge plates of pasta and seafood grills just steps from the sea.

ⓘ Getting There & Away

Ifaty village lies 22km north of Tuléar along a sandy, potholed road. Several *taxis-brousses* leave daily from the northern *taxi-brousse* station in Tuléar, usually between 6am and early afternoon. The trip costs Ar8000 and takes two hours. Transfers provided by the hotels for their clients cost around Ar30,000 per person, while taxis in Tuléar charge around Ar60,000.

Ambolimailaka

You might consider this a smart alternative to the village of Mangily, if you really want to get away from it all on the northern reef. There are plenty of activities on offer, including zebu-cart trips, forest excursions, kitesurfing, diving, whale watching, fishing, quad biking and horse riding. Stay or not, it's definitely worth stopping by here around noon to watch the return of the fishing fleet, over 200 pirogues strong, just below Hôtel Belle Vue.

🛏 Sleeping & Eating

Au Soleil Couchant BUNGALOW €€
(☏032 47 360 15; www.hotelsoleilcouchant-ifaty.com; bungalow €30; P🛜) With rondavel bungalows on the beach, this place sprawls down a sand dune to the water's edge and is terrific value for money. The bungalows have thatched roofs, mosquito nets and wood floors.

Hôtel Belle Vue BUNGALOW €€€
(☏034 11 112 11; d Ar120,000; 🛜) This hotel is aptly named, as it overlooks the sea, with a panoramic view of the fishermen's village shared by rooms and bungalows alike. The whitewashed walls have murals painted by local artists and there's a decent on-site restaurant.

Hotel de la Plage BUNGALOW €€€
(☏032 04 346 63, 032 04 362 76; www.hotelplage-tulear.com; bungalow €49-85) Located between two fishing villages, this resort offers some neat circular bungalows strung along an elegant arc of beach. The rooms are fine, if unspectacular. The local dive centre is located here and whale watching and windsurfing are possible.

Ankasy

With barely a village to speak of, Ankasy, 100km north of Tuléar, has an excellent upmarket lodge and a palpable sense of blissful isolation.

🛌 Sleeping

Ankasy Lodge
LODGE €€€

(☑032 05 400 42; www.ankasy-lodge-spa.com; s all-inclusive €125-140, d €190-210) With four massive (100-sq-metre) high-end bungalow on a broad and beautiful 1.3km of private beach, the family friendly Ankasy Lodge operates on an all-inclusive model. All accommodation, food and local activities – and there are a lot of options, including a small spa – are included. Food is straight off the pirogue and room prices drop when it's quiet.

Salary

The sandy village of Salary, 129km from Tuléar, sits amid sand dunes just back from the water, with the Salary Bay resort a few kilometres further north.

🛌 Sleeping

Salary Bay
RESORT

(☑020 75 514 86, 032 49 120 16; www.salarybay. com; d bungalow €75-90, 8-person villa €280) 🕑 This resort sits high on a sandy peninsula, affording a spectacular 270-degree view from the restaurant, taking in a broad turquoise lagoon and the resort's own 7km of beach! It's a popular choice for honeymooners and divers (the local dive centre is here). It can also organise whale watching (€50 per person, minimum four people). Rooms are lovely and white. It's a long trip here unless you come in by private plane (it has its own airfield), but once you have arrived it is heavenly. Transfers available from north or south.

ℹ️ Getting There & Away

It may not look like far, but the 78km drive to Andavadoaka takes at least three, possibly four hours by 4WD. The sand can be deep, the bumps are like a funfair ride, the baobab forest is dramatic and you may even pass through shallow mangroves en route.

Andavadoaka

Yes, it's a long 78km from Salary, but this remote and laid-back outpost of 1500 people is one of the more interesting spots north of Tuléar. After passing through the tidy local village, you end up at the tip of a sandy peninsula spotted with ramshackle beach bungalows and a basic restaurant enlivened at night by the staff and volunteers of NGO Blue Ventures.

🏃 Activities

Blue Ventures
VOLUNTEERING

(☑+44 20 7697 8598; www.blueventures.org) Based in London, with a field site in Andavadoaka, this hugely impressive organisation coordinates teams of volunteer divers to work with local NGOs and biologists in marine-conservation programs that are spreading throughout the length of the reef, helping staunch its decline. Volunteering stints range from three to 12 weeks (£1900 to £4075) and include PADI scuba-diving certification. Volunteering stints must be organised in advance through the London office.

🛌 Sleeping & Eating

Coco Beach
BUNGALOW €€

(☑034 14 001 58; nassim.tahora@gmail.com; d/ tw bungalow Ar50,000/70,000) This set of basic bungalows that seem to lean into the wind supports many Blue Ventures personnel and is the only budget accommodation around. A friendly place, the restaurant does simple chicken or fish dishes and teases with a sign advertising the rarely working pizza oven.

Manga Lodge
LODGE €€€

(☑032 58 266 26; s/d Ar75,000/125,000) Three cheers for the best entrance to a lodge on this coast: you arrive by pirogue on the resort's little white powder beach and sink your toes in the sand. The beachfront bungalows are suites that sleep four, while the kitchen offers fresh crabs and lobster (set menus Ar30,000). Excursions include snorkelling and pirogue trips. If you stay somewhere else, take a pirogue here for dinner.

Laguna Blu
RESORT €€€

(☑032 70 569 13, 034 05 814 10; www.resort madagascar.com; d bungalow full board €142) Laguna Blu is an excellent Andavadoaka choice, blissfully isolated and with good if unexciting-for-the-price beachfront bungalows.

ℹ️ Getting There & Away

A taxi-brousse leaves from the central market in Morombé almost daily. It is also possible to take a pirogue from Morombé or Salary (Ar65,000, five to eight hours depending on wind) as long as you depart early in the morning.

Morombé

The northern end of the Great Reef peters out at Morombé, 280km north of Tuléar. Most travellers visit as part of the three-day epic road trip between Morondava and Tuléar (p120) and there is a handful of surprisingly decent accommodation options.

🛏 Sleeping & Eating

★**Chez Katia**   GUESTHOUSE €€
(☎ 033 01 769 30, 032 74 273 40; d Ar60,000, without bathroom Ar50,000, tr Ar80,000, f Ar120,000) This charming beachside *chambre d'hôte* is warm and welcoming and the large, spotless rooms are outstanding and look like they've been freshly painted. The restaurant, on an elevated wooden platform so you can see the beach, serves up meals from Ar20,000.

Pirogue d'Or   GUESTHOUSE €€
(☎ 032 05 888 56, 032 02 147 24; www.pirogue dormorombe.com; d/tr/f €30/45/55; 🅿 🛜) The Pirogue d'Or has big, clean rooms by the sea, but they're pretty bare and careworn these days. The bar that sits in the middle of the restaurant is built out of a wooden pirogue and the meals (mains Ar20,000, set menu Ar28,000) are OK. Don't count on the wi-fi working.

Southern Reef

There are some interesting places to visit on the reef south of Tuléar, including its best overall tourist destination, Anakao. But after that, places of interest are fewer and further between. The area inland contains a massive spiny forest, which can be vast and monotonous, but it does house two excellent protected areas: Parc National de Tsimanampetsotse and Réserve Spéciale de Beza-Mahafaly.

How far you go along this coast depends on how much time you have. For those with limited time, a day trip to Sarodrano and St Augustine, or one or two days in Anakao, will suffice. For those wanting to unearth an unknown gem in a more remote location, consider Ambola. Long-haulers have to decide between the inland route to Ampanihy, on the RN10, or the coastal route via Beheloka, Itampolo and Saodona, before continuing on to the cape. The latter is preferable, but only doable in the dry season between May and late October.

Sarodrano

Sarodrano, the first stop south of Tuléar, is a fishing village of grass huts on a sandy peninsula that extends into the ocean beneath some cliffs. It's a short distance from the city, on a good road, but worlds away in every other respect.

🏃 Activities

Grotte de Sarodrano   SWIMMING
(admission Ar2500) The Grotte de Sarodrano, near La Mangrove, is worth a look (and swim). It's a bi-level natural pool jointly fed by tidal flow and freshwater springs, so it contains both fresh and saltwater fish at different depths (and lots of them). From here you can take an interesting pirogue ride to Sarodrano. If one isn't waiting, call Auberge de Pecheur.

🛏 Sleeping & Eating

Auberge de Pecheur   BUNGALOW €
(☎ 032 42 903 90; d Ar30,000, without bathroom Ar18,000) You can rent a very basic hut at this place right on the beach, and do nothing the rest of the day.

La Mangrove   BUNGALOW €€
(☎ 020 94 936 26; d Ar40,000) For the closest Sarodrano comes to midrange accommodation, try this place, which appears on the right side of the road just before the peninsula. Putting the wobbly dock and muddy swimming hole aside, the bungalows are good value and the grounds are well kept and shady.

❶ Getting There & Away

From Sarodrano you can go on to Anakao by sail pirogue for only Ar20,000 – far less than the Ar50,000 speedboat trip from Tuléar – or back to Tuléar for the same amount. Either way it's 45 minutes to two hours, wind depending. Daily *taxis-brousses* from Tuléar are Ar5000.

St Augustine

St Augustine lies at the mouth of the Onilahy River, on the other side of the cliffs from Sarodrano, on a good road. It's an excellent drive through switchbacks and down into the lost valley – the site of the very first English settlement in Madagascar in 1645 – beyond. Only 12 of 140 people survived that brief stay. The little tropical town sits on a sandy former floodplain and is very scenic from above, with an alluring end-of-the-world feel. Daily *taxis-brousses* from Tuléar cost Ar10,000.

🛏 Sleeping & Eating

Longomamy   LODGE €
(☎ 020 94 444 56; d Ar20,000) Longomamy is perched at the end of the Onilahy River, where local fishermen practice their time-

less rhythm. It's a place where hours slip past unnoticed. The hotel offers great seafood straight from the sea, and can arrange a pleasant pirogue trip (Ar11,000) upriver to a crystal-clear natural pool.

Anakao

Strung out along a series of perfect semicircles of white-sand beaches and looking out over turquoise waters, Anakao is laidback in the finest tradition of small seaside Malagasy settlements. It's our pick of the options along the southern reef coastline. Excellent sleeping and eating options complete a fine all-round destination.

🏃 Activities

Activities here are mostly arranged through the hotels, with at least one excellent independent operator. In addition to the full range of water activities, most hotels can also arrange excursions to Parc National de Tsimanampetsotse, as well as **whale-watching trips** (per person from Ar75,000) to see humpback whales from mid-June or early July to September.

Il Camaleonte   DIVING, WATER SPORTS
(☑032 63 672 34; http://ilcamaleonteanakao. wordpress.com) Just a short walk along the sand from Auberge Peter Pan, this excellent Italian-run place organises diving, snorkel-

WATCHING WHALES

Anakao is one of the best places along the Great Reef to watch humpback whales from mid-June or early July to September. You'll spend around two hours on the water and the whales are regularly seen, sometimes not far beyond the reef. Check the wind conditions – it's not really worth going if seas are choppy.

Most hotels offer whale watching, but the experience (and cost) vary. If you organise your trip through Auberge Peter Pan, it will cost you Ar75,000 to Ar100,000 per person (depending on the number of people) and you'll go out with local fishers in a small, motorised pirogue. You don't have to be staying here to take its trip. At most other hotels, the cost starts at €50 per person, and most excursions use larger, more modern boats.

ling, kitesurfing, stand-up paddleboarding, kayaking and numerous combinations of the same to fill your days. Andrea and Nicoletta are warm and welcoming and simply love what they do, which helps make it all the more enjoyable.

Anakao Club   DIVING, ADVENTURE SPORTS
(☑020 94 921 77; www.anakaooceanlodge.com) One of the better activity centres, at the Anakao Ocean Lodge, Anakao Club arranges boat excursions to the islands, mangroves and whales (in season), diving, kitesurfing, windsurfing and extensive quad excursions that are a great way to see the area.

Longo Vezo   DIVING, BOAT TOUR
(☑020 94 901 27; www.longovezo.com) Longo Vezo, which has a CMAS-certified dive centre, also does numerous water sports, can organise whale watching and runs 4WD trips that go as far south as Parc National de Tsimanampetsotse.

🛏 Sleeping & Eating

Chez Emile   BUNGALOW €
(☑032 04 023 76; chezemile.anakao@yahoo.fr; d bungalow Ar45,000, without bathroom Ar30,000) These bungalows are set back from the beach near the local village, in a well-kept sandy garden. The beach restaurant serves fast and cheap seafood.

★ Auberge Peter Pan   BUNGALOW €€
(☑032 82 614 54, 034 94 437 21; www.peterpan hotel.com; d bungalow Ar30,000-70,000, f bungalow Ar70,000-90,000; 🛜) This creative burst of liberal personality is the best budget hotel south of Tana. Dario and Valerio, the young Italian owners who have made this place their life's work, have crafted a funky selection of eight warmly eclectic bungalows, set in a playful yard of political art contained by a fence of enormous crayons.

All of this on a beautiful beach and with strong ties to the local community.

The dynamic bar within is a fusion of revolutionary and hip, with Che Guevara looking on while you sip a deadly rum drink from an enormous green coconut. Apart from understanding the science of cool, these boys know how to cook. The spectacular ever-changing menu (mains Ar18,000 to Ar25,000), a mixture of Italian and Malagasy, is precisely what is missing in hotels three times the price. The problem is that word has got out, and people are staying for weeks if not months. So book ahead and be careful of that Molotov cocktail. English spoken.

WORTH A TRIP

RÉSERVE SPÉCIALE DE BEZA-MAHAFALY

Southwest of the RN7 from Andranovory, the **Réserve Spéciale de Beza-Mahafaly** (www.parcs-madagascar.com; adult/child Ar45,000/25,000) is better known as a scientific venture than a tourist destination, but travellers are welcome. The spiny and riverine forest here harbours four species of lemur (ring-tailed, white-footed and mouse lemur, as well as Verreaux's *sifaka*), four species of tenrec (including the large-eared tenrec), fossa and more than 100 bird species.

There are six circuits through the park, with the pick being:

➡ **Circuit Ihazoara** (4km, three hours) Natural botanical garden, canyons and good lemur viewing.

➡ **Circuit Parcelle 1** (2km, two hours) Gallery forest, excellent lemur viewing, a riverside bird hide and the chance to see radiated tortoises.

➡ **Circuit Parcelle 2** (12km, four hours) Spiny forest, diurnal lemurs and a sweeping viewpoint.

Visitors can pitch a tent near the scientific station and simple rooms may be available if not in use by the scientists, both for a small fee. To get here and around you'll need a 4WD (the reserve is 35km east of Betioky on rough tracks; the turn-off is signposted at the southern end of Betioky). You'll need to bring your own food and supplies.

The roads between Andranovory and Betioky and south of Betioky are considered unsafe after dark.

Lalandaka   BUNGALOW €€

(☑ 032 05 622 80, 020 94 922 21; www.lalandaka. com; d bungalow Ar75,000-85,000, f bungalow Ar110,000; 🐾) 'Upscale beach shack' sounds like a contradiction in terms, but this place manages to pull it off. The family versions are claustrophobic, but the doubles on the beach have a charming verandah where you can float in your hammock for hours, while the classy central lodge is just as attractive.

Longo Vezo   BUNGALOW €€

(☑ 020 94 901 27; www.longovezo.com; d bungalow off/on beach €20/25; 🐾) A secluded location overlooking the spiny forest to Nosy Ve, a private stretch of beach, bungalows discreetly hidden in the dunes with hammocks and bucket showers, and convivial family-style dining all combine to form a unique, casual beach-camp ambience. The shacks on the beach, which sleep five, are ubercool.

★ Anakao Ocean Lodge   LODGE €€€

(☑ 020 94 921 76, 020 94 919 57; www.anakao oceanlodge.com; s/d/f bungalow €110/143/162, ste €175; 🐾) This is the premier resort on the Great Reef. It's not that any of the elements are unique, but that each one is carried off to perfection. The bungalows, with enormous baths, are beautiful, the smiling uniformed staff are always there when you need them and the food (set menus €16) is a work of art.

From the moment you step off the boat, greeted with a drink, you descend into an ambience of effortless laid-back refinement, where attention to detail is of the highest calibre. Neither commerce nor mechanics are to be seen; just stone walkways, a light surf, a serene half-moon bay and the sight of pirogues sailing past.

Safari Vezo   BUNGALOW €€€

(☑ 020 94 413 81, 034 07 602 52; www.safarivezo. com; s half board €50-68, d half board €68-86; 🐾) Lots of nice touches set these beach bungalows apart from the crowd, including stone steps, grass matte walls, drapes, shady terraces and well-appointed bathrooms with seawater toilets. There's also a lively beach bar with Bahamian shutters for a bit of Caribbean vibe.

❶ Getting There & Away

Almost everyone coming to Anakao arrives by speedboat. By 'road' (a relative term), it's a rough, bone-shaking seven- to eight-hour drive from Tuléar.

Transfert Anakao (☑ 034 91 468 36; www. transfert-anakao.com; per person one-way/ return Ar50,000/100,000) This enjoyable speedboat connects Tuléar with Anakao, leaving the former every day at 9am. It leaves Anakao at 7.30am (or earlier to connect with Air Madagascar's unpredictable timetable).

Anakao Express (☑ 034 91 468 36; www. anakaoexpress.com; per person one-way/return Ar50,000/100,000) This speedboat company leaves Tuléar around 9.30am and arrives in Anakao an hour later. It leaves Anakao at 7.30am, unless Air Madagascar decides to push its Tana departure earlier, in which case the speedboats adjust.

Beheloka

If you're thinking of staying here, either to access the reef or Parc National de Tsimanampetsotse, we recommend pressing on the 20km to Ambola.

🛌 Sleeping

Canne à Sucre   BUNGALOW €€
(☑ 064 74 860 44; www.la-canne-a-sucre.com; camping/d/bungalow   Ar8000/40,000/70,000)
Canne à Sucre has some decent accommodation with wooden rooms and bungalows just back from the beach. There's better accommodation further south in Ambola, but it's still a good place to spend a few days.

Ambola

The town of Ambola is found on a remote corner of the reef. While not on many maps, it is home to a charming boutique hotel.

Le Domaine d'Ambola (☑ 032 43 555 74; www.ambola-madagascar.com; d Ar140,000-200,000) is one of those special places that lingers in the mind for its serenity – you know you're somewhere special when a place lists its address as 'Beach'. The hotel sits up high on a bluff overlooking the reef, with pleasant breezes.

It's also set apart by its design, with its white walls and blue accents looking inspired by the Greek islands. The simply furnished rooms are brightly coloured, with tiled floors and distant views. The restaurant serves up great seafood fresh from the village. Perhaps most surprising is the resident dive operation, which gets high marks from customers who come a long way to use it. There is no pampering here, but if you want a few days of low-key charm in pristine surroundings, this is worth the trip from Tuléar.

Parc National de Tsimanampetsotse

This 432-sq-km **park** (www.parcs-madagascar.com; adult/child Ar45,000/25,000, guide per person Ar15,000) makes a good day trip if you're in the area. While it may not be a generalist's first stop, it's certainly worth a detour as you follow the remote coastline south. The park's large and ancient salt lake hosts some part-time resident flamingos (April to October) and the lake doubles in size during the rainy season. There's a sacred cave pool, the **Grotte Mitoho**, with some endemic blind catfish. Locals believe the cave is home to the Antambahoka, an invisible people, and animal sacrifices still occur here from time to time.

Amid the rampant spiny forest, watch also for a large banyan tree full of parrots and ring-tailed lemurs and whose tendrils fall several storeys into a flooded sinkhole. Verreaux's sifaka are commonly seen during daylight hours, and keep an eye out for sleeping nocturnal species such as the tiny grey-brown mouse lemur, fat-tailed dwarf lemur and white-footed sportive lemur.

The MNP office is in Efoetse, 3km from Ambola. You can arrange a mandatory guide and itinerary here, and a map of all the current routes is on display. There are several circuits, from 30 minutes to 3½ hours in length.

Itampolo

The reef ends here, around 75km from Ambola, and the main attraction is a gorgeous beach and decent diving. There are some basic bungalows available at **Gîte d'Etape Sud Sud** (Chez Alain; ☑ 020 94 415 27; www.chez-alain.com; camping Ar10,000, r Ar25,000-40,000, bungalow Ar60,000, set menu Ar22,000) if you choose to stay. It's run by the same people as Chez Alain in Tuléar.

THE CAPE

The south of Madagascar narrows to a wild cape and the sense of isolation here is palpable. This feeling grows the further south you go, until you finally reach the cliff at Cap Sainte Marie, where there's nothing between you and Antarctica. Then it's back to civilisation – sort of. After many hours driving through dense spiny forest and one-zebu towns, the trail ends on the doorstep of Fort Dauphin, a city isolated by hundreds of kilometres of tortuous roadways in all directions.

Ampanihy

While Ampanihy is a lively place, it looks a little rough around the edges. The only reason to go here is to get petrol or fix a flat.

The road is particularly bad between here and Tranoroa to the east. If you're driving straight to Fort Dauphin, it may be faster to

---

ℹ️ GETTING TO THE CAPE

The lack of sealed or easily passable roads in this part of the country may be part of the region's appeal, but it does make getting around an arduous process that requires careful planning.

Unless you're flying from Tana to Fort Dauphin, the best way to get here is to come south from Itampolo. If coming this way, you will need to drive through the Linta River (only possible during the dry season) to Saodona, on the river's eastern bank. There is an arduous roadway for about 85km to the northeast, where you join the RN10 at Ampanihy. Alternatively, check locally to see if you can cross the Menarandra River further south and continue along the coast to Lavanono.

---

turn northeast at Tranoroa towards Bekitro, then head southeast to Antanimora on the RN13, which rejoins the RN10 at Ambovombe. If you must stay in Ampanihy, **Hotel Angora** (☑ 033 12 232 82; d Ar20,000) is surprisingly hospitable, with basic rooms and en-suite bathrooms with bucket showers.

Lavanono

This secluded surfer paradise has some of the best waves in Madagascar, and no reef to interfere with them.

Run by the hard-working Eveline, the atmospheric **Tea Longo** (☑ 033 23 076 86, 032 04 105 45; d bungalow without bathroom Ar25,000) has some tidy beach shacks that reverberate to the roar of the sea, and communal dining with fresh seafood. There's an interesting assortment of guests, as you don't end up here without a decent story.

Réserve Spéciale de Cap Sainte Marie

Madagascar's southernmost tip, Cap Sainte Marie, is a thought-provoking climax to the 'eighth continent', a stark and windswept place that, like so many places down here, feels like the end of the earth. There's an 18-hectare reserve (☑ 032 40 934 03) here, partly created to protect radiated and spider tortoises, which ends at some cliffs.

A small MNP office lets you know that you have arrived. Here you'll need to pick

up a park guide (Ar20,000). A further drive takes you to the edge of the cliffs, where there is a lighthouse complex, a religious statue and, if your timing is right, a memorable sunset beneath a huge sky. Whales are also often visible offshore between July and November. A longer circuit takes you to a beach strewn with eggshell fragments of the extinct elephant bird, *Aepyornis*.

There are no hotels, but camping (sites Ar15,000) can be arranged at the park office. Otherwise the nearest accommodation is in Lavanono, a two-hour journey by 4WD.

Faux Cap

If you thought there was only one end to Madagascar, and the earth, guess again. As the name suggests, Faux Cap is another, even if it is a shade further north. Here you'll find a little lobster-fishing town hiding behind some windswept dunes, *Aepyornis* eggshell fragments littering an endless beach, the ever-present sound of the sea and little else. But there is some decent accommodation.

While a bit storm-ravaged in spots, **Mada Libertalia** (☑ 032 07 560 41; www.madalibertalia. com; d/tr bungalow €36/45, meals from €10) offers five solar-powered bungalows in stone buildings that are simple but not uncomfortable and a sense of isolation that's as strong as the wind. Pirogue trips, snorkelling and local village visits are all possible.

Ambovombe

Ambovombe is an important regional crossroads town and, as such, it's marginally better equipped than Ampanihy – we were able to find a Snickers bar in the petrol station. One. So fuel up and move on. But do so carefully, as the cratered road from here to Fort Dauphin is the worst in the south – and that's saying something.

Réserve Privée de Berenty

This well-known private reserve (☑ 033 23 210 08; www-personal.umd.umich.edu/~fdolins/ berenty/; admission €20) contains nearly one-third of the remaining tamarind gallery forest in Madagascar, nestled between the arms of a former oxbow lake on the Mandrare River. It was one of Madagascar's first ecotourism destinations and it has an international reputation, helped along by the friendly ring-tailed lemurs that greet you in the parking lot. Visitors can walk forest paths unguided in search of other lemurs. There is also an excellent **anthropological museum** that provides unique insights into local Antandroy culture.

Times have changed, however. The worsening road from Fort Dauphin now means that half of a day's excursion is spent driving, leading 80% of visitors to stay overnight. Meanwhile, a similar reserve, Réserve de Nahampoana (p99), has opened in Fort Dauphin, while much of the wildlife here can be seen at other parks.

There's on-site accommodation in simple but well-tended bungalows (double €50) with mosquito nets and en-suite bathrooms, and a reasonable restaurant (set menus €10).

For many years Berenty would not allow admission unless you bought an expensive transfer from its own agent in Fort Dauphin. It has since widened its net to three locations: **Chez Gigi** (☑033 07 971 64) in Lavanono, **Croix Sud** (☑033 23 210 08) in Fort Dauphin and **Hotel Capricorn** (☑020 24 743 49) in Tuléar. Still, why not simply sell tickets at the entrance?

Parc National d'Andohahela

This 760-sq-km **park** (www.parcs-madagascar. com; adult/child per day Ar55,000/25,000, guides from Ar10,000) northwest of Fort Dauphin protects some of the last remnants of mountainous rainforest in southern Madagascar, as well as spiny forest and a remarkable 12 species of lemurs. It also boasts more than

---

ℹ **PARC NATIONAL D'ANDOHAHELA**

....

Best time to visit April to December, ie outside cyclone season.

Key highlight Circuit Tsimelahy.

Wildlife Three-cornered palm (only found here), spiny iguanas, harrier hawks, lemurs.

Habitat Humid rainforest, spiny forest, transitional forest.

Gateway town Tsimelahy village.

Transport options Rental 4WD (Ar175,000); *taxi-brousse* and hike in.

Things you should know Best to stay overnight at Tsimelahy to give yourself enough time.

---

120 species of birds, as well as a variety of amphibians and reptiles, including crocodiles. In short, this is one of Madagascar's most diverse parks when it comes to both landscapes and wildlife. Questionable security is our only explanation for why the park remains so little known.

The rainforest section of the park offers the best lemur-viewing possibilities. Daytime species include the collared brown lemur, southern lesser bamboo lemur and possibly even the Milne-Edwards' sifaka. Among the occasionally seen nocturnal lemurs, there's the Fleurete's sportive lemur, and rumours persist that the park has a population of aye-ayes... see one and you've hit the jackpot. There's a handful of cheap and extremely basic hotels and guesthouses in Tsimelahy village.

🏃 Activities

The park currently maintains three main circuits for visitors and, with an early start, it's possible to visit the park on a day trip, but it is advisable to camp overnight. If you are interested in longer hikes across the rainforest mountains, visit the MNP office in Fort Dauphin.

➡ **Circuit Tsimelahy** (3.7km, two to 2½ hours) The most popular route is an excellent trail in the bird-rich transition zone between the humid east-coast forest and the dry vegetation of the central region. There are campsites and some natural bathing pools. From Fort Dauphin, turn right at the signpost 48km along the RN13, then proceed 8km along a rough road. Check the security situation before setting out.

➡ **Circuit Malio** A bird- and amphibian-rich loop of 10km (four to five hours) through low-altitude humid forest with waterfalls and natural bathing pools that may be inaccessible during rainy season. From Fort Dauphin, turn right after 25km on the RN13, then proceed 13km on a dirt road (4WD advisable).

➡ **Circuit Mangatsiaka** A gentle loop of 4km (two hours) in bird-rich dry forest. From Fort Dauphin, follow the RN13 for 54km, then turn right and proceed 4km on a dirt road.

Fort Dauphin (Taolagnaro)

If you've driven for days through the spiny forest to get here, the prosperous mining

Fort Dauphin (Taolagnaro)

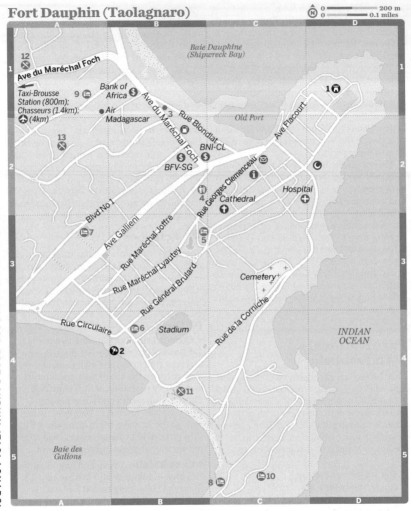

Fort Dauphin (Taolagnaro)

⊙ **Sights**
1 Fort Flacourt..D1
2 Libanona Beach B4

🏃 **Activities, Courses & Tours**
3 Air Fort Services B1
4 Ankoba Watersports B2
  Lavasoa..(see 8)

🛏 **Sleeping**
5 Chez Anita...B3
  Chez Georges..................................(see 11)

6 Chez Jacqueline B4
7 La Croix du Sud A3
8 Lavasoa..C5
9 Népenthès A1
10 Talinjoo C5

🍽 **Eating**
11 Chez Georges...B4
12 Mami Jo A1
13 Restaurant Mirana/Chez
   Bernard...A2

centre of Fort Dauphin, with its sealed roads and street lights, looks for all the world like a mirage of civilisation. And whichever way you arrive, it can look like a gateway to some tropical paradise, strung out along a peninsula between sea and mountains – if it looks vaguely familiar, it may be because it's pictured on the back of the 5000 ariary note.

Apart from some great beaches, the city proper has little to offer travellers and you need to keep your wits about you. But there is much to see in the surrounding area, so your best bet is to enjoy the decent in-town accommodation options and organise excursions or car hire through your hotel and then get out and explore the dramatic hinterland.

◉ Sights & Activities

Libanona Beach   BEACH
What luck for locals to have this fine beach right in the city! It's known for its surfing, both board and wind. Don't leave your belongings unattended on the sand or they may just disappear. And don't even think about wandering around here at night.

Fort Flacourt   FORTRESS
(admission Ar10,000; ☉ 8-11am & 2-5pm Mon-Sat, 2-6pm Sun) This fort is currently used as a military base and the soldiers at the entrance endlessly discuss whether or not to let you in, how much it should cost and who should get the money. If they do let you in, they'll insist on a guide. There's not much to see except for a few cannons, a small museum with some antique maps and some fine views, so consider these negotiations a highlight of your visit.

Ankoba Watersports   SURFING
(☑ 020 92 215 15; www.ankoba.com; surfboard per hr €2, teacher per hr €2) If you've always longed to learn to surf, what better place to do so than here, where staff also organise windsurfing lessons and rental? Most of the action takes place at in-town Ankoba Beach.

☞ Tours

Lavasoa   TOUR
(☑ 033 12 517 03; www.lavasoa.com) The Lavasoa hotel offers trips to Evatra and Lokaro, including stays at its sister property, Pirate Camp, and can also organise surfing and kitesurfing.

Goulzar Tours   DRIVING TOUR
(☑ 033 12 516 14) A reliable choice for a rental car with driver.

Air Fort Services   DRIVING TOUR
(☑ 020 92 212 24; www.airfortservices.com; Ave du Maréchal Foch) Reputable company that rents vehicles and arranges a variety of excursions in the southeast.

🛏 Sleeping

Chez Jacqueline   BUNGALOW €
(☑ 033 12 839 15; d Ar35,000) Jacqueline has cute little bungalows with high ceilings close by Libanona Beach. The rooms are small and breezy and have bucket hot water.

Chez Georges   GUESTHOUSE €€
(☑ 032 48 097 38; georgesliban@yahoo.fr; Libanona Beach; d/tr Ar50,000/75,000) There are only two rooms here, but they are right on Libanona Beach. The triple, a studio, is the town steal. The adjacent bar and restaurant, which share a log-cabin ambience, make this a mini-resort.

Népenthès   BUNGALOW €€
(☑ 032 04 455 54, 034 60 832 54; lenepenthes@ yahoo.fr; Ampasikabo; d Ar60,000) These charming chalet-style cottages in their own compound are clean, have hot water and are situated on spacious grounds.

Chez Anita   BUNGALOW €€
(☑ 020 92 904 22, 033 12 679 83; anita@ fort-dauphin.com; Bazarikely; d/tr bungalow Ar40,000/45,000) Somewhat worse for wear, but still comfy, these A-frame bungalows with attached restaurant, arranged around a quiet garden, are the best budget option in town. Pay the extra Ar5000 for a triple with loft.

★ Talinjoo   BOUTIQUE HOTEL €€€
(☑ 034 05 212 35, 032 05 212 35; www.talinjoo. com; d incl breakfast €75; 🖥🏊) This is the only stylish hotel in Fort Dauphin, with an attractive contemporary design and classy horizon pool. Located high on a hill overlooking Libanona Beach, it has a postcard view, too. Rates include airport transfer and there's an on-site spa.

Lavasoa   BUNGALOW €€€
(☑ 033 12 517 03; www.lavasoa.com; d bungalow €40-45; 🖥) This friendly, well-run guesthouse has brightly painted bungalows in a superb location on the edge of a steep peninsula looking back over Libanona Beach and Pic St Louis – room 6 has one of the best views in Madagascar. The hotel also runs a tour company and owns Pirate Camp (p99) on the Lokaro Peninsula. Book in advance.

SOUTHERN MADAGASCAR FORT DAUPHIN (TAOLAGNARO)

La Croix du Sud
HOTEL €€€

(☑ 032 05 416 84, 033 23 210 08; www.madagascar-resorts.com; d Ar135,000-175,000) The sister hotel to the adjacent Le Dauphin, and the better choice. It's like a large plantation house, with a big metal roof and porches. Painted in solid colours, the rooms manage to be cheery and the best have baths and balconies, while an attractive lobby ties it all together. A good and unpretentious all-round package.

✖ Eating

Chez Georges
SEAFOOD €

(mains Ar9000-14,000; ⊘ 8am-9pm) This popular local eatery and adjoining bar enjoys a laid-back surf atmosphere in cabins overlooking Libanona Beach. Catch of the day and crab farci are house specialities, but expect a wait. People swim after putting in an order and the sunset views are simply magical.

Chasseurs
MADAGASCAN €

(☑ 033 14 368 61, 032 81 172 43; mains Ar6000-12,000; ⊘ 8am-10pm) Near the *taxi-brousse* station, this friendly neighbourhood institution offers traditional Malagasy fare, but is well above a *hotely*.

Mami Jo
CHINESE, MADAGASCAN €

(☑ 033 18 551 36; mains from Ar5000; ⊘ 8am-8pm) The place to come for no-frills fried rice and other Chinese-Malagasy approximations. Also offers great juices, yogurt and a patisserie.

ℹ FORT DAUPHIN BY ROAD

Unless you fly in, it's a very difficult journey to/from Fort Dauphin. The shortest route, from Ihosy on the RN7 to Ambovombe was considered unsafe at the time of research, due to the very real and not-to-be-underestimated threat of banditry, especially after dark.

The two possible approaches require a 4WD and you should take plenty of back-up food and water (especially along the coast):

➡ From Itampolo to Ambovombe via Ampanihy. It's a long journey on rough tracks and should take two days from Itampolo, or three from Tuléar.

➡ Along Madagascar's east coast from Vaingaindrano, with numerous ferry crossings and still a long road to civilisation from there. Count on two to three days.

Restaurant Mirana/ Chez Bernard
EUROPEAN €€

(☑ 034 01 637 04; mains Ar15,000; ⊘ 11am-8pm Mon-Sat) This single room off a narrow side street is an insider spot known for its pizza, seafood and beef.

ℹ Information

Hotels Talinjoo, Lavasoa and Kaleta (in the centre) all offer free wi-fi. There are plenty of banks and ATMs sprinkled around the city; some of the ATMs even work.

MNP Office (☑ 020 92 904 85; Villa Dalia, Esokaka) Has information about Parc National d'Andohahela and other areas, but is hard to find; take a taxi.

Tourist Office (☑ 032 02 846 34; www.fort-dauphin.com; Rue Realy Abel) Useless except for a map – but you have one.

ℹ Getting There & Away

AIR

Air Madagascar (☑ 020 92 211 22) flies from Fort Dauphin to Antananarivo (from €245, two hours, daily) and Tuléar (€479, one hour, weekly). These are ridiculously high fares, which may be cheaper to purchase in-country.

TAXI-BROUSSE

Fort Dauphin's *taxi-brousse* station is in Tanambao, in the northwestern part of town, along the road leading to the airport.

Although *taxis-brousses* connect Fort Dauphin with Ihosy (and beyond) along the RN7, we recommend against travelling this route for security reasons. Between Ambovombe and Ihosy, most *taxis-brousses* travel in convoy, but that doesn't eliminate the risk entirely and we recommend against overnight stops along this section. The roads are also appalling and facilities almost nonexistent.

Safer destinations include Ambovombe (Ar12,000, three to four hours) and the daily *camion-brousse* to Tuléar (Ar45,000, two to three days).

ℹ Getting Around

The airport is 4km west of town. Taxis to/from the centre cost around Ar7500 to Ar15,000 per person. Taxis within town, including to the *taxi-brousse* station, cost Ar2000 per person.

Around Fort Dauphin

You didn't come all this way to restrict yourself to Fort Dauphin, and the town's hinterland has plenty to keep you occupied, including isolated beaches, one of southern

THE ELEPHANT EGG

Elephant birds were a species of flightless birds unique to Madagascar that included the massive *Aepyornis*. Over 10m tall and weighing 400kg, it was the largest bird ever to walk the earth. Scientists disagree as to the cause of its disappearance, which occurred sometime in the 17th century, but it seems clear that humans were responsible, either from eating the eggs or hunting the bird. Today the most poignant sign of these magnificent creatures is the shards of their eggshells, which litter the beaches of the cape. These were suitably enormous, with a circumference of 1m, and contained the equivalent of 160 chicken eggs. They have been made famous by Sir David Attenborough, who featured his own reconstructed egg in his films on Madagascar. Complete eggs are also found. There is one at reception in Réserve de Nahampoana near Fort Dauphin, and one at the National Geographic Society headquarters in Washington, which contains the skeleton of an unborn bird. Sensing commercial opportunity, people on the cape and elsewhere sell eggs made from various reconstructed fragments, usually using a great deal of plaster. It is not legal to remove these from the country.

Madagascar's most underrated wildlife reserves and some fine natural vantage points.

⊙ Sights

Réserve de Nahampoana   NATURE RESERVE
(☑020 92 212 24; www.nahampoana.com; admission incl guide Ar30,000; ☉sunrise-sunset) This 67-hectare forest reserve, 7km north of Fort Dauphin, deserves much greater recognition. Its exotic tropical setting, with mountains for a backdrop, is prettier than Berenty. Add to this a robust and varied lemur population, including ringtail, sifaka, brown, bamboo and mouse species (some with the habit of dropping from trees to say hello), more humane crocodile pens, extraordinary bamboo groves, night walks and a cooling sea breeze, and you wonder why so many people are driving west. There are also bungalows (€28) and a restaurant, making this a peaceful alternative to staying in Fort Dauphin itself. Just grab a taxi.

Domaine de La Cascade   NATURE RESERVE
(☑032 07 678 43; admission Ar15,000) This gorgeous park, about 9km from the Total station on the road to Ambovombe from Fort Dauphin, is an easily overlooked spot. Almost 100 hectares in size, it consists of a nursery set in a paradisiacal valley with several walking trails, including one to a pretty waterfall where you can take a dip. Most people come on a day trip, but there's a large bungalow (q Ar120,000) with kitchen for rent – you'll probably have the whole place to yourself.

Pic St Louis

The summit of Pic St Louis (529m), which you can see around 3km north of Fort Dau-phin, offers good views of the town and coast. From the base, allow 1½ to three hours for the ascent and 1½ hours for the descent. A dawn climb is ideal, before the going gets too hot or windy. You'll need a guide to show you the way – ask in town, or contact an agency – and you should travel in a group as there is a security risk here.

Evatra & Lokaro Peninsula

Lokaro Peninsula is a spectacular and well-preserved area of inland waterways, green hills and barrier beaches. It lies about 15km northeast of Fort Dauphin along the coast, or about 40km by road. Day excursions begin with a 3km drive from Fort Dauphin to the shore of Lac Lanirano then continue by boat to Lac Ambavarano and the tiny fishing village of Evatra. From here it is about 20 minutes on foot over the hills to a good beach. Once at Evatra, you can arrange a pirogue to visit nearby Lokaro Island, or just stay and explore the peninsula itself, which has numerous opportunities for canoeing and walking.

Pirate Camp (Evatra; s/d €25/28) ✐ is run by Lavasoa (p97) in Fort Dauphin. It also has a campsite and hires equipment. Accommodation is made from local materials and there's solar electricity. The transfer here from Fort Dauphin costs €70 one way. If arriving under your own steam, call ahead.

To reach the Lokaro area by road, you'll need a 4WD; allow about two hours from Fort Dauphin. If you go by foot it will take a full day and require food and water. You should also walk with a group, as security can be a problem along this route.

Western Madagascar

Why Go?

Madagascar's western region – divided in two, with no roads linking the south and north – is filled with adventurous possibilities and it's from here that so many iconic Madagascar images originate. There are incredible highlights, from soulful river journeys to the otherworldly limestone spikes and crippled spires of the Tsingy de Bemaraha, the fabulous birdwatching of Parc National d'Ankarafantsika and the stomping ground of the fossa at the Réserve Forestière de Kirindy. Throw in the Allée des Baobabs, world-class resorts and so many opportunities to go out into the wilderness and you have a region that showcases all that's memorable about this remarkable country.

Best Places to Eat

➡ Mad Zebu (p111)

➡ Chez Madame Chabaud (p105)

➡ Le Masoandro (p118)

Best Places to Stay

➡ Antsanitia Beach Resort (p101)

➡ Le Soleil des Tsingy (p114)

➡ Karibu Lodge (p105)

➡ Chez Maggie (p117)

➡ Princesse Tsiribihina (p109)

When to Go
Majunga

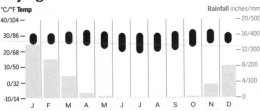

Apr–Oct The region's dry season and only time to see Parc National des Tsingy de Bemaraha.

Nov Fossa mating season at Réserve Forestière de Kirindy and your best chance to spot one.

Dec–Apr Despite the (relatively light) wet season, good for wildlife in Parc National d'Ankarafantsika.

ℹ Getting There & Around

With the exception of the well-maintained RN4 between Antananarivo (Tana) and Majunga (Mahajanga), and the RN35 between Antsirabe and Morondava, there are no sealed roads in this region so 4WD is imperative to explore sights off the RN network. The only way to get from Morondava in the south to Majunga in the north is to backtrack through Antananarivo.

BOENY REGION

The area around the regional centre of Majunga allows you to tick some of western Madagascar's most important boxes, from the country's finest cave system at the Grottes d'Anjohibe to the much-photographed Cirque Rouge. Other reasons to explore include the sedate charms of Katsepy and the bird-rich destinations of easily accessible Parc National d'Ankarafantsika, or the far-more-difficult-to-reach Mahavy-Kinkony Wetland Complex. For real adventurers there's the off-the-map allure of Parc National Tsingy de Namoroka and Parc National Baie de Baly.

Majunga (Mahajanga)

POP 232,730

Majunga is a sprawling and somnolent port town with one of the prettier waterfronts of Madagascar's seaside cities – a palm-lined seaside promenade, as well as shady arcades and walls draped with gorgeous bougainvillea. With its large Comoran and Indian populations, and historical connections with Africa, it is one of the most colourful and ethnically diverse places in Madagascar. It is also the gateway to one of western Madagascar's most diverse regions, from stunning caves and rock formations to sacred lakes and bird-rich wetlands.

History

Arab traders established a number of trading posts along the coast here in the 13th and 14th centuries, and the area became a thriving commercial crossroads between the Malagasy highlands, East Africa and the Middle East. Swahili and Gujarati traders settled in Majunga and the nearby town of Marovoay in the 19th century, and these communities were known for the exquisitely carved wooden doors that adorned their houses. A few can still be admired in Majunga and Marovoay.

◉ Sights

La Corniche AREA

Majunga is all about the Corniche, the palm-lined promenade bordering the sea made up of Blvd Poincarré and Blvd Marcoz. In the evening, residents come here to enjoy a stroll under the setting sun, sip a soft drink or nibble kebabs from numerous street carts. During school holidays (July to September) it has a fair-like atmosphere, with makeshift (and slightly scary-looking) Ferris wheels, horses to ride on and families at play.

At the T-junction with Ave de France, there is an enormous **baobab tree** (circumference, 21m!) thought to be well over 700 years old. It is considered *fady* (taboo) to touch it.

☞ Tours

La Ruche des Aventuriers ADVENTURE TOUR

(☑ 033 07 631 27, 020 62 247 79; www.laruchedesaventuriers.net; Rue Richelieu) Affordable excursions to all the main sights around Majunga, including three-day camping trips to the hard-to-reach Lac Kinkony.

Aventure & Découverte ADVENTURE TOUR

(☑ 034 08 521 96, 020 62 934 75; www.aventure-decouverte.com; 401 Rue Ampasika) Specialises

ANTSANITIA BEACH RESORT

About 40 minutes' drive north of Majunga, along an isolated stretch of coast, **Antsanitia Beach Resort** (☑ 020 62 911 00, 020 62 023 34; www.antsanitia.com; r/bungalow/ste from €28/39/70; ☎), ✆ pronounced 'An-tsan-tee', is a fantastic place to stay. As well as lovely bungalows with wood and raffia furniture, a gorgeous pool, open-air bar, fabulous restaurant and a wonderful setting, guests enjoy numerous activities, from sailing to hiking, snorkelling, pirogue trips and cultural excursions.

The hotel has put sustainability at the heart of everything it does, so many of the activities on offer involve trips to local villages or outings with local fishers. The resort also employs and trains a number of people from the area, and it donates part of the fees from activities to the local communities' fund. Antsanitia is also doing its bit for the environment: hot water comes courtesy of the sun, 'air-con' courtesy of the sea breeze.

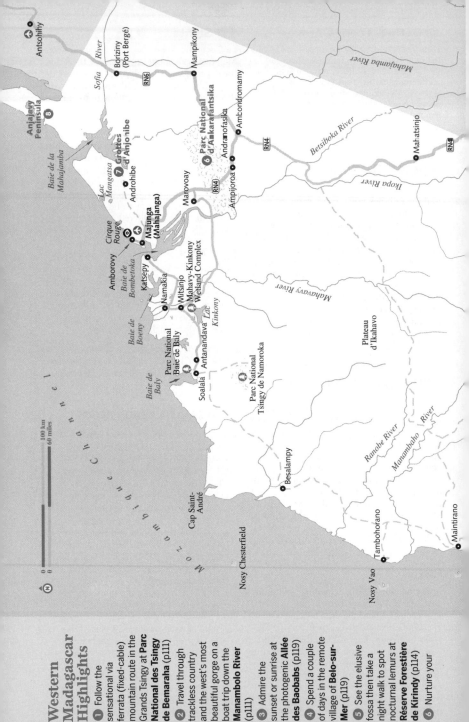

Western Madagascar Highlights

1 Follow the sensational via ferrata (fixed-cable) mountain route in the Grands Tsingy at **Parc National des Tsingy de Bemaraha** (p111)

2 Travel through trackless country and the west's most beautiful gorge on a boat trip down the **Manambolo River** (p111)

3 Admire the sunset or sunrise at the photogenic **Allée des Baobabs** (p119)

4 Spend a couple of days in the remote village of **Belo-sur-Mer** (p119)

5 See the elusive fossa then take a night walk to spot nocturnal lemurs at **Réserve Forestière de Kirindy** (p114)

6 Nurture your

inner birder at the easily accessible **Parc National d'Ankarafantsika** (p108)

7 Splash about in the emerald-green water of the natural swimming pools at **Grottes d'Anjohibe** (p109)

8 Put down your bags for a few days of remote rest on the **Anjajavy Peninsula** (p106)

ANTANANARIVO

Arkazobe

Lac Tsiazompaniry

RN7

Ambatolampy

Antsirabe

Ambositra

Lac Itasy

RN1

RN34

Mahajilo River

Mania River

Malaimbandy

Tsiroanomandidy

Ankavandra

Manambolo River

2 Manambolo River

RN35

Miandrivazo

Tsiribihina Gorge

Tsiribihina River

Morondava River

Parc National des Tsingy de Bemaraha **1**

Antsalova

Bekopaka

Manambolo Gorge

Réserve Forestière de Kirindy **5**

3 Allée des Baobabs

Belo-sur-Tsiribihina

Morondava

Parc National de Kirindy-Mitea **4**

4 Belo-sur-Mer

Manja

Nosy Barren

Nosy Andryhovo

Nosy Andriangory

Nosy Andriamitaroka

Majunga (Mahajanga)

◉ Sights
1 Baobab Tree A2
2 La Corniche A2

✪ Activities, Courses & Tours
3 Aventure & Découverte D2
4 La Ruche des Aventuriers C3

🛏 Sleeping
5 Coco Lodge B3
6 Hôtel Chez Chabaud D1
7 Hôtel du Phare B1
8 Karibu Lodge B1

✖ Eating
Chez Madame Chabaud .... (see 6)
9 Fishing Residence B1
10 Parad'Ice A3

in quad-bike excursions to nearby attractions. Also organises 4WD and pirogue trips.

🛏 Sleeping

Hôtel Chez Chabaud HOTEL €

(☑ 032 40 530 05, 020 62 233 27; off Ave du Général de Gaulle; r Ar25,000-40,000, without bathroom Ar20,000; ❄) With neon light and white-and-blue walls, rooms at Chez Chabaud have the charm of prison cells. That said, the hotel is immaculate, the staff are friendly and you won't find better value anywhere else. The cheaper rooms have fans and shared facilities.

Hôtel du Phare HOTEL €€

(☑ 033 37 000 20, 020 62 235 00; hotelduphare@ moov.mg; Blvd Marcoz; r Ar40,000-62,000; ❄ 🛜) Overlooking the Corniche, this friendly establishment has simple but spacious and spotless rooms, with tiled floors. Rooms at the back are equipped with fans, those at the front (with sea views) have air-con. There is a nice garden where breakfast can be served.

WESTERN MADAGASCAR MAJUNGA (MAHAJANGA)

★**Karibu Lodge**   LUXURY HOTEL €€€
(☑020 62 247 05, 020 62 247 10; www.karibulodge.
net; Blvd Marcoz; ste from €60; ❄☷☎) The
rather lovely Karibu offers 15 duplex suites
with sea views, TV lounge and terrace/
balcony. The rooms have been furnished to
very high standards and the pool and bar-
restaurant overlooking the sea are prime
spots to enjoy the sunset.

Coco Lodge   HOTEL €€€
(☑020 62 230 23; www.cocolodgemajunga-
madagascar.com; Ave de France; d/f €49/69;
❄☷☎) A well-designed, personable little
hotel, Coco Lodge has pretty pink buildings
built around a small pool and bar. The rooms
are huge, very comfortable and individually
decorated, with attractive bathrooms.

✗ Eating

Parad'Ice   CAFE €
(Rue du Maréchal Joffre; mains Ar7000-12,000;
☺8am-9.30pm Tue-Sun) This cheerful cafe-
restaurant serves simple but well-prepared
meals, including salads you can tuck into
without hesitation and rotating *plats
du jour* such as *ravitoto* (pork stew with
manioc greens) and zebu stew. It also does
burgers and croque-monsieurs (ham-and-
cheese grilled sandwiches), excellent homemade ice creams and breakfasts.

★**Chez Madame Chabaud**   FUSION €€
(☑032 40 530 05; off Ave du Général de Gaulle;
mains Ar11,000-16,000; ☺11am-3pm & 6-9pm
Wed-Mon) Small, intimate and oh-so-
delicious, Chez Madame Chabaud is a Majunga institution. Christiane (the original
Madame Chabaud's daughter) prepares a
divine fusion cuisine mixing Malagasy, Creole and European influences that befit the
city's heritage. Try the *camaron* (large freshwater prawn) or the *ouassous* (a huge crayfish) and the mean cocktails.

Fishing Residence   SEAFOOD €€
(www.fishingresidence.com; Blvd Marcoz; mains
Ar13,000-16,000) This hotel-restaurant is well
known for its exquisite seafood, such as calamari and prawns in *combava* (wild lemon)
sauce or grilled swordfish.

Marco Pizza   PIZZA €€
(☑032 11 110 32; Ave d'Amborovy; pizzas from
Ar10,000; ☺11am-9pm) This friendly joint
with street seating churns out excellent –
and absolutely huge – pizzas with a variety
of meat, fish and vegetarian toppings. It's a
couple of kilometres from the centre, but
every taxi knows where it is so you won't
have trouble finding it.

❶ Information

Espace Médical (☑034 02 172 26, 020 62
248 21; www.espacemedical.mg; Magarivotra;
☺24hr) The best place for medical treatment.
Tourist Office (☑034 08 088 80; www.
majunga.org; 14 Ave Philibert Tsiranana) Can
recommend excursions, arrange guides and help
with all manner of bookings. Also sells city maps.

❶ Getting There & Away

AIR
Air Austral (☑020 62 227 65; www.air-austral.
com; Rue des Messageries Maritimes) Flies
twice a week between Majunga and Saint-Denis
in Réunion (€680).
Air Madagascar (☑032 05 222 06, 020 62
224 61; www.airmadagascar.com; Rue Girard)
Flies several times weekly to Antananarivo (one
hour, €245) and once a week to Diego Suarez
(€479).

BUS
Transport Première Class (☑033 07 601
67; www.malagasycar.com; Blvd Marcoz) To
travel in luxury, Transport Première Class runs
comfortable, air-con vehicles between Tana
and Majunga (Ar78,000, 10 hours, daily). The
buses sit just two people to a row and a packed
lunch is included in the price. Departure is at
7am, close to CNAPS; drop-off is at its office at
Hôtel Le Grand Mellis (p43) in Tana. Bookings
essential.
Transpost (post office) A good alternative to
standard *taxi-brousse* rides is Transpost, run by
Madagascar's postal service. It has minibuses
between Majunga and Tana (Ar25,000, 12
hours, Tuesday, Thursday and Saturday).

TAXIS-BROUSSES FROM MAJUNGA

DESTINATION	COST (AR)	DURATION (HR)	DEPARTURE TIME (APPROXIMATE)
Ambanja	50,000	13	5pm
Antananarivo	30,000	12	8am & 5pm
Diego Suarez	50,000	15	5pm

ANJAJAVY'S FLY-IN RESORTS

For those looking for something truly off the radar, the remote resorts on the Anjajavy Peninsula are the answer. Getting there alone costs an eye-watering €200 to €600.

Anjajavy (☑ France +33 1 44 69 15 03; www.anjajavy.com; s/d incl meals €437/690; ☺ Mar–mid-Jan; 🛏 🛜 🍽) is part of the prestigious Relais & Châteaux network, and the quintessential desert-island idyll. The guest villas are luxurious, with polished wood, fine linen and their own private terrace. There are myriad activities – snorkelling, swimming, guided walks through the forest and to local villages – many of them free. Massages, fishing and boat excursions are also available. The hotel leases 450 hectares of native dry deciduous forest and protects it as a nature reserve. A three-day minimum stay is required; transfer is by private plane from Antananarivo.

La Maison de Marovasa-Be (☑ 032 07 418 14, France +33 6 22 85 71 54; www.marovasabe.com; per person all-inclusive from €250; ☺ Mar-Jan; 🍽) is an exquisite villa offering beautiful suites and bedrooms, all with balconies. The house has a 1930s colonial retro feel about it. The surrounding environment is more arid than for other Anjajavy resorts, but Marovasa is involved in local reforestation projects. The hotel is also powered by wind and solar energy rather than generator. Access is by private plane from Antananarivo, Majunga or Nosy Be.

Pick-up and drop-off is at the central post office in both cities. Departure is at 7.30am sharp. Bookings required.

TAXI-BROUSSE

There are two *taxi-brousse* stations in Majunga: one on Ave du 14 Octobre near the town hall and the other, much bigger, one on Rue George Ranaivoson, close to the Jovenna petrol station.

For Nosy Be, change at Ambanja for Ankify (Ar6000, 30 minutes), where you'll find boats for Nosy Be.

ⓘ Getting Around

TO/FROM THE AIRPORT

The airport is 6km northeast of town. A taxi to/from town costs Ar15,000. *Taxis-brousses* (Ar1000) stop about 300m from the airport.

CAR

Upmarket hotels and tour companies in Majunga can arrange car or 4WD rental. Expect to pay Ar150,000 to Ar200,000 per day for a 4WD and around Ar80,000 for a regular car. Petrol is extra.

TAXI

The standard rate for a taxi ride in town is Ar3000, but drivers can ask as much as Ar5000.

Around Majunga

Majunga stands in the heart of some stirring country, with just the right combination of accessibility and remote wilderness experience to satisfy most travellers. Highlights around here include Grottes d'Anjohibe (p109), which is one of Madagascar's most spectacular caves, and the stunning natural formation of Cirque Rouge.

Cirque Rouge

Dramatic Cirque Rouge is one of western Madagascar's most famous sights. This amphitheatre of eroded rock is tinted in a rainbow hue of colours, including red, pink, ochre and white – for the full effect, arrive late afternoon and stay until sunset. A stream runs along the bottom of the valley and through a small ravine down to the sea (a lovely 10-minute walk).

Cirque Rouge is just 12km north of Majunga. A charter taxi will cost around Ar60,000 for the return trip, including waiting time.

Katsepy

Katsepy *(kah-tsep)* is a small, sleepy fishing village across Bombetoka Bay from Majunga with a couple of swimmable beaches. Most visitors are likely to go *through* Katsepy on their way to Kinkony, but there are a couple of low-key sights to visit and an excellent hotel-restaurant.

◉ Sights

Katsepy's Lighthouse   LIGHTHOUSE
(admission Ar5000) About 8km southwest of Katsepy, Katsepy's Lighthouse has sweeping views of Bombetoka Bay and Mozambique

Channel. It's a hot, two-hour walk to get here from Katsepy. Otherwise you can charter a *taxi-brousse* to take you there and back (Ar45,000, with 30 minutes at the site).

🛏 Sleeping & Eating

Chez Mme Chabaud   BUNGALOW €€
(☑020 62 233 27; bungalow Ar35,000, mains Ar10,000-17,000) Run by the same family as the eponymous restaurant in Majunga, Chez Mme Chabaud serves the same delicious blend of Malagasy and French cuisine with fresh, local ingredients. The seven pretty bungalows have been built and decorated with local materials and are right by the beach, in a lovely garden.

To preserve the site's peacefulness, the hotel has eschewed generators in favour of wind and solar energy.

ℹ Getting There & Away

The Majunga–Katsepy ferry (passenger/car Ar3000/35,000, one hour) leaves Majunga at 7.30am daily, then sets out for the return journey from Katsepy around 9am. If there are many cars and/or trucks waiting in Katsepy, it sometimes does a second trip in the afternoon. If the ferry doesn't come back, private motor-boats (Ar3500, 30 minutes) ply the crossing in both directions between Majunga and Katsepy several times a day until about 3pm.

Mahavy-Kinkony Wetland Complex

The Mahavy-Kinkony Wetland Complex gained temporary protection status in 2007. It incorporates a diverse and fragile ecosystem consisting of marine bays, river, delta and 22 lakes, including Madagascar's second-largest, Lac Kinkony. The reserve is also home to dry deciduous and gallery forest, savannah, marshland, mangrove, caves and lots of wildlife.

What most people come to Lac Kinkony for, however, are the birds. Indeed, if you've

OFF THE BEATEN TRACK

TWO REMOTE PARKS

West of Majunga, Madagascar's western bulge is one of the island's least trampled corners. It's a land of adventurers and well-equipped expeditions and it's only accessible in the dry season, from May to October.

Parc National Tsingy de Namoroka (www.parcs-madagascar.com; adult/child per day Ar45,000/25,000, guide per circuit Ar15,000) is an isolated park home to that peculiarly Madagascan landform, the *tsingy*, a dense forest of jagged rocky pinnacles interwoven with deep canyons filled with streams and trees. It's a bit like visiting the more-famous Tsingy de Bemaraha (p111), but without the crowds. Trails weave among the rocks, and rope bridges cross the canyons.

There are three circuits through the park. The 70km Circuit Ambovonomy combines walking with 4WDing and there are fine panoramic views and a good chance of seeing Decken's sifaka or red lemurs. Circuit Mandevy (70km) is similar, with good baobab views, while the Circuit Antsifotra (60km) is also similar, if slightly shorter and with less chance of spotting lemurs. Most circuits take four to six hours.

Other lemur species include eastern lesser bamboo lemur, fork-crowned lemur, grey mouse lemur, Milne-Edwards' sportive lemur, fat-tailed dwarf lemur and the oh-so-elusive aye-aye. More than 80 bird species have also been recorded here.

To get here, it's a rough 150km, eight-hour 4WD expedition from Katsepy to Soalala, from where it's a further 50km south. Count on four days' round trip from Majunga, plus time spent here.

Parc National Baie de Baly (www.parcs-madagascar.com) is best known as the home of the critically endangered ploughshare tortoise, and has dense dry, bamboo and mangrove forests, sand dunes and beaches, lakes and rivers. In addition to eight lemur species (Decken's sifaka and brown lemurs are most commonly sighted), the beaches are nesting grounds for green, hawksbill, Madagascar big-headed and loggerhead turtles. The four circuits through the park take from one to six hours; the longer circuits usually include a pirogue ride. More than 120 bird species have also been recorded here.

Access to the park is only possible from Soalala. It's a two-day 4WD expedition from Majunga.

no interest in birds, there's little reason to come. There are 143 species and it is the only place where all of western Madagascar's waterfowl species can be seen in the same location.

Getting to Lac Kinkony is virtually impossible under your own steam and there is no tourism infrastructure. Travel agencies in Majunga organise all-inclusive camping trips, but you'll need at least three days (the roads are *very* rough) and a minimum of Ar600,000 for the 4WD, fuel and guide (for two to four people).

Parc National d'Ankarafantsika

Ankarafantsika (www.parcs-madagascar.com; adult/child per day Ar55,000/25,000, guides from Ar15,000) is the last strand of dry western deciduous forest in Madagascar, and the need for its protection is obvious – as you drive to Ankarafantsika, whether from Tana or the north, there isn't a tree in sight for hundreds of kilometres. The combination of accessibility (the park straddles the RN4 and is accessible even by public transport) and excellent wildlife viewing makes it one of western Madagascar's most popular and rewarding parks.

🏃 Activities

Wildlife Watching

Ankarafantsika is home to eight lemur species, many easily seen, including Coquerel's sifaka and the recently discovered golden-brown mouse lemur. You're also likely to see brown lemurs and four nocturnal species:

sportive, woolly, grey mouse and fat-tailed dwarf lemurs. More elusive is the rare mongoose lemur, which is observed almost exclusively here.

Ankarafantsika is one of Madagascar's finest birdwatching venues, with 129 species recorded, including the critically endangered Madagascar fish eagle and the raucous sickle-bill vanga. There are also more than 70 species of reptiles, including small iguanas, a rare species of leaf-tailed gecko and the rhinoceros chameleon (the male sports a large, curious-looking, bulb-like proboscis).

The **Durrell Wildlife Conservation Trust** (www.durrell.org) has been operating a very successful captive-breeding program for the critically endangered ploughshare tortoise in Parc National d'Ankarafantsika for 25 years. Because poaching is a problem, you'll only be able to watch the tortoises through a chain-link fence.

Hiking

Hiking is the name of the game here. There are eight short circuits in the park, some of which can be combined into a half-day hike. Circuits in the western half of the park go through dense forests on a sandy plateau and are great for lemur spotting (sifakas and brown lemurs in particular) and birdwatching. There's also a breathtaking canyon that is well worth the hike in baking heat across the grassland plateau.

The northern half of the park is all about the lake and the baobabs. The birdwatching is excellent here (and completely different from the south) and there are more reptiles, including crocodiles. If you have time, try to see both sides.

🛏️ Sleeping & Eating

Gîte d'Ampijoroa   CAMPGROUND, BUNGALOW €€
(☑ 020 62 780 00; akf.parks@gmail.com; camping Ar6000, r without bathroom Ar35,000, bungalow Ar80,000) The national park's privately run accommodation is adequate and improving, if uninspiring – reasonable but exposed camping facilities, basic rooms with poor shared facilities and large, simple bungalows. The redeeming feature is the restaurant, which serves delicious three-course meals for a bargain Ar12,000.

★ Blue Vanga Lodge   BUNGALOW €€€
(☑ 034 08 522 22; www.bluevanga-lodge.com; d Ar105,000) In the village of Ampijoroa, around 5km south of the park entrance, friendly Blue Vanga Lodge has large, spot-

WORTH A TRIP

GROTTES D'ANJOHIBE

These caves, about 73km east of Majunga, are among the most impressive in Madagascar. A series of subterranean rooms and galleries, some of them the size of buildings, they are adorned with stalactites and stalagmites and stretch over 5km. Shafts of light penetrate every room from passageways and holes in the ceiling, giving the caves an eerie feel.

What most people now come to Anjohibe for, however, are not the caves, but the stunning **natural swimming pools** (admission Ar15,000). Of a deep emerald-green colour and framed by luxuriant vegetation and *ravinala* trees fanning their leaves like parading ostriches, they are the most improbable find in an otherwise arid landscape. The first pool you come to is shallow, while the second pool, at the foot of a spectacular waterfall, is deep and wonderful for swimming.

It takes a good 3½ hours to get to Anjohibe from Majunga and to do it as a day trip you'll need to leave at first light to be back by sunset. Local guide **Rivo** (☏032 45 839 28), who speaks basic English, can organise two-day visits, with a night of camping by the pool (Ar5000 per person). If you don't have your own vehicle, catch a *taxi-brousse* to Majunga from Tana (Ar35,000, eight hours) or a *taxi-brousse* towards Andranofasika from Majunga (Ar6000, three hours) and ask to be dropped off at the park. You'll have no problem flagging a *taxi-brousse* to go to Majunga whatever the time of day, but you may have to go to Majunga to find a *taxi-brousse* to Tana as many are likely to be full by the time they pass the park.

TSIRIBIHINA RIVER REGION

One of Madagascar's top wilderness destinations, the region between Antsirabe and Morondava is home to the beautiful Tsiribihina and Manambolo Rivers, the spectacular Unesco World Heritage–listed Parc National des Tsingy de Bemaraha and the Réserve Forestière de Kirindy with its population of fossa (Madagascar's largest predator).

Miandrivazo

Miandrivazo (mee-an-dree-vaaz), which lies along the main RN34 road between Antsirabe and Morondava, is the starting point for boat trips down the Tsiribihina River to Belo-sur-Tsiribihina. If you're coming from Antsirabe, there are fine views over the town and surrounding river plains on the final approach into town.

Riverboat guides will generally find you not long after you arrive in town.

🛏 Sleeping & Eating

La Pirogue   BUNGALOW €€
(☏ 032 07 508 37; d bungalow Ar35,000-60,000) Simple but clean bungalow rooms, with good views from the restaurant. It's the best Miandrivazo choice for those on a tight budget. It's also a reputable organiser of riverboat trips.

★**Princesse Tsiribihina**   HOTEL €€€
(☏ 033 11 301 72; www.madagascar-circuits.com; s/d Ar90,000/100,000; ✿ Mar Nov; ▣🅟📶🅼) Opened in 2012 and easily the best place to stay in Miandrivazo, Princesse Tsiribihina is run by one of the better river-trip operators. Rooms are attractively painted,

RIVER TRIPS: TSIRIBIHINA OR MANAMBOLO?

Drifting down the Tsiribihina (tsi-ree-been) or Manambolo has become one of the most popular activities in western Madagascar and for good reason. The trip between Miandrivazo and Belo-sur-Tsiribihina, or between Ankavandra and Parc National des Tsingy de Bemaraha, allows you to see a slice of the country where life is ruled by the river, not the roads. There is excellent birdwatching along the rivers, as well as occasional lemurs, crocs and chameleons. You'll also see Malagasies going about their daily life: men fishing or attempting to cross the river with their loaded zebu carts, women washing clothes by the riverside and children playing and swimming. Camp is set on sandbanks every night, complete with campfire and prime viewing of the Milky Way. Most operators will also organise short walks and visits to local villages.

But which river do you choose? It all depends on what kind of trip you're looking for.

Ease of access It's much easier to reach the start of the Tsiribihina River – the gateway town of Miandrivazo lies along a sealed road well served by public transport. To reach the Manambolo involves a rough, day-long 4WD trip from the capital. On the other hand, the Manambolo descent leaves you in Bekopaka, which is more convenient for Parc National des Tsingy de Bemaraha.

Scenery Both are beautiful, peaceful river journeys, although we reckon the Manambolo descent is the more spectacular of the two, especially for its final passage through the Manambolo Gorge.

Crowds In high season the Tsiribihina River can be extremely popular. The Manambolo remains, for the time being at least, the quieter option.

Choice of operators You're likely to have far more choice of who takes you down the Tsiribihina River and what boat you'll travel in – Miandrivazo is filled with guides and boat owners. For the Manambolo, you'll need to arrange everything in advance through a tour operator.

Security Although the overwhelming number of travellers experience no problems, we received an unconfirmed report of visitors being robbed and assaulted while camping remotely on a Tsiribihina River boat trip in 2014. Check the situation with your tour operator or guide, as well as what precautions are being made, before undertaking this trip.

spacious and come with terrific bathrooms, the location takes advantage of the town's fine riverside location with sweeping views and there's a decent restaurant and swimming pool. It's 1km south of town.

ⓘ Getting There & Away

There are daily *taxis-brousses* to Antananarivo (Ar24,000, nine hours), Antsirabe (Ar15,000, seven hours) and Morondava (Ar24,000, six hours). *Taxis-brousses* from Antananarivo leave the capital around 5pm or 6pm and reach Miandrivazo in the middle of the night.

Tsiribihina River

Trips down the Tsiribihina generally start close to Miandrivazo and cover 146km of lazy bends all the way to Belo-sur-Tsiribihina. It takes about 2½ days to cover the distance at a leisurely pace. The scenery is beautiful

and varied: the river is in turns broad in the plains and narrow through the Tsiribihina Gorges, with vast sandbanks converted to paddy fields alternating with tall, red cliffs and beautiful deciduous forest. Day one generally finishes with a visit to lovely waterfalls, and most trips arrive at Belo-sur-Tsiribihina by lunchtime on day three.

Belo-sur-Tsiribihina

Belo-sur-Tsiribihina, lost in the marshes and mangroves of the Tsiribihina Delta, is a dusty collection of two-storey buildings. It's halfway between Morondava and Parc National des Tsingy de Bemaraha and has that incongruous combination of utter remoteness and tourist hub. It's often referred to as 'Belo' and is not to be confused with the coastal village of Belo-sur-Mer, which lies further south.

🛏 Sleeping & Eating

Hôtel-Restaurant du Menabe HOTEL €
(☎032 42 635 35; http://hoteldumenabe.free.fr;
d/tw/tr/f Ar25,000/35,000/40,000/80,000) In
an old, colourful colonial building, Hôtel du
Menabe offers some grand rooms with huge
double beds. Most have bathrooms and all
are impeccably clean. The hotel is run by a
friendly Frenchman, Bruno, and there is a
great atmosphere, notably in the evenings
when the dining room fills up with travellers swapping stories of Tsingy ascents and
Tsiribihina descents.

★Mad Zebu INTERNATIONAL €€
(☎032 07 589 55, 032 40 387 15; restaurantmad
zebu@yahoo.fr; mains Ar12,000-18,000; ⊗9am-
9pm) The 'crazy zebu' is the most incongruous find in dusty Belo, possibly in all
Madagascar. Dishes seem to come straight
out of a Michelin-starred restaurant (the
chef trained in prestigious kitchens in
Madagascar and Europe), with exquisite
creations such as pan-fried shin of zebu
with roast cherry tomatoes, or Nile perch
in coconut sauce, all elaborately presented.

Every travel agent in Madagascar books
its clients here for lunch on their way between Morondava and the Tsingy de Bemaraha, so book ahead.

❶ Information

There is no bank or internet access in Belo. The
nearest facilities are in Morondava.

❶ Getting There & Away

BOAT

Belo is on the northern side of the Tsiribihina
River so vehicles (and passengers) coming from
Morondava need to use the ferry (passenger/
vehicle Ar750/22,000, 45 minutes, 6am to 7pm).

CAMION-BROUSSE

These huge, 4WD army-style trucks go to
Bekopaka (for Parc National des Tsingy de
Bemaraha) every few days in the dry season
(May to October). The trip (Ar25,000) takes
anywhere from 10 to 24 hours and is extremely
rough.

TAXI-BROUSSE

There are daily taxis-brousses between Belo-
sur-Tsiribihina and Morondava (Ar12,000, four
hours). Departures are from the Morondava side
of the river. The road is unsealed but in good
condition.

Manambolo River

The descent of the Manambolo River is a
quieter alternative to the better-known Tsiribihina River, although things are changing.
Journeys begin at Ankavandra, a remote
village west of Antananarivo and Tsiroanomandidy – to reach the starting point, it's
a very long 4WD journey from the capital.
Once on the river, it generally takes three
days to reach Bekopaka, the gateway town
to the Parc National des Tsingy de Bemaraha. The final stretch of the descent passes
through the Manambolo Gorge, a gorgeous,
broad canyon walled by red limestone cliffs.

Parc National des Tsingy de Bemaraha

If you visit one place in western Madagascar,
make it the **Parc National des Tsingy de
Bemaraha** (www.parcs-madagascar.com; adult/
child per day Ar55,000/25,000, guide per circuit
Ar15,000). A Unesco World Heritage–listed
site, its highlights are the jagged, limestone
pinnacles known as *tsingy* and the impressive infrastructure – via ferrata (mountain

---

❶ PARC NATIONAL DES TSINGY DE BEMARAHA

Best time to visit April to October.

Key highlight The dramatic, dark grey,
serrated pinnacles of the *tsingy*.

Wildlife The park's main draw is its
geology rather than wildlife, although
you're bound to come across some of
the park's 11 species of lemurs.

Habitat Humid and dry forests, grassland, limestone rock formations.

Gateway town Bekopaka.

Transport options Access to Bekopaka
is possible by 4WD between April and
October from Morondava.

Things you should know It is *fady*
(taboo) to smoke, go to the toilet outside designated areas, or point at the
tsingy with your finger outstretched.

Top tip During peak season (July and
August), there aren't enough guides
and harnesses, so arrange everything
the day before. This also allows you
to depart around 5am and avoid the
human traffic jams along the via ferrata
(fixed-cable route).

routes equipped with fixed cables, stemples, ladders and bridges, and organised through your guide), rope bridges, walkways – the park has put in place to explore them. Formed over centuries by the movement of wind and water, and often towering sever-

RIVERBOAT TRIPS

The main time for river descents is from April to November. During the rainy season, you'll sleep in villages rather than on the sandbanks.

Packages: Pirogue or Motor Boat?

Most river-trip packages include all camping equipment, food, (nonalcoholic) drinks, a guide and, of course, the boat. For the last, you have two options: traditional wooden pirogue or motorised boat.

Purists argue that traditional wooden pirogues are the genuine experience. Except for the splash of the paddle, silence reigns and your chances of seeing wildlife are greatly enhanced. Pirogues also only take three to four people (including the *piroguier*, or paddler), offering a more intimate experience. The downside is comfort: once you've boarded the pirogue, you're stuck in that position until your next stop, exposed to the beating sun. Allow about €300 for a group of three or four for the whole trip.

The *chaland* (or motor boat) is a narrow, barge-like boat with two decks and must be arranged through a tour operator. The lower deck has the engine room, kitchen, dining area and storage, while the upper deck is basically a viewing platform with loungers, seats and an awning for shade. They generally fit eight to 12 people. The biggest downside is the noise of the engine, but they make up for it in comfort and conviviality by allowing you to move around and chat with fellow passengers. Most operators will stop the boat for lunch so that you can eat in peace. Trips generally cost €200 per person.

On the Tsiribihina River, motor boats arrive at the ferry landing in Belo, but pirogues generally stop 40km upstream and travellers finish the last stretch either by zebu cart or 4WD.

Tour Operators

Most agencies can combine the river trip with a visit to Parc National des Tsingy de Bemaraha (well worth doing), with a 4WD coming to pick you up from the landing and delivering you in Morondava three days later. These trips cost around €900 per person on the basis of two people, but around €500 per person with four people (the biggest cost is the 4WD).

You'll also find plenty of hotels and local operators in Miandrivazo and Antsirabe (see p52) that can organise pirogue trips. Do try to inspect the camping equipment before setting off and make sure you confirm what is included, the kind of food you will be served and how much water will be available.

For security reasons, you must visit the police station in Miandrivazo with your passports and your *piroguier* before setting off. At the end of the trip, the *piroguier* will ask you to sign a discharge confirming that the trip went well, which they will hand back at the police station.

Mad Caméléon (☑ 020 22 630 86; www.madcameleon.com) Dizzying array of options, including an eight-day trip with a three-day descent of the Manambolo, two days in the Parc National des Tsingy Bemaraha and a return to Tana from Morondava by air.

Espace Mada (☑ 020 22 262 97; www.madagascar-circuits.com) Three-day descents of the Tsiribihina from €135 to €390 per person (depending on the number of people).

Remote River Expeditions (☑ 032 47 326 70, 020 95 523 47; www.remoterivers.com) Range of options on the river from budget to relative luxury.

Treading Lightly

The increased traffic on the Tsiribihina River in particular has taken its toll: trash and improper burial of human waste are real issues in this fragile ecosystem. Please take responsibility for yourself. Make sure you bury any waste in a hole at least 15cm deep and 30m from the river.

al hundred metres into the air, the serrated peaks would definitely look at home in a Dalí painting.

✶ Activities

Wildlife Watching

Although better known for its landscapes, the park's wildlife is exceptional. There are 11 lemur species in residence, with the most commonly sighted species being the Decken's sifaka and the red-fronted brown lemur; your best chances come while hiking in the Petits Tsingy. Even by day, you might chance upon fat-tailed dwarf lemurs and grey mouse lemurs catching up on sleep in tree hollows. If you're really lucky, you'll happen upon the Cleese's woolly lemur (also known as the Western woolly lemur) and the Sambirano lesser bamboo lemur, both of which are only found in this park.

More than 100 bird species are also present in the park, including the critically endangered Madagascar fish eagle. Other important raptors include Henst's goshawk, Madagascar sparrowhawk and Madagascar harrier, while sightings of the crested ibis and Madagascar grey-throated rail are also greatly prized among birders.

Some 45 reptiles and amphibians round out an impressive portfolio – watch in particular for the Antsingy leaf chameleon and Madagascar iguana.

Hiking

Although there are a few 4WD circuits, you'll miss the best bits if you don't explore the park on foot. At a bare minimum, we recommend at least a day in the Petits Tsingy and a day in the Grands Tsingy – more, of course, if time allows.

➡ **Petits Tsingy** Near Bekopaka, this is the most accessible section of the park. There are seven hiking circuits in this area, ranging from an easy 1½-hour walk with walkways and easy bridges, to a pretty serious six-hour circuit requiring you to abseil a 30m cliff. Many involve a section by pirogue through the stunning Manambolo River Gorges.

➡ **Grands Tsingy** The largest and most impressive expanse of limestone pinnacles, the Grands Tsingy lie 17km north of Bekopaka. Most visitors drive to the start of the two circuits (four hours each), which follow a fantastic via ferrata – no climbing experience required, you just wear a

harness, which you clip to cables and ladders as you go.

🍴 Sleeping & Eating

Park visitors stay at the small village of Bekopaka, a ramshackle collection of huts with bright-green paddy fields stretching under immense skies at the entrance of the gorges of the Manambolo River. If you'd like to escape your hotel, head to the ferry crossing for a cold beer in one of the atmospheric *gargotes* (cheap restaurants).

Le Relais des Tsingy   BUNGALOW €
(☑ 032 02 049 48; www.tsingy-de-bemaraha.com; dm/d from Ar15,000/40,000) The thatch-roofed bungalows are fairly standard, but the views from this property, particularly the public areas, are outstanding.

Tanankoay   BUNGALOW €€
(☑ 034 18 251 93; www.tanankoay.com; Bekopaka; camping Ar5000, d Ar40,000-68,000, without bathroom Ar20,000; ☺May-Nov) This super-friendly hotel offers everything from camping to spacious en-suite bungalows. There is a lovely garden and the restaurant serves excellent food in the evening (the Ar22,000 three-course meal is great value) – although it must be said that the packed lunches are rather sorry looking. Tanankoay is 900m north of Bekopaka, on the road to the Grands Tsingy.

Camp Croco   CAMPGROUND €€
(☑ 020 22 630 86; www.madcameleon.com; s/d/tr Ar40,000/45,000/60,000) This lovely tented camp, run by the reputable tour operator Mad Caméléon, has an atmospheric location with epic sunsets on the southern

---

ⓘ WALKING THE TSINGY

Much of the walking in the *tsingy* area of the park can be pretty strenuous and requires careful conversations with your guides before setting out. Gaps between the rocks are sometimes narrow and bridges are high. Anyone with a low level of fitness or vertigo might find exploring the *tsingy* challenging, particularly the Grands Tsingy, where hauling, squeezing, crawling and pulling are all part of the fun and guides have developed an arsenal of tricks to coax even the most vertigo-struck hikers across the rope bridges.

banks of the Manambolo River. The large canvas tents are mounted on decks; inside you'll find proper beds and basic furniture. They're comfortable, but considering you have to share bathrooms and toilets, overpriced.

Travellers rave about the food (Ar25,000 for a three-course meal).

★ **Le Soleil des Tsingy**   LODGE, BUNGALOW €€€
(☏ 033 15 719 68, 034 14 719 68; www.soleil destsingy.com; d €79; P❈🛜🛗) ✎ Set in a 200,000-sq-metre garden, with infinity views out over the surrounding wilderness, Le Soleil des Tsingy is easily the best place to base yourself for visiting the national park. The beautifully appointed bungalows are spacious and have expansive terraces with fine views. There's a good restaurant, lovely swimming pool and even a children's playground. Service is attentive.

Orchidée du Bemaraha   HOTEL €€€
(☏ 032 50 898 79; www.orchideedubemaraha.com; Bekopaka; camping per tent Ar35,000, bungalow from Ar40,000, r Ar80,000-140,000, f Ar220,000; 🛗) With beautiful grounds, a pool and a lovely bar, this is a fantastic place to come back to after scaling the pinnacles of the *tsingy*. Both the tents and rooms are good value and well appointed. The latter have tiled floors, mosquito nets and plenty of space.

Le Grand Hôtel du Tsingy du Bemaraha   BUNGALOW €€€
(☏ 034 99 389 99; www.legrandhotel-du-tsingy. com; d/tr Ar120,000/130,000; ⊘ mid-Apr–Nov; P🛜🛗) Set amid expansive grounds, this three-star lodge has circular brick rondavel-style bungalows with good bathrooms, a shaded entrance terrace and 24-hour electricity. It's a good upmarket option with a reasonable price tag and a decent restaurant.

ℹ Information

MNP Office (☏ 034 49 401 30; www. parcs-madagascar.com; ⊘ 6-11am & 1-4pm) The MNP office, at the entrance to Bekopaka, arranges guides, payment of park fees and climbing harnesses if required. Most guides speak French, English and Italian.

ℹ Getting There & Away

You need a 4WD to access the Tsingy and it's a seven-hour drive from Morondava. Bekopaka and the national park are on the north side of the **Manambolo River ferry crossing** (passenger/vehicle free/Ar10,000; ⊘ 6.30am–noon & 2-6pm). The crossing is about 80km of very rough track north of Belo-sur-Tsiribihina (four hours) and passable only from April to October. Bekopaka is about 3km from the ferry crossing. A car and driver from Morondava will set you back around €75 per day, including fuel.

In the dry season, there are infrequent *camions-brousses* between Bekopaka and Belo-sur-Tsiribihina (Ar30,000, 10 hours) and Maintirano (Ar68,000, one to two days) in the north. There's no public transport from Morondava.

Réserve Forestière de Kirindy

Réserve Forestière de Kirindy (adult/child Ar25,000/12,500, day/night guide per 2hr per group Ar20,000/30,000), 60km northeast of Morondava, covers about 125 sq km and was established in the late 1970s as an experiment in sustainable logging and forest management. It's now a protected area, popular with scientists and travellers for its amazing wildlife. Night walks are a highlight.

🏃 Activities

Everyone comes here for the wildlife, with both day and night, guided two-hour circuits possible. Mornings (7am to 9am) are best for the day walks, while night walks set out just after sunset.

Kirindy is one of the few places in Madagascar where you are very likely to see the fossa (*Cryptoprocta felix*), the country's largest predator, a cat-like creature with oversized ears and a strangely elongated body. The best time to see them is in the mating season (September to November), although your chances are good year-round since they tend to hang around the Ecolodge

---

ℹ RÉSERVE FORESTIÈRE DE KIRINDY

Best time to visit Year-round.

Key highlight The profusion of wildlife, including some of Madagascar's rarest mammals; night walks.

Wildlife Fossa, eight lemur species, tortoises and many birds.

Habitat Deciduous dry forest.

Gateway town Morondava.

Transport options Private vehicle or *taxi-brousse*, plus a 5km walk.

in the hope of stealing goodies from the kitchen and rubbish dump.

Kirindy also has eight lemur species and you're likely to see three or four of the following nocturnal species on a night walk: grey mouse lemur, red-tailed sportive lemur, fork-marked lemur, fat-tailed dwarf lemur, Coquerel's giant dwarf lemur and the Madame Berthe's mouse lemur, which is considered the world's smallest primate and weighs around 30g.

The highlights of day walks are less likely to be lemurs – the reserve's Verreaux's sifaka and red-fronted brown lemur are commonly seen in other parks – but the 45 recorded bird species. Birding highlights include the rare crested ibis, the nocturnal white-breasted mesite and the Madagascar pygmy kingfisher.

There are also 32 reptile species. Watch out for tenrecs and the giant jumping rat, too.

🛏 Sleeping & Eating

Le Camp Amoureux   BUNGALOW €€€
(☑ 032 02 120 08; m.ravaroson@fanamby.org.mg; d safari tent from Ar80,000) Run by the local community, Le Camp Amoureux is, despite being an hour's drive south of Kirindy, many people's preferred base for visiting the reserve – the accommodation is much better value here, with tidy, thatch-roofed safari tents on raised wooden platforms. Water runs hot (sometimes) and cold in the ensuite bathrooms. Night walks in the surrounding forest are possible.

Ecolodge de Kirindy   LODGE €€€
(☑ 033 16 303 78, 032 40 165 89; www.kirindy forest.com; dm/bungalow Ar40,000/120,000) Friendly Ecolodge de Kirindy has oh-so-basic, overpriced wooden bungalows with mosquito nets, uncomfortable mattresses and questionable plumbing. Camping is no longer possible due to the rather brazen fossa, but you still may find one sleeping under your bungalow...lullabies are courtesy of the forest residents. There's a small, slow on-site restaurant serving ample meals (mains Ar20,000) and cold beer.

Bring a good torch.

ℹ Getting There & Away

Kirindy is about 60km northeast of Morondava, signposted off the Belo-sur-Tsiribihina road. If you're travelling by taxi-brousse (Ar10,000, two hours), this is as far as they will take you.

SAKALAVA EROTICA

The western part of Madagascar has traditionally been the area with the strongest African influence. The language of the dark-skinned western peoples contains many words taken from mainland African languages. The dominant tribe in the area is the Sakalava, who venerate the relics not of their own ancestors, but of their ancient royal families. This belief, plus the use of spirit mediums to communicate with dead royalty, also has an African base (Bantu).

The Sakalava are perhaps best known for covering the tombs of their dead with elaborate, erotic carvings, often depicting oral sex or other acts considered *fady* (taboo) in life. Although Sakalava tombs were once visible throughout the entire western region, many were pillaged for their valuable carvings. Following this desecration, the Sakalava now understandably keep the location of those burial grounds still containing intact tombs top secret. It's important to respect their privacy. If you are lucky enough to see these erotic artworks, please take photos only.

The forest camp and office are 5km into the reserve – you'll have to walk to it if you don't have your own vehicle.

MORONDAVA REGION

Out here it's all about what lies beyond the end of the sealed road, and the area that surrounds the remote western town of Morondava is at once worth visiting in its own right and the starting point for so many adventures into the wild. Close to town, the Allée des Baobabs is the sunrise or sunset photo that defines a nation. Away to the south is the wonderfully sleepy Belo-sur-Mer and the rarely visited Parc National de Kirindy-Mitea – this combination of wild isolation and somnolent seaside living is a beguiling mix. It's from the Morondava region, too, that the gruelling three-day, off-road 4WD adventure (p120) that connects western Madagascar to Tuléar in the country's south begins and ends.

Morondava

Morondava is a terminally laid-back seaside town with sandy streets and gently decaying clapboard houses. There is not much to do or see in the town itself, and most people come here on their way to/from Parc National des Tsingy de Bemaraha or Réserve Forestière de Kirindy. It's also the starting point for the gruelling three-day, off-road 4WD adventure that connects western Madagascar to Tuléar in the country's south. Closer-to-town attractions include the iconic Allée des Baobabs (p119).

☞ Tours

Local agents can help you organise trips to Belo-sur-Mer, Parc National des Tsingy

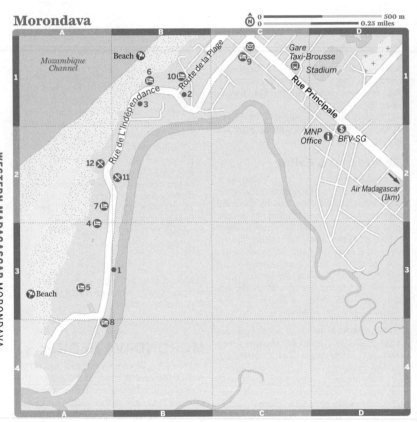

de Bemaraha and Réserve Forestière de Kirindy, as well as deep-sea fishing trips and sailing excursions.

François Vahiako ADVENTURE TOUR
(☏ 034 04 703 54, 032 04 703 54; visk_fr@yahoo.fr) Vahiako is the head of the Morondava Guides Association and the best person to go to for affordable vehicles (4WD with driver) for trips to the Tsingy de Bemaraha, Belo-sur-Mer, or pirogue trips anywhere along the coast. Your best bet for finding him is at Les Bougainvilliers.

Chez Maggie ADVENTURE TOUR
(☏ 032 47 326 70, 020 95 523 47; www.chezmaggie.com; Rue de l'Indépendance) Chez Maggie is an agent for **Remote River Expeditions** (☏ 032 47 326 70; www.remoterivers.com), which runs sustainable-travel-focused trips down the little-explored Mangoky, Mahavavy and Manambolo Rivers. The hotel also organises trips to local attractions and it has some cutesy bungalows.

Jean le Rasta ADVENTURE TOUR
(☏ 020 95 527 81, 032 04 931 60; L'Oasis, Rte de la Plage) Charismatic Jean le Rasta, or Rasta Jean, speaks English, is reliable and owns a 4WD. He runs a range of tours in the region and across southern Madagascar. Look for him at L'Oasis.

Loic Tours ADVENTURE TOUR
(☏ 032 20 009 89; Rue de l'Indépendance) A full portfolio of activities from 4WD rental to national park trips.

Baobab Cafe BOAT TOUR
(☏ 032 07 405 07; www.baobabcafe-hotel.net) For a boat transfer to Belo-sur-Mer (Ar2.1 million), or a day out fishing (Ar2.77 million), this hotel's 12-person motor launch is good, but only if there are enough of you to keep per-person costs down.

🛏 Sleeping

★Trecicogne GUESTHOUSE €
(☏ 034 51 636 66, 020 95 924 25; www.hotel trecicogne.com; Rue de l'Indépendance; d/tr from Ar43,000/60,000, d with air-con Ar60,000, d/tr without bathroom Ar27,500/38,500; ❄) This Italian-run guesthouse, right at the end of Nosy Kely peninsula, is a lovely place. The rooms all have polished wooden floors, whitewashed walls, blue curtains and are absolutely spotless. The cheaper ones share bathrooms and only have fans. The restaurant is on a verandah overlooking the

mangrove canal at the back; room 18 does likewise.

The hotel can organise trips to most regional attractions, including pirogue trips to Belo-sur-Mer.

Zoom Hôtel HOTEL €
(☏ 032 46 298 35; Rte de la Plage; r Ar35,000, without bathroom Ar24,000) If you can tear the receptionist away from his mobile phone, he might just rouse himself to show you the basic, clean rooms with fan but no mosquito nets (a concern in Morondava). No frills at all, but at this price did you really expect otherwise?

Les Bougainvilliers HOTEL €€
(☏ 034 50 797 75, 032 97 787 37; bol_nd@yahoo.fr; Rue de l'Indépendance; r without bathroom Ar30,000, bungalow with bathroom Ar50,000) The bungalows here, right on the beach, are starting to show their age, but at this price they remain among the best lower-midrange value in town. The cell-like cheap rooms are only for those who are really saving their ariary. There's an atmospheric restaurant.

Vezo Hotel HOTEL €€
(☏ 032 11 220 00; menage.a@gmail.com; Rue de l'Indépendance; r Ar60,000-120,000) This place could be so much more. The lovely large, whitewashed rooms have high ceilings and a vaguely colonial air, but are a little bare. The downstairs bar-restaurant has a whiff of urban cool, but service veers between absent and borderline civil. Still, we reckon the price is about right and you won't mind coming back here at day's end.

★Chez Maggie BUNGALOW €€€
(☏ 032 47 326 70, 020 95 523 47; www.chezmaggie.com; Rue de l'Indépendance; r Ar116,000-190,000; ❄☏) Whether you sleep in the atmospheric captain's cabin with its marine-themed decor, or the well-appointed bungalows or the superb mezzanine 'chalets', Chez Maggie is a delight and fabulous value. You could spend many hours reading in the garden, lounging by the pool or admiring the ocean.

★Hôtel Palissandre Côte Ouest LODGE €€€
(☏ 020 95 520 26, 033 15 349 74; www.palissandrecote-ouest.com; Rue de l'Indépendance; s/d/tr incl breakfast €135/170/195; P❄@☏☏) Morondava's premier address has supremely comfortable wood-floored bungalows away from the town's clamour. There are ample terraces from which to watch the setting sun, a stylish boutique, restaurant,

swimming pool and excursions can be arranged. We feel the food lets things down a little and the water's edge is a long way across the sand.

Renala Au Sable D'Or
BUNGALOW €€€

(☑ 032 04 976 88; Rue de l'Indépendance; d €40; ✻ @ 🕿) Renala's pretty rooms and clapboard bungalows, with their brightly coloured bedspreads and curtains, have a girly quality that won't be to everyone's taste, but they're excellent Morondava value.

🍴 Eating

★ Le Masoandro
EUROPEAN €€

(☑ 032 47 326 70; www.chezmaggie.com; Rue de l'Indépendance; mains Ar10,000-18,000; 🕙 7.30am-10pm) At Chez Maggies's thatch-roof restaurant, you can't fault the service, or the food. House specialities revolve around the grill: be it steak, jumbo shrimp or the catch of the day, everything comes out cooked to perfection. The bar has a wide selection of Scotch, whiskey and delicious homemade coconut rum.

Renala
EUROPEAN €€

(☑ 032 04 976 88; Rue de l'Indépendance; mains Ar13,000-18,000, 3-course menu Ar36,000; 🕙 noon-2.30pm & 6-10pm) In a tall wooden building on stilts overlooking Morondava's beach, Renala serves delicious Franco-Malagasy cuisine. Seafood is the name of the game: try the *camaron*, the crab or whatever fish is on offer that day. All side dishes are beautifully crafted, too, including delicious sautéed potatoes if you fancy a change from rice. Come early to get an upstairs table.

Les Bougainvilliers
MADAGASCAN €€

(Rue de l'Indépendance; mains Ar11,000-17,000, set menu Ar25,000; 🕙 7.30am-10pm) The Bougainvilliers has made a name for itself by serving excellent Malagasy dishes and therefore attracting travellers as well as locals.

You'll find traditional dishes such as *ravitoto, romazava de la mer* (a seafood stew) and coconut crab. The three-course *menu du jour* is excellent value. The breakfast (Ar7500) also includes very good croissants.

Le Kazaléa
INTERNATIONAL, MADAGASCAN €€

(☑ 032 43 877 43, 032 59 875 27; off Rue de l'In dépendance; mains from Ar12,000; 🕙 10am-11pm Tue-Sun) This quiet place, signposted from the main road and just back from the beach, serves up excellent steaks and brochettes, but its real speciality is foie gras with balsamic vinegar.

La Capannina
ITALIAN €€

(☑ 020 95 527 49; Rue de l'Indépendance; mains Ar11,500-17,000; 🕙 9am-11pm Wed-Mon) Run by an Italian-Malagasy couple, this place serves consistently yummy Italian food – think lots of pastas and different sauces, and pizzas straight out of the wood-fired oven. Other good choices include crab spaghetti or the seafood brochette. It's all served in a thatched dining room overlooking the river.

ℹ Information

MNP Office (☑ 020 95 921 28; www. parcs-madagascar.com; Ny Havana Bldg; 🕙 7.30am-noon & 2.30-6pm Mon-Fri) National park office.

ℹ Getting There & Around

AIR

Air Madagascar (☑ 032 07 222 14, 020 95 920 22; www.airmadagascar.com; Amahora) Flies several times weekly between Morondava and Antananarivo (€252, one hour) and once a week between Morondava and Tuléar (€252, one hour).

BOAT

Morondava is connected with the villages to the south, including Belo-sur-Mer, by pirogue and *boutre* (single-masted dhow used for cargo) –

TAXIS-BROUSSES FROM MORONDAVA

DESTINATION	COST (AR)	DURATION (HR)	FREQUENCY
Antananarivo	44,000	16	daily
Antsirabe	35,000	15	daily
Belo-sur-Mer	35,000	4	several times weekly Apr-Oct
Belo-sur-Tsiribihina	12,000	3	daily
Miandrivazo	24,000	6	daily
Tuléar	60,000	48	several times weekly Apr-Oct

ALLÉE DES BAOBABS

One of Madagascar's most recognisable images, this small stretch of the RN8 between Morondava and Belo-sur-Tsiribihina is flanked on both sides by majestic *Adansonia grandidieri* baobabs. Some of the trees here may be 1000 years old, with huge, gnarled branches fanning out at the top of their trunks – it's easy to see why they've been nicknamed 'roots of the sky'. The actual stretch of road is shorter than many visitors expect, but even this brief concentration in honour-guard formation is without parallel anywhere else in the country.

The best times to visit Allée des Baobabs are at sunset and sunrise, when the colours of the trees and surrounding earth deepen and the long shadows are most pronounced. That said, every vehicle driving down from Parc National des Tsingy de Bemaraha aims to get here around sunset and it can therefore be very busy, particularly during the park's high season (July to September).

With popularity has arisen a small-scale local industry, with a small information centre run by the local community, souvenir stalls, stands selling baobab fruits and even paid parking (Ar2000 per vehicle).

If you don't plan to see the Allée on your way to/from attractions north of Morondava (Tsingy, Tsiribihina or Réserve Forestière de Kirindy), a taxi from Morondava town costs around Ar50,000 return. All tour operators in Morondava can also help you out.

ask your guide to help with the arrangements and remember that safety is a concern on these boats, there are no facilities and you'll need to carry your own supplies.

TAXI
Taxis between town and the airport cost Ar15,000; taxis within town cost Ar2500.

Belo-sur-Mer

Few places will make you feel so far away from anywhere than Belo-sur-Mer. The village, sitting on the edge of a small lagoon, appears to have been swallowed up by the dunes and in the heat of the midday sun, time literally seems to stand still.

This is a regional shipbuilding centre and huge cargo vessels are still constructed on the beach just as they were four centuries ago. It's also one of the country's main salt-producing areas, with vast salt marshes a few kilometres inland.

◎ Sights & Activities

As the name of the village suggests, life in Belo is all about the sea, so spend a morning or an afternoon wandering along the beach. Watch fishermen prepare their gear or bring their catch, admire the craftsmanship of pirogue and *boutre* builders, or look for beautiful shells on the beach.

Nosy Andrahovo   SNORKELLING
Belo-sur-Mer's star attraction is this string of coral-fringed islands, some semi-submerged. The islands are uninhabited and offer fabulous snorkelling. All hotels in Belo can organise trips to Nosy Andrahovo with local pirogues. Allow around Ar18,000 per person for a half-day, or Ar40,000 for a full day with picnic lunch.

Menabe Plongée   DIVING
(☑ 033 09 436 32; www.menabelo.com; 1/2 dives €50/75; ⊘ Oct-Jun) The diving around Belo is excellent thanks to the proximity of a deep passage through the Mozambique Channel (humpback whales are not uncommon) and the coral reefs of Nosy Andrahovo. This dive centre, operated by the owners of Ecolodge du Menabe, operates largely outside the dry season, when transfers to Belo are done by boat from Morondava.

🛏 Sleeping & Eating

Dorohotel   BUNGALOW €
(☑ 033 01 863 54; r without bathroom from Ar20,000) These small bungalows, right in the centre of the village, sit so close to each other that they look like a row of terraced houses. They're generally clean, as are the toilets and shower rooms, and good value. There is a good atmosphere in the restaurant in the evening.

MORONDAVA TO TULÉAR

The road from Morondava to Tuléar cuts inland via Manja and rejoins the coast at Morombé. This road is only passable in the dry season (usually from April to October) and it takes three bone-shaking days – more if you linger along the towns of the northern reef. The *taxis-brousses* that do the route are 4WD *bâchés* (small, converted pick-up trucks) or *camions-brousses* – even more uncomfortable than normal *taxis-brousses*. Whichever way you travel, the reward is an adventure that'll be worth telling the grand-kids, with beautiful landscapes, remote villages, makeshift ferries and heavenly beaches.

Day 1: Morondava to Manja (six to eight hours) The tracks here are less rough than those further south, but there are five wide, shallow rivers to cross and numerous streams to ford. Your prize at the end is Manja, a lively provincial town with a pretty church. The only place to stay is **Manja Hotel** (☑ 033 08 567 43; Main St; r Ar50,000), a friendly spot with a surprisingly good restaurant, but basic rooms with shower water that barely trickles from the wall. Toilet seats seem optional. Try to avoid weekends when the downstairs bar bumps and grinds until the wee small hours. At around 2am, we gave up trying to sleep and went down to join them...

Day 2: Manja to Morombé or Andavadoaka (10 hours) This is a long, punish-ing day of off-road driving with a rickety vehicle ferry crossing at Bejoavy (per vehicle Ar10,000). You'll have to set off at first light and carry a picnic lunch.

Day 3: Morombé or Andavadoaka to Tuléar (eight to 10 hours) This splendid stretch of coastline hugs Madagascar's Great Reef, with the toughest section of the road a 30km, baobab-lined stretch of sand south of Andavadoaka. There are numerous gor-geous hotels and lots of good snorkelling and diving, so you may well want to split this into two days.

★**Ecolodge du Menabe** LODGE €€
(☑ 033 09 436 32; www.menabelo.com; d Ar75,000) Remote, scenic and peaceful, the Ecolodge is Belo's best accommodation op-tion. The nine bungalows are simple but comfortable and right on the beach. Meals (fixed menu Ar25,000) are served under a large canopy and the food is good, with plen-ty of fresh fish. The Ecolodge is right at the end of the peninsula.

Tsara Belo BUNGALOW €€
(☑ 033 02 911 64; www.tsara-belo.com; r €23-39, d bungalow €26; ⊗ Mar-Dec) Simple thatch bun-galows, just back from the water's edge, are a good choice and will be even better once the lemon-and-baobab garden has time to mature. The bungalows sleep three to five people and are great for families.

Corail BUNGALOW €€
(☑ 033 20 326 87; r Ar65,000) A handful of hap-hazard but coquettish bungalows, the Corail is a family-run outfit right by the beach just south of town. There are some nice touches throughout, such as the hammocks on the porch, open-roof (cold-water) showers and raffia-decorated mirrors, and the home-cooked food is delicious.

ⓘ Information

There are no banking facilities in Belo – the nearest bank is in Morondava – nor is there electricity, apart from that generated by the hotels.

ⓘ Getting There & Away

BOAT
From November to May, the only way to access Belo-sur-Mer is by sea. Local pirogues ply the route, but journey times are entirely dependent on winds. It's much faster (2½ hours), but also

MASONJOANY

In many areas of western and northern Madagascar, you will see women with their faces painted white. This facial mask, known as *masonjoany,* is sup-posed to protect skin from the sun, make it softer and suppler and remove blemishes. It's applied during the day and usually removed at night. *Mason-joany* is made by grinding a branch from a tree of the same name against a stone with a small amount of water to form a paste.

more expensive, to arrange a motor boat transfer with one of the tour operators in Morondava or Ecolodge du Menabe in Belo.

CAR

Access to Belo-sur-Mer by road is only possible by 4WD from May to November. There are irregular *taxis-brousses* (Ar30,000, four hours) between Belo-sur-Mer and Morondava in 4WD *bâchés* (small, converted pick-ups).

Parc National de Kirindy-Mitea

Not to be confused with the Réserve Forestière de Kirindy, the deliciously remote 722-sq-km **Parc National de Kirindy-Mitea** (www.parcs-madagascar.com; adult/child per day Ar45,000/25,000, guide per circuit Ar15,000), which surrounds Belo-sur-Mer, is one of Madagascar's newest parks and it's well worth the effort to get here. It's isolated and beautiful, with little infrastructure, and for that reason, seldom visited. What this means for visitors is that those making the effort to get here will be rewarded with a more personal experience in an environment rarely disturbed by visitors. Out here it's all about sand dunes, mangroves and untouched coastline, with some fine wildlife viewing thrown in.

🏃 Activities

The main draw at Kirindy-Mitea is the birdlife – 58 recorded species in total, 18 of which are endemic to the region – although there are lemurs and reptiles, too. Of the park's nine lemur species, only three are easily seen by day: Verreaux's sifaka, the red-fronted brown lemur and the ring-tailed lemur. The nocturnal species are Madame Berthe's mouse lemur (the world's smallest primate), fork-marked lemur, grey mouse lemur, Coquerel's dwarf lemur, fat-tailed dwarf lemur and red-tailed sportive lemur. Also present, if rarely seen, is the fossa.

There are three hiking circuits through the park:

🛈 PARC NATIONAL DE KIRINDY-MITEA

Best time to visit May to November.

Key highlight Brackish lakes and sand dunes.

Wildlife Birdlife, including flamingos.

Habitat Dry deciduous forest.

Gateway town Belo-sur-Mer.

Transport options By boat year-round; by 4WD from May to October.

Things you should know It is easier to arrange a visit to the park from Morondava, where the MNP office has admin staff. In Belo, ask at Dorohotel.

➡ **Circuit Agnolignoly** (2km, one hour) Easy walk through mangroves and coastal estuaries with an emphasis on waterbirds.

➡ **Circuit Ambondro-Sirave** (3km, two hours) With sand dunes, spiny forest, baobabs, the beach and plenty of waterbirds, this is our pick if you only have time for one walk.

➡ **Circuit Maetsakaloe** (4km, two hours) Baobabs, birds, dry forest and lemurs are the highlights on this relatively new walk.

There is also the possibility of doing a pirogue trip (Ar35,000) along the estuary and the mangrove; the park staff in Morondava can help you arrange it.

🛈 Information

MNP Office (☑ 020 95 921 28; www.parcs-madagascar.com; Ny Havana Bldg, Morondava; ⊙7.30am–noon & 2.30–6pm Mon-Fri)

🛈 Getting There & Away

You'll need your own transport to access Kirindy-Mitea. The park can be reached by road between May and October or November (it's just off the rough Morondava–Belo-sur-Mer road). Access is by boat, which must be arranged with the park, for the rest of the year.

Northern Madagascar

Why Go?

If you're unable to decide between a discovery trip and a 'lace up your boots and forge a new trail' kind of trip, you'll love travel in northern Madagascar. Activity junkies will be spoilt for choice with everything from diving to kitesurfing, while all travellers will revel in the region's diverse landscapes.

The area around Nosy Be is Madagascar's premier beach destination, with more sea-based activities than you'll have time to try, excellent seafood and idyllic scenery. It couldn't be more different from the mainland, where arid plains are fringed with lush ylang-ylang plantations, and two top parks feature both strange geological formations and rainforest. As for the Sava region, those who make it to this isolated part of the country will be rewarded with vanilla-scented air and world-class mountain hiking.

The region also hosts Madagascar's flagship cultural events, the Donia and Zegny'Zo – unique chances to discover Malagasy artists.

Best Places to Eat

➡ La Table d'Alexandre (p134)
➡ La Bodega (p143)
➡ Les Bungalows d'Ambonara (p129)
➡ Chez Maman (p132)

Best Places to Stay

➡ Le Jardin Exotique (p142)
➡ Camp Two, Parc National de Marojejy (p155)
➡ Le Grand Bleu (p133)
➡ 293 On Komba (p136)

When to Go
Hell-Ville

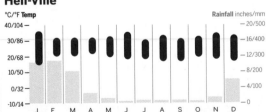

May & Jun Festivals bring together artists from across Madagascar and the Indian Ocean.

Jul–Sep Humpback whales make their annual visit to Madagascar and can be seen around Nosy Be.

May–Nov Guaranteed access to the Tsingy Rouges and the western part of Réserve Spéciale Ankarana.

NOSY BE

Despite being Madagascar's number-one beach destination, the island of Nosy Be remains relatively low-key. It's the most expensive destination in Madagascar, and rooms can cost twice as much here as on the mainland. Still, compared to Europe, prices are competitive (except for the most exclusive resorts), and many visitors find the lack of major development and *mora mora* (literally, slowly slowly) lifestyle worth the extra euros.

The climate is sunny year-round, and Nosy Be is paradise for water-based activities. Diving is the island's top draw, and there is plenty of swimming, snorkelling and sailing for those keen to stay close to the surface.

Once you've had enough of seascapes, head for the rolling landscapes of the little-explored hinterland: as well as the brilliant Réserve Naturelle Intégrale de Lokobe, there are cocoa, ylang-ylang and vanilla plantations, crater lakes and waterfalls, and miles of dirt tracks accessible only by foot or quad bike.

Despite all these assets, Nosy Be has a history as the capital of sex tourism. It's true that Ambatoloaka is seedy in places but it is by no means representative of the whole island, and definitely not of the surrounding islands, which are all tiny, remote and heavenly. It's also worth knowing that tourism operators and the authorities in Nosy Be have come down hard on prostitution; perpetrators face heavy prison sentences.

History

Nosy Be's first inhabitants are believed to have been 15th-century Swahili and Indian traders. Later, the island served as a magnet for refugees, merchants and settlers of all descriptions.

In 1839 the Sakalava queen Tsiomeko fled to Nosy Be and turned to the French for help in resisting her Merina enemies. In 1841 the Sakalava ceded both Nosy Be and neighbouring Nosy Komba to France.

In recent years, with increasing tourism development and local environmental pressures, deforestation has become a problem on the island, as has destruction and damage of offshore coral reefs.

🏃 Activities

Nosy Be has a plethora of activities. Most are sea-based (diving, snorkelling, fishing, day trips to islands etc), but operators also offer activities exploring the island's beautiful hinterland.

Diving

Nosy Be and the surrounding islands are home to a rich diversity of marine life and offer world-class diving. Boxfish, surgeonfish, triggerfish, damselfish, clownfish, yellowfin, barracuda, eagle rays, manta rays and humpback whales (July to September) can all be spotted. Around Nosy Sakatia you're likely to see clownfish, barracuda, turtles, and perhaps dolphins and whale sharks.

On average, visibility on dives is about 15m year-round – much more on good days. The best months are April to December. July and August can be windy, especially to the north around Nosy Mitsio. The best months for seeing whale sharks are October and November, while manta rays are more prevalent from April to June and October to November.

ℹ️ NOSY BE ON A BUDGET

Nosy Be is expensive compared to the rest of Madagascar. Accommodation is particularly pricey, with most hotels falling squarely in the top-end category. There are, however, a number of ways to visit Nosy Be on a budget and still enjoy the very best of the island.

Accommodation Look carefully and you'll spot a few midrange options in Hell-Ville and Ambatoloaka, and even one on Nosy Komba.

Eating Food is generally good value in Madagascar, and Nosy Be has a couple of excellent budget eating options. The market in Hell-Ville is a good place to pick up picnic supplies.

Transport Use shared taxis or tuk-tuks between Hell-Ville and Ambatoloaka. For touring the rest of the island, rent a motorbike rather than a car: they're super cheap (Ar20,000 per day plus about Ar3000 of petrol for a day's riding) and ideal for exploring Nosy Be.

Northern Madagascar Highlights

1 Locate the silky *sifaka* in **Parc National de Marojejy** (p155)

2 Assault your senses with a visit to the **Millot Plantations** (p137), where cocoa and spices are grown

3 Sail to some of the small **islands around Nosy Be** (p135)

4 Watch black lemurs, boa constrictors, owls and more in Nosy Be's stunning **Réserve Naturelle Intégrale de Lokobe** (p133)

5 Marvel at the geological work of art that is **Tsingy Rouges** (p152)

6 Hike around **Les Trois Baies** (p146)

7 Snorkel off the tiny island of **Nosy Tanikely** (p136)

8 Take a self-guided walk through the history-filled streets of **Diego Suarez** (p140)

Mozambique Channel

Nosy Lava

Bevoaka

Marimbe

Grande Mitsio

Androvorony

Nosy Mitsio Archipelago

Nosy Fanihy

Islands Around Nosy Be 3

Andilana

Befetika

Nosy Sakatia

Nosy Faly

Djamandjary

Nosy Be

Ambondrona

Réserve Naturelle

Ambatoloaka

Intégrale de Lokobe

Baie des Russes

Hell-Ville

Nosy Komba

RNE

Nosy Iranja Be

7

Ankify

Maherivara

Nosy Tanikely

Anjanojano

2

Nosy Iranja Kely

Ampasindava Peninsula

Millot Plantations

Ambanja

Maevatanana

Nosy Radama

Maromandia

Befotaka

Nosy Be & Surrounding Islands

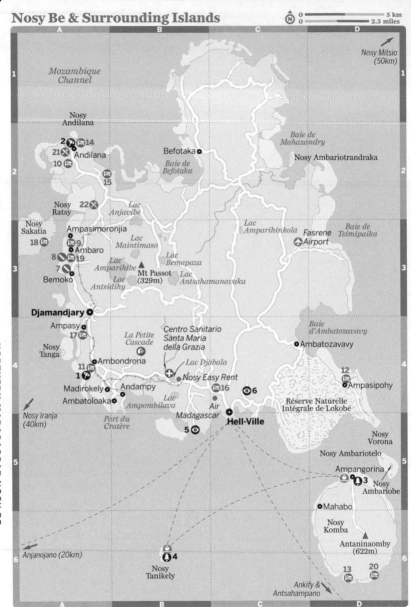

Most operators run daily morning trips long enough for two dives, with boats leaving around 8am and getting back in time for lunch. Prices are about €50 for a *baptême* (first dive), €38/70 for one/two dives, and €50 for a night dive. Many operators also run all-inclusive, catamaran sailing trips (from two to five days) to surrounding archipelagos such as Nosy Iranja, Nosy Mitsio and Nosy Radama, with two dives a day (€400 to €850, depending on the num-

Nosy Be & Surrounding Islands

ber of people on the boat, the length of the trip and the number of dives).

Courses are conducted in French or English, with many staff also speaking Italian. A PADI course costs around €400; it's best to book certification courses in advance.

Nosy Be now boasts a recompression chamber at the new hospital, **Centro Sanitario Santa Maria della Grazia** (Map p126; ✆ 034 86 925 55; Rte de l'Ouest; ⊗ 24hr).

Océane's Dream   DIVING
(✆ 032 07 127 82; www.oceanesdream.com; Ambatoloaka) One of the most well-established and recommended operators on the island, Océane's Dream offers single and introductory dives along with diving cruises to neighbouring islands. A minimum of two people (previous certification required) is needed. It also does CMAS and PADI dive courses.

Madaplouf   DIVING
(Map p126; ✆ 033 14 248 33; www.divingin madagascar.com; Bemoko) Madaplouf runs PADI and CMAS courses in Spanish, German and Italian, as well as in French and English. It also offers excursions to various other islands.

Tropical Diving   DIVING
(✆ 032 49 462 51; www.tropical-diving.com; Hôtel Coco Plage, Ambatoloaka) Offers a variety of diving excursions to nearby islands, including a one-day trip to Nosy Iranja.

Forever Dive   DIVING
(✆ 032 84 913 81; www.foreverdive.com; Madirokely) Forever Dive is run by the friendly Rolland and Sylvia, who've been living in Nosy Be since 1999. They speak French,

English and Italian. It delivers NAUI courses as well as four- to six-day diving cruises to Nosy Mitsio and Nosy Radama.

Sakalav' Diving   DIVING
(Map p126; www.sakalav-diving.com; Bemoko) Sakalav' Diving is operated by Alain and Natalie, who speak French, English and German. They offer diving cruises of three to eight days to surrounding islands, as well as PADI courses, including for children aged eight and over.

Snorkelling
Snorkelling is best at Nosy Tanikely, Nosy Mitsio and Nosy Sakatia. All tour operators on Nosy Be run trips to Nosy Tanikely, generally combined with a visit to Nosy Komba.

Fishing
The best time for fishing is March to June and October to December. Fishing excursions aren't cheap – expect to pay at least €480 per day per boat, including equipment, for up to four people. The hotel Sakatia Lodge (p136) specialises in sportfishing.

Quad Biking
Quad bikes are a great way to explore Nosy Be. Popular routes include a circuit around the crater lakes, remote beaches in the north, and cocoa plantations to the south. Some hotels also have their own quads and offer excursions to their guests.

Nosy Bikes Center   DRIVING TOUR
(✆ 032 07 761 24; www.mada-services.com; Ambatoloaka) This outfit has a wide range of quad bikes to hire from €28 to €47 per day. Guides are available, too, at €40 per day.

☞ Tours

Nosy Be is home to dozens of tour companies, some specialising in sailing trips exploring the surrounding islands, others providing day trips of all kinds on and around the islands, including Nosy Be, Komba and Tanikely (Ar90,000), Lokobe (Ar95,000), Nosy Sakatia (Ar120,000) and Nosy Iranja (Ar130,000).

MadaVoile   BOAT TOUR
(☑020 86 065 55; www.madavoile.com; Ambatoloaka) One of the best sailing operators on Nosy Be, with a superb fleet of sailing boats, offering highly recommended cruises – from day trips to Nosy Sakatia or Nosy Komba to five-day trips to Nosy Mitsio or Nosy Radama including diving and fishing. Find it at the top of the hill in Ambatoloaka, opposite Le Coucher du Soleil bungalows.

Nosy Be Original   TOUR
(Map p126; ☑032 05 524 90; www.nosybe-original.com; Bemoko) A tip-top operator organising a range of excursions on and around Nosy Be, including lovely sailing trips on an 18m catamaran, and horse riding. It is also one of the few organisations to run whale-watching trips during the humpback whale migration (July to September). Also has a branch at Vanila Hôtel, Ambaro.

Evasion Sans Frontière   TOUR
(☑032 11 005 96; www.mada-evasion.com; Hell-Ville) This tour operator, one of the biggest in Madagascar, specialises in the north; it's a well-oiled machine, and their Diego–Nosy Be circuits take in all the highlights. They also organise excursions on Nosy Be, including a day trip around the island and excursions to Lokobe.

❶ Getting There & Away

Be aware that offers of 'direct' transfer from Nosy Be to Diego Suarez are often a scam. Resist all offers on Nosy Be, take the boat to Ankify (Ar12,000) and then choose your *taxi-brousse* (Ar14,000) as you would anywhere (the one in best condition and/or the fullest).

AIR
Air Austral (Map p130; ☑020 86 612 32; www.air-austral.com; Blvd de l'Indépendance, Hell-Ville) Flies direct to Réunion (two hours) and Mayotte (45 minutes).

Air Madagascar (Map p126; ☑020 86 613 60; www.airmadagascar.com; Route de l'Ouest, Hell-Ville) Flies daily to/from Antananarivo (one hour, €264) and weekly to Diego Suarez (25 minutes, €178).

BOAT
➡ Sailing yachts regularly come into Nosy Be, and many are prepared to take passengers. Their principal destinations are Mayotte, Mozambique and South Africa.

➡ Small speedboats shuttle between the mainland port of Ankify and Hell-Ville on Nosy Be (Ar12,000, 40 minutes, 5.30am to 4pm). They work like *taxis-brousses* and leave when full. Trade winds pick up in the afternoon, so the crossing is smoother, and therefore more popular, in the morning – you'll never have to wait long for your boat to depart. Life jackets are provided.

➡ If you're travelling with a vehicle, ferries sail between Ankify and Hell-Ville in Nosy Be (from Ar80,000, two hours, 6am to 4pm).

❶ Getting Around

Nosy Be's main road, which goes all the way around the island and takes in the airport, Hell-Ville, Ambatoloaka, the west coast and Andilana, is sealed but not in good condition.

YLANG-YLANG

The low, gnarled ylang-ylang (e-lang-e-lang) tree is seen in plantations all over Nosy Be. Its scented green or yellow flowers are distilled to make essential oil for perfume. The trees are pruned into low, rather grotesque shapes to make harvesting easier.

Distillation at the large **ylang-ylang distillery** (Map p126; admission Ar15,000; ⊙8am-3.30pm Mon-Fri, 7.30am-2.30pm Sat) at Lemuria Land takes place on Monday, Wednesday and Friday year-round, or daily in the rainy season (January to the end of March). The whole process of turning these somewhat insignificant flowers into a valuable essential oil is explained.

The distillery is also home to a small zoo, including a large lemur park. It's a shame to see these animals in cages or confined to tiny islands (lemurs can't swim) when they can be viewed in their natural environment just a few kilometres away at Lokobe.

To reach the distillery head east from Hell-Ville along the Route de Marodokana for 3km. All taxi drivers know where the place is (Ar50,000 for the return trip, including an hour waiting time).

TO/FROM THE AIRPORT

Nosy Be's Fasrene Airport (Map p126) is on the island's east side, about 12km from Hell-Ville. A taxi fare from the airport to Hell-Ville is around Ar15,000. It is about Ar40,000 to Ambatoloaka or Andilana.

BOAT

For the ultimate freedom to explore Nosy Be's shores and the surrounding islands, you can charter one of the speedboats doing the Hell-Ville–Ankify transfer for around Ar250,000 a day.

CAR & MOTORCYCLE

The best way to get around Nosy Be is by motorcycle (helmets are compulsory): roads are not bad, traffic is light, distances are short and the weather is lovely – perfect conditions to ditch the car, which rules on the mainland. If you'd rather have a vehicle, a sedan (saloon) car is perfectly adequate.

Location Jeunesse (☑ 032 59 055 26; Ambatoloaka; ⊙7am-6pm) Rents out motorbikes (Ar20,000) and mountain bikes (Ar15,000).

Nosy Easy Rent (Map p126; ☑ 033 11 611 00; www.nosyeasyrent.com; Route de l'Ouest) Rents Dacia Logan/Mitsubishi/Pajero vehicles for €30/50/70 per day, with a 150km mileage, and motorbikes from €20 per day. It's 3km from Hell-Ville in the direction of Ambatoloaka.

TAXI

➡ Collective taxis (Ar2000) travel between Hell-Ville and Ambatoloaka (15 minutes) and between Hell-Ville and Djamandjary (25 minutes), from 6am until 7pm. Pick them up near the market in Hell-Ville, and flag them down on the main road of Ambatoloaka as they cruise (and beep) for customers.

➡ A chartered taxi between Hell-Ville and Ambatoloaka costs Ar25,000, between Hell-Ville and Andilana Ar30,000. From Hell-Ville's centre to the jetty costs Ar2000.

➡ Tuk-tuks whizz around the towns of Hell-Ville and Ambatoloaka and are a cheap alternative to taxis. They cost Ar500 during the day, and Ar1000 after 8pm.

Hell-Ville (Andoany)

Despite the off-putting moniker (named for Admiral de Hell, a French governor of Réunion), Nosy Be's main town is anything but hellish. Rather, it's an upbeat, comparatively smart place where frangipani and bougainvillea frame crumbling ruins of old colonial buildings, pavement cafes bustle with tourists and expats sip strong espresso.

🛏 Sleeping

Hôtel Plantation   HOTEL €€
(Map p130; ☑032 07 934 45; plantation_b@yahoo.fr; Rue Fortin, Hell-Ville; r Ar55,000-75,000; ❄ 🛜 🏊) Housed in an old colonial mansion, this is a charming little place with a small pool. Ask to see a few rooms before you settle as the cheaper ones can be a little dark, while the nicest have parquet floors and sea-facing balconies. The restaurant serves reasonable food and is equipped with wi-fi.

Hôtel Belle Vue   HOTEL €€
(Map p130; ☑020 86 613 84; bellevuehotel-nosybe@yahoo.fr; Rue R Tsiomeko; d Ar50,000, without bathroom Ar27,000; ❄ 🛜) The Belle Vue is an excellent budget option right in the centre of Hell-Ville. Cheaper rooms have fans and share a toilet, but all are immaculate and cheerful. The ones at the back of the building are the best – brighter, airier and with nice views. However, you might not feel comfortable with the somewhat seedy atmosphere.

★**Les Bungalows
d'Ambonara**   GUESTHOUSE €€€
(Map p126; ☑020 86 613 67; www.nosy-be holidays.com; off Route de l'Ouest, Hell-Ville; bungalow Ar85,000; ❄ 🛜 🏊) Bungalows here nestle in a luxuriant garden and are beautifully decorated using local materials. Owner Jean-Michel makes his own *rhum arrangé* (rum with fruit) and the restaurant is excellent (mains from Ar16,000). To find it, head out in the direction of Ambatoloaka; it is signposted just before the Air Madagascar office. Take a tuk tuk to go into Hell-Ville or to the beach.

Hell-Ville (Andoany)

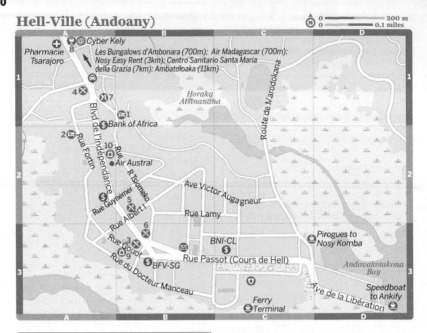

Hell-Ville (Andoany)

⊕ Sleeping
1 Hôtel Belle Vue	B1
2 Hôtel Plantation	A2

⊗ Eating
3 Le Papillon	B3
4 Marché de Hell-Ville	A1
5 Nandipo	B2
6 Oasis Café	B3
7 Restaurant Manava	A1

⊖ Drinking & Nightlife
8 Bar Ankoay	A1

⊕ Shopping
9 Le Jardin des Sens	B3
10 Société de Rhum Arrangé	A2

🍴 Eating & Drinking

Marché de Hell-Ville　　　　　MARKET €
(Map p130; Place du Maré; ⊙6am-5pm) Hell-Ville's market is a good place to pick up fruit and vegetables for picnics, as well as spices.

Restaurant Manava　　　MADAGASCAN €€
(Map p130; Rue R Tsiomeko; mains from Ar15,000; 🕾) On the top floor, Restaurant Manava is an unexpected gem. The fare is simple but incredibly tasty, including grilled meat or fish with seasonal vegetables, and rice or chips. The balcony terrace is an atmospheric place to people-watch, and there is always a good atmosphere at the bar, with people playing pool, and live music several times a week.

At ground level is the Makoumbe Disco, which doesn't get started until late.

★ Le Papillon　　　　　　　ITALIAN €€€
(Map p130; 🖀020 86 610 08; Blvd de l'Independance; mains Ar16,000-25,000; ⊙7am-3pm) Highly recommended by locals, Le Papillon is *the* place to eat (and be seen) in town. It is set in a beautiful, old colonial house with a verandah in the heart of Hell-Ville. The Italian owner changes the menu according to the season and the fresh pasta dishes are particularly good. Breakfast is also served.

Nandipo　　　　　　　　　　　PIZZA €€€
(Map p130; Rue Albert 1; mains Ar16,000-20,000; ⊙breakfast, lunch & dinner; 🕾) This very cool place is an expats' favourite, even though it's now looking a bit frayed at the edges. It serves excellent wood-oven pizzas and has friendly staff, a great selection of drinks and the best ambience in town. ✦

Oasis Café CAFE €€€
(Map p130; Blvd de l'Indépendance; mains
Ar17,000; ⊗8am-9pm; 🐾) Oasis' pavement
seating is prime people-watching territory. The cafe serves food all day, but it does
breakfast best, with excellent baguettes,
good pastries and proper coffee, including
espresso. It's very quiet in the evenings.

Bar Ankoay BAR
(Map p130; Galerie Ankoay, Blvd du Général de
Gaulle) Spilling onto the street, the Ankoay
(ank-way) is Hell-Ville's most popular bar.
Inside a shopping gallery, it's done up like
the interior of a ship with lots of wood. It's
hard to spot its name from the street, but
you can't miss the early evening crowds
and the large thatched building.

🛍 Shopping

Le Jardin des Sens BEAUTY
(Map p130; 📱034 02 223 23; Villa Locullus, 37 La
Batterie; ⊗10am-5pm Mon-Sat) Local essential
oils of ylang-ylang, black pepper, *katrafay*
and more scent the air here, where you can
also stock up on honey, spices, soaps and
skin products. Set in a beautiful old house,
Le Jardin des Sens has knowledgeable staff
who offer massage (one hour Ar45,000) and
reflexology (half hour Ar30,000).

Société de Rhum Arrangé DRINK
(Map p130; Blvd de l'Indépendance; ⊗8am-6pm
Mon-Sat) If you'd like to take a taste of Madagascar home with you, why not plump for
a bottle of *rhum arrangé*? There are more
than 20 flavours to choose from at this
little place, from vanilla to cinnamon, liq-
uorice to coconut. The 180ml plastic bottles
(Ar10,000) make perfect presents.

ℹ Information

Bank of Africa (BOA; Map p130; Blvd de
l'Indépendance) ATM.
BFV-SG (Map p130; Rue Gouot) ATM (Visa);
changes travellers cheques; Western Union.
BNI-CL (Map p130; Rue Passot) ATM (Visa and
MasterCard).
Cyber Kely (Map p130; Galerie Ankoay, Blvd
du Général de Gaulle, Hell-Ville; 30min/2hr
Ar1500/5000; ⊗7am-10pm; 🐾) Wi-fi.
Pharmacie Tsarajoro (Map p130; Blvd du
Général de Gaulle) Well-stocked pharmacy.
Post Office (Map p130; cnr Blvd de l'In-
dépendance & Rue Passot)

Ambatoloaka

Nosy Be's southernmost beach is one of the
island's most touristy, although not its best.
Its popularity with foreign men of a certain
age in search of young Malagasy love is what
gave Nosy Be a bad name. Many travellers
will feel uneasy about the sleazy atmosphere, particularly in bars and restaurants.
That said, Ambatoloaka can be fun: the
nightlife is good by Madagascar standards,
and the village comes into its own on Sundays when locals come en masse to enjoy a
day at the beach. A number of hotels have
taken a very firm stand against sex tourism
and their efforts deserve to be supported.

Ambatoloaka is a snazzy small town,
stretched along one long street, with most
of the hotels, bars and restaurants clustered
at the beach end. The beach itself, which
becomes Madirokely at its northern end, is
pretty, but the constant flow of touts, diving
boats coming in and out, and noise from
seafront establishments, means it's not that
relaxing; head north if that's what you're
after.

🛏 Sleeping

Accommodation is often full, so it's best to
reserve in advance. Lots of places quote in
euros.

Le Coucher du Soleil BUNGALOW €€
(📱032 02 087 21; www.coucherdusoleil-nosybe.
com; bungalow Ar55,000-75,000; 🐾) This is the
best budget option in Ambatoloaka. The
bungalows come with or without running
water; those without actually have more
charm than the more modern ones, if you
don't mind bucket showers. There are also
three very-well-appointed apartments (€70
for four people). It's signposted from the
main street in Ambatoloaka, and there's a
shortcut down to the beach.

Coco Plage HOTEL €€
(📱032 67 385 88; www.cocoplage-nosybe.com;
bungalow sea-facing Ar80,000-100,000, in garden
Ar60,000; ✳🐾) If you're interested in diving,
this is a good choice; the long-established
Tropical Diving (p127) is based here. There
are 12 rooms right on the beach and another
six facing a pretty garden at the back. All are
well appointed (though without mosquito
nets), and the sea breezes provide natural
air-con at night.

★ **Hôtel Gérard et Francine** GUESTHOUSE €€€
(☎032 07 127 93; www.gerard-et-francine.com; d €55; ☜) ✐ A beautifully decorated family guesthouse with wooden floors and a verandah overlooking the beach. The rooms come in all shapes and sizes – some are in the main house and some in the garden. The hotel uses solar power, and the owners are very involved in environmental initiatives in Nosy Be. They also lobby actively against sex tourism. Rates include breakfast.

Hôtel Benjamin BUNGALOW €€
(☎032 02 408 13; www.hotelbenjamin-nosy-be.com; bungalow €33; ☜) ✐ Situated in a beautiful garden and quiet location back from the main road, this is a pretty good deal for Nosy Be. The bungalows are furnished simply, and each comes with a petite verandah. Some have hammocks.

L'Heure Bleue BOUTIQUE HOTEL €€€
(☎020 86 060 20; www.heurebleue.com; Madirokely; bungalow €100; ❄☜☜) On a hill overlooking the beach of Madirokely, this gorgeous hotel has a terrace with great views and a sensational saltwater pool just above the sea. The bungalows are on the small side, but have giant sliding-glass doors, which open on to balconies with distant ocean views and armchairs for private sunbathing.

✖ Eating

★ **Chez Maman** MADAGASCAN €
(mains Ar5000-6000) For a true Madagascan eating experience, try Chez Maman, located on Ambatoloaka's main street. Mama buys her ingredients at Hell-Ville's market every morning, and everything she cooks is fresh, tasty and incredibly cheap. Try some of the local staples such as *romazava* (beef and vegetable stew) or *poulet sauce* (chicken in tomato sauce).

Baobab Kafé Restaurant ASIAN €€€
(mains Ar16,000-20,000; ☜) This popular place puts an Asian twist on the usual fare, offering plenty of seafood (try the tempura prawns), noodles and rice dishes. It's upstairs on a breezy verandah, while there are take-outs on offer downstairs.

Chez Teresa ITALIAN €€€
(mains Ar15,000-35,000; ☺Wed-Mon; ☝) Run by the ebullient Teresa, this Italian restaurant is an eye-catching place, with its candy-colour

decor and fairy lights. The menu features plenty of pizza and pastas that make good use of the plentiful supply of seafood, and there are vegetarian options, too. The house limoncello is a delight.

🍷 Drinking & Nightlife

Le Taxi-Be BAR
(☺Wed-Mon) This lively bar is very popular with local *vazaha* (foreigners) and young Malagasy women. For all that, it's not a creepy place. There's live music every night and a cut-out Renault 4L decorating the stage.

Djembe Disco CLUB
(admission Ar5000; ☺from noon Mon, Wed & Sat) This is Nosy Be's favourite nightclub, located at the end of the village on the road leading to Madirokely. It's the place to be seen in the evenings – popular with local couples, expats and foreign men on the prowl. Besides having a dance floor, Djembe regularly hosts live music events. There are also pool tables.

La Sirène Disco CLUB
(admission Ar5000; ☺from noon Tue, Thu, Fri & Sun) La Sirène draws the crowds on the nights of the week when Ambatoloaka's other disco, Djembe Disco, is closed.

ℹ️ Information

BNI-CA ATM accepting MasterCard and Visa.
Pharmacie Nourdine (☺8am-noon & 2-6pm Mon-Sat)

> **WORTH A TRIP**
>
> ### SACRED BANYAN TREE
>
> On the coast beyond the tiny village of Mahatsinjo, there's an enormous **Sacred Banyan Tree** (Map p126; Mahatsinjo Village) planted by the Queen of the Sakalava tribe in 1836. Nowadays, the Queen of Nosy Be makes an annual pilgrimage to sacrifice a zebu and gain benediction. Shoes must be removed before approaching the tree, and if you have bare legs, a wrap will be provided.
>
> The tree is signposted from the Route de l'Ouest just north of Hell-Ville, and easily reached by quad- or motorbike. The guide charges Ar7000.
>
> Black lemurs play in the branches, making great photo opportunities.

RÉSERVE NATURELLE INTÉGRALE DE LOKOBE

The **Réserve Naturelle Intégrale de Lokobe** (www.parcs-madagascar.com; entry permits per day Ar55,000) protects most of Nosy Be's remaining endemic vegetation. The reserve is home to the black lemur (the male is dark brown, almost black, while the female is a lovely chestnut colour with white tufts around her ears and cheeks) and several other lemur species. You're also likely to spot boa constrictors, owls, chameleons and many wonderful plants, from ylang-ylang trees to vanilla, orchids, travellers' palms and more.

You will need a guide to visit Lokobe (only the periphery of the reserve is actually accessible to visitors). The best guide is **Jean Robert** (☑ 032 02 513 85; jean.robert lokobeapphy@yahoo.fr). As well as knowing the reserve intimately and being a mine of information on all things fauna and flora, Jean is a real character, who will have you singing a Malagasy version of 'Old McDonald's Farm' before you set off but then insist on silence during the visit to minimise disruption to Lokobe's wildlife (he'll just whisper the names of the animals as you go). Jean organises lovely day trips to Lokobe that cost Ar90,000 per person. They include taxi between your hotel and Ambatozavavy, transfer in pirogue from Ambatozavavy to Ampasipohy (the starting point for walks), a two-hour walk in the forest, lunch, drinks and admission fees to the reserve. Most tour operators in Nosy Be organise similar packages, often through Jean Robert.

If you would like to spend the night in Lokobe, **Hotel Paradisa Kely** (Map p126; ☑ 032 59 700 36; www.madagascar-paradisakely.com; Ampasipohy; d €55; ☜☒) is an excellent option in the tiny village of Ampasipohy.

Nosy Be's West Coast

With its lovely beaches and postcard sunset views, it's no surprise most hotels on Nosy Be have decided to set up shop on this part of the island. It stretches from Madirokely to Andilana in the north. The further north you go, the more isolated and quieter it gets, so you'll need to eat where you sleep (or take a taxi to go out) if you stay up there. If you yearn for company, you'll be happier in Ambatoloaka or Hell-Ville.

Beaches

Andilana   BEACH
(Map p126) Far and away Nosy Be's best beach, Andilana, at the island's northwest tip, is a long stretch of pearly white sand, with water that's true turquoise and clear as gin. It's ideal for swimming and chilling for an afternoon, with gorgeous sunsets.

Andilana ignites on Sundays, when French expats and Malagasy from around Nosy Be come for a lazy day in the sun. Families lay out picnics on a shaded bit of sand, tuck into a crate of beers, turn on their stereo, and swim and dance until the sun goes down.

Ambondrona   BEACH
(Map p126) On a small bay just north of Madirokely, Ambondrona is more tranquil than its southern neighbours, with lovely views of the mainland hills across the sea.

🛏 Sleeping

Accommodation on this bit of the coast is almost exclusively top end.

⭐ **Le Grand Bleu**   GUESTHOUSE €€€
(Map p126; ☑ 032 02 194 84; www.legrandbleu nosybe.com; Antanamitarana Village, near Andilana; bungalows €30-65; ❋☜☒) 🖉 On a hill overlooking the sea, Le Grand Bleu has spectacular views from its terrace restaurant. The star attraction is the dazzling infinity pool; the hotel is also three minutes' walk from a lovely beach. The bungalows are very pretty, with wood floors, four-poster beds and mosquito nets. Each has its own terrace and hammock. Simpler bungalows are €30 a night. Half- and full-board plans are available.

Le Grand Bleu offers all sorts of excursions and activities including sailing, scuba diving, snorkelling, kayaking and cycling, as well as massage. A kitchen garden supplies the restaurant, and owners Jacques and Céline are involved in supporting the local community. The hotel is about 3km from Andilana.

★ **Nosy Be Hôtel & Spa** RESORT €€€
(Map p126; ☑ 020 86 061 51; www.nosybehotel.
com; Ampasy; d €110-250; ❋ 🛜 ⛱) ✦ The top-
notch Nosy Be Hôtel stands out from the
competition thanks to its highly original
decor – stunning wooden furniture made
on Nosy Be and lots of local artwork – and
lush garden on the edge of the beach. All
rooms are different, each offering European
mattresses and pillows, and beautiful bathrooms. The hotel offers various plans, from
half board to all inclusive.

For diving, Madaplouf (p127) has an office
on site, and quad bike and island-hopping
trips can be arranged. Kayaks and pedalos
are free for guests. There are three pools,
one of which is in the spa.

Le Belvédère GUESTHOUSE €€€
(Map p126; ☑ 032 76 751 99; www.belvedere-nosy
be.com; Andilana; d Ar150,000; 🛜) ✦ Perched
on a bluff overlooking the blissful Andilana
beach, this is a small, simple hotel – there
are no TVs, minibars or fridges. But the
lack of modern amenities makes Belvédère
charming: you can just enjoy the sunsets
and tranquillity. The decent-size rooms each
come with a front porch – complete with
chairs and tables – overlooking the ocean.
Rates include breakfast.

The restaurant is down on the beach.
Next door is a crèche for local children that
was built by Virginie, the manager and owner's sister.

Vanila Hôtel RESORT €€€
(Map p126; ☑ 032 03 921 01; www.vanila-hotel.
com; Ambaro; d €92-122, ste €295; ❋ 🛜 ⛱) One
of the top beach hotels on this stretch of
the coast, Vanila caters more to couples and
families than tour groups, and its design –
small buildings with thatched roofs, and lots
of local art – gives the Vanila a boutique feel.
Rooms are charming, with salmon-coloured
walls and wooden furniture. As well as the
two pools and beach, there is a sensational
spa.

Nosy Be Original (p128) has an office
here that organises a range of excursions in
Nosy Be and nearby islands, and excellent
talks on whales during the migration season (July to September).

Sambatra GUESTHOUSE €€€
(Map p126; ☑ 032 67 251 17; www.sambatra.net;
Ambaro; d incl breakfast €50) With a handful
of simple but cheerful rooms right on the
beach, Sambatra is overpriced by Madagas-

can standards but not bad for Nosy Be. The
sunsets and views of Sakatia are gorgeous
and the restaurant serves excellent food
(mains from Ar18,000).

Domaine de Manga Be APARTMENT €€€
(Map p126; ☑ 032 42 092 82; www.domaine
mangabe.com; Ambondrona; d €30-50, tr/q
€55/70) A rather stylish and original self-
catering complex aimed predominantly at
families. The beautifully decorated studio
apartments, villas, rooms and bungalows
come in all shapes and price ranges, but all
have kitchens or kitchenettes, nets and fans.
You can also hire a cook to prepare your
meals, and there's a restaurant overlooking
the beach (mains from Ar15,000).

Chanty Beach GUESTHOUSE €€€
(Map p126; ☑ 020 86 928 16; www.chanty
beach-hotel.com; Ambaro; r/bungalow incl breakfast €66/82; ❋ 🛜) This German-run place
is a charming, if slightly staid, white colonial-style guesthouse in a neat garden on
the beach facing Nosy Sakatia. Some of the
bungalows have their own kitchenettes,
and there's a small restaurant-bar serving
mostly seafood. Activities include sailing
trips and boat rentals, and excursions can
be arranged. There is snorkelling nearby.

Nosy Sakatia is opposite: take a motorised pirogue from Ambaro Village (15
minutes, Ar5000).

Chez Eugénie GUESTHOUSE €€€
(Map p126; ☑ 032 40 634 48; www.chez-eugenie.
com; Andilana; r incl breakfast €30-40, bungalow incl breakfast €60) There are just five
rooms at this little hotel and restaurant
owned by a French and Malagasy couple. It
has two separate wings joined under one big
thatched roof to form a dining room (menu
Ar35,000). Abodes are small, but pretty,
with firm mattresses and high-quality lin-
ens. There are no sea views, but the hotel is
200m from Andilana beach.

✕ Eating

★ **La Table d'Alexandre** FRENCH €€€
(Map p126; ☑ 033 14 247 22; Ambaro; mains from
Ar22,000; ⊙ lunch, dinner by reservation only) For
a decadent lunch on a day trip around the
island, stop at Alexandre's. The debonair
French chef here serves exquisite cuisine
in a dining room that wouldn't have looked
out of place on the set of *Out of Africa*: a
gazebo perched on a low hill overlooking
mangroves and Nosy Sakatia, decorated

with traditional china and 19th-century paintings. Splendid.

Chez Loulou
SEAFOOD €€€

(Map p126; 032 96 141 44; Andilana; set menu Ar35,000) Right on the beach, this casual restaurant and bar is best known for its gargantuan Sunday seafood buffet lunch (Ar40,000). Seafood also gets pride of place in the daily three-course meal. If you want to linger after dessert at lunch, grab a sun-lounger and an ice-cold THB, and relax with a good book. Bookings are essential for the Sunday buffet.

Mt Passot & Crater Lakes

Mt Passot (329m), Nosy Be's loftiest point, lies about 15km northwest of Hell-Ville (somewhat further by road). It's a good spot for admiring sunsets and the sweeping panorama. It's also one of the best places to see Nosy Be's crater lakes. Unfortunately, the viewing area is now packed with souvenir stalls, which somewhat detracts from the experience.

If you have your own wheels, the summit is easily accessible by car or motorbike (allow 45 minutes from Ambatoloaka); otherwise you could charter a taxi from Hell-Ville or Ambatoloaka (allow Ar90,000 for the return trip, including time at the top).

There have been muggings in the area so if you're on your own or on a motorbike, ensure that you drive back before it gets dark.

ISLANDS AROUND NOSY BE

If money is no object, the islands surrounding Nosy Be – particularly Nosy Iranja and Nosy Mitsio – are home to some idyllic resorts, ideal for a few days of remote tranquillity. If you're on a tighter budget, take a day trip to check out the palm-fringed white beaches and do some excellent snorkelling.

Nosy Komba

This island rises off the ocean floor midway between the mainland and Nosy Be in an almost perfect cone shape and looms above the turquoise sea: its summit reaches a mighty 622m (much higher than that of Nosy Be). There are no roads, no banks and

no electricity on the island. Hotels operate on solar power backed up by generators.

Nosy Komba is often included in an organised tour from Nosy Be along with Nosy Tanikely, with just a couple of hours at the village of **Ampangorina**. If you'd like to stay, the choice of accommodation is between relatively isolated top-end resorts, and less expensive options along the beach at Ampangorina village.

◉ Sights

Ampangorina Craft Market
MARKET

Ampangorina is Nosy Komba's main village. It has an interesting craft market with beautiful cut-work embroidered tablecloths and curtains, excellent wood carvings and paintings spilling out of almost every house.

Lemur Park
NATURE RESERVE

(Map p126; Ampangorina; admission Ar4000) In this small park, the black lemurs are wild, but locals feed them bananas so that the animals will eat off your hand or jump on your shoulder for that perfect photo op. The practice is detrimental to the animals but generates substantial revenue for the village, which has helped protect the forest. So if you'd like to support the village, pay the admission fee to admire the lemurs, but decline the offer to feed them.

☂ Activities

Nosy Komba's interior is remarkably well preserved and is prime hiking territory. It takes about five sweaty hours to walk up to the summit from Ampangorina and back down. Madame Yvonne is the recommended guide (Ar30,000 including lunch): ask for her at any of the shops. When you are an hour from the top, Yvonne will yell out to the next village so that lunch will be ready when you arrive. She is very knowledgeable about local medicinal plants.

🛏 Sleeping & Eating

Chez Yolande
GUESTHOUSE €€

(020 86 921 40; www.hotel nosykomba.com/contact-chez-yolande; Ampangorino; d Ar75,000;) The simple yet comfortable rooms at Chez Yolande offer very good value for Nosy Komba. They are attached to the restaurant (mains from Ar12,500) and bar, and have sea views. Yolande speaks English, French and Italian. Wi-fi is available (30 minute, Ar3000).

★ **293 On Komba** GUESTHOUSE €€€

(☑034 09 417 01; www.293onkomba.com; Ampangorina; per person half board €63-83; ☎) 𝄢 This delightful guesthouse is set among mango trees at the end of the beach at Ampangorina. South African owner Marcine is a mine of information on all things local. The stylish rooms are spacious, and each has a verandah and hammock. Local wood carvings are dotted about the lounge and garden. The food here is superb.

There are various nooks in the garden for relaxing with a book or gazing out to sea.

Floraly Komba GUESTHOUSE €€€

(☑034 09 583 61; www.floralykomba.com; Ampangorina; d Ar90,000-125,000; ☎) Floraly Komba is situated on the beach at Ampangorina. Rooms are quite small, but there's a variety of accommodation ranging from upstairs or ground-floor rooms to bungalows. There's a convivial bar and restaurant, and the owner, Xavier, can arrange transfers, excursions and diving.

Tsara Komba LODGE €€€

(Map p126; ☑020 86 921 10; www.tsarakomba. com; d full board per person €270; ☎) 𝄢 With just eight bungalows, this superb lodge is about as exclusive and secluded as you can get. The polished wood floor rooms come with king-size beds and a porch looking out to the sea. The garden is a work of art, as is the food served in the dining room with panoramic views. Minimum three-night stay.

Tsara Komba has a fantastic program of activities, including walks on Nosy Komba, visits to the cocoa plantations in Ambanja, day trips to Nosy Be, and all the usual sailing and snorkelling trips.

Jardin Vanille LODGE €€€

(Map p126; ☑032 07 127 97; www.jardinvanille. com; d with half/full board €144/174) This lovely lodge offers cute and comfortable Madagascan-style bungalows located on Nosy Komba's beautiful Anjiabe beach. The restaurant serves a very fine menu and overlooks the sea. Numerous excursions can be arranged, along with Nosy Be transfers.

Chez Madio MADAGASCAN €€

(Ampangorina; mains Ar10,000) Alfredo and Madio make the most of local ingredients to produce excellent dishes. Seafood is a speciality – order the fish of the day with a platter of delicious chips. Eat upstairs to catch the breeze.

❶ Getting There & Away

➜ Organised tours to the island are available from most tour operators in Nosy Be and cost around Ar120,000 in combination with Nosy Tanikely.

➜ Motorised pirogues (Ar5000) leave the small harbour in Hell-Ville when full for the 40-minute journey. Pay on the boat, not the touts on the quay. Ask to be dropped off at your hotel, or at the village of Ampangorina.

Nosy Tanikely

Nosy Tanikely is 10km west of Nosy Komba. It is a protected **marine reserve** (Map p126; admission Ar10,000; ☺8am-5pm) and one of the best snorkelling sites in the area, with coral, numerous fish and sea turtles.

Snorkelling is best in the morning, before the wind picks up. Although the reserve officially opens at 8am, you are allowed to come earlier – just stick around until the reserve officials arrive so that you can pay your admission fees. Snorkelling equipment is available from the reserve's cabin for Ar10,000.

Most organised day tours combine Nosy Tanikely with Nosy Komba, using the beach on Nosy Tanikely for a lunchtime picnic.

Nosy Sakatia

At a mere 3 sq km, Nosy Sakatia, just off the west coast of Nosy Be, is quiet and tiny. It's famous for its orchids and is an easy place to wander around. There is also good snorkelling and a couple of good diving sites off the island.

Sakatia Lodge (Map p126; ☑032 02 770 99; www.sakatia.co.za; d bungalow €58-99) offers a variety of accommodation in garden bungalows, larger sea-view bungalows and family villas. A raft of activities – sailing, snorkelling, walking, fishing (the hotel's speciality) and diving – can be arranged, making it ideal for families.

To get to Sakatia, make your way to the Nosy Be beach of Ambaro, next to the Chanty Beach hotel, where you'll find motorised pirogues to Sakatia (Ar5000). Negotiate a price for a tour of the island (depending on the length of the excursion).

Nosy Mitsio

Nosy Mitsio is a small, beautiful archipelago about 55km northeast of Nosy Be, where

EDEN LODGE, MAINLAND PARADISE

The eight luxury tents at **Eden Lodge** (☎034 86 93 119; www.edenlodge.net; Anjanojano; d full board €480; ☎) 🌊 are equipped with beautiful mahogany beds, colourful fabrics, and, wait for it, private massage cabins. Meals are served in the atmospheric thatched dining room–lounge (complete with fairy lights); the menu changes daily and makes the best of the hotel's vegetable garden and the abundant seafood.

Eden Lodge is on a remote peninsula, accessible only by boat transfer (40 minutes) from Nosy Be or Ankify (p138).

Designed to minimise impact on the environment, the lodge effortlessly blends with its surroundings: lemurs roam the garden, birds nest in the baobabs and resident green turtles lay their eggs on the beach in front of the tents. Seeing these marine giants labour over their nests or witnessing the eggs hatching is a once-in-a-lifetime experience.

There is plenty to do around the lodge: snorkelling off the beach is a must, plus there's sailing, canoeing and windsurfing. The resident guide can take you on walks around the peninsula, and the lodge can organise excursions to Nosy Be and other islands. Sociable types shouldn't miss the opportunity for a game of soccer with local villagers on the bumpy pitch, or try a game of pétanque: a word of warning, the locals are very good!

The lodge is powered by solar energy and the staff use only organic cleaning products.

---

the main attractions are the still relatively virgin dive sites and the picture-perfect beaches.

Most diving and tour operators in Nosy Be organise multiday diving trips or cruises to Nosy Mitsio (€400 to €850, depending on the number of people on board, the number of dives and number of days).

Like to treat yourself to a few nights of remote idyll? Stay at the relaxed **Tsarabanjina** (☎034 02 152 29; www.tsarabanjina. com; bungalow from €500; ☎). There are no TVs or phones here (the only concession to modern living is wi-fi in the communal areas) – just the sea, the beach and the hills, into which the thatched wooden bungalows blend effortlessly. Most people come here to dive: Tsarabanjina has a PADI and NAUI-certified club. A three-night minimum stay is required. The boat transfer from Nosy Be or Ankify takes two hours.

Nosy Iranja

The gorgeous Nosy Iranja, southwest of Nosy Be, consists of two islands: the larger, inhabited Nosy Iranja Be (about 2 sq km) and the tiny Nosy Iranja Kely (0.13 sq km). The islands are connected by a 1.5km-long sand bar, negotiable on foot at low tide. Sea turtles regularly lay their eggs on the beaches.

Nosy Iranja is a popular sailing day trip from Nosy Be (Ar130,000; check tour operators in Nosy Be). The excursion generally includes snorkelling, swimming and a good lunch on board the boat.

AMBANJA REGION

This lush region produces mangoes, cashew nuts, ylang-ylang, vanilla, cocoa and spices. Mango trees line the RN6 all the way from Diego Suarez to Ambanja; you will pass through the area if you are heading to Nosy Be.

Ambanja

Ambanja is a small, tree-lined town on the Sambirano River, and the junction for overland travel to and from Nosy Be. It is famous for its large cocoa, spice and vanilla plantations, some of which can be visited.

◉ Sights

★**Millot Plantations**   FARM
(www.cananga.fr; 4hr tours €10, farmhouse 3-course meal incl drinks €15; ☉8am-5pm Mon-Sat) This beautiful plantation, established in 1904, is a leading producer of organic cocoa, spices and essential oils, and a visit to this little slice of paradise is not only highly informative but a true festival of the senses. The tour can be topped off with lunch in the beautiful old farmhouse.

Against a backdrop of stunning scenery, the formidable Mado, your guide, will invite you to taste or smell every plant on the farm, from the lychee-like raw cocoa beans straight out of their husk, to potent green peppercorns soaking in brine and vinegar. You'll also poke your nose in the distillery, where ylang-ylang essential oils or freshly picked vetiver roots will fight for your olfactory attention. During your visit, you'll see how each plant is grown, picked and processed (the distillery for perfume plants, and preparation areas for cocoa and spices). Millot employs more than 800 people, the majority of them women. The plantation also supports the village school, which most of the employees' children attend.

Lunch includes dishes prepared with products from the plantation, including a wondrous chocolate cake with vanilla cream. Make sure you try Mado's exquisite chocolate-flavoured rum (made with the plantation's cocoa, of course). You can also sleep at the farmhouse, where there are simple and atmospheric rooms (doubles €55, including dinner).

Because the plantation spreads over 15 sq km, you'll need a vehicle. If you don't have your own, you can hire the plantation's for the length of your visit (€50).

ℹ Getting There & Away

From Ambanja there are regular *taxis-brousses* to Ankify (Ar2000, 30 minutes), where you'll find the ferry to Nosy Be. *Taxis-brousses* also go to Diego Suarez (Ar30,000, six hours), Majunga (Ar50,000, 13 hours) and Tana (Ar50,000, 24 hours).

Ankify

Ankify is the main port for boats and ferries between the mainland coast and Nosy Be. If you arrive too late for the crossing to Nosy Be (4pm) or the last *taxi-brousse* to Diego Suarez (noon), there are a couple of nice but expensive places to stay. There are no banks and no electricity here.

🛏 Sleeping & Eating

Ankify Lodge BUNGALOW €€€
(☎ 032 45 334 61; www.ankifylodge.com; d Ar150,000-180,000) This lodge has great colonial charm. Surrounded by a tropical garden with stunning views, the bungalows are enormous with good bathrooms. Each has its own terrace to make the best of the fine setting, and there is a small beach below. The hotel is 4km from the port of Ankify; a taxi is around Ar10,000. The menu of the day will set you back Ar46,200.

Les Baobabs BUNGALOW €€€
(☎ 033 07 208 87; bungalow garden/sea-facing Ar115,000/150,000) Les Baobabs has modern round bungalows on a gorgeous beach with superb views across to Nosy Komba. They lack charm, but are comfortable, and are set in a pretty garden. The restaurant is on an enormous, atmospheric verandah (mains Ar20,000 to Ar30,000). A taxi to the port costs around Ar10,000.

ℹ Getting There & Away

When heading to the port via taxi from local accommodation, allow a staff member to accompany you to offset the touts at the port. The road between Ankify and Diego Suarez is badly potholed. Allow four hours in a private vehicle, five hours by *taxi-brousse*.

ANTSIRANANA REGION

Madagascar's northernmost region is an alluring place: it's remote, host to weird and wonderful geological sights, and has disarming contrasts between very wet and very dry.

Diego Suarez (Antsiranana) is the main gateway town, although it's by no means the only place in which to base yourself when exploring the region. There is plenty of excellent hiking to do in the two national parks of Montagne d'Ambre and Ankarana, and a growing niche of more adventurous sports to try, such as quad biking and kitesurfing.

Some travellers decide to base themselves in Diego or Joffreville (Ambohitra) and do day trips from there; others prefer to do a couple of days in Diego and then work their way down (or up) the RN6, sleeping in Joffreville for Montagne

TAXIS-BROUSSES FROM ANKIFY

DESTINATION	PRICE (AR)	DURATION (HR)	DEPARTURE TIMES
Ambanja	2000	½	All day
Ambilobe	20,000	2	Morning
Diego Suarez	30,000	5	Morning

Baie de Diego Suarez

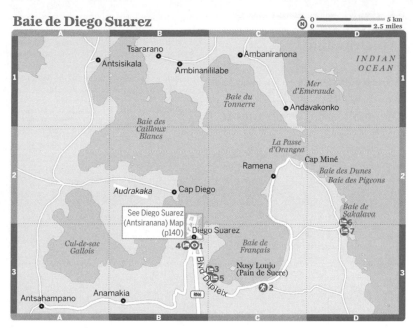

d'Ambre, and in Réserve Spéciale Ankarana, to minimise travelling time.

History

The history of the area around Diego Suarez is intimately linked to its enormous bay; its strategic location on the Indian Ocean trade routes and the natural shelter it provides have been prized by generations of pirates, slave traders, merchants and navies.

The earliest evidence of human settlement in Madagascar was found here. The bay was frequently visited by East African and Arab traders, but it wasn't until the 16th century that Portuguese explorers landed here. In 1885, France, which had gradually increased its presence on the big island, signed a treaty with Madagascar granting France the right to occupy the territories of Diego Suarez and Nosy Be, a precedent which eventually led to colonial occupation.

In 1942, during WWII, British forces seized Diego Suarez from the French, fearing that Vichy-supporting troops (who had capitulated to Hitler) might support the Japanese navy, allied to Germany. The area was handed back to the French at the end

of the war in 1946. Madagascar finally obtained independence from France in 1960, but the French Foreign Legion retained a base in Diego until 1975.

ⓘ Dangers & Annoyances

There have been a number of muggings in isolated areas popular with travellers such as Montagne des Français and Les Trois Baies. To minimise chances of things going wrong, never go alone. Even if you're part of a couple or small group, take a guide, tell your hotel where you're going and don't take valuables with you.

NORTHERN MADAGASCAR ANTSIRANANA REGION

Diego Suarez (Antsiranana)

POP 121,320

With its wide streets, old colonial-era buildings, and genteel air, Diego is a lovely base from which to explore Madagascar's northern region. It's a slow-moving place; nearly everything shuts between noon and 3pm while residents indulge in long afternoon naps.

Diego is an important port in Madagascar; the town notably exports tinned fish,

Diego Suarez (Antsiranana)

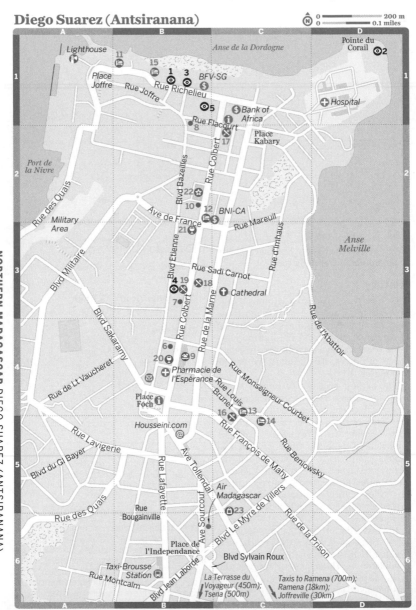

and soft and alcoholic drinks – there is an important Star (THB) bottling plant on the outskirts of town. Thanks to its deep-water anchorage, Diego has also become a firm favourite of cruise ships, which visit between December and March. The ships are a magnificent sight as they cross the bay, although the outpouring of thousands of visitors for just one day turns the usually sleepy Diego into a bit of a madhouse.

There are no beaches in Diego itself, but plenty of amazing views of the bay, and the town encourages visitors to explore its fascinating architecture and history.

◉ Sights & Activities

Diego's tourist office and local heritage association, **Ambre** (http://ambre.cyber-diego.com), have designed five self-guided walking tours of Diego Suarez, the **Dans les Rues de Diego Suarez**; the History of the City; Architecture; The Port and Military Area; Businesses, Markets and Artisans; and Culture and Traditions. The walks take in the main historical and architectural highlights of the city. Each itinerary (1½ to two hours) is featured in a booklet (Ar5000), complete with map, photos and detailed explanation about each highlight of the itinerary. Booklets are available from the tourist offices in Diego.

Le Grand Hôtel SWIMMING
(Map p140; Rue Colbert; half day per person weekdays/weekend Ar15,000/20,000) This hotel's pool has been beautifully landscaped, with tropical plants all around and an attractive deck for loungers.

☞ Tours

Diego tour companies offer a variety of activities and excursions to Ankarana, Montagne d'Ambre, Les Trois Baies, Tsingy Rouges and Mer d'Emeraude. They're also the best place to go to if you'd like to hire a 4WD to explore the region under your own steam, notably between Diego and Nosy Be, and also the vanilla coast (Vohémar, Sambava and Antalaha). Allow Ar175,000 to Ar220,000 per day for a 4WD with driver plus fuel, depending on the distance.

Diego Raid DRIVING TOUR
(Map p140; ☎ 032 40 001 75; www.diegoraid.com; Rue Colbert; tours per day Ar321,000-480,000) This operator organises highly recommended quad bike excursions to areas such as Les Trois Baies, Windsor Castle and Montagne des Français. It also offers half-day 4WD trips to the Tsingy Rouges (Ar90,000), and hires out mountain bikes at Ar45,000 per day. As well as taking in the main sights, the trips tend to leave the tarmac well behind and take the scenic route instead.

Evasion Sans Frontière TOUR
(Map p140; ☎ 020 82 230 61; www.mada-evasion. com; Rue Colbert) This well-respected company runs day trips to all the main regional sights, including Mer d'Emeraude. It also has a branch in the Grand Hôtel.

New Sea Roc ADVENTURE SPORTS
(Map p140; ☎ 032 04 724 46, 020 82 218 54; www. newsearoc.com; 26 Rue Colbert) 🛇 New Sea Roc specialises in climbing and camping trips (Corail Camp tent/hut/troglodyte room

Diego Suarez (Antsiranana)

€50/60/90, full board per person) on the remote Nosy Hara archipelago, a marine park. Its Tree Camp at Jungle Park has tents/tree houses/eco-houses at €30/60/90 full board per person. Biking, rock climbing and kayaking is €70 per day. It supports village development, environmental education and tree planting.

Paradis du Nord TOUR

(☑032 04 859 64, 020 82 214 05; www.leparadis dunord-diego.com; Ave Princesse Fatima Achimo) Run by the affable Eric, this agency has a large fleet of quality vehicles and offers the cheapest rates in town. Find it behind the Tsena (covered market).

King de la Piste TOUR

(Map p140; ☑032 04 908 10; www.kingdelapiste. de; Ave Bazeilles) A German-run company, King runs excursions along the Diego–Nosy Be corridor. It has its own hotel in Ankarana and one on the outskirts of Diego. It also does car hire.

🎎 Festivals & Events

Zegny'Zo Festival PERFORMING ARTS

(☑032 02 358 15, 032 04 931 81; www.zolobe.com; ☺May) In the third week of May, street theatre and traditional music are showcased in the streets of Diego Suarez.

🛏 Sleeping

There are few budget hotels in Diego, but the midrange category has some great options.

Hôtel Valiha HOTEL €€

(Map p140; ☑032 07 789 95; 33 Rue Colbert; d Ar35,000-45,000) Well-located, this hotel is one of the cheapest in town. It is elderly but clean and well-kept. Opt for a room upstairs, as the cheapest rooms on the ground floor have no windows. There's a bar and restaurant, too.

La Belle Aventure GUESTHOUSE €€

(Map p140; ☑032 44 153 83; www.labell aventure-diego.com; 13 Rue Freppel; d Ar60,000-100,000; ❉☎) Gilles and Elisabeth built their Beautiful Adventure in a great neighbourhood of Diego: quiet, yet close to the centre, and with good views of the bay. Everything is bright, fresh and impeccable, with colourful sheets, and lemur and baobab friezes on the walls. Rooms upstairs have a balcony and sea view. There's a friendly bar and restaurant at street level.

Perle de la Baie GUESTHOUSE €€

(Map p140; ☑032 04 434 50; perledelabaie@gmail. com; Rue Richelieu; d Ar60,000, without bathroom Ar50,000; ☎) This hotel probably has the most jaw-dropping view of the Bay of Diego Suarez in Diego; breakfast or a sundowner on the balcony really takes some beating. You can sometimes spot dolphins, and watching container or cruise ships come in is majestic. The rooms are sparsely furnished but spacious and light (opt for one upstairs). Some share bathrooms.

La Terrasse du Voyageur HOTEL €€

(Map p139; ☑020 82 240 63; www.terrassedu voyageur-hotel.com; Rue du Mozambique; s/d/tr Ar35,000/45,000/55,500; ❉☎) 🌿 Right in the centre of the Tsena, Diego's market district, La Terrasse du Voyageur is not exactly in a postcard location, but the hotel offers a chance to be a little closer to the local community. Rooms are simple and colourful, with old-fashioned bathrooms, and can be noisy. Add Ar35,000 per room for air-conditioning.

The building has become an important community focal point: neighbourhood associations have their offices here, there are movie nights on Tuesdays, a kids' club on Wednesdays, and karaoke on the terrace on Fridays.

★Le Jardin Exotique BOUTIQUE HOTEL €€€

(Map p140; ☑020 82 219 33; www.jardin exotique.hotel-diegosuarez.com; Rue Louis Brunet; r Ar75,000-160,000; ❉☎) Rooms at this quirky boutique place all come with parquet floors, four-poster beds, mosquito nets, bold and creative paint jobs, and Italian showers in the bathrooms. The rooftop terrace has picnic tables, and the views over the bay of Diego Suarez are awesome. The garden, with its indigenous plants and tumbling bougainvilleas, is wonderful. Massage is available.

Allamanda Hôtel BOUTIQUE HOTEL €€€

(Map p140; ☑020 82 210 33; www.allamanda-hotel. com; Rue Richelieu; d from Ar190,000; ❉@☎✉) The swanky Allamanda is just steps from the sea and has all the luxuries you would expect from a top-end hotel. The exterior of the building itself is a bit bland and boxy, but the rooms are spacious and elegantly decked out in nautical-themed decor.

🍴 Eating

Diego has some excellent restaurants, but as with accommodation, they're not the cheapest in Madagascar. In the early evenings, there are good **street-food stands** along Rue Colbert.

Pâtisserie Le Grand Hôtel
BAKERY €

(Map p140; Rue Colbert; cakes & sandwiches Ar3000-9000; ⊙5am-9.30pm) This excellent bakery doubles up as a cafe that's popular with tourists. It's a great choice for an economical and light breakfast, or a cheap lunch of salad or a sandwich. There are some lovely pastries, too, which you can devour with real espresso.

Score
SUPERMARKET €

(Map p140; Rue Colbert; ⊙8.30am-1pm & 3-7.30pm Mon-Fri, 8.30am-7.30pm Sat, to 11.30am Sun) Very well-stocked supermarket.

★La Bodega
MADAGASCAN €€

(Map p140; cnr Rues Colbert & Flacourt; mains Ar10,000-35,000; ⊙noon-3pm & 6-11pm Mon-Sat) The name suggests Spanish influence, but owner Cyrille is from France and the colourful restaurant is in Madagascar, so it's hardly surprising the menu is a mix of all three nationalities. We loved the tapas à la Malagasy, the fish carpaccio with avocado and lime mousse, and the amazing rum cocktails. It's always busy, and has a great atmosphere.

Balafomanga
INTERNATIONAL €€

(Map p140; 18 Rue Louis Brunet; mains Ar11,000-45,000; ⊙noon-2.30pm & 6.30-10pm Mon-Sat) The big menu at Balafomanga offers a bit of everything, although the delicious food definitely has a big French and Madagascan influence, with dishes such as sea bass in pink peppercorn sauce, barbecued prawns and garlic calamari. It's a funky dining environment, with Chinese lanterns, multicoloured walls and rows of home-brewed fruit-flavoured rum in big pots on the low-lit bar.

La Rosticceria
ITALIAN €€

(Map p140; ☑032 67 637 03; 47 Rue Colbert; mains Ar13,000-35,000) This Italian restaurant has a good selection of risottos, gnocchi, lasagne and fresh-made pasta with pesto, cream, meat or seafood sauce. The restaurant decor follows a nautical theme, with intricately carved wooden vessels and old maps for decoration. Outside tables sit on a verandah.

La Terrasse du Voyageur
MADAGASCAN €€

(Map p139; ☑020 82 240 63; www.terrassedu voyageur-hotel.com; Rue du Mozambique; set menu Ar30,000; ⊙dinner) ✐ The 4th-floor restaurant at hotel La Terrasse du Voyageur has sweeping views of Diego. It's a cosy and convivial space, with a TV lounge, library and bar. The set taster menu of Madagascan dishes is good value: portions are gargantuan and the food delicious. The restaurant is only open for dinner and you must book.

Le Melville
FRENCH €€€

(Map p140; ☑032 05 606 99; Allamanda Hôtel, Rue Richelieu; mains Ar16,500-40,000; ⊙7am-10.30pm; 🕸) Right by the sea, with a fabulous patio that's particularly alluring at sunset, the atmosphere at Melville is romantic and sophisticated without being stuffy. The food is delicious, featuring zebu and seafood: fish-lovers will be spoiled for choice. Service is also top-class. Booking is recommended for weekends.

🍷 Drinking & Nightlife

Diego has good nightlife by Madagascan standards, so make the best of it!

Vahinée Bar
BAR

(Map p140; Rue Colbert) A local favourite, Vahinée has something for everyone: a widescreen TV showing football and rugby, a pool table, and live music every night. The atmosphere is excellent, and there is a range of drinks, from beer to cocktails.

Boîte Noire
LOUNGE

(Map p140; Rue Colbert) With big fauxleather couches, pool tables and intimidating bouncers, this is Diego's fanciest disco. It attracts a chic, wannabe crowd.

🛈 ANKIFY TO DIEGO SUAREZ BY 4WD

The popular northern circuit from Diego Suarez (Antsiranana) to Nosy Be offered by travel agents means that a number of 4WDs often drop their clients in Ankify for the final leg of their trip and head back to Diego Suarez empty. As a result, **Evasion Sans Frontière** (☑032 11 005 96; www.mada-evasion.com; Hell-Ville) accepts passengers on the way back for Ar50,000 per person (Ar20,000 more than the *taxi-brousse* and so much more comfortable). Just ring ahead to find out when a vehicle might be available.

NORTHERN MADAGASCAR DIEGO SUAREZ (ANTSIRANANA)

TAXIS-BROUSSES FROM DIEGO SUAREZ

DESTINATION	PRICE (AR)	DURATION (HR)	DEPARTURE TIMES
Ambilobe	8000	5	All day
Ankify	4000	9	1am
Antananarivo	74,000	24	Morning & afternoon
Joffreville	5000	1½	All day
Majunga	50,000	15	Afternoon
Ramena	3000	1	All day
Sambava	60,000	24	Afternoon

☆ Entertainment

Alliance Française   PERFORMING ARTS
(Map p140; www.alliancefr.mg; Rue Colbert) The
Alliance Française is housed in a magnifi-
cently restored art-deco-style building, formerly the Grande Bazaar, which is worth a
look on its own. There are regular art exhibitions here, along with film screenings,
concerts and shows.

🛍 Shopping

Ateliers de l'Artisanat   ARTS, CRAFTS
(Map p140; Ave Tollendal) This boutique has a
huge selection of handicrafts and artwork
from all over Madagascar.

ℹ Information

All banks have ATMs and money-changing
facilities.
Bank of Africa (BOA; Map p140; Rue Colbert)
BFV-SG (Map p140; Rue Richelieu) Changes
travellers cheques.
BNI-CA (Map p140; cnr Ave de France & Rue
Colbert)
Housseini.com (Map p140; Ave Tollendal; inter-
net per 30min/2hr Ar1500/5000; ⊙8am-9pm
Mon-Sat, 3-8.30pm Sun) The fastest internet
option in town.
Pharmacie de l'Espérance (Map p140; Rue
Colbert)
Post Office (Map p140; Place Foch)
Tourist Office (Map p140; www.office-
tourisme-diego-suarez.com; Place Foch;
⊙8am-noon & 3-6pm Mon-Fri, 8.30-11.30am
Sat) Sells a booklet of self-guided itineraries
taking in Diego's historical and architectural
highlights. There is a second branch that's
located at the corner of Rue Colbert and Rue
Flacourt, though it's not open on Saturdays.

ℹ Getting There & Away

Air Madagascar (Map p140; ☑ 020 82 214 74;
Ave Sourcouf) flies from Diego to Antananarivo
(€266, two hours, daily), Sambava (€179, 45
minutes, twice weekly) and Nosy Be (€179, 30
minutes, weekly).

The Gare Routière is 6km south of town behind
the Jovenna petrol station.

For destinations on the northeast coast, it can
be quicker to get a *taxi-brousse* to the junction
town of Ambilobe and change to a 4WD *taxi-
brousse* heading east. The road from Ambilobe
to Vohémar was badly degraded by the 2015
rains and the journey will take about 18 hours,
much more in the rainy season.

The road journey from Diego Suarez to Antananarivo is a long and arduous one.

ℹ Getting Around

TO/FROM THE AIRPORT
Diego's Arrachart Airport is 6km south of the
town centre. Taxis charge Ar12,000 to get from
there to town; otherwise, you can walk out to the
main road and catch a tuk-tuk (Ar5000).

TAXI
➜ Taxi journeys in Diego cost a flat Ar1000,
Ar1500 at night. Tuk-tuks are Ar500, Ar1000
at night.
➜ A popular alternative to an expensive 4WD
trip is chartering a taxi to Les Trois Baies
(Ar80,000) and Parc National Montagne
d'Ambre (Ar100,000).

Baie des Français

The road between Diego and Ramena
hugs the coastline of this bay, part of the
immense Baie de Diego Suarez. The sea is
an ethereal turquoise colour that contrasts
beautifully with the ochres and browns of
the towering Montagne des Français.

The bay and mountain were named so in memory of the Malagasy and French forces killed in 1942 in Allied resistance to the pro-German Vichy French forces.

🏃 Activities

Circuit Anosiravo HIKING

(Map p139; per person Ar10,000, plus guide Ar10,000) This new trail on the Montagne des Français has something for everyone: the 6km (three hours) route is definitely for the fit, climbing the mountain and negotiating a tunnel, but there's a gentle 1km route for those less energetic. You can see lemurs, chameleons, snakes, tortoises and lots of birds, including the drongo. Baobabs stud the mountain and all around are magnificent sea views. Note that it's *fady* (taboo) to answer the call of nature here.

🛏 Sleeping & Eating

Le Suarez BOUTIQUE HOTEL €€€

(Map p139; 📞 032 07 416 17/8; www.suarez-hotel.com; Route de Ramena; s/d incl breakfast Ar140,000/196,000; ❋ 🛜 ☒) Owners Philippe and Sophie have created a country boutique hotel with a gorgeous pool. The 12 bungalows have thatched roofs and red-brick-and-stone walls. Inside you'll find a breezy space with whitewashed walls and wooden beams on the ceiling; there's more local wood in the dark polished floors and matching four-poster beds. It's about 4km from Diego's centre on the road to Ramena.

The open-air restaurant serves exceptional food (mains from Ar15,500), and excursions can be arranged.

La Note Bleue Park Hotel HOTEL €€€

(Map p139; 📞 032 07 125 48; www.diego-hotel.com; Route de Ramena; d/ste €90/160; ❋ 🛜 ☒) The large, family friendly Note Bleue offers spacious rooms with balcony or terrace. The huge pool has waterslides and there's a good

---

---

restaurant, all being refurbished at the time of our visit. La Note Bleue runs loads of excursions. It also has a free shuttle to Diego Suarez for hotel guests. It is about 3km from Diego's centre on the road to Ramena.

Ramena

A sleepy fishing village for most of the week, Ramena (located 18km northeast of Diego) wakes up on Sundays, when seemingly half the population of Diego Suarez comes here for a knees-up on the beach: restaurants fill up for the traditional Sunday buffet and the beach at the northern end of the village becomes picnic central (complete with stereos, crates of beer and some quality dancing!).

For visitors, coming here on Sundays is a great opportunity to partake in Madagascan fun. But staying in Ramena is also a good alternative to staying in Diego, particularly if you're after some beach time.

🛏 Sleeping & Eating

La Case en Falafy BUNGALOW €€

(📞 032 02 674 33; www.case-en-falafy.com; Chez Bruno; bungalow Ar40,000, mains Ar8500-11,000; 🛜 ☒) One of the best-value options in the Diego Suarez area, La Case en Falafy is about 200m up the hill from the beach. It has a great bar, pool and restaurant (mains Ar8500 to Ar11,000). The thatched-roof bungalows sit in a lovely garden but have no sea views. Try for one situated at the back of the property – they are a bit quieter.

Tours and excursions can be arranged.

Badamera Park GUESTHOUSE €€

(📞 032 07 733 50; www.badamera.com; r Ar47,500, d bungalow Ar50,000) A few hundred metres up a hill from the beach, this popular and laid-back budget place has a stylish terrace, and a restaurant that gets good reviews for its food (the musical Sunday buffet, Ar40,000, is particularly popular). The rooms and bungalows are spread out in the exotic garden; though basic, they're clean and come with nets.

Le 5 Trop Près SEAFOOD €€

(📞 032 07 740 60; www.normada.com/5trop; mains Ar14,000-16,000; ⏰ Tue-Sun) Ramena is a fishing village so it's hardly surprising that seafood is plentiful. Right on the beach at Le 5 Trop Près (pronounced like St Tropez, a wink to the glitzy French Riviera town), it comes in many guises and everything is delicious. There's a buzzy, friendly vibe. It is especially popular on Sundays, when booking is recommended.

L'Emeraude SEAFOOD €€
(mains Ar10,000-13,000) This restaurant, with its lovely deck on Ramena's beach, has a great reputation for its excellent food and Saturday-night disco. It follows a nice formula of fish, crab or calamari, offered in sauce, curried, fried or grilled.

❶ Getting There & Away

Taxis-brousses run between Diego Suarez and Ramena (Ar3000) each day – although you sometimes have to wait a while for the vehicle to fill. Chartering a taxi is an easier option, but will cost about Ar60,000 return.

Les Trois Baies

On the eastern side of the peninsula that juts into the bay east of Diego is a series of beautiful bays with stupendous beaches. There are many coves and inlets along this stretch of the coast, but the area is named after three majestic bays: **Baie de Sakalava** (Sakalava Bay), the **Baie des Pigeons** (Pigeon Bay) and the **Baie des Dunes** (Dune Bay). It's a wild, harsh and starkly beautiful environment, with not a village in sight; expect strong winds from April to November and baking heat from December to March. You will need a 4WD for the sandy tracks.

🏃 Activities

Hiking
The walk from Baie de Sakalava (the southernmost of the three bays) to Ramena has become a popular excursion. 'Les Trois Baies Circuit' takes roughly half a day to walk from one end to the other, more if you include stops for swimming and/or a picnic. Many tour operators in Diego offer it as a package, with transfer from Diego in 4WD, drop-off at one end and pick-up at the other, plus a guide and a picnic on the way.

Around the lighthouse at Cap Miné, you'll come across rusting military installations (cannons, bunkers, buildings in ruins) dating back to WWII. The cape dominates La Grande Passe, the entrance of the bay of Diego Suarez, and waves crash below the cliffs with thunderous might.

The area between Cap Miné and Ramena is a military base and you'll need to pay an admission fee (Ar5000 per person, Ar2000 for a vehicle) at the main gate.

If you're staying in Diego, a cheaper way of doing it is to charter a taxi for the day (Ar90,000), have it drop you off at Baie de Sakalava and then pick you up in Ramena (or vice versa). It's recommended that you take a guide (Ar50,000; ask at your hotel or the tourist office, as the route is not always obvious and there have been muggings in the area.

Swimming & Water Sports
Between December and March, when the wind has died down, swimming in the three bays is blissful: beaches are deserted and the sea is calm, with a translucent, pale turquoise colour that contrasts with the dark blue of the depths. There is good snorkelling too. Baie des Dunes is the most sheltered of the three main bays.

LIBERTALIA

The first mention of the Pirate Republic of Libertalia was in a 1726 story by Daniel Defoe. According to Defoe, Libertalia was founded around the Baie des Français by Captain Misson, a French adventurer with a Robin Hood bent who sailed the seas freeing slaves and avoiding bloodshed whenever possible. He teamed up with a defrocked Dominican priest, Father Caraccioli, to set up a communist Utopia.

They began building with the help of freed African slaves and British, French, Dutch and Portuguese pirates. A parliament was formed, a printing press was started, crops were planted, stock was reared and a new international language was established.

All seemed to be going well until the Malagasy people living around the 'International Republic of Libertalia' descended en masse from the hills and massacred the Libertalian population. Caraccioli was killed, but Misson escaped. His eventual fate remains a mystery.

As yet, there is no physical evidence of Libertalia, and some historians have relegated it to the realms of fantasy. Sceptics argue that Robinson Crusoe's creator could easily have invented a pirate republic.

From April to November, when the winds blow so strong you'll struggle to retain ownership of your hat, the Baie de Sakalava is a prime kitesurfing spot. The two hotels based in the bay offer equipment rental and courses.

🛌 Sleeping & Eating

The only accommodation in the area is on Baie de Sakalava, right by the beach. Close by are several *gargottes* (local eateries).

Sakalava Lodge BUNGALOW €€€
(Map p139; ☑ 032 67 385 95; www.sakalava.com; bungalow full board €60-75; 📶) There are two types of bungalows at the Sakalava Lodge. The cheaper, brick garden bungalows have whitewashed walls and colourful soft furnishings. The seaside bungalows, however, are made of local materials. Both have bags of charm, and the whole place has a languid beach feel to it. Kitesurfing rules (equipment and lessons are available); excursions can also be organised.

Royal Sakalava BUNGALOW €€€
(Map p139; ☑ 020 82 926 36; www.royalsakalava. com; d incl breakfast €45; 📶) The concrete bungalows at Royal Sakalava are functional but devoid of charm. There's a nice communal area/dining room, with sofas, a pool table and a TV. Royal Sakalava's French kitesurfing instructor is IKO-affiliated (International Kiteboarding Organisation), and the hotel offers courses from beginners to advanced (€40 per hour). If you know what you're doing, you can rent equipment.

La Mer d'Emeraude

On the northern side of the entrance to the Baie de Diego Suarez lies the gorgeous Mer d'Emeraude (Emerald Sea), a sheltered bay of the Indian Ocean with the colour and translucence of a rare gemstone. The shelter is provided by a series of small islets, which make ideal picnic stops and have good swimming and snorkelling.

Thanks to this idyllic setting, La Mer d'Emeraude has become a popular day trip from Diego Suarez. Standard packages include transport to Ramena, the sailing from Ramena to La Mer d'Emeraude (generally in a local sailing boat), three hours on an islet to sunbathe, swim and snorkel (equipment is normally included) and a lunch that includes alcoholic drinks. It's worth knowing

that the package from Ramena onwards normally only costs about Ar60,000 per person plus the Ar10,000 entrance permit, yet many agencies charge around Ar250,000 for two because of the 4WD transfer from Diego to Ramena; so if you're on a budget, tell the tour operator you'll arrange transport to Ramena yourself (and take a *taxi-brousse* or charter a taxi for the day).

The sailing from Ramena to La Mer d'Emeraude can be very rough between May and November when trade winds are strong, and you're pretty much guaranteed to get wet. Make sure you arrange this excursion with a reputable agency.

Joffreville (Ambohitra)

Joffreville (Ambohitra), established in 1902, was once a pleasure resort for the French military. Today it's a sleepy but incredibly atmospheric place, with crumbling colonial buildings, ever-changing weather and gorgeous views of the valleys and mountains.

Most people use the town as a jumping-off point to visit the fabulous adjacent Parc National Montagne d'Ambre, but Joffreville also makes a brilliant base from which to explore northern highlights such as the Tsingy Rouges, Diego, Ankarana and Les Trois Baies.

🛌 Sleeping & Eating

The village store sells a few basics, but if you plan on camping in the park you'll need to get food and other supplies in Diego. All the hotels do meals.

**Le Relais de la
Montagne d'Ambre** PENSION €
(☑ 032 88 475 06; r without bathroom Ar30,000; bungalow Ar60,000) Sisters Henriette and Louise run this basic pension from their atmospheric 1932 colonial house. The rooms are no-frills, with just a bed and a wardrobe. The garden is pretty, though the captive crocodile down the well is off-putting. The three-course lunch (Ar25,000) is good value.

★Litchi Tree BOUTIQUE HOTEL €€€
(☑ 033 12 784 54; www.thelitchitree.com; d €85; 📶) ✍ Built in 1902 and once home to Marshall Joffre, this exquisite house was painstakingly restored by French owner, Hervé Dumel. Its elevated position gives it breathtaking views over the Suarez bay. The furniture was all made locally using sustainable

WORTH A TRIP

WINDSOR CASTLE & BAIE DU COURRIER

Windsor Castle is a 391m-high rock formation about three-hours' drive (and about 50km) northwest of Diego Suarez. The mountaintop is flat and served as a French fort and lookout, which was taken by the occupying British in 1942. You'll understand why it was fought over when you get to the summit: the 360-degree views, including Diego and the Bay of Diego Suarez to the east, Baie du Courrier to the west, the archipelago of Nosy Hara to the southwest and Cap d'Ambre to the north, are breathtaking.

Although Windsor Castle is impressive, what really makes the trip worthwhile is the journey there. The site is remote and can only be accessed by 4WD; you'll pass beautiful and varied scenery along the way, and get a fascinating insight into the local economy and what life is like in remote areas.

After driving through Diego's industrial estate, you'll reach the salt marshes run by the Compagnie Salinière de Madagascar. This is one of Madagascar's most important salt-producing areas, with an annual production of 80,000 tons destined for food and industrial markets. You'll also drive through paddy fields (some producing three crops a year thanks to irrigation, others relying on the rain for their annual crop), forests of mango trees (reputed to be the best in the country) and miles of arid bushland with wandering zebus. The villages on Baie du Courrier make their living from fishing; a pick-up truck takes the catch to Diego daily. If you get to the bay before lunchtime, you'll have a chance to see the weighing and trading of the goods by the waterside.

Since this trip is all about local knowledge and anecdotes, the key is a good guide. One of the best ways of doing the excursion is by quad bike with Diego Raid (p141), as the terrain is fun and varied. All tour operators in Diego can also organise the trip with a 4WD, driver and guide (Ar321,000 for up to three people); shop around and ask to meet the guide before you go.

wood, and complements the rough-hewn walls and muted colours. Hervé produces excellent food and arranges excursions into the Montagne d'Ambre park.

Nature Lodge LODGE €€€
(☑ 034 20 123 06; www.naturelodge-ambre.com; bungalow Ar230,000) A couple of kilometres north of Joffreville, Nature Lodge boasts magnificent views of the valley and lovely wooden safari-lodge-style cottages. The interiors are very chic, with colourful batiks, original sculptures and raffia matting on the walls. Meals are served in the large thatched dining room and bar (meals Ar35,000).

ⓘ Information

There is no electricity in Joffreville; hotels generally turn on their generators from 5pm to 10pm. The nearest bank is in Diego Suarez.

ⓘ Getting There & Away

The road from Diego Suarez is in bad condition. It is easy to catch a *taxi-brousse* to Joffreville (Ar3000, 1½ hours) from Diego. Vehicles depart from the Gare Routière behind the Jovenna petrol station. It is unlikely you'll find a vehicle back to Diego after 4pm.

Parc National Montagne d'Ambre

This wonderful **national park** (www.parcs-madagascar.com; permit per day Ar55,000, guides Ar30,000-Ar80,000) is literally a breath of fresh air from the arid northern plains: at 1000m, it is generally 10°C cooler than in Diego or Ankarana, even more in winter, and its luxuriant forests could not contrast more with the mineral beauty of the lower grounds.

It rains almost every day in Montagne d'Ambre, and the park (182 sq km) and adjacent massif act as Diego's water reservoir: hydrologists have calculated that the area contributes 50 million cu metres of water annually to northern Madagascar, enough to support 700 sq km of rice paddies.

For visitors, the park provides lovely walks in gorgeous forests, with plenty of waterfalls and lakes to rest by. The summer season (December to April) is the best for seeing reptiles and amphibians, but birdwatching and views from the summit are better in winter months. One day is enough to get a good sense of what the park and the wildlife are like, and two days will give you time to hike to the summit and discover many of the lakes and waterfalls that dot the park.

🏃 Activities

Wildlife Watching

Of the seven species of lemur found in the park, the most notable are the crowned lemur and Sanford's lemur. Others include the rufous mouse lemur, the dwarf and northern sportive lemurs, the aye-aye (rarely seen) and the local Montagne d'Ambre fork-marked lemur. Among other mammals, the ring-tailed mongoose is probably the most frequently observed.

Reptile and amphibian life thrives in the park's humid conditions, and Montagne d'Ambre is where you'll find the diminutive Brookesia chameleon, the world's smallest. It lives in leaf litter and you'll need your guide's well-trained eyes to find it.

Hiking

There are six hiking trails in Montagne d'Ambre ranging from easy one-hour walks to more strenuous eight-hour hikes. Many can be combined to tailor your own circuit: ask your guide to recommend the best itinerary.

Highlights include the Voie des Mille Arbres (Path of a Thousand Trees), a majestic alley planted with tall exotic species (Montagne d'Ambre was an important research centre for forestry and tree plantations during the 20th century); the Petit

---

> ### ℹ️ PARC NATIONAL MONTAGNE D'AMBRE
>
> **Best time to visit** Year-round.
>
> **Key highlight** Beautiful waterfalls and streams; the world's smallest chameleon (if you manage to see it!).
>
> **Wildlife** Lemurs, amphibians, birds, wild orchids.
>
> **Habitat** Humid forest.
>
> **Gateway town** Joffreville.
>
> **Transport options** From Joffreville, 4km by foot or private vehicle.
>
> **Things you should know** It rains almost every day at Montagne d'Ambre, and temperatures can drop to a nippy 3°C at night and reach just 10°C or 15°C on winter days (June to September) – take warm clothes and a waterproof jacket.

Lac, a small crater lake also known as Lac de la Coupe Verte; and Cascade Antankarana, a beautiful waterfall flowing into a tranquil pool surrounded by fern-covered cliffs. Nearby is the path known as Jardin Botanique, a forest track lined with orchids, palms, lianas and bromeliads. Not far away, another trail leads to the small Cascade Sacrée, a sacred waterfall where locals often make offerings.

A longer track leads to the viewpoint over Cascade Antomboka (or Grande Cascade), a narrow waterfall that plunges 80m into a forest grotto.

The summit of Montagne d'Ambre (Amber Mountain; 1475m) is reached via an 11km trail heading south from the park entrance. From the campsite at Grand Lac, it's a relatively easy three- to four-hour hike, and it's less than an hour from the base to the summit. On clear days (sadly, a rare event), there are wonderful views of the lush forests. Just below the summit is Lac Maudit, where local *fady* (taboo) prohibits swimming, and to the southeast is the larger Grand Lac, where you are allowed to camp.

🛏️ Sleeping

There are three campsites (per tent Ar2000, under cover Ar4000) in the park, all in gorgeous locations. The campsite near the Cascade Sacrée has the best facilities, with picnic tables, showers and water. The other two sites, near Grand Lac and Lac Maudit, only have pit toilets. Reserve your spot through the national park headquarters.

Gîte d'Etape   CABIN €

(dm Ar10,000) Run by the park, this cabin has a kitchen and a sitting area. It's located near the Cascade Sacrée, in a beautiful clearing. Bookings are via the national park headquarters.

ℹ️ Information

The park's **headquarters** (📞 032 41 646 06, 032 49 925 54; www.parcs madagascar.com; ⊗ 7.30am-4pm), at the park entrance, 4km southwest of Joffreville, can help with information, permits and compulsory guides. Most guides speak French and English.

ℹ️ Getting There & Away

The park entrance is about 4km southwest of Joffreville. There are no *taxis-brousses* from Joffreville to the park entrance so if you don't have a private vehicle, you'll have to walk. A chartered taxi for the day from Diego costs Ar80,000.

Réserve Spéciale Ankarana

Réserve Spéciale Ankarana (www. parcs-madagascar.com; entry permit per day Ar65,000, compulsory guides for up to 6 people Ar25,000-50,000) is a striking and undeveloped fantasy-land that's home to uniquely Madagascan sights: psychedelic fields of spiky *tsingy* (limestone pinnacle formations) sitting next to dry forests. Running through and under the *tsingy* are hidden forest-filled canyons and subterranean rivers.

The park is famed for its bat-filled grottoes and mysterious caves steeped in legend and history, where the Antakarana (the predominant tribal group in northern Madagascar) took refuge from the Merina (the traditional ruling elite from the highlands) during the 18th-century tribal wars.

🏃 Activities

Hiking

Ankarana is best known for its serrated, dark-grey *tsingy* (the word means 'walking on tip-toes') and its caves, and there are a variety of circuits taking in the highlights.

ℹ️ RÉSERVE SPÉCIALE ANKARANA

Best time to visit June to December, when both the eastern and western parts of the park are accessible (the west is cut off in the rainy season).

Key highlight Dark-grey *tsingy* (limestone pinnacle formations) and magnificent caves.

Wildlife Bats, birds and lemurs.

Habitat Dry deciduous forest.

Gateway town Mahamasina.

Transport options *Taxi-brousse* to Mahamasima (between Ambilobe and Diego), or private vehicle.

Things you should know Most lakes and rivers are sacred in Ankarana, so bathing and swimming are not permitted. Bring a torch for visiting the caves. Guides are compulsory.

The park is split in two halves, which are distinct and not easily linked, so plan on two days to visit both sides.

The eastern half is the most accessible, via the village of Mahamasina, and the best place to admire the strange-looking *tsingy*. The easiest way to see these surreal pinnacles is to do the two- to three-hour **Grotte des Chauves-Souris** (Bat Cave) circuit. This impressive cave has superb stalactites and stalagmites, and thousands of bats; nearby is a small viewpoint from where you can look over the **Petits Tsingy**.

The route to the **Grands Tsingy** is longer – five hours return – with some interesting sights on the way, including **Perte des Rivières**, a massive rock chasm into which three of the park's rivers plunge during the rainy season (they emerge 20km later in the Mozambique Channel). There are some good viewpoints and a rope bridge to cross. The hike to the pretty **Lac Vert** is the longest circuit (nine hours in total) and takes in all the main sights in the eastern half of the park.

The western half of Ankarana is different and only accessible from June to December. Here the focus is on three sets of caves – **Grotte Squelette** (Skeleton Cave), **Grotte Cathédrale** (Cathedral Cave) and **Grotte d'Andrafiabe** – which you can visit through a subterranean circuit (if this doesn't appeal, another circuit links two of the caves via a 'normal' path). There are beautiful canyons along the way, including **Canyon d'Andohalambo**.

Wildlife & Flora

The dry *tsingy* are full of strangely shaped succulents such as *Euphorbia* and *Pachypodium*, while the sheltered intervening canyons are filled with leafy cassias, figs, baobabs and other trees typical of dry deciduous forest.

Of the area's more than 10 species of lemur, the most numerous are crowned, Sanford's and northern sportive lemurs. Tenrecs and ring-tailed mongooses are also common, the latter particularly around campsites where they come in search of food (make sure you pack everything away).

More than 90 species of bird have been identified in the reserve, including the orange-and-white kingfisher, crested coua, Madagascan fish eagle, crested wood ibis and banded kestrel. Many of the park's guides are keen birders and will relish the opportunity to tell you about them.

Réserve Spéciale Ankarana

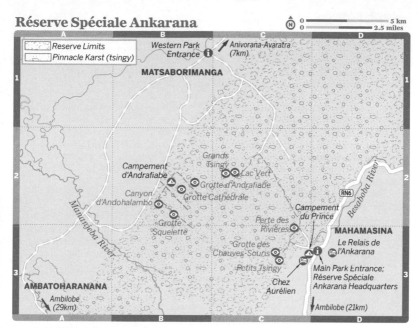

Fourteen of Madagascar's 33 species of bat live here, of which you're bound to see at least half a dozen (no vampires!) in the park's numerous caves.

And finally, one animal you're very likely to see, even though you'd probably rather not, is the scorpion: they thrive in Ankarana, living under rocks and logs. To make sure that you find them, rather than them finding you, don't leave your bag on the forest floor and check where you sit. Campers will have to be especially careful with their shoes and when packing their tent.

🛏 Sleeping & Eating

The reserve has two basic campgrounds with pit toilets and no drinking water: **Campement d'Andrafiabe** (Andrafiabe; per tent Ar5000) and **Campement du Prince** (Grottes des Chauves-Souris; per tent Ar5000).

Chez Aurélien BUNGALOW €
(☑ 032 40 630 14; aurelien_ank@yahoo.fr; Mahamasina; bungalow Ar25,000-50,000) A brilliant option for independent budget travellers, Chez Aurélien is located right next to the park entrance on the RN6 – perfect for those travelling by *taxi-brousse*. Bungalows are basic and clean, and the restaurant is excel-

lent, with a lovely dining room in a small thatched shelter. The *menu* (a three-course meal with a choice of mains; Ar15,000) is good value.

★ Iharana Bush Camp LODGE €€€
(☑ 032 11 062 96, 020 22 312 10; www.iharana bushcamp.mg; d ½-board per person €92; ☺ closed Dec-Mar; 🖥🏊) 🍴 Although not far from Ambilobe, this gorgeous lodge is perfectly placed for exploring the Réserve Spéciale Ankarana. Wattle and daub bungalows are widely spaced for privacy and are beautifully appointed; each has its own deck with views over a lake and the *tsingy*.

Find the lodge by turning west 7km north of Ambilobe; follow the signposts along the sandy track for 12km.

Electricity is all solar-powered and there are no power points in the bungalows. Excursions include taking a *pirogue* on the lake and walks into the *tsingy*. For extra romance, champagne is served at the Ambatomiloloha *tsingy* lookout point on full-moon nights. An open-air restaurant and bar, massage room and pool complete the picture.

Le Relais de l'Ankarana GUESTHOUSE €€€
(☑ 032 02 222 94; http://relaisdeankarana. unblog.fr; Mahamasina; d Ar0,000) Run by the

DON'T MISS

TSINGY ROUGES

About 65km southeast of Diego lies one of Madagascar's most awesome natural wonders, the **Tsingy Rouges** (Red Tsingy; admission Ar10,000). These scraggly pinnacles, erosion's work of art, are made of laterite, an iron-oxide-rich soil with an intense red-brick colour.

These surreal formations stand on the edge of beautiful canyons: it's a fragile environment, and local authorities have thankfully stepped in to protect the site. There are three areas you can access, including a breathtaking viewpoint.

The most stunning site is at the bottom of a small ravine, where *tsingy* (pinnacle formations) line an entire bank like an army of sentinels. If you're here with a guide, ask him or her to show you the three natural pigments found in the soil – ochre, vermilion and magenta – which northern Malagasies use for face paints and natural dyes.

Because of their colour, the *tsingy* are best admired early in the morning (around 7am or 8am) or late in the afternoon (around 4pm), when the light is low and warm.

You will need a 4WD to access the Red Tsingy: the turn-off on the RN6 is 45km south of Diego and signposted. It's then 20km eastwards along a dirt track that's pretty good in some places, dismal in others. En route, you'll cross a number of eucalyptus plantations destined for charcoal production. (The majority of Malagasies use charcoal for cooking and its production is a leading cause of deforestation, so these plantations help preserve primary forests.) You'll also be treated to sweeping views of the Indian Ocean. The dirt track can be impassable during the rainy season (December to April).

hospitable Hobaya family, the Relais is a wonderful halt on the Diego–Nosy Be route. The rooms are comfortable and elegant, with exquisite wood-clad ceilings. The garden is planted with drought-resistant plants to allow for limited water resources. The food is superb, too (three-course meals Ar24,000). The Hobayas speak English, Spanish and Italian, as well as French.

ℹ Information

→ The park's **headquarters** (⊘7.30am-4pm) is located at the eastern entrance of the park in the village of Mahamasina on the RN6. Entry permits and compulsory guides must be arranged here.

→ There are no park offices at the western entrance of Ankarana, so make sure you make all arrangements in Mahamasina. The western entrance is unreachable during the rainy season.

ℹ Getting There & Away

Mahamasina village is approximately 100km southwest of Diego Suarez and about 40km north of Ambilobe along the RN6. The main park entrance at Mahamasina is accessible year-round and easily reached by *taxi-brousse*; drivers can drop you off at your hotel or at the park entrance, and you won't have problems flagging a vehicle for your onward journey. Be aware that you'll likely have to pay the whole Diego–Ambilobe fare (Ar18,000).

To reach the western half of the park, you'll need your own vehicle. All tour operators in Diego Suarez can arrange 4WD hire to Ankarana, as well as multiday excursions or day trips from Diego.

Ambilobe

Ambilobe is a junction town for transport between the northeast coast (Vohémar, Marojejy, Sambava) and Madagascar's north (Diego Suarez) and northwest coast (Ambanja). As with junction towns the world over, it is neither attractive nor interesting, but if you need to stay the night, **Floridas Eden** (✉032 05 033 83; www.floridas-eden-ambilobe.com; d Ar60,000-80,000; ✳🛜) is the best of a sorry bunch.

You'll find vehicles to Diego Suarez (Ar15,000, three hours) and Ambanja (Ar15,000, 1½ hours) throughout the day; *taxis-brousses* for Vohémar (Ar30,000, 18 hours) leave daily.

SAVA REGION

The Sava region (known for its four principal towns, Sambava, Antalaha, Vohémar and Andapa) is disconnected from the rest of the country, with the exception of the airports at Sambava and Antalaha, and one rough road: the 157km piste between Ambilobe and Vohémar, for which you will need a 4WD, has been badly degraded by the rains of 2015. Count on 10 hours, or 18 by *taxi-brousse*. It is virtually impassable in the rainy season – the huge trucks you'll see navigating the potholes can take up to a month to get through at that time of year.

The only overland route from Maroantsetra to Antalaha is on foot, requiring several days of hiking. Having said that, the airports make the region's principal attraction, the superb Parc National de Marojejy, easily accessible. The area is economically better off than most, as its main crop is the valuable vanilla bean. You can enjoy a decent beach break here, too. So this is a pleasant place to be marooned, particularly as there are very few tourists to be found.

Vohémar (Iharana)

The small town of Vohémar lies on the coast and has beautiful, if wild, beaches. Swimming is not usually possible along this coast because of strong currents, but Vohémar is protected by a reef. Ask locals where it's safe to swim. The town has a couple of banks on the main road.

Vohémar is a good place to stay if you want to visit the Loky Manambato Protected Area in Daraina. Cheapest is **Hôtel Sol-y-Mar** (☑ 032 60 202 27; bungalow small/ large Ar26,000/51,000), a row of ramshackle bungalows on a beautiful beach. Also in a stunning location is the **Baie d'Iharana Hôtel** (☑ 032 43 806 35; d Ar70,000-100,000; ❋ 🛜).

Sambava

Capital of the vanilla industry, Sambava also produces cocoa, cloves, coconuts and coffee. The road between Sambava and Antalaha is not only beautiful, but the air is redolent with the scent of vanilla. There is little tourism, but there are some good places to stay, particularly at the beach. The beach itself is very long, and almost unoccupied, with enormous crashing waves. Take care with currents (and, some say, sharks). If you have been travelling hard, Sambava is an inexpensive place to recharge your batteries, particularly after a tough hike in Marojejy. It is also the best place to stay prior to visiting the park, as it can be reached by taxi from Sambava with an early start, so you don't need to overnight in Andapa.

⊙ Sights & Activities

The helpful staff at the **Office Régional de Tourisme Sava** (☑ 032 27 123 81; ort.sava. bureau@gmail.com) can organise trips to the Parc National de Marojejy and vanilla plantations, cultural walking or cycling tours, photographic expeditions and pirogue trips.

Domaine d'Ambohimanitra FARM
(☑ 032 07 411 07; admission Ar80,000) Meaning 'hill of a thousand perfumes', the Domaine d'Ambohimanitra produces various types of vanilla along with coffee, cinnamon, pepper, ylang-ylang and cloves. On a four- to five-hour visit you will learn about production and processing. Lunch at the gracious colonial farmhouse is included.

Soavoanio Coconut Plantation FARM
(☑ 032 04 871 40, 020 88 966 35; contact@ soavoanio.mg; admission Ar10,000; ⊘ 9am-1pm Mon-Fri) This enormous coconut plantation extends across 50 sq km, where the trees march away into the distance in strict lines. On the two-hour visit you will see germination, seedlings and processing of the nuts into copra and coconut oil. Beehives produce coconut-flavoured honey.

⨋ Sleeping & Eating

Staying on the beach is highly recommended. Otherwise there is some very inexpensive budget accommodation nearby.

KHAT: A LEGAL HIGH?

The area between Ambilobe and Diego is a big *khat*-growing area. This small flowering shrub produces a compound that is an amphetamine-like stimulant. Chewed, the plant's leaves cause hyperactivity and euphoria, and are a popular drug, particularly among *taxi-brousse* drivers, who often work very long hours.

Although the authorities largely turn a blind eye to *khat* production and consumption, it is worth knowing that it is still illegal. Before the political turmoil of 2009, there had been talk of the government taking a stand to either legalise *khat* so that its trade could be included in the formal economy, or enforcing its illegality and encouraging growers to produce other crops. Unfortunately, the political crisis has left the matter unsettled for now.

WORTH A TRIP

LOKY MANAMBATO PROTECTED AREA

Madagascan NGO Fanamby manages the **Loky Manambato Protected Area** (http://association-fanamby.org; permit Ar10,000, guide Ar27,000-40,000), 56km west of Vohémar, to support local villages and protect flora and fauna. Most spectacular are the critically endangered golden-crowned Tattersalli sifakas: about 1000 of them live only in the seven forested areas of this reserve.

Hire a Fanamby guide through **Hôtel Lémurien Blanc** (☑ 032 81 947 60; www.lemurien blanc.com; Daraina; d Ar30,000) in the village of Daraina (the price should be no more than Ar15,000 plus the entry permit of Ar10,000) or stay at Fanamby's new **Camp Tattersalli** (☑ Narcisse Amavatra 032 26 219 27; per person incl breakfast Ar125,000, menu Ar30,000) in the forest. Set out early, as the lemurs sleep during the heat of the day. It's a 50-minute drive from Daraina into the forest, then 20 to 30 minutes' easy walking; you will most likely see the lemurs. Allow at least three hours. But don't expect a pristine forest experience: the area is home to around 100 gold panners: you'll meet them and see the holes they've dug throughout the forest. It's *fady* (taboo) to harm the sifakas, so they are not afraid of humans.

You will need a 4WD to reach Daraina from Vohémar; it's not accessible during the rainy season.

Hotel Flamboyant
HOTEL **€**
(☑ 032 80 047 37; d Ar15,000) For the budget-minded, the Hotel Flamboyant is clean and incredibly cheap. It's just two blocks from the beach; there's no sign, but it's the second pink house down the alley to the right of the Victoria Hotel.

Las Palmas
BUNGALOW **€€**
(☑ 032 40 073 72; laspalmas.hotel@gmail.com; bungalow/r Ar68,000/75,000; ❄️🛜) Las Palmas is not signposted, but is the most southerly of the beach hotels. It is a well-manicured property in a great location across from the beach, offering nice rooms with great bathrooms, and some bungalows. The accommodation is spacious and comfortable. Staff rustle up some good food (mains from Ar12,000), served on the wide terrace.

Mimi-Hôtel
HOTEL **€€**
(☑ 032 07 610 28; www.mimi-hotel.marojejy.com; r Ar40,000-45,000, bungalow Ar55,000; 🛜) This is a pleasant hotel in a garden setting. Rooms have fans and nets. It might not be on the beach, but the added bonus is the tea room: Patisserie Mimi is the best place for breakfast and cakes. The restaurant serves Madagascan and Chinese dishes (mains Ar9000). The owner's son, Bruno Lee, is involved with tourism in the region.

★ Hôtel Orchidea Beach II
HOTEL **€€€**
(☑ 032 04 383 77; http://orchideabeach.marojejy.com; Plage des Cocotiers; d/bungalow Ar84,000/44,000; ❄️🛜) This is a charming, quiet, leafy hotel, with whitewashed buildings and a manicured courtyard tucked away on a pleasant side street across from the beach. The brightly painted rooms have nice tiled baths (but no nets), and the amiable staff serves up excellent food (mains Ar9000). The two beachfront bungalows are a steal, with crashing surf right outside your door.

Boule d'Or
PIZZA **€**
(pizza from Ar10,000; ⏱ 4-9pm Tue-Sun) The only pizzeria, it's behind the Hôtel Orchidea Beach II, opposite La Terrasse.

La Terrasse
MADAGASCAN **€**
(mains from Ar12,000; ⏱ 8am-1am Tue-Sun) Has good Madagascan seafood and fun karaoke at night.

❶ Information

➤ There are several banks with ATMs at the northern end of town.

➤ Internet access is available at BIC (Ar1500 for 30 minutes).

❶ Getting There & Around

AIR

Air Madagascar (☑ 020 88 920 37; Route Principale) flies from Sambava several times weekly to Antananarivo (€265, one hour). There are also flights to Diego Suarez (€178, 30 minutes), and weekly flights to Maroantsetra via Tamatave (Toamasina; €312, 30 minutes).

Sambava airport is about 2km south of town; a taxi is Ar5000.

TAXI-BROUSSE

→ *Taxis-brousses* to Antalaha (Ar5000, two hours) depart from the southern *taxi-brousse* station in the market.

→ The northern *taxi-brousse* station handles transport to Andapa (Ar8000, 3½ hours), Vohémar (Ar8000, four hours) and Diego Suarez (Ar60,000, 18 hours).

→ A private car to Andapa will cost you Ar90,000; buying the two front seats in a *brousse* is a far less expensive while still comfortable proposition.

Parc National de Marojejy

The **Parc National de Marojejy** (www. marojejy.com; entry permit per day Ar45,000) is one of Madagascar's great undiscovered parks, a fact all the more astonishing because it is one of the best managed and easiest to get to. You can fly from Antananarivo to Sambava or Antalaha, jump in a taxi, and within an hour or two you are off on a world-class hike.

The park consists of over 550 sq km of pristine mountainous **rainforest** – an often thick, steep, and root-filled jungle with numerous streams and **waterfalls**. It is a primordial place, where the astonishing 'angel of the forest', the silky *sifaka*, inhabits misty mountains, and spectacular views of the Marojejy Massif peek through the canopy. For naturalists, the area is noted for its extraordinary biodiversity, including 2000 types of plants, 147 species of reptile and amphibian, 118 species of bird, and 11 species of lemur, about 70% of which are

---

ⓘ PARC NATIONAL DE MAROJEJY

Best time to visit August to November: it's dry season, and birding is best.

Key highlight Silky *sifaka*.

Wildlife Massive millipedes, paradise flycatcher, mantella frog.

Habitat Four levels of forest: low altitude, dense montane, high montane, high altitude.

Gateway towns Sambava and Andapa.

Transport options Taxi from Sambava or Andapa (Ar7000).

Things you should know Minimum four days' hike to scale the summit.

---

endemic to Madagascar. It also ascends through four levels of forest, enhancing the variety of experience. In 2007 the park was designated a Unesco World Heritage Site.

Assisted by American researcher Erik Patel, whose **Simpona** (www.simpona.org) organisation works to protect the silky *sifaka*, the local MNP office has constructed three quality camps at different altitudes, each set in an attractive location. Trained guides, cooks, and porters provide excellent service. Cabins are cleaned regularly. Revenue is distributed to local communities, helping turn conservation into a winning enterprise. There is also an excellent interpretation centre at the park office (with signs in English), a model for parks elsewhere. For more information see www. marojejy.com.

🏃 Activities

The park has a single trail ascending through three camps to the summit of Mt Marojejy. The trail officially begins at the park boundary, about a 1½-hour walk from the park office at Manantenina. If you want to cut down your hiking time, you can arrange for a ride to the trailhead, but it is a beautiful walk to get there, along a dirt road through lush mountains, small villages and rice paddies.

Camp One (Mantella), at 450m, takes about two hours to reach, and has six cabins (wooden frames with canvas walls) and a campground. This is an area of lowland rainforest.

Camp Two (Marojejia), at 775m, takes an additional two hours and a bit more work to reach. It has four cabins with fully made beds, and a large covered kitchen and dining area. This is a transition area between lowland and montane rainforest, and is the best place to see wildlife, including colourful millipedes the length of your hand (a lot more enjoyable than it sounds), leaf-tailed geckos and paradise flycatchers. It is also a wonderful place to hang out, surrounded by the sounds of the forest and the rush of a nearby stream.

Camp Three (Simpona), at 1250m, is the base camp for ascents to the summit, and has two cabins with a sheltered dining area. It is a very steep and strenuous climb to get there, requiring both hands and feet as you surmount one root after another, a challenge magnified when it's wet. The final leg to the summit, 2132m high, stretches

OFF THE BEATEN TRACK

RÉSERVE SPÉCIALE D'ANJANAHARIBE-SUD

The entry permit for Marojejy includes entry to Réserve Spéciale d'Anjanaharibe-Sud. This 182.5-sq-km area to the southwest is little visited. It is 20km from Andapa by rutted dirt road, has no facilities, and offers much of the same vegetation and wildlife as Marojejy. That said, it is a place of outstanding beauty and solitude, where the wail of the *indri* can be heard. More information is available at the park office in Manantenina.

2km and can take up to four or five hours to traverse.

Note: the hike from the park boundary to the second camp is a nature expedition. The trail from Camp Two is a climbing expedition. If you prefer the former, there is no need to go past Camp Marojejia, which anyone in decent shape can reach. Beyond it you must be very fit, and prepared for cold weather.

🛏 Sleeping

Accommodation in the Parc National de Marojejy is found at three levels along the single trail to the summit (p155): Camp One (Mantella) is at 450m and has six cabins (wooden frames with canvas sides) and a campground. Camp Two (Marojejia) is at 775m and has four cabins, and Camp Three (Simpona) at 1250m has two cabins. Cabins are Ar10,000 per bed, and the campsite Ar4000 per person.

If you have to stay outside the park, Sambava is recommended. The only other option is Andapa, a small town nestled in the hills some 40km away on the way to Réserve Spéciale d'Anjanaharibe-Sud. It is closer to the park, but further from Sambava (to which you must return), lacks the appeal of the beach, and has little accommodation.

If you do choose Andapa, the best place to stay is the surprising **Hotel Beanana** (☑ 020 88 070 47, 032 40 226 10; http://beanana. marojejy.com; Andapa; d Ar38,000), a bright-white drive-in motel that is clean and inexpensive. **Hotel Vatosoa** (☑ 032 52 990 87, 020 88 070 78; d Ar20,000) offers more-basic rooms and a good restaurant (mains Ar7000).

ℹ Information

The **MNP office** (☑ 033 49 403 38; www. marojejy.com) is located 60km from Sambava, and 40km from Andapa, in the village of Manantenina, and arranges entry permits (per day Ar45,000). Guide/cook fees are Ar25,000/15,000 per day if you provide the guide's food, Ar30,000/20,000 otherwise. Porters are Ar4000 to Ar7000 per day depending on the length of the hike. An excellent English-speaking guide is Mosesy, the head of the local guide organisation. To maximize your chance of seeing a silky *sifaka*, an additional specialist guide is necessary.

ℹ Getting There & Away

Taxis-brousses run daily between Andapa and Sambava (Ar7000, 2½ hours), and will drop you off at the park office en route.

Antalaha

A relatively affluent city, thanks to the vanilla bean, Antalaha surprises with its street lights, proper drainage and excellent roads. Beyond lies the Masoala Peninsula, which can only be crossed by foot. Consequently, Antalaha is a starting point for hikes into Masoala, although most people begin in Maroantsetra, which offers better access to the coastal lodges and Nosy Mangabe, as well as the relative calm of the Baie d'Antongil.

⦿ Sights & Activities

Macolline   NATURE RESERVE
(☑ 032 55 127 71, 032 07 161 01; www.macolline. org; admission Ar33,500-61,500) Billed as a botanical hiking trail, Macolline is an arboretum on the banks of the River Ankavanana, 3km north of Antalaha. Guided walks of three to six hours can include lunch and a pirogue ride. There are fruit trees and medicinal plants, as well as frogs, chameleons, millipedes and butterflies. For Ar5500 you can plant a tree and make a contribution to the organisation. Proceeds go towards local villages and support former leprosy sufferers through the organisation Comité d'Aide aux Lépreux d'Antalaha (CALA).

**Bureau de Liaison du
Parc National de Masoala**   HIKING
(☑ 032 41 800 81; Ave de l'Indépendance) Arranges hikes into Masoala (p191) park, including permits and guides. Fees are the same as for entering from Maroantsetra.

🛏 Sleeping & Eating

Hôtel Florida   HOTEL €

(📞 032 41 555 12; d from Ar20,000; ❄) Your best budget option, the Florida has a cheery yellow and red paint job in the bar/reception area. It's on the main road opposite Pharmacy Kam-Hyo. Some more expensive rooms with air-con are also available.

Hazovola   HOTEL €€

(📞 032 41 287 11; www.hotelantalaha.com; d incl breakfast from Ar65,000; ❄ 🛜 🏊) This is a lovely hotel with a gorgeous pool. Rooms have nice tiled baths, balconies and flat-screen TVs. Locals praise the restaurant (mains from Ar15,000), and there's an ice-cream parlour (Ar2000 per scoop).

★ Hôtel Océan Momo   BUNGALOW €€€

(📞 032 02 340 69; www.ocean-momo.com; d Ar80,000, mains Ar12,000; ❄ 🛜) Readers recommend this elegant hotel set in gardens about 250m south of the port. It has imposing white bungalows in rows beside the beautiful beach, with dark wood furniture and four-poster beds. The restaurant is large and tastefully decorated, with a range of seafood on offer (mains Ar12,000). More expensive bungalows have air-conditioning. Staff can arrange various excursions.

Jeannick Gargotte   MADAGASCAN, EUROPEAN €

(pizza Ar9000-13,000; 🕙 dinner Tue-Sun) This expat hang-out is a popular spot for pizza and a range of Madagascan/European food. It's one block back from the Jovenna petrol station.

ℹ Information

There are banks and ATMs in town.

ℹ Getting There & Around

AIR

➨ Air Madagascar flies twice weekly to Antananarivo (€265, 1½ hours) and to Tamatave (Toamasina; €221, 1½ hours).

➨ Antalaha's Antsirabato airport is regularly damaged by cyclones, in which case you can fly to Sambava.

BOAT

➨ Cargo boats sail regularly on the rough and sometimes dangerous journey between Antalaha and Maroantsetra, sometimes also stopping near Cap Est. There are no set schedules; inquire at the port about sailings.

➨ There are also cargo boats to other areas along the east coast, including Tamatave (Toamasina), Sambava and Vohémar.

TAXI & TAXI-BROUSSE

➨ A taxi to the airport costs Ar3000.

➨ Heading north, there are usually several *taxis-brousses* each day between Antalaha and Sambava (Ar7000, three hours) and Vohémar (Ar8000, four hours). Departures are from the *taxi-brousse* stand about 2km north of town.

➨ Heading south, two *taxis-brousses* daily go to Cap Est (Ar15,000, four hours) in the dry season. *Taxis-brousses* towards Cap Est depart from the *taxi-brousse* station on the airport road.

Eastern Madagascar

Best Places to Eat

➡ La Véranda (p172)

➡ Piment Banane (p172)

➡ Mangrove Le Gourmand
(p183)

➡ Idylle Beach (p181)

Best Places to Stay

➡ Hôtel Feon'ny Ala (p162)

➡ Chez Sica (p185)

➡ Dounia Forest Lodge
(p192)

➡ Libertalia (p183)

➡ Ony Hôtel (p168)

Why Go?

Eastern Madagascar is travel the way it used to be. There is a wildness here of primordial allure, from the misty mountains of Masoala, down the huge coastline with its pounding sea and overhanging palms, to the lush waterways of the Pangalanes Lakes. When you arrive back home, it all has the quality of a dream.

This part of the country is largely cut off from the rest, and from itself, by a degraded transportation network, including some roads out of an engineer's nightmare. Travelling here requires a combination of plane, car, 4WD, dirt bike, scooter, pirogue (dugout canoe), ferry, cargo boat, *taxi-brousse* (bush taxi) and motorboat. This inaccessibility results in isolated communities and, for the traveller, a constant sense of coming upon undiscovered locales, including entire national parks. There's no doubt it can be frustrating at times, but eastern Madagascar produces more travellers' tales than anywhere else. If you value that, come here first.

When to Go
Tamatave (Toamasina)

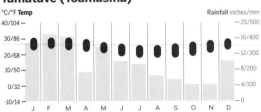

Jun–Oct Vanilla season. Flights can be full in the northeast.

Jul–Sep Whale watching in the Baie d'Antongil.

Dec–Mar Hold onto your hat, it's cyclone season.

Eastern Madagascar Highlights

1 Wake to the wail of the *indri* in **Parc National Andasibe Mantadia** (p162)

2 Drift along **Lac Ampitabe** (p166) on a solar-powered boat from Vohibola

3 Drive the infamous **RN5** (p177) from Soanierana-Ivongo to Maroantsetra

4 Watch the elusive aye-aye eat a coconut during a night walk on **Aye-Aye Island** (p187)

5 Camp out on the tropical jungle island of **Nosy Mangabe** (p190)

6 See breaching humpbacks on a **whale-watching trip** (p180)

7 Explore the island of **Île Sainte Marie** (p177) by quad or dirt bike

8 Stay in an ecolodge at **Parc National de Masoala** (p191)

9 Do absolutely nothing on **Île aux Nattes** (p184)

ℹ Getting There & Away

Air Madagascar (www.airmadagascar.com) serves Tamatave (Toamasina), Antalaha, Sambava, Maroantsetra and Île Sainte Marie, largely in a circuit from Antananarivo (Tana). From Réunion, Air Madagascar flies to Île Sainte Marie and Air Austral flies to Tamatave, both three times weekly.

Almost all land access to eastern Madagascar is via a single road, the RN2 from Antananarivo. It is possible to drive up the coast from Fort Dauphin (Taolagnaro), but this is 4WD adventure travel, not transportation.

There is a train service running from Moramanga north to Ambatondrazaka, and east from Moramanga to Tamatave. The line also has a limited service from Tana to Andasibe.

EAST OF ANTANANARIVO

Leaving Antananarivo and heading east, the RN2 passes through gloriously diverse landscapes, from the wooded hills around Lac Mantasoa, to the major-attraction rainforest parks of Andasibe, and onwards to the peaceful, tropical Pangalanes canals that follow the east coast. The road is in good condition, though you will meet many trucks on their way to and from the major port of Tamatave, negotiating the twists and turns along the way. The climate is as varied as the topography: you'll need rain gear in the parks and swimwear on the coast.

Lac Mantasoa

This 20-sq-km artificial lake, built in 1931, is a good place for fishing, sailing and picnicking, and is a popular weekend retreat for Antananarivo residents. The hotels on the lakeside all offer boating, waterskiing, pedalos, fishing and more. The lake also holds a special place in history as being the site where Madagascar's industrial revolution started.

In 1833 Frenchman Jean Laborde built a country palace for Queen Ranavalona I, as well as carpentry and gunsmith shops, a munitions factory, an iron forge and a foundry. The primary aim was to supply the monarch with swords, arms and ammunition. Much of this was destroyed in 1851 when slaves rebelled, whilst other parts now lie underwater, but some notable buildings can still be seen and visited in the village of Mantasoa, offering a fascinating insight into Madagascar's heyday as an industrial powerhouse.

Laborde's home (⊙8am-4pm Mon-Sat, noon-4pm Sun) is a lovely traditional, wood-clad house. Inside there are old photographs and a fair amount of biographical information (in French). His **grave** lies in the local cemetery surrounded by 12 soldiers' tombs. All that remains of the industrial complex are the munitions factory, now a school, some staff houses and an impressive stone furnace.

With its country club feel, **Domaine de l'Ermitage** (☑034 04 960 64, 020 42 660 54; www.ermitagehotel-mg.com; d Ar150,000) attracts a wealthy Tana crowd who come here on weekends. It is rather quiet during the week (when good discounts can be negotiated).

ℹ Getting There & Away

Mantasoa village lies about 60km east of Antananarivo. If you're going by *taxi-brousse* (Ar3000), plan to spend the night here, as it is impossible to know whether you'll find a *taxi-brousse* heading back to Tana in the afternoon.

Moramanga

The first major stop in the east after leaving Antananarivo on the RN2, this commercial centre has little tourism value, but you'll have to pause here if you're heading to the Andasibe parks on public transport. Take a pousse-pousse (rickshaw) around.

⊙ Sights

Musée de la Gendarmerie Nationale

MUSEUM

(Police Museum; ☑020 56 821 39; Camp Tristany; admission Ar5000; ⊙8-11am & 3-5pm) Exhibits cannons, police uniforms, a vintage *taxi-brousse*, and an enormous bunch of dried marijuana.

🛏 Sleeping & Eating

Hotel Nadia

HOTEL €

(☑020 56 822 43; s/d/tr Ar20,000/ 30,000/40,000) A basic budget option in the middle of the busy market, with its own cafeteria. Serviceable, but could be cleaner.

THE DEAD ZONE

With the exception of Manakara, the southeast coast of Madagascar is basically a dead zone for travellers, unless you want pure 4WD adventure. Heading south from Brickaville, Vatomandry, Mahanoro and Nosy-Varika there as virtually no sights or attractions, with the exception of some waterfalls.

In Mananjary the beach is used as a latrine and the market floods in heavy rains. After Manakara, the RN12 is paved as far as the frontier town of Vaingaindrano, and easily traversed save for a 30km stretch of unpaved road north of Farafangana. However, the unpaved 220km between Vaingaindrano and Fort Dauphin (Taolagnaro) is notoriously treacherous and should only be attempted in the dry season with a trustworthy 4WD. The route contains 10 ferry crossings, five motorised and five hand-powered, and two nature reserves. **Parc National de Midongy Sud**, located 100km inland of Vaingaindrano, requires a difficult trip through dense jungle, and is only for specialists. **Manombo Reserve**, 30km to the south of Farafangana, is the only worthwhile stop, home to a patch of coastal forest and the rare white-collared brown lemur.

Swimming is dangerous along the entire coastline due to sharks and strong currents.

Hôtel Restaurant
Espace Diamant   HOTEL €€
(☑ 020 56 823 76; d Ar60,000) This spick-and-span hotel has tiled rooms, big beds and a large restaurant.

Bezanozano   HOTEL €€€
(☑ 032 69 769 03; www.bezanozanohotel.com; d Ar80,000; ▣) This sprawling complex is the best choice in this town. The rooms are large, with balconies, and the restaurant serves Madagascan, European and Chinese fare. Management is helpful, and the huge pool is most welcome in summer. Prices negotiable.

Le Coq d'Or   CHINESE, MADAGASCAN €
(☑ 020 56 820 45; mains from Ar12,000; ☺ lunch & dinner Tue-Sat, lunch Sun) A neat painted cafe off the main road, serving *soupe chinoise* (noodle soup with fish, chicken or vegetables), fried chicken and other Madagascan meals. Highly rated by locals.

❶ Information

The helpful **Regional Tourism Office** (☑ 033 11 413 21; www.ortalma.org) is located above the Bezanozano restaurant and covers Moramanga, the Andasibe parks and Lac Alaotra.

❶ Getting There & Away

TAXI-BROUSSE

Taxis-brousses leave regularly from Antananarivo's eastern *taxi-brousse* station for Moramanga (Ar7000, 2¾ hours).

There are direct *taxi-brousse* connections from Moramanga to Andasibe (Ar2000, 1½ hours) every few hours. To get to Tamatave

(Ar12,000, five to seven hours), you will need to wait until a vehicle coming from Antananarivo arrives with space.

TRAIN

A slow passenger train departs Moramanga for Tamatave (Ar10,000, 10 hours) every Monday at 7am. The return train leaves Tamatave at 8.20am every Tuesday. On Thursday, a train leaves Moramanga for Ambila-Lemaitso (Ar8000, seven hours) at 3pm, and returns on Friday, leaving Ambila-Lemaitso at 8am. A train also leaves Moramanga at 10.30am on Wednesday and Saturday to Ambatondrazaka, returning at 7am on Thursday and Sunday. The journey takes four to five hours and costs Ar14,000 in Palissandre class or Ar9000 in ordinary class. It's best to check the schedule with Madarail (www.madarail.mg) ahead of time, either at the station (best), or online.

Andasibe

The small town of Andasibe is surrounded by several parks and reserves whose unique wildlife and close proximity to the capital have made this area extremely popular with travellers.

The largest is the Parc National Andasibe Mantadia. This is actually the organisational union of two separate parks, the northern Parc National de Mantadia and the much smaller Réserve Spéciale d'Analamazaotra. To these are added Parc Mitsinjo, Réserve de Torotorofotsy and Mahay Mitia Ala (MMA).

Back on the RN2 about 8km east of Andasibe lie two further parks: the Vohimana Forest and the Réserve de Maromizaha.

In and around Andasibe, accommodation is more or less centralised along a single main road. Bring warm clothing in winter, and enough cash to see you through, as the nearest banks/ATMs are in Moramanga.

🛏 Sleeping & Eating

Vohitsara Guest House   GUESTHOUSE €
(✆ 034 60 089 69; vohitsara@hotmail.com; d/tr Ar20,000/30,000) This family-run operation, on the edge of the village near the station, offers a varied selection of spick-and-span budget rooms with external showers and Madagascan food on request. Reception is in the Mitsinjo building.

MNP Campsite   CAMPGROUND €
(camping per site Ar5000, tent hire Ar10,000) Camping is available behind the MNP office. The more expensive site has better toilets. You can also hire a tent if you reserve in advance.

★ Hôtel Feon'ny Ala   BUNGALOW €€
(✆ 020 56 832 02, 033 05 832 02; d/tr bungalow Ar73,200/78,000, camping Ar10,000) Whoever named this garden hotel 'Song of the Forest' was absolutely right: the site is virtually part of the forest in Réserve Spéciale d'Analamazaotra, so close that you can hear the *indris*. The thatched bungalows are close together but comfortable enough, and they have hot showers. The restaurant does all meals well (menu Ar27,000), and can provide picnic lunches for walkers.

There are also twin rooms for Ar37,200.

Hôtel Les Orchidées   HOTEL €€
(✆ 020 56 832 05; hotelorchideeandasibe@yahoo. fr; d Ar40,000) This wooden hotel-restaurant in the centre of Andasibe village seems intent on proving that you can't judge a book by its cover. Once you get past the rough exterior, it feels like a charming cabin, with spartan but clean rooms upstairs. The restaurant offers simple Madagascan staples in a cosy atmosphere (mains Ar15,000).

★ Andasibe Hotel   LODGE €€€
(✆ 034 14 326 27; www.andasibehotel-resto.com; d/f Ar205,000/245,000; ❷❸) This hotel on the west side of the village shines: it has the best double rooms around, with split levels, bold Asian styling, and knockout views across a verdant rice paddy. The restaurant (mains from Ar22,000) has creative French cuisine, and there's a nice pool deck. Located on a forest lake, the hotel also offers kayaking.

Hôtel Mikalo   BUNGALOW €€€
(✆ 034 11 817 85; new bungalow d Ar94,000) This hotel on the south side of the village has a roadside restaurant (set menu Ar25,000) that gets high marks for design. But sort carefully through the bungalows, which come in three levels of varying quality and attention to detail. Pass on the old chalets near the train station in favour of the wooden bungalows with balconies in the forest.

Vakôna Forest Lodge   LODGE €€€
(✆ 034 15 705 80, 033 02 010 01; www.hotelvakona. com; d Ar225,400, mains from Ar20,000; ❷❸) This forest resort has everything – a lake with an island full of lemurs and a crocodile park (entry for both Ar15,000), an equestrian centre, a beautiful lodge, golf and squash, massage and a private airstrip. However, the bungalows are only average. Be aware of the location 2km north of Andasibe: it's a long hike from the park office and you will probably opt for a transfer (Ar40,000).

ℹ Getting There & Away

From Tana, the best way to reach Andasibe is to take a *taxi-brousse* to Moramanga first, then another to Andasibe (Ar2000, 1½ hours). Ask the driver to drop you at your hotel. Otherwise, you can take any *taxi-brousse* along the RN2 for 26km to the Andasibe junction at Antsapanana, then walk or hitch the 3km to the village itself.

If you're leaving Andasibe, you either have to return to Moramanga first, or wait for a *taxi-brousse* on the RN2. This can be difficult going east as *brousses* from Tana tend to be full. If you hire a car or taxi from Tana, keep in mind that you'll have to leave by 6am in order to hear the *indris*. If you hear a clickety-clack, it's the tiny Moramanga–Tamatave passenger train, which passes through Andasibe every Monday and Tuesday.

Parc National Andasibe Mantadia

The Parc National Andasibe Mantadia comprises two distinct parks. More accessible and fairly flat for easy walking is the Réserve Spéciale d'Analamazaotra (8 sq km; formerly known as Périnet), with its entrance and large information centre on the main road to Andasibe. Some 17km to the north lies the wilder, primary forest of Parc National de Mantadia (155 sq km). This is harder terrain but worth the effort.

Analamazaotra gets the most visitors, and tends to fill up from July to October,

Andasibe Area Parks

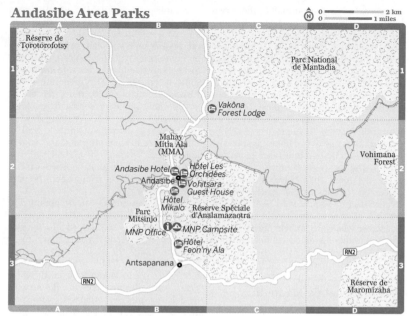

Madagascar's tourist high season. Because the reserve is small, most of it can be covered in short walks, including to two small lakes, **Lac Vert** (Green Lake) and **Lac Rouge** (Red Lake). The best time for seeing (and hearing) *indris* is early in the morning, from 7am to 11am.

ℹ Information

The **MNP office** (⊘ 6am-4pm) for Parc National Andasibe Mantadia is located at the entrance of the Réserve Spéciale d'Analamazaotra and contains a helpful interpretation centre. Entrance permits and guides are available here. The office also sells an informative booklet (Ar5000).

Réserve Spéciale d'Analamazaotra

The real draw of this reserve (entry permit per day Ar45,000) is the rare *indri*, Madagascar's largest lemur, whose unforgettable wail can be heard emanating from the misty forest throughout the day, most commonly in the early morning. There are about 60 resident family groups of two to five *indris* each. You may also see woolly lemurs, grey bamboo lemurs, red-fronted lemurs, black-and-white ruffed lemurs and diademed *sifakas*. In 2005 the Good-

man's mouse lemur was discovered here and identified as a distinct species. Eleven species of tenrec, the immense and colourful Parson's chameleon and seven other chameleon species are also found here. More than 100 bird species have been identified in the park, together with 20 species of amphibian. The park is also home to the endemic palm tree *Ravenea louvelii*, found nowhere else on the island.

There are four organised walking trails, all of which are generally easy going. The easiest, most popular trail is the **Circuit**

ℹ ANDASIBE AREA PARKS

Best time to visit October to November, when orchids are blooming.

Key highlight *Indris*.

Wildlife Diademed *sifaka*, Parson's chameleon, leaf-tailed gecko, paradise flycatcher.

Habitats Primary and secondary mid-altitude rainforest.

Gateway town Andasibe.

Transport options *Taxi-brousse* or car.

Things you should know Bring a raincoat at any time of year.

Indri 1 (guide for four Ar20,000, about two hours), which includes the main lakes and the territory of a single family of *indris*. The moderate Circuit Indri 2 (guide for four Ar30,000, three hours) visits the lakes and encompasses the patches of two separate families. The Circuit Aventure (guide for four Ar40,000, four to six hours) does all of the above, plus some more strenuous walking. Join these circuits together for an 8km trail of about six hours. The Palmier Circuit (2km, one to two hours) is specially designed for children and takes in palms, orchids and two *indri* families.

On the main road between the MNP office and Andasibe is the small Parc des Orchidées (⊘ 7.30am-noon & 1.30-4pm) FREE, which is at its most attractive in October to December when the orchids are in bloom. By late summer it's almost completely dried up. There's no signage so you need a good guide to fully appreciate it.

Parc National de Mantadia

Parc National de Mantadia (entry permit per day Ar45,000), located about 17km north of Andasibe, was created primarily to protect the *indri*, and also hosts the black-and-white ruffed lemur. A quiet, beautiful area with numerous waterfalls and wonderful landscapes, it is undeveloped and seldom visited compared with its popular neighbour to the south, so if you're here in high season it's well worth the detour to escape the crowds. If the weather has been wet (which it often is), watch out for leeches on the trails.

---

❶ BRICKAVILLE: TRANSIT TOWN

Brickaville, reached by train or *taxi-brousse* from Moramanga (Ar12,000, three hours), Antananarivo (Ar17,000, 5½ hours) or Tamatave (Ar5000, 1½ hours), is a ramshackle transit point. From here you can transfer to Ambila-Lemaitso or Manambato in the Pangalanes Lakes, or head direct to Tamatave. There are two *taxi-brousse* stations, north and south, both of which serve the same destinations, except only the north station serves Andasibe (Ar12,000, 2½ hours). There is a BOA bank with ATM on the main street.

Established circuits include the easy 1km Circuit Rianasoa (Ar20,000, one hour) to see *indris*, orchids and a natural pool where you can swim. This can be combined with the Sacred Waterfall for a 2km, two-hour moderate walk with some steep slopes. The moderate 2.8km Circuit Tsakoka (Ar50,000, three hours) is especially good for seeing frogs, birds and plants, while the Trekking Circuit (Ar40,000, 10 hours), a difficult trail of 15km, offers diverse altitudes and superb landscapes. For more of a challenge, you can also embark on an Adventure Circuit of two to three days, camping in the park (Ar50,000 per day).

Permits and guides can be obtained at the MNP office (p163) in Réserve Spéciale d'Analamazaotra. You'll need all your own camping equipment if you're planning to stay the night; the MNP campsite (tent sites free), just outside the park, has no facilities. To get to Mantadia from the MNP office, you will most likely need your own vehicle or bicycle; otherwise, transport can usually be arranged with park staff, or sometimes through guides and local hotels.

Parc Mitsinjo

Located on the main road opposite the MNP office (p163), Mitsinjo is a private reserve run by Association Mitsinjo (✆ 034 68 674 72; www.mitsinjo.com; ⊘ 7am-9pm), set up by guides to promote conservation and community tourism. It's a great idea to add this to your itinerary before or after visiting Parc National Andasibe Mantadia.

There are three circuits: a short circuit (guide per person Ar25,000), a medium circuit (Ar35,000) and a long circuit (Ar50,000). An excellent night hike (Ar15,000, 1½ hours), within the forest, gives you a much better chance of seeing the smaller nocturnal lemurs, sleeping chameleons and rare leaf-tailed lizards. You can also visit the reforestation area and plant a tree (Ar30,000; one ot two hours); there's no separate entry fee. The *Accrobranche* (zipline) through the forest canopy is fun (Ar30,000; 1½ to two hours), and you can try out the hammock 25m up into the trees (both activities Ar50,000).

For more information visit Mitsinjo's small handicrafts shop next to the Parc Mitsinjo office.

Réserve de Torotorofotsy

A varied and attractive landscape of wetlands, forests and small villages, this private reserve is known for its greater bamboo lemurs and excellent birdwatching. A visit here to see the birds, and perhaps the golden mantella frog, costs Ar60,000 per person for four to five hours, including transport.

Like Parc Mitsinjo 12km south, Torotorofotsy is managed by Association Mitsinjo. Information is available at its handicrafts shop next to the Parc Mitsinjo office.

Mahay Mitia Ala

The Mahay Mitia Ala (MMA) park opened in 2011 and is managed by a local association to promote biodiversity, conservation and local development. The same species are found here as in the other parks nearby, including the *indri* and the elusive aye-aye. The main benefit of this park is accessibility. The trails are clear and wide, allowing better views of wildlife, and there are no steep hills such as exist elsewhere. The park entrance is 1km north of the MNP office in the Réserve Spéciale d'Analamazaotra, where guides can be found. There is a small circuit (guide Ar20,000, two hours) and a large circuit (Ar30,000, three hours). Two-hour night hikes are Ar15,000.

Réserve de Maromizaha

The Réserve de Maromizaha is a 100-sq-km ecotourism reserve, about 8km southeast of the Parc National Andasibe Mantadia. It offers good camping, numerous walking tracks, stands of rainforest and panoramic views. The area is home to 11 somewhat elusive lemur species, including diademed *sifakas* and black-and-white ruffed lemurs, both of which are also found at Parc National de Mantadia. Visits here can be organised with the guides at Réserve Spéciale d'Analamazaotra. The reserve is accessible via an easy trail from the park gate. No permit is necessary.

Vohimana Forest

Established as a private reserve in 2001, the crucial Vohimana Forest (permit Ar10,000, guide per person Ar8000) corridor of 1.6 sq km links the Andasibe area parks with the for-

ⓘ LAC ALAOTRA & AROUND

The trip from Antananarivo via Moramanga to Lac Alaotra, Madagascar's largest body of fresh water, has historically been of interest to Malagasy and other visitors. However, major environmental damage around the lake, difficult access, negative feedback on the Route des Contrabandiers hiking trail from Lac Alaotra to the east coast, and the underdevelopment of the nearby Parc National de Zahamena reduce the attractiveness of this area for most visitors.

ests of the south. It's administered by the NGO Man and the Environment (MATE; ☏ 034 05 737 28, Tana 020 22 674 90; www. madagascar-environnement.org), which is developing it as an ecotourism site in conjunction with its conservation work. At present facilities include around 20km of walking trails, from two hours to three days in length, taking in lemurs, birds and the pointy-nosed columma gallus chameleon (not found elsewhere), plus three picnic areas and a botanical garden. Local guides have been trained in some interesting specialist circuits highlighting such subjects as medicinal plants. They also have a distillery for making essential oils for which they have some famous customers, including the perfume house Chanel. Contact MATE for all details on accommodation tariffs and facilities; volunteer placements are also available.

PANGALANES LAKES

The Pangalanes Lakes are one of Madagascar's lightly visited natural wonders, where half the fun is getting around. Travel here is done largely by long, narrow metal canal boats, which ply the waters from end to end, leaking all the while. Some carry tourists to the lake hotels, others cargo, villagers and the occasional off-the-beaten track traveller. Cruising in this placid freshwater network is a fascinating journey through time and history, not to mention luxuriant vegetation.

In the villages of the Betsimisaraka people, traditional life goes on as ever. People cast nets, paddle by in pirogues, dry eels in the sun, and invariably wave a greeting. Fishing weirs appear at intervals, like gates

Pangalanes Lakes

across the waterway. The lakes themselves are very placid and picturesque, with nice beaches and no development apart from a handful of beach bungalows. The canal creates an interesting topographical effect, too; a long and very narrow outer beach separates it from the Indian Ocean, such that a brief walk takes you from placid lake to tempestuous sea. Oddly, for such extensive wetlands, there are few animals of any kind to be seen from the water, not even birds.

For the most part, this is a destination supported by European travellers who come on tours. As a result, prices have risen, and there is no regularly scheduled transport system – boats come with tour groups. This means that solo travellers have to find space in one of these boats, or hire an entire boat for the ride.

Never fear, if you are a single traveller or small group, you can do it yourself (see box opposite), make reservations if possible. The best times to visit are from March to May and September to December. For travellers, the most popular section of the extensive Pangalanes Canal is the region between Ambila-Lemaitso and Tamatave, where the canal links several large lakes together.

Lac Ampitabe (Akanin'ny Nofy)

With two private reserves, an interesting village and several hotels (including some well-hidden budget options), Lac Ampitabe is the most popular lake – it's accessible only by boat.

◎ Sights & Activities

Vohibola Forest   NATURE RESERVE
Vohibola is one of the last pieces of littoral forest in the country. There are three rewarding hiking trails here: the **Discovery Trail** (Ar20,000), a half-day immersion in forest conservation; the **Forest Trail** (Ar50,000, minimum five people), which allows you to see some rare plants and perhaps even the *calumma vohibola,* a chameleon discovered in 2009; and the **Village Trail** (Ar35,000, minimum five people). The NGO Man and the Environment (p165) also offers solar-powered boat canal trips, such as Vohibola to Tampino (Ar120,000 for up to six people, plus Ar2000 per person).

Visits (and accommodation) are arranged through the MATE office near the entrance to Andranokoditra village.

Andranokoditra   VILLAGE
Thanks to Man and the Environment the village of Andranokoditra is a tourist-friendly destination. Besides being the jumping off point for MATE's canal trips and hiking trails in Vohibola, there is an essential oil distillery and a small market for local jewellery.

Palmarium Reserve   NATURE RESERVE
(Ankanin'ny; ☑ 033 14 847 34; admission Ar15,000; ☺ dawn-night) This private reserve next to Palmarium Hotel on Lac Ampitabe is a great place to test your inner guide. There are 500,000 sq m of dense forest cut with wide trails, and seven species of lemur to

GETTING TO & AROUND THE PANGALANES LAKES

The easiest, though not necessarily the cheapest, way to get to the lakes is to arrange a transfer through your hotel. If you can find a seat on a tour group's boat this should greatly reduce the cost. Calypso Tours (p169) can also arrange this. The other way is to do it yourself.

Brickaville to Ambila-Lemaitso & Manambato

The southern point of entry to the lakes begins at Ambila-Lemaitso. There's a turn-off from the RN2 about 11km north of Brickaville, and a 17km track thereafter. A two-wheel drive is sufficient if there is no mud. You will then need to cross the canal by hand-operated ferry (Ar8000) to Ambila-Lemaitso. Either call Nirvana d'Ambila (p168) for a transfer, or ask around for a private car at the *taxi-brousse* station in Brickaville. Take this option if you intend to stay in Ambila-Lemaitso overnight.

Manambato is also accessible from the RN2: turn off 30km north of Brickaville and follow a 7km sandy track. From Manambato you have to charter a boat to your hotel; talk to the people at the beach. They will start negotiating at Ar150,000, and will go as low as Ar50,000. Or wait until the next tour group shows up and see if they are going your way, as a single seat will be much cheaper.

Tamatave to Lac Ampitabe via Cargo Boat

The northern point of entry to the lakes is the *gare fluviale* (river station) in Tamatave, where canal boats carrying cargo depart daily around 10.30am. Any pousse-pousse (rickshaw) or tuk-tuk can take you there, but do not confuse the cargo boat dock, which is midway down a polluted waterway, with the empty canal boats at the very end of it, as the latter are rented to tour groups. If you can, confirm your departure the afternoon prior, otherwise show up by 9.30am. For around Ar16,000 you will be given a space to occupy, although it may mean sitting on cargo. The river odyssey that follows is a *National Geographic* photo op, with a boatload of locals for company, although you should bring a raincoat and visit a bathroom first. It takes all day to reach Andranokoditra village, from where you can walk or take a pirogue (dugout canoe) to a hotel.

Train

An inexpensive option for reaching the lakes is the passenger train. The train departs Tamatave every Tuesday at 8.20am, travels down the barrier beach past the lakes, stopping at various villages along the way, and continues inland to Moramanga. Ask for the stop nearest your destination. Conversely, one can take the train from Moramanga on Monday at 7am and expect to reach the lakes by midafternoon. The total fare is Ar10,000. Alternatively, the same train departs Moramanga every Thursday at 3pm, but only goes as far as Ambila-Lemaitso, arriving at 10pm. It returns Friday at 8am, arriving Moramanga at 6.55pm. The cost of this shorter journey is Ar8000. It is always wise to check the schedule with Madarail (www.madarail.mg) ahead of time, either at the station (best), or online.

Getting Around

Once you are at the lakes, getting around can be expensive unless you are careful. You can walk around any single lake easily enough, but you'll need a boat to travel between them, unless you want to hike down the barrier beach. If hiring a boat, it is best to deal with the locals, not the hotels, who quote in euros for transport; negotiations are best done in the local village or on the beach. For example, an entire canal boat from Manambato to Lac Ampitabe can be had for Ar70,000 direct from the operator, whereas hotels charge Ar180,000 for the same journey. A boat from Manambato to Ambila-Lemaitso should be about the same.

spot, including Coquerel's *sifaka*, aye-ayes and some tame black-and-white ruffed lemurs. Access is only by boat.

🛏 Sleeping & Eating

Chez L'Habitant   BUNGALOW €
(d Ar11,000) Run by the NGO Man and the

Environment (p165), Chez L'Habitant has six bungalows located in the middle of Andranokoditra. Inquire at the MATE office at the village entrance.

Orchidées
BUNGALOW €

(d Ar25,000-45,000) This option has five bungalows that are a short walk from Andranokoditra. It offers a set menu for Ar12,000.

Bush House
BUNGALOW €€€

(☑020 22 248 47, 033 12 441 27; www.boogie pilgrim-madagascar.com/hotels/bush-house; d bungalow €50) ✦ These quality bungalows with cheery porches have an elevated location that affords views across the lake, with stairs winding down to the beach. The hotel also owns a great viewpoint on the top of a hill from where you can see the interesting landscape of lakes, peninsula and sea around you.

Bush House is on Lac Ampitabe and is accessible by boat. Activities are well managed, with lots of options; free kayaks are a plus. Bush House is Fair Trade in Tourism accredited. Half board is available for an additional €18.

Hôtel Pangalanes Jungle Nofy
BUNGALOW €€€

(☑034 47 931 58; www.hotelpangalanes-jungle nofy.com; d bungalow €35-50) Everything is done well at Hôtel Pangalanes Jungle Nofy.

WORTH A TRIP

ONY HÔTEL

At the north end of Lac Rasoamasay, the **Ony Hôtel** (☑020 53 994 56, 033 11 587 25; http://onyhotel.free.fr; d/q Ar75,000/100,000) occupies an interesting location in the middle of three different lakes. This is a very family-friendly place, with nice thatched log cabins on the beach, plenty of hot water, and a very kind and diligent staff that gets high marks from guests. It's the most secluded of the lake hotels, giving it a very peaceful ambience.

The surprise is how much there is to do here, including forest walks, village visits, swimming, pirogue trips and hikes to the sea (only 40 minutes away) – more than enough to keep you busy for several days. This conscientious hotel sponsors local conservation efforts. A set menu is Ar30,000.

There's a nice lodge, good food (set menu Ar30,000), attentive management and clean bungalows, all at a very attractive price. Half board is an extra €15. Access is by boat.

Palmarium Hotel
BUNGALOW €€€

(☑033 14 847 34; www.palmarium.biz; d bungalow Ar150,000) The Palmarium Hotel is adjacent to the private Palmarium Reserve (p166) on Lac Ampitabe and is accessible only by boat. The bungalows are expensive at this package-tour destination, but the lemurs that crash dinner are great company, and there is a nice bar to hang out in where staff know how to make a decent mojito. Rates include entry into the reserve. Set menu meals are Ar30,000.

Lac Rasobe & Manambato

To get to Manambato, an access town for the Pangalanes Lakes, turn east off the RN2 30km north of Brickaville. It's a 7km sandy track and you'll need a 4WD in the rainy season. Pretty Lac Rasobe has a beautiful white-sand beach and a good place to stay. **Acacias** (☑033 12 338 35; www.acaciasbungalows. com; d/tr bungalow Ar55,000/60,000) has cute bungalows on the beach connected by sandy paths, and management that pays attention to the details. Picnics packed on request.

Ambila-Lemaitso

The main attraction in this sleepy region is **Nirvana d'Ambila** (☑032 91 423 06, 033 15 017 78; nirvanabckvlle@gmail.com; d bungalow Ar60,000), which faces the ferry crossing at the end of the Brickaville piste. The hotel enjoys a captivating location astride the barrier beach, with its canal dock on one side, the roaring ocean on the other, and barely 50m in between. The clean and basic bungalows, with private bathrooms and hot water, have all been renovated, and the atmospheric restaurant (breakfast Ar10,000, set menu Ar40,000) features lots of fresh seafood.

From the ferry crossing, it's another 4km north along a sandy track to Ambila-Lemaitso, where you can inquire about boats heading up or down the canal. Less expensive but even simpler accommodation can be found at **Tropicana** (☑033 08 037 39; d

THE PANGALANES CANAL

The Canal des Pangalanes is one of the quiet wonders of Madagascar, a collection of natural and artificial waterways that stretches over 645km along the east coast from Foulpointe to Farafangana. It was constructed between 1896 and 1904, during the French colonial period, in an effort to create a safe passage for cargo boats to Tamatave; one look at the waves on the nearby Indian Ocean explains why.

Since then the navigability of the canal has ebbed and flowed like the tide. After WWII the canal was expanded and 30-ton barges could travel the 160km from Tamatave to Vatomandry. After a long period of silting in, renovations began in the 1980s, including a new barge network. Today the canal is slipping backwards again. Sections north of Tamatave, between Vatomandry and Mahanoro, and south of Mananjary have grown in. The remains of the old barge network are rotting by the pier in Tamatave. It all makes one wonder: could the depth of the canal be an economic barometer for Madagascar?

bungalow Ar30,000). The most incongruous sight here is the two large French canal boats straight from the Canal du Midi, which are rented out for Ar250,000 per four hours, Ar750,000 per full day. Three days sailing to Tamatave (excluding food) costs Ar1 million.

TAMATAVE (TOAMASINA)

POP 289,730

Tamatave is very much like its cousin on the western coast, Tuléar (Toliara). It is a hot, dusty and chaotic port town full of decaying colonial buildings, roadside markets and throngs of pousse-pousse carts. The emphasis is on commerce, not tourism, apart from being an important transit point.

There are some bright spots amid the fading grandeur if you know where to find them, meaning that you can have a good time here for a day or two. It's a convenient spot to break the journey between Antananarivo and Île Sainte Marie, or to organise a trip down the Canal des Pangalanes. Avoid walking at night, however, particularly alone, and don't leave articles where they can be snatched. At night, take a tuk-tuk rather than a pousse-pousse.

◉ Sights & Activities

Place de Colonne   PLAZA
A monument to those killed in the 1947 uprising against the French, this plaza is in a sad state of disrepair.

Place Bien Aimé   PLAZA
At Place Bien Aimé, you'll find the remains of a once grand park; a dozen magnificent banyan trees weep before a crumbling colonial mansion.

Musée du Port   MUSEUM
(admission by donation; ⊙9am-4pm Tue-Sun) The small university museum at the entrance to the port constitutes barely 2½ rooms of farming tools, fishing implements, archaeological finds and tribal charms, along with poster displays on deforestation and local conservation projects. Some of the captioning is in English, including translations of some typically cryptic Madagascan proverbs.

Bazary Be   MARKET
(Big Market; Rue Amiral Billard) Tamatave's colourful Bazary Be sells fruit, vegetables, spices, handicrafts and beautiful bouquets of flowers (should you feel the need to brighten up your hotel room).

Bazary Kely   MARKET
(Little Market; Blvd de la Fidelité) Bazary Kely sells fish and produce in the ruins of a commercial complex, west of the train station.

Swimming

For around Ar6000 you can swim at various hotels, including **Hôtel Neptune** and **Sharon Hotel**, but the big pool at Le Bateau Ivre (p172) is more fun, and free if you eat there.

☞ Tours

Calypso Tours   BOATING
(☑032 04 628 82, 032 40 247 78; www.tourisme-tamatave.com; Hôtel Eden, Blvd Joffre; tour incl lunch Ar70,000) Day-long (10am to 5pm) tours of the Canal des Pangalanes from Tamatave. Located in Hôtel Eden (p170).

Tamatave (Toamasina)

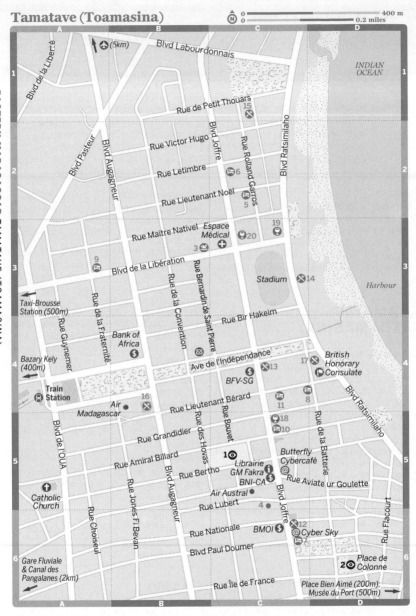

N
0 ——————— 400 m
0 ——————— 0.2 miles

INDIAN OCEAN

Blvd Labourdonnais

Rue de Petit Thouars

15

Rue Victor Hugo

Rue Letimbre

6

5

Rue Lieutenant Noël

Rue Maitre Nativel

Espace Médical

20

19

3

Blvd de la Libération

9

Stadium

14

Harbour

Bank of Africa

Rue Bir Hakeim

Ave de l'Indépendance

13

17

British Honorary Consulate

BFV-SG

Air Madagascar

16

Rue Lieutenant Bérard

11

8

18

10

Rue Grandidier

Rue Amiral Billard

1

Librairie GM Fakra

Butterfly Cybercafé

BNI-CA

Rue Bertho

Rue Aviate ur Goulette

Catholic Church

Air Austral

Rue Lubert

4

Rue Nationale

BMOI

12

Cyber Sky

Blvd Paul Doumer

2

Place de Colonne

Gare Fluviale & Canal des Pangalanes (2km)

Rue Île de France

Place Bien Aimé (200m); Musée du Port (500m)

Taxi-Brousse Station (500m)

Bazary Kely (400m)

Train Station

Tropical Service TOUR
(☎ 020 53 336 79; www.croisiere-madagascar.
com; 23 Blvd Joffre) Top-end local tours, plus
cruises to Mauritius and Réunion, transfers
and travel services.

🛏 Sleeping

Hôtel Eden HOTEL €
(☎ 020 53 312 90; calypsotour@netcourrier.
com; Blvd Joffre; r Ar25,000, without bathroom
Ar16,000) This popular backpackers' hotel is
a good budget choice, with a mix of shared

Tamatave (Toamasina)

and private bathrooms, and helpful staff. Expect slightly higher rates, as it was being upgraded at the time of research. Calypso Tours (p169) is based here, so it's a good place to organise a tour of the Canal des Pangalanes.

Génération Hôtel   HOTEL €€
(☏ 020 57 220 22; www.hotel-generation.com; Blvd Joffre; d/ste Ar60,000/70,000; ❋🛜) At this slightly cluttered but genial hotel all rooms have balconies and fridges; the good-value suites are larger. Furnishings are old-style, but it all works and the staff are friendly. The restaurant serves reasonable food (mains from Ar11,000) and has a pleasant terrace.

Hôtel Fréderic   HOTEL €€
(☏ 020 53 347 40; Rue Lieutenant Bérard; d from Ar35,900; ❋🛜) This good option on a quiet corner has a mixture of tiled and parquet rooms, some with fridges but none with nets. Corner rooms 101 and 201 (Ar42,900) are easily the best, with lots of light and great balconies. A pizza restaurant and bar are helpful additions.

Hôtel Les Flamboyants   HOTEL €€
(☏ 020 53 323 50, 032 71 093 51; hotelflamboyants @gmail.com; Blvd de la Libération; r with fan/ air-con Ar45,000/50,000; ❋🛜) This is your typical concrete box hotel done moderately well, with air-conditioning that is welcome in summer. Rooms are large, and some have decent balconies (add an extra Ar5000), but the hot water struggles at times.

La Véranda   HOTEL €€€
(☏ 020 53 340 86; www.hotel-laveranda-tamatave. com; 5 Rue Lieutenant Bérard; d Ar100,000; ❋🛜) The highly successful restaurant La Véranda has morphed into a rather nice hotel in a new location. Rooms here are smart and spacious; some have balconies and even bathtubs. The restaurant (p172) operates on the ground floor.

Java Hotel   HOTEL €€€
(☏ 020 53 316 26, 034 12 252 53; www.java-hotel-tamatave.com; 34 Blvd Joffre; d Ar140,000; 🛜) An antiseptic business hotel, but given the competition, a bit of mouthwash feels refreshing. Rooms and hallways sparkle, while the brand new elevator leaves the hardened traveller dumbstruck. Interior parking is another welcome touch, particularly in Tamatave. Discounts are possible. Le Verseau restaurant is on the ground floor.

Calypso Hotel & Spa   HOTEL €€€
(☏ 020 53 304 59, 032 07 131 33; www.hotel calypso.mg; Rue Lieutenant Noël; d incl breakfast Ar295,000, ste Ar460,000; ❋🛜☀) As the price suggests, this is the top hotel in the city, and the only one with this level of finish. It offers elegantly appointed rooms with glass showers and attractive island-style decor, a beautiful indoor pool, a gym, a spa and a posh restaurant. Clients are a mix of business people and high-end tour groups.

Next door is the new building, Ulysse, where a double room including breakfast costs Ar330,000. Access to the spa and pool is included. Nonguests can use the pool for Ar40,000.

🍴 Eating

Self-caterers and treat-seekers should check out Score (Ave de l'Indépendance; ⏰ 8.30am-1pm & 2.30-7pm Mon-Sat, to 12.30pm

Sun) or **Shoprite** (Ave de l'Indépendance) supermarkets.

★ **La Véranda**　　　　INTERNATIONAL €
(☑ 020 53 334 35; Rue Lieutenant Bérard; mains from Ar9000; ☺ breakfast, lunch & dinner Mon-Sat; ☏) A popular choice for French expats and visitors thanks to its wide-ranging menu of European, Chinese and Madagascan dishes, and very reasonable prices. The three-course set menu (Ar15,000) changes daily, and is far too tempting to settle for less. Eat inside or on the lovely colonial-style terrace.

Adam & Eve Snack Bar　　　　CREPERIE €
(☑ 020 53 334 56; Blvd Joffre; mains from Ar8000; ☺ breakfast, lunch & dinner Tue-Sun) A popular budget option, though getting a little tacky, the open bar and terrace has a loyal following for the Madagascan dishes, juice, ice cream and crêpes. No alcohol.

La Terrasse　　　　PIZZA €€
(Blvd Joffre; mains/menus Ar14,000/12,000; ☺ breakfast, lunch & dinner; ☏) This hopping streetside bistro with tasty pizza and grills is the go-to lunch spot for people on the move.

★ **Piment Banane**　　　　FRENCH €€€
(Rue de l'Ourd; mains from Ar15,000; ☺ lunch & dinner Mon-Sat; ☏) You wouldn't expect to find a sophisticated brasserie in Tamatave, but we are in the land of exceptions. And exceptional is how to describe this chic place, from the stylish decor to the innovative cuisine to the extensive wine list, all of which has garnered rave reviews from those discerning culinary travellers, the French.

Le Bateau Ivre　　　　INTERNATIONAL €€€
(Blvd Ratsimilaho; mains Ar19,000-45,000; ☺ lunch & dinner; ☏) This sprawling beach-front enterprise manages to do everything well. There is a central restaurant and bar, beach bar with BBQ, hamburger bar, pizza oven, 25m swimming pool, and even beach volleyball. Beneath the central big top, you'll find a diverse mix of clientele, from miner expats to Malagasy families, all there for the excellent food.

It's all charmingly cluttered with statuary, fossils and parasols. The seafood is particularly good, and there are creative drinks and nightly live music. This eclectic mix is not only stimulating, it manages to define a vibe for the whole city that seems entirely appropriate, like a Cotton Club for Tamatave. If you're only in town one night, spend some time here, although given the options, there is little reason to leave. Very busy on weekends.

☕ Drinking & Nightlife

Apart from hotel restaurants, bar-restaurants, and Le Bateau Ivre, Tamatave's surprisingly dynamic nightlife centres on a few swinging discos.

Pandora Station　　　　CLUB
(Route d'Ivoloina) On the road to the airport, this is Tamatave's favourite club. It has two large rooms: the Tropical, and the Clubbing with live DJs.

Queens Club　　　　CLUB
(Blvd Joffre) There's a laid-back ambience at this centrally located club, set in an old house with a verandah.

THE WAILING INDRI

The wondrous *indri* has been described as looking like 'a four-year-old child in a panda suit'. It's famous for its eerie cry, a whooping siren that can be heard over a mile away. It is used mainly to define a particular group's territory, though there are also distinct mating and alarm calls. *Indris* are active on and off throughout the day, beginning about an hour after daybreak, which is usually the best time to see them. Despite the incredible cacophony of sound that comes out of the forest, each individual only calls for about four or five minutes per day.

Indris eat complex carbohydrates, and therefore need to spend much of their day in a sedentary manner digesting their food. They spend most of their time high in the forest canopy, feeding, sleeping and sunning themselves. Their powerful hind legs make them capable of 7m horizontal leaps from tree to tree, and they are perfectly balanced despite their stump-like tails. *Indris* are very sensitive to any change in environment, which is the main reason for their endangered status – not only does deforestation threaten their habitat, but no *indri* has ever survived in captivity, as they simply stop eating and die.

Neptune Nightclub CLUB
(☎ 020 53 322 26; www.hotel-neptune-tamatave.
com; Blvd Ratsimilaho; ☺from 10pm Mon-Sat) A
very popular nightclub in the large Hotel
Neptune on the seafront.

City Pub CLUB
(Blvd Joffre; ☺Mon-Sat) This large venue in
the centre of town features videos, lighting
effects and DJs.

ⓘ Information

There are many banks in the centre with ATMs;
BNI-CA (Blvd Joffre) takes MasterCard. There
are also plenty of exchange bureaus.
Butterfly Cybercafé (Blvd Joffre; per hr
Ar3000; ☺8.30am-noon & 2.30-6pm Mon-Fri,
to noon Sat)
Cyber Sky (Blvd Joffre; per 10min Ar500;
☺8am-8pm Mon-Sat)
Espace Médical (☎ 020 53 315 66; Blvd de la
Libération; ☺24hr)
Librairie GM Fakra (Blvd Joffre; ☺closed Mon
morning) A few English news magazines, plus
maps of the region and postcards.

ⓘ Getting There & Away

AIR

Air Madagascar (☎ 020 53 323 56; Ave de
l'Indépendance) flies most days between
Tamatave and Antananarivo (€221, one hour),
and three times weekly to Île Sainte Marie
(€221, 30 minutes). Other services connect
Tamatave with Antalaha (€221, 1½ hours) and
Maroantsetra (€221, 1¼ hours). Be forewarned
that during the vanilla season (June to October), flights in the northeast fill up quickly.

Upstart **Madagasikara Airways** (☎ 034 05
970 09, 032 05 970 09; www.madagasikara
airways.com; Airport Ambalamanasy), which
commenced operations in late 2015, has five
weekly flights to Antananarivo (€104, one hour).
There is also a weekly service to Île Sainte Marie
(€74, 30 minutes).

Air Madagascar has a weekly flight (€286, 1¾
hours), and **Air Austral** (☎ 020 53 300 26; Rue
de Lattre de Tassigny) flies three times weekly
(€328), to St-Denis on Réunion.

BOAT

To Île Sainte Marie If you are heading to Île
Sainte Marie via Soanierana-Ivongo, your boat
company will provide a shuttle service from
Tamatave.

To the northeast Cargo boats without set
schedules also ply the waters of the northeast. This type of travel is generally slow and
uncomfortable, and potentially dangerous,
particularly during cyclone season (December

DON'T MISS

THE ENDS OF THE EARTH

The end of the earth: it's a term you'll
hear used to describe many a place in
Madagascar. But what does it mean?
There seem to be several factors: isolation, natural beauty, the sea, and a distant horizon forming a reflective place
where the world appears to stop, and
the spirit deepens. With that in mind,
here are our favourite end-of-the-earth
hotels in Madagascar:

Le Domaine d'Ambola (p93), Ambola

Analatsara Eco-Lodge (p185), Île aux
Nattes

Tea Longo (p94), Lavanono

Longomamy (p90), St Augustine

Masoala Forest Lodge (p192),
Masoala Peninsula

Sakatia Lodge (p136), Nosy Sakatia

Ecolodge du Menabe (p120), Belo-
sur-Mer

Anjajavy (p106), Majunga

to March); always check forecasts and ask
local advice before travelling. Those prone
to motion sickness should not attempt it.
Standards vary widely; cabins are sometimes
available, but on most boats you can expect
to be bedding down on deck, and you will
need to bring your own food and water. If
you're still interested, ask any pousse-pousse
driver to take you to the bureau of boats
going to Mananara or Maroantsetra. This is an
obscure shed by the port that you will never
find on your own.

PRIVATE 4WD

Taxi-brousse company **Mbola Tsara Voyage**
(☎ 033 75 629 35; contact@mbolatsara
voyage.com; *taxi-brousse* station) rents
private 4WDs for travel on the RN5. Published
prices for car and driver from Tamatave include Mananara and Maroantsetra (Ar2
million) but with any luck, aggressive bargaining might reduce this.

TAXI-BROUSSE

➡ The *taxi-brousse* station at the northwestern
edge of town serves Antananarivo, as well
as points north as far as Soanierana-Ivongo
(Ar10,000, four hours) and south as far as
Mahanoro (Ar20,000, four hours).
➡ Minibuses and coaches run along the RN2
throughout the day to Moramanga (Ar15,000,
seven hours) and Antananarivo (Ar20,000

ℹ BY SEA TO RÉUNION & MAURITIUS

For an interesting itinerary twist, consider this ocean voyage. The mixed cargo and passenger ships MS Mauritius Trochetia and Mauritius Pride (www.croisiere-madagascar.com/en/indian-ocean-cruise) depart Tamatave once every two weeks or so for the islands of Réunion and Mauritius. One-way/return fares to Réunion (24 hours) are €295/420 per adult, and €360/490 to Mauritius (36 hours). More expensive deluxe cabins are also available. Tickets are available from Tropical Service (p170).

to Ar23,000, at least seven hours). It is best to leave early to ensure that you reach your destination during daylight hours.

➤ If road conditions permit, you may be able to find a camion-brousse (truck) or similar large vehicle heading towards Mananara (Ar60,000) or Maroantsetra (Ar90,000, two to three days). A 4WD to Mananara or Maroantsetra will likely cost Ar2 million (one or two days).

TRAIN

A slow passenger train departs Moramanga every Monday at 7am, arriving in Tamatave at 4.50pm (Ar10,000). It returns on Tuesday at 8.20am, arriving in Moramanga at 6.55pm. It is always wise to check the schedule with **Madarail** (ℹ 020 22 345 99; www.madarail.mg) ahead of time, either at the station (best), or online.

ℹ Getting Around

➤ Taxis between town and the airport (5km north of town) should cost around Ar25,000. Taxi rides within town are Ar3000.

➤ Some local minibuses shuttle passengers around town for Ar300, if you can work out the routes; service No 4 goes to the Bazary Kely and the port.

➤ To hire a car locally, inquire at any hotel, restaurant or travel agency, or ask around at the taxi-brousse station. It may be more expensive if you want to take the vehicle beyond Foulpointe.

➤ Pousse-pousse drivers charge from Ar1000 per trip within the town centre. The drivers are fairly friendly, but agree on the fee before you climb in. Tuk-tuks are the same price and a much safer option at night.

NORTH OF TAMATAVE

Beaches north of Tamatave make a great escape from the city, with Mahambo being the best option. Soanierana-Ivongo is the ferry port for those heading to Île Sainte Marie by boat. Beyond lies the daunting RN5 that can only be traversed by a reliable 4WD.

Parc Zoologique Ivoloina

This **park** (ℹ 020 53 01217; www.seemadagascar.com; admission Ar20,000; ◷ 9am-5pm) is a very well-run zoo and botanical garden set on a lovely lake just north of Tamatave. The beautiful grounds of Ivoloina (ee-va-la-*ween*) cover 2.82 sq km and contain more than 100 lemurs from 10 different species, both caged and semiwild, as well as chameleons, radiated tortoises, tree boas and tomato frogs. The botanical garden contains more than 75 species of native and exotic plants, and a model farm designed to demonstrate sustainable agricultural methods. Visitors can enjoy four walking trails with booklets in English, a snack bar and an education centre. An optional guide is Ar10,000 for a basic two-hour tour, or Ar40,000 for a full day. Book in advance for a night tour (5.30pm) to see the nocturnal lemurs (Ar10,000). There is dormitory accommodation, too (for two Ar30,000); order dinner in advance (Ar5000).

The park is run by the **Madagascar Fauna & Flora Group** (ℹ 032 05 103 07, 020 53 308 42; www.madagascarfaunaflora.org; Rte de l'Aéroport), located 4km north of Tamatave. It's a worldwide conservation association headquartered in St Louis, USA. In addition to hosting tourists, the park has captive breeding programs for endangered species, and a halfway house for animals being reintroduced into the wild. The park also raises local awareness of wildlife and conservation issues – around 70% of the estimated 14,000 annual visitors are Malagasy.

To reach the park from Tamatave, take the RN5 north, go 9km past the airport, and turn left on the unpaved road in front of the Ivoloina Bridge. Continue on until you see the park entrance sign (the trip takes half an hour). A charter taxi from town costs around Ar70,000 for a return trip; taxis-brousses to Ivoloina village (Ar7500) leave every hour or two. From Ivoloina village it's a scenic 4km walk to the park entrance.

Alternatively, **Bamboo Adventure** (www.facebook.com/bambooadventure) will take you to the park on a bamboo raft from its hut near the junction of the RN5 and the road to the park (Ar5000, one hour).

Foulpointe (Mahavelona)

Foulpointe (fool-*pwant*) is a nondescript town with some nice white-sand beaches, and a strip of accommodation and dining; it's certainly enough for a weekend. If you're looking for a quick sun 'n' fun escape from Tamatave, this is a worthy option.

◉ Sights

Fort Manda FORTRESS
(☉9am-noon & 2.30-4.30pm) The ruins of this 19th-century Merina fort, built for Radama I, are about 500m north of Foulpointe. Its walls, which are 8m high and 6m thick in places, are made from coral, sand and eggs.

🛏 Sleeping & Eating

Le Grand Bleu BUNGALOW €€
(☎034 07 220 06, 020 57 220 06; www.grandbleu-tamatave.com; d bungalow Ar72,000, 6-person villa Ar134,000; ✻🛜) The 'Big Blue' complex fronts directly onto the beach, and the rooms here come well equipped. If you're any judge of character, however, you'll forgo the air-con rooms for the subtler breezes of the cute wickerwork bungalows.

Génération Hôtel Foulpointe BUNGALOW €€
(☎020 53 328 34, 033 21 615 90; www.generationhotel-tamatave.com/foulpoint; r with/without aircon Ar74,000/47,000, bungalow Ar51,500; ✻🛜) This garden site towards the southern end of the strip offers a choice between standard concrete rooms and nicer thatched bungalows – some two-tier models sleep up to six people (Ar101,500). It's not directly on the beach but the big terraced restaurant, which serves Chinese and French food, is only 20m from the shore.

Manda Beach Hôtel HOTEL €€€
(☎034 11 220 00; www.mandabeach-hotel.com; d/bungalow Ar77,500/112,500; ✻🛜🏊) With its central pool, concrete rooms, tennis courts, Western music and long stretch of parasols on the sand, not to mention the nearby golf course, this place feels more like an upscale beach motel in Florida

than a hotel in Madagascar. Choose the beachfront bungalows over the industrial rooms. Menu Ar27,500; nonguests can use the pool for Ar7000.

❶ Getting There & Away

➤ Foulpointe lies 58km north of Tamatave. Minibuses depart from the Tamatave *taxi-brousse* station daily, generally in the mornings (Ar5000, 1½ hours).

➤ For short hops, such as to Mahambo or Fenoarivo-Atsinanana, you can try flagging down just about any vehicle going in the right direction; hotel vehicles may be able to take you all the way to Tamatave, but you'll have to pay at least the equivalent of the *taxi-brousse* fare.

➤ Several vehicles daily pass Foulpointe on their way between Tamatave and Soanierana-Ivongo. Heading south, when they pass Foulpointe depends on what time the ferry from Île Sainte Marie arrives at Soanierana-Ivongo. Heading north, wait by the roadside before 9am to get to Soanierana-Ivongo in time for the best boats.

Mahambo

Mahambo is a coastal village with a safe swimming beach and luxuriant vegetation that comes right down to the shore in some places. It's much quieter and generally more enticing than Foulpointe, primarily because it's further from the main road, and while facilities are expanding it should still be some time before resort life starts to take over.

🛏 Sleeping & Eating

Zanatany BUNGALOW €
(☎033 15 324 73; d bungalow Ar30,000) This little restaurant in the centre of the village has the cheapest digs in town. It's very basic, but a good deal.

Ylang-Ylang BUNGALOW €€
(☎033 76 659 96; petalepirogue@yahoo.fr; bungalow Ar40,000) If you can't be on the beach, then this wonderfully scented garden with its well-kept row of wooden cottages is a fine substitute.

★La Pirogue LODGE €€€
(☎033 08 768 10, 033 08 768 18; www.pirogue-hotel.com; r Ar99,500, bungalows Ar145,000-295,000; 🛜) This elegant resort has a fascinating reef-front location and a

beautiful garden setting complete with two resident lemurs. The bungalows are delightful with local wood carvings and deckchairs on the porch. There's a wonderful outside dining area with the sea lapping nearby, although the food is pricey and could be improved.

Kayaks and pedalos are free for guests. Motorbikes (half day, Ar20,000) and quad bikes (30 minutes Ar50,000) are available, and fishing trips can be arranged.

❶ Getting There & Away

Mahambo is 30km north of Foulpointe (Ar2000, 45 minutes) and about 90km from Tamatave (Ar6000, 2½ hours) on the RN5. If taking a *taxibrousse*, ask the driver to drop you at the intersection (you'll see the hotel signs), then walk about 2km down the sandy track heading east.

Fenoarivo-Atsinanana (Fénérive Est)

Unless you have a great interest in cloves, or need to visit a bank, there's really no reason to come to this agricultural market town (usually just called 'Fenoarivo' or 'Fénérive').

If you must stay, the best place is the **Hôtel Restaurant Belle Rose** (☑020 57 300 38; d Ar20,000).

Soanierana-Ivongo

The riverside port of Soanierana-Ivongo (son-ee-ran-*ee-vong*) is the most practical of places: you go there to get a boat to or from Île Sainte Marie. The road down to the jetty has recently been paved.

The crossing here is dangerous, as the boats exit a shallow river mouth with incoming breaking waves. There have been several fatal accidents in recent years.

The danger is particularly pronounced between June and September, when water levels are low and the weather is bad – often boats don't run at all at this time. Thus our warning: travellers on a tight schedule, who are not otherwise driving the coast road, should consider flying from Tamatave to Île Sainte Marie, even if it is more expensive. Otherwise you risk spending several days in what is definitely not paradise waiting for the weather to clear. Having said that, if the weather complies, it is a pretty and inexpensive trip.

🛏 Sleeping & Eating

All the hotels here are basic. There is no internet connection anywhere.

Hôtel Les Escales   BUNGALOW €
(☑033 17 403 03, 033 08 486 38; bungalow Ar20,000) This is the obvious choice, as it is located right next to the boat jetty, with a tiny porch where you can have a beer and watch the madness when the boats arrive.

Relais   HOTEL €
(☑034 47 257 04; d Ar20,000-30,000) This hotel has basic rooms and the best restaurant in the neighbourhood (mains from Ar5000, open Tuesday to Sunday).

❶ Getting There & Away

BOAT

➜ There are four main shuttle boats from Soanierana-Ivongo to Ambodifotatra on Île Sainte Marie. All have offices on the waterfront in both towns.

➜ On average boats leave Ambodifotatra around 6am and Soanierana-Ivongo around 10am. Crossing time is 1¼ hours for the fastest boat, *Melissa Express*. Transfers from Tamatave take another hour.

➜ There is usually a price reduction of Ar10,000 on a return ticket.

➜ Before sailing out to the island, passengers are asked to go to the gendarmerie (police station) across the street from the Hôtel Les Escales to register.

➜ If you have no reservation, make sure you know when the boats leave (all in the morning). Arrive early to get your pick of the litter. There's not a lot to discriminate between them except when they depart (departures take place over an hour or so) and how long they take (*Melissa Express* saves a half hour on the slowest alternative). The important thing is to assess which boat will arrive first.

Cap Sainte Marie (☑032 05 118 08, 020 57 404 06; www.cap-sainte-marie.com; each way €28) Shuttle from Tamatave leaves from Tanambao V, next to Jesosy Mamonjy church and costs €12 each way. Return ticket with shuttles is discounted to €70.

El Condor (☑Tamatave 034 70 433 01, Île Sainte Marie 034 70 433 02; www.bluemarine-madagascar.jimdo.com; each way €35, shuttle bus Tamatave to Soanierana-Ivongo €5) El Condor's shuttle bus leaves from Tanambao V in Tamatave. This new catamaran also plies the Mahambo/Ambodifotatra route at the same price.

Gasikara (☑Soanierana-Ivongo 034 43 856 13, Tamatave 020 53 987 49; www.sainte-

THE INFAMOUS RN5

Depending on how you look at it, the RN5 from Soanierana-Ivongo to Maroantsetra is either the worst road in Madagascar, or the best 4WD adventure in the country. The very idea of calling it a 'National Route' is so hysterical that only the sight of your 4WD being floated across a river on a few oil drums will stop you laughing.

The trip has two legs, Soanierana-Ivongo to Mananara, and Mananara to Maroantsetra, of which the first one is the most difficult. There are sections of sheer rock, sections of deep sand, and everything in between, particularly mud. In January/February the entire route is impassable. At the same time, much of the trip is adjacent to, and sometimes even on, an endless stretch of sublime coastline, with bright white sand and overhanging palms.

Best of all are the numerous river crossings, some with dilapidated bridges that require close inspection (walk across these *before* the car), others with ferries both real and homemade, where you get out and everyone pulls a rope to get across. At one end or the other you'll find a rickety village where you can pick up dried fish, bread and soda. With luck, the entire adventure takes two days, with an overnight stay in Mananara, leaving time to do a night walk on Aye-Aye Island.

As you can imagine, the drivers who do this 240km journey day in and day out are some of the most talented 4WD captains anywhere. Try Mbola Tsara Voyage (p173) in Tamatave, where the published cost for this stretch is Ar2 million, but you might get the price reduced with some hard bargaining. The price can be further minimised by taking on extra passengers. Alternatively, take a 4WD *taxi-brousse* (Ar150,000, two to five days).

marie-tours.mg; 40 Blvd Joffre, Tamatave; one way €24) Shuttle from Tamatave leaves from Gare Routière Transport Vatsy and costs €11 each way. There's a 10% reduction on a return ticket.

Melissa Express (☑ 032 02 073 64; melissaexpress1@gmail.com; one way incl shuttle Ar80,000) Shuttle from Tamatave leaves from the suburb of Valpinson in the north of the city, west of the airport road. The *Melissa Express* also offers a service (Tuesday and Saturday) from Soanierana-Ivongo to Maroantsetra (Ar180,000 including the shuttle from Tamatave). This is the only service of its kind on this coast but is subject to interruptions, particularly from June to September.

PRIVATE 4WD

The RN5 north from Soanierana-Ivongo to Mananara and Maroantsetra is a Pandora's box of potential delays, as well as a tremendous 4WD adventure. A private 4WD will cost Ar2 million, though this could be negotiable if you bargain hard.

TAXI-BROUSSE

Taxis-brousses depart Tamatave for Soanierana-Ivongo (Ar10,000, three to four hours) around 6am every morning. However, they are not necessarily coordinated with boat departures, so you could end up getting stuck in Soanierana-Ivongo. It makes more sense to book a transfer with your boat company. Returning to Tamatave, vehicles wait for the arrivals from Île Sainte Marie, so a *taxi-brousse*

makes more sense. For *taxis-brousses* going north, inquire at the station.

Manompana

This small coastal village 38km north of Soanierana-Ivongo is where to head if you want to ditch beach tourism in favour of rural isolation. Nearby attractions include the scenic **Point Tintingue**, the protected **Ambodiriana forest** (www.adefa-madagascar.org) and the even smaller fishing village of **Antanambe**. A French charity, **Marmaille a la Case** (http://marmaillealacase.free.fr), has set up an education and cultural centre here, staffed partly by volunteers.

Au Bon Ancrage/Chez Wen Ki (☑ 020 53 957 72, 033 19 746 41; d bungalow Ar15,000) offers basic bungalows on the beach, with bucket showers, and a convivial restaurant with fresh seafood.

ÎLE SAINTE MARIE

The best thing about Île Sainte Marie is that it contains all the ingredients for a great vacation *and* great travel. This is a very long (57km), thin, lush and relatively flat tropical island surrounded by beaches and reef, and spotted with thatched villages.

Île Sainte Marie

N

0 —————— 5 km
0 —————— 2.5 miles

Ambodiatafana

Pointe des Cocotiers
(Lohatanjona Antsirakaraiky) 9

3 4

Antsirakaraiky

Ambatoroa

Androrangatsara

15
Forêt
d'Ambohidena

11 Anivorano

Ankirihiry

13
Sahasifotra

Loukintsy
18
Forêt
d'Ikalalao

Forêt
d'Ampanihy

Baie
d'Ampanihy

Maromandia
Agnafiafy
22
Baie d'Ankoalabe

Davolo
(112m)
Ampanihy
Peninsula

Ankobahoba
Sandroavoahangy

Ambohitra

Launches to
Soanierana-Ivongo

Ilot Madame &
Main Port

Ilampy

Cargo Boats to
Tamatave,
Mananara &
Maroantsetra

Ambodifotatra
Betona
Saint Joseph

17
1
21
Baie des
Forbans
Île aux Forbans

Mahavelo
Ambodiforaha

12
10
Ankoalamare

6
16
Ilots aux Sables
(Isles of Sand)

INDIAN
OCEAN

Vohilava
2

20
Ravoraha
23
Nosy Rinditra

Madagasikara
Airways
Airport
Ankarena

19 14
Île aux Nattes
(Nosy Nato)
La Pointe Sud

5 8
7

Île Sainte Marie

The port of Ambodifotatra, a quarter of the way up the western coast, is the only sizeable town. South of here, the shore is lined with a great variety of hotels and resorts, which don't overpower the setting, culminating in the small island of Île aux Nattes, a postcard tropical paradise, where one can easily imagine pirates coming ashore with treasure chests in tow. In contrast, the upper half of the island is quite wild, and its great length means that there is plenty of room for exploration. There is a fantastic adventure to be had by buggy, quad or dirt bike through remote villages and along beautiful paradisiacal shoreline, culminating in the natural pools at the island's northern tip. If you just sit on the beach, you'll greatly miss out.

Some key dates: July to September is whale-watching season, and December to March is cyclone season. There are many times (mid-December to mid-January, April and May, July to October, as well as week-ends and Madagascan holidays) when it would be wise to make reservations. There is also a tourist tax of Ar10,000 per person per stay, and up to Ar1500 per person per night, although sometimes this is included in the quoted room rate.

⊙ Getting There & Away

AIR

Air Madagascar (Map p181; ☑ 020 57 400 46) flies four times weekly between Île Sainte Marie and Antananarivo (€264, one hour) and weekly to Tamatave (€221, 35 minutes). Flights to Maroantsetra and destinations further north involve a stopover at Tamatave. Flights up the northeast coast are often full; in the vanilla season (June to October) book as far in advance as possible, and reconfirm all bookings.

As of late 2015, the new airline **Madagasikara Airways** (Map p178; ☑ 034 05 970 10, 032 05 970 10; www.madagasikaraairways.com; Airport Ravoraha) has two weekly flights to Antananarivo (€124, one hour) and a single weekly service to Tamatave (€74, 35 minutes).

BOAT

Boats leave Ambodifotatra for Soanierana-Ivongo as early as daybreak. Cargo boats leave from a different port on Ilot Madame, the tiny island at the entrance to Baie des Forbans, sailing to Mananara, Maroantsetra and Tamatave. There are no set schedules for these; departures from Île Sainte Marie are often in the evening or at night, and you will likely have to wait several days for something to turn up.

⊙ Getting Around

There is a good paved road on the western side between the airport and the northern tip, and between Ambodifotatra and Ilampy. A paved circuit of the island is promised by government. For now, the remaining roads are dirt, rock or sand.

TO/FROM THE AIRPORT

The airport (Map p178) is located at the southern tip of the island, 13km south of Ambodifotatra. A tuk-tuk or *taxi-brousse* for this route costs Ar5000 per person, and a taxi Ar20,000 for up to three people. To Loukintsy, a tuk-tuk is Ar7000 per person and a taxi Ar35,000.

BICYCLE

Virtually every hotel and all kinds of other places have bikes of varying quality for hire. The going rate is from Ar15,000 per day. Once off the paved road you need a mountain bike, and even then going will be difficult in stretches.

EASTERN MADAGASCAR ÎLE SAINTE MARIE

CAR & MOTORCYCLE

➤ The whole food chain of motorised vehicles – including cars, buggies, quads, motorcycles and scooters – is available for hire. If you wish to travel in a group, you can hire a car and driver through any high-end hotel; negotiations start at Ar300,000 per day.

➤ The well-run **Quad Sainte Marie** (Map p181; ☑ 032 40 745 39; www.quadsainte marie.com; Ave I a Bigorne) has quads and buggies from Ar300,000 per day including fuel and a guide, and the experience of open-air driving around the island is priceless.

➤ That same experience, or perhaps an even better one, can be had *much* more cheaply by renting a dirt bike from a mere Ar54,000 per day plus petrol from the rental agent near the Bank of Africa in Ambodifotatra. If you know how to ride a motorcycle, and have the right insurance, you can handle this upgrade, but you must be careful of sudden sand traps in the road.

➤ Finally, for those who wish to putt-putt along sealed surfaces, you can pick up a scooter from around Ar40,000 per day, which is a lot of fun too. If your hotel doesn't have any, you'll see them for rent along the main road in Ambodifotatra.

TAXI & TAXI-BROUSSE

There are a few *taxis-brousses* on Île Sainte Marie. A ride north along the road from Ambodifotatra to the northern tip is Ar15,000 (two hours). Private taxis are more common, though disproportionately expensive. They usually hang out by the harbour in Ambodifotatra. You have a reasonable chance of flagging one down along the airport road. Tariffs are fixed and posted at the tourist office and hotel receptions: it's Ar20,000 to the airport, Ar35,000 to Loukintsy.

Ambodifotatra

Ambodifotatra (am-bodi-*foot*-atr) is Île Sainte Marie's only real town and has all the island's practical facilities. You'll find everything you need to organise your stay, plus some interesting restaurants.

🏃 Activities

Most activities on the island are offered by hotels; diving is one exception. The scuba season runs from July to January, with the best time being October to December. Dive centres are often closed between February and May.

Il Balenottero DIVING
(Map p181; ☑ 020 57 400 36; www.il-balenottero.com; Ambodifotatra) A large operation with five boats. It also offers PADI courses, whale watching, yacht cruises and fishing trips.

Le Lémurien Palmé DIVING
(Map p181; ☑ 020 57 040 15, 032 04 816 56; www.lemurien-palme.com; Ave La Bigorne) Dives start at Ar120,000. It also offers dive training, sea excursions and whale watching.

CetaMada WILDLIFE WATCHING
(Map p181; ☑ 020 57 912 29, 020 81 973 00; www.cetamada.org; Port Barachois) 🐋 This association promotes conservation of the humpback whales that visit Sainte Marie between July and October. Some members offer whale-watching expeditions. Artisanal products are sold at the office here to raise money for educational projects.

🧭 Tours

Sainte Marie Consulting TOUR
(Map p181; ☑ 032 40 084 43, 034 01 793 81; www.saintemarieconsulting.com) If you are looking to put together any type of itinerary on the island, the best person to call is Orpheu. This dynamic young gentleman speaks fluent English, makes things happen and knows everyone. Formerly head of the tourism office, he now runs his own agency.

🎊 Festivals & Events

Whale Festival PARADE
(Festival des Baleines; www.festivaldesbaleines.com; ☉ Jul) If you're on Île Sainte Marie during the first two weeks of July, you can't miss the Whale Festival. It's a huge event that takes place just as the humpback whales arrive: there's a big parade, games, stalls, exhibitions, concerts and a conference, all to raise awareness about these enormous mammals.

🛏 Sleeping

Ambodifotatra is generally good for inexpensive hotels near the port and stand-alone restaurants (which may close by 9pm). If you're looking for a bungalow on an idyllic beach, head south or north.

Les Palmiers BUNGALOW €
(Map p181; ☑ 032 04 960 94; hotel.palmiers@yahoo.fr; d/tr bungalow Ar26,000/30,000; @ 🖵) A little compound with smart, good-value bungalows with fans, up a path from the centre of town. The studio triples are a bargain.

Ambodifotatra

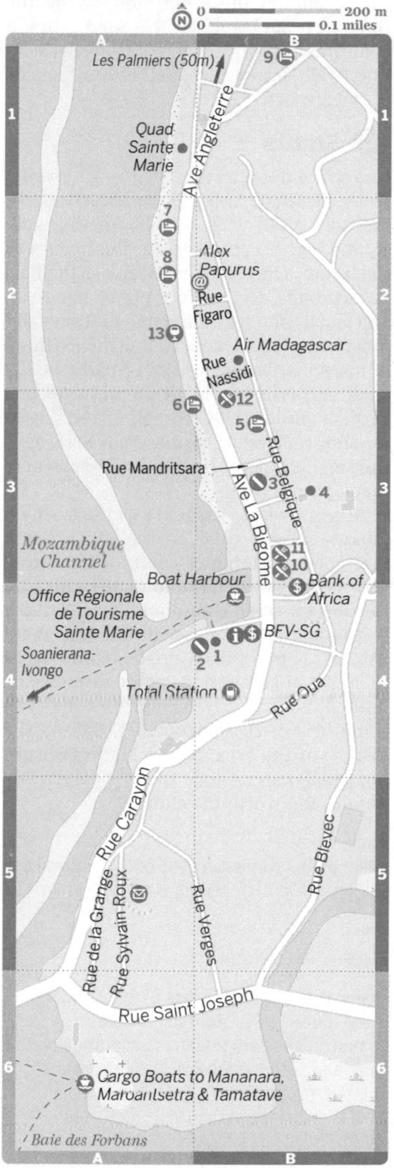

Ambodifotatra

⊙ Activities, Courses & Tours
1	CétaMada	B4
2	Il Balenottero	B4
3	Le Lémurien Palmé	B3
4	Sainte Marie Consulting	B3

⊖ Sleeping
5	Hôtel Freddy	B3
6	Hotel Hortensia	A3
7	Idylle Beach	A2
8	La Banane	A2
9	Les Palmiers	B1

⊗ Eating
10	Du Quai	B3
11	La Paillote	B3
12	Pizza Mama Santa	B3

⊙ Drinking & Nightlife
13	Baramix/La Polina	A2

Hôtel Freddy HOTEL €€

(Map p181; ☏ 032 83 079 50; Rue Belgique; d Ar40,000, without bathroom Ar30,000; ❋) This midrange hotel, conveniently located in the town centre, does all the basics right. Rooms are clean and sizeable with hot water, a shared balcony, lots of light, and even air-con. Try for the corner room first.

Hotel Hortensia HOTEL €€

(Map p181; ☏ 032 02 578 09; d Ar41,000, breakfast Ar6000) Nice large balconies face the ocean at this spacious and reasonably priced two-storey hotel.

★ Idylle Beach HOTEL €€€

(Map p181; ☏ 032 48 684 81; www.idyllebeach. com; r Ar135,000-150,000; ❋) A wonderful little place on the beach, this hotel has village-side rooms and more expensive sea-view rooms. Choose fans rather than air-con and get a reduction in price. There's a casual yet sophisticated bar-restaurant (menu Ar60,000) with a creative menu, and you can eat under the umbrellas on the white sand or retreat into the shadows of the multicoloured verandah. Water sports available.

✗ Eating

For the cheapest eats on the island, try the food stalls that appear in the market area around 6pm daily. There are some small food shops facing the harbour with limited supplies.

La Banane HOTEL €

(Map p181; ☏ 032 02 280 26; dm Ar5000) Backpackers take note: a dorm bed in this decent hotel by the sea is a rare find. The bar is a lively expat hang-out.

La Paillote EUROPEAN €€
(Map p181; mains from Ar10,000; ☺ breakfast, lunch & dinner; ☎) This *vazaha* (foreigner) hang-out entices with its very attractive open-air floor plan, street-front location (great for people-watching), and broad menu, from pizza to langouste. Try the thick zebu fillets. English spoken.

Du Quai CHINESE, MADAGASCAN €€
(Map p181; mains from Ar10,000) The food here is way above average, but the prices aren't.

Pizza Mama Santa PIZZA €€
(Map p181; pizza Ar8000-12,000) Great wood-fired pizza.

🍷 Drinking & Nightlife

Baramix/La Polina CLUB
(Map p181; admission Ar4000; ☺ closed Tue) Nightlife is best found at Baramix/La Polina, a disco that starts up after 8pm.

ℹ️ Information

There are banks and ATMs in the centre of town.
Alex Papurus (Map p181; Ave Angleterre; per min Ar50) Internet access.
Office Régionale de Tourisme Sainte Marie (Map p181; ☎ 034 03 804 55, 034 48 441 98; www.saintemarie-tourisme.mg; harbour; ☺ 8am-noon & 2-6pm Mon-Sat) This excellent office has information about all activities on the island.

South of Ambodifotatra

The area between Ambodifotatra and the airport contains most of the island's hotels and a variety of restaurants. The beach is narrow on this western shore, but on the other side, facing the Ilots aux Sables (Isles of Sand), lies a beautiful unspoilt stretch of tropical coastline. Walk across the small hill to the east of the airport.

◉ Sights

Cimetière des Pirates CEMETERY
(Pirate Cemetery; Map p178; Ambodifotatra; admission Ar2000) This is a fascinating spot from which to contemplate the history of the island. The cemetery overlooks the Baie des Forbans, the perfect pirate hang-out, and smells of a very different era. Ironically, most of the gravestones are actually those of missionaries, but you can clearly see the skull and crossbones on the grave of one English pirate. The crumbling piers used for ship repairs are visible from here, as is the small island of Île aux Forbans, where many pirates lived.

Access is via an isolated foot track, which crosses several tidal creeks and slippery logs about 10 minutes south of the causeway. Guides hang around at the entrance to collect a small community fee, to which they add their own fee if you hire them (Ar5000 is more than ample). However, as their actual knowledge and English may be limited, we strongly recommend that you come here with someone who knows the history of the area. Sainte Marie Consulting (p180) can arrange this. It's completely unique and worth the effort.

Endemika ZOO
(Map p178; admission Ar15,000; ☺ 8am-noon & 2-5pm Mon-Sat) About halfway down the

---

SHIVER ME TIMBERS

In the late 17th and 18th centuries, Île Sainte Marie was the headquarters of the world's pirates, who enjoyed its proximity to maritime trade routes, its protected harbour (a great place to hide), its abundant fruit and its women. Legendary brigands including William Kidd once brought their boats here for repairs, and set up house on Île aux Forbans, near Ambodifotatra. At one point the pirate population topped 1000. Today the remains of several pirate ships still lie within a few metres of the surface in the Baie des Forbans, including Kidd's *Adventure* and Captain Condent's famous *Fiery Dragon,* while the skull and crossbones can be seen engraved at the nearby pirate cemetery.

In May 2015, to great excitement, a 50kg silver bar was discovered off Île Sainte Marie by US explorer Barry Clifford, who claimed it was part of Kidd's long-lost treasure from the *Adventure*. It was presented to the Madagascan president with much fanfare. There was hope that tourism to the island would soar as more people searched for 'X marks the spot'. Next up, Unesco sent a team to investigate that scuppered this romantic tale: they say the silver bar is 95% lead, and definitely not old enough to be part of Kidd's bounty.

WORTH A TRIP

AMPANIHY BAY

If you look at the map of Saint Marie, you'll see a long narrow bay on the east side of the island, and a peninsula to match. Baie d'Ampanihy is a wild and untouristed place, where village life goes on as it has for centuries. It makes for a great day trip, or even an overnight, assuming you have hired a vehicle. The typical route is to drive north from Ambodifotatra to Loukintsy, where you can cross the island to Agnafiafy. Here you'll see a sign for **Mangrove Le Gourmand** (Map p178; ☑ 020 57 901 98; mains from Ar12,000), a bungalow restaurant in a clearing overlooking the bay. The food here is fresh from the sea, and fabulous. By fresh, we mean it has wicker baskets of live fish and mangrove crabs from the nearby creek, while the morning's catch of shrimp is still kicking. Ask for coconut milk, and the cook will climb the adjacent palm tree to get you one. Call ahead to book fresh food.

After lunch, you can hire a pirogue to take you across the bay to the peninsula (Ar5000). You'll probably see local women wading up to their necks as they fish for shrimp.

Now consider this: the locals report that every year from mid-November through December enormous sharks, larger than your pirogue (dugout canoe), enter the mostly shallow bay through a very deep channel in order to give birth. They never attack anyone, although their young are sometimes netted by accident, and the sight of a huge dorsal fin can prompt an early bathroom break. Once you reach the peninsula, you can walk across to the ocean, where you can look for miles in either direction, probably seeing no one. You can spend as much time as you'd like beachcombing here before returning.

southern road, just before Vohilava, this small private zoo and botanical garden showcases regional flora and fauna. It takes about an hour to see.

🛏 Sleeping & Eating

La Baleine BUNGALOW €
(Map p178; ☑ 032 40 257 18; www.hotel-la-baleine. com; d bungalows from Ar30,000, with hot water Ar40,000-50,000; ⊚) Basic beachfront bungalows close to the water, with the world's most rickety dock.

Vanilla Café BUNGALOW €€
(Map p178; ☑ 032 40 239 43; d incl breakfast Ar60,000) A small place with basic bungalows, all with bathrooms and hot water. A bit pricey, but it has some very pleasant waterfront dining.

Chez Pierrot BUNGALOW €€
(Map p178; ☑ 034 01 060 91; chezpierrot@moov. mg; d/f Ar60,000/120,000) These spick-and-span, mismatched bungalows, with bright bedcovers and deckchairs, are arranged in a neat garden next to the sea, but there's no real beach, just an elevated artificial replacement.

★**Libertalia** BUNGALOW €€€
(Map p178; ☑ 034 18 997 27, 020 57 923 03; www. lelibertalia.com; d Ar144,000; ☎) 🕿 The lascivious whistles of the house parrot welcome

you to this popular hotel named after the mythical pirate kingdom. The setting is unique, with a small private island connected to the lovely beach, and a great swimming dock. A sophisticated kitchen, friendly staff, and special touches such as hydrophones for listening to the whales singing are all part of a winning personality.

Owners Didier and Martine are founder members of CétaMada and can arrange whale-watching excursions, other boat trips and diving. Kayaks, mountain bikes, motor bikes and scooters are also available. Accepts credit cards.

Les Villas de Vohilava VILLA €€€
(Map p178; ☑ 032 04 757 84, 020 57 900 16; www.vohilava.com; d bungalow €35, villa €70-110) These five large and very-well-done beachfront villas, with two to three rooms, a kitchen and a chef, are designed for groups of four to 10 people. There's a bungalow and a double room, too. The attentive owner, Henri, ensures a quality stay. You can hire bikes and scooters, and kayaks are free. Whale-watching trips and other excursions can be arranged.

**Princesse Bora
Lodge & Spa** LUXURY HOTEL €€€
(Map p178; ☑ 020 57 040 03; www.princessebora. com; d half board per person Ar270,000; ❄@🏊) One of Madagascar's top resorts. Creative

touches here include an extraordinary spa with pirogue tubs and its own essential-oil laboratory, an extensive wine cellar with a private label, a nearby tropical nursery featuring the island's diverse species, huge bungalows with suspended wooden beds, enamel bathrooms and serpentine corridors reminiscent of a reef. There's also an airy pool and an elegant restaurant.

Set on a nice beach with comfortable sunloungers and outdoor showers, none of this comes cheaply, but this is one high-end property where you really do get what you pay for. The secret is the extraordinary Swiss family behind it, for whom the lodge is not just a business but a ruling passion extending well beyond the normal boundaries of tourism. Prices increase to Ar310,000 during whale-watching season.

Hôtel Lakana　　　　　BUNGALOW €€€
(Map p178; ☑ 032 07 090 22; www.sainte-marie-hotel.com; d bungalow Ar120,000-132,000; 🔊) This hotel and restaurant is known for its bungalows on stilts over the sea, each with its own bathroom back on land. Smarter bungalows (with bathrooms) are clustered in a well-tended garden.

Jardins d'Eden　　　　BUNGALOW €€€
(Map p178; ☑ 034 09 265 76; www.jardins deden-saintemarie-madagascar.com; d bungalow Ar85,000) If you want to be away from the main coastal road, and enjoy some cooler weather, the only option, and it's a good one, is this guesthouse with grand views,

high up on a hill overlooking the pirate cemetery. Botano-philes will be particularly pleased with the grounds. Clients arrive by pirogue and gain free access to the pirate cemetery.

Once you've finished treasure-hunting, pop in for brunch (Ar21,000).

☆ Entertainment

Casa à Nono　　　　　　　　　　CLUB
(Map p178; ☉ Thu & Sun) The main night spot – it's near the airport.

Île aux Nattes (Nosy Nato)

What a lovely place this is. Île aux Nattes is a classic tropical island, with curving white beaches and overhanging palms, a turquoise sea with waves breaking over the reef, a gentle breeze and a lush green interior. While only a brief pirogue ride (Ar5000 return) from the tip of Sainte Marie, or a mere walk at low tide, there's a palpable sense of isolation and adventure. Numerous sand pathways (beware the crab holes!) open the way for exploration without the possibility of getting too lost in an area only 2km across. Surprisingly, there is also some great, wonderfully quirky accommodation. So if you are suffering from visions of tropical paradise, here is your medicine.

There is no electricity on the island; hotels use solar panels.

HUMPBACK SEASON

Every year several hundred humpback whales make their way from the Antarctic northward to the warmer Madagascan waters around Baie d'Antongil, where they spend the winter months breeding and birthing before the long journey back. En route they swim past Île Sainte Marie, where they are often sighted between July and mid-September. Getting to see these amazing creatures close up can be a highlight of a visit to Madagascar.

Humpbacks can measure up to 15m in length and weigh as much as 35,000kg. Despite their size, they are exceptionally agile, and capable of acrobatic moves such as breaching (launching themselves out of the water). These whales are also renowned for their singing, which is presumed to be related to mating patterns. Humpback songs can last up to an hour, and are considered the most complex of all whale songs.

During humpback season you can go on 'whale safaris' around the island for about €45 for a half-day trip. Inquire at the dive centres and shuttle-boat companies, as hotels without their own boats often arrange trips through them. The business is informally regulated by **CétaMada** (☑ 033 65 656 56; www.cetamada.org), a Madagascan conservation organisation that promotes responsible whale watching. Participating hotels agree to respect a code of approach, assure security protocols on board, and have a qualified guide. You can help by hiring a boat with a CétaMada sticker on it.

🛏 Sleeping & Eating

⭐ Chez Sica
BUNGALOW €€

(Map p178; ☑032 42 478 86, 032 41 656 98; www.chezsica.com; Île aux Nattes; d/f Ar35,000/60,000) Wow. If you are looking for inexpensive accommodation, look no further: here it is. The hotel is like an open park beneath the palms, with an absolutely gorgeous location on a fringing reef. These bungalows are the best value anywhere on Sainte Marie, with a thatched porch, a hammock with dreamy views and the clever use of pirogues as shelving.

Only breakfast is served, but there is a kitchen for guests (and plenty of other hotels nearby). Best of all, management has not crafted a system for extracting as much money from you as possible. They actually *lend* you snorkel equipment, and spearfishing trips are free. A refreshing choice from every perspective.

A pirogue from Île Sainte Marie to Chez Sica costs Ar10,000, or you can walk (30 minutes) from the northern drop-off point.

Chez Tity
BUNGALOW €€

(Map p178; ☑034 04 065 80; cheztity@gmail.com; d Ar40,000, without bathroom Ar10,000-30,000) This is a laid-back, friendly Malagasy-owned place, popular with backpackers, with a bit of wisdom thrown in: all the bungalows are named after philosophers. The more expensive bungalows have been renovated and have en-suite bathrooms. Main dishes from Ar10,000.

Analatsara Eco-Lodge
BUNGALOW €€€

(Map p178; ☑032 02 127 70; www.analatsara.net; bungalow Ar90,000-150,000; 🖥) The owner of Analatsara has crafted a high-quality miniresort basically for the love of sharing it. A couple of bungalows share a bathroom, others have their own. A six-person house with housekeeper, chef and 24-hour electricity is €600 per week. The standout option is the tree house, replete with trapdoor entry. A pirogue to Analatsara costs Ar8000, or you can walk (30 minutes) from the northern drop-off point. Credit cards accepted. Set menu is Ar55,000.

La Petite Traversée
BUNGALOW €€€

(Map p178; ☑032 42 360 52, South Africa +27 72 827 7158; www.madxperience.com; d €45, f €80-95) This is one of the island's wonderfully personable offerings. Castaway South African Ockie Snyman has created more of a community than a hotel, including family-style dining, and music and movies at night. The menu changes constantly, with seafood a recurring theme, and pizza cooked in an oven built into the prow of an old dhow. Try the Passion Island cocktail.

Meva Paradis
BUNGALOW €€€

(Map p178; ☑034 98 471 23, 032 46 802 81; www.mevaparadis.com; d/f bungalow €35/65) In a garden setting by a great stretch of beach, these are pleasant en-suite bungalows. Hot water on request.

North of Ambodifotatra

Sometimes it's easy to forget, but north of Ambodifotatra lies three-quarters of the island. In terms of accommodation, almost all is on the west coast, which is more sheltered from cyclones. There is a good paved road to the northern tip, after which the road down the eastern side gets rough, and the real adventure begins.

It will take several enjoyable hours, but you can drive all the way to the **Piscine Naturelle d'Ambodiatafana** (Map p178), a natural pool at the northeastern tip of the island, where there are some basic bungalows. The **Fanilo Albrand lighthouse** (Map p178) lies to the southwest. From the ridge, Maroantsetra and Baie d'Antongil are sometimes visible.

🛏 Sleeping

Le Bon Endroit
GUESTHOUSE €€

(Map p178; ☑033 09 624 38, 020 57 906 62; www.lebonendroit.net; d/f Ar45,000/66,000) This guesthouse is off the beaten track, and offers a good deal. The simple en-suite bungalows occupy a rugged coral beach, and there's a central restaurant (menu Ar19,500). There is a full range of activities (deep-sea fishing, snorkelling, kayaking, spearfishing and more). Bikes are Ar10,000 per day. You could easily stay here a week and have plenty to do. Transfers arranged.

Cocoteraie Robert
BUNGALOW €€

(Map p178; ☑020 57 901 76, 034 29 666 98; cocoteraierobert@gmail.com; d bungalow Ar50,000) This long-established hotel has rebuilt itself after the tragic cyclone that struck here several years ago. The beach is the main selling point, one of the best in Sainte Marie, with sweeping horizon views encompassing miles of shoreline.

Hôtel Sainte Marie Lodge
BOUTIQUE HOTEL €€€

(Map p178; ☑034 19 059 52; www.hotel-sainte
marielodge-madagascar.com; per person from €58;
🛜📶) This elegant lodge on a large piece of
waterfront is a big step above the competition, with a charming ambience that is part
safari lodge and part piano bar. The simple rooms are very comfy, with thick euro-
mattresses and balconies overlooking the
sea. The owners have paid great attention
to the details; there are sophisticated touches throughout. English is spoken. Minimum
three-night stay.

Quads and other activities are available,
including water aerobics.

Masoandro Lodge
LODGE €€€

(Map p178; ☑020 57 910 43, 034 44 416 28; www.
masoandro.mg; standard d bungalow €76, menu
€17; ❄🛜📶) This beautiful wooden lodge
is located on a hillside with great long-
range views, and there's a fantastic pool
area with an adjacent waterfall. It's well
situated at the end of the good road heading north, equally convenient for town and
adventure. The deluxe bungalows are much
larger than the standard ones, but the latter are half the price. Multiple excursions
available.

La Crique
BUNGALOW €€€

(Map p178; ☑034 03 117 25, 020 57 902 63; www.
lacrique-saintemarie.com; d/f bungalow per person Ar63,000/41,000) The rooms at La Cri-
que have verandahs with deckchairs from
which you can look out over the garden and
a magnificent stretch of beach. Most bungalows are en suite.

BAIE D'ANTONGIL & THE MASOALA PENINSULA

In February 2015, with the support of the
Wildlife Conservation Society, the Madagascan government declared the Baie
d'Antongil a marine sanctuary to protect
19 shark species and fishing rights for local
communities. The remote bay lies north of
Soanierana-Ivongo; its boundaries stretch
from Mananara around Maroantsetra to
the Masoala Peninsula, forming a deep blue
U teeming with fish and surrounded by
mountainous forest. Cut off from easy road
access to the south, and with nothing but
hiking trails elsewhere, this is a place whose
only reliable contact with the outside world
is the intermittent flights into Maroantsetra. As a result, there is a captivating sense of
timelessness here, as if one has been flung
back into 1950s Madagascar. Disconnected
from the wheels of progress, one turns to
the mountains, the sky and the sea.

Mananara

Mananara is a small and very out-of-
the-way town set in a clove- and vanilla-
producing area at the southern entrance
to Baie d'Antongil. This is the place to stay
if you wish to explore the nearby Parc National de Mananara-Nord. There's also some
decent snorkelling off the peninsula behind
the (nonfunctioning) airport, and internet
access at the Boutique Orange.

If staying the night (likely if you're heading down the RN5), be sure not to miss the
night walk at Aye-Aye Island, which is the
easiest way to see Madagascar's most reclu-
sive and bizarre lemur.

👁 Sights & Activities

Parc National de Mananara-Nord   PARK

(entry permit per day Ar45,000) The remote
240-sq-km Parc National de Mananara-Nord
encompasses some of the last remaining
lowland rainforest in the country. An additional 10 sq km of islets and surrounding
reefs are protected as a marine park, the
largest being Nosy Atafana. While lemurs
are not always seen, Mananara-Nord contains *indris*, brown lemurs, ruffed lemurs
and aye-ayes, and is the only known habitat of the hairy-eared dwarf lemur. There
is also a variety of geckos, including the endemic uroplatus and day geckos. Offshore
there are dugong.

The **MNP office** (☑033 12 768 97, 033 12 692
60; mananara_nationalpark@yahoo.fr; Sahasoa) is
in Sahasoa, about 30km south of Mananara.
Come here first to arrange your visit. Guide
and porter fees start at Ar12,000/8000 per
day. Many guides speak some English. They
will print out a map upon request.

The park has two main circuits, one terrestrial and the other marine. The terrestrial
circuit begins 6km south of the park office by
foot. It takes two hours to get there, two to
do the circuit, and another two to get back.
The marine circuit includes a trip to Nosy
Atafana, and costs an additional Ar120,000
to Ar150,000 for boat and fuel. The cost per
person thus declines with the size of the
group (maximum eight). A third circuit takes

Baie d'Antongil & the Masoala Peninsula

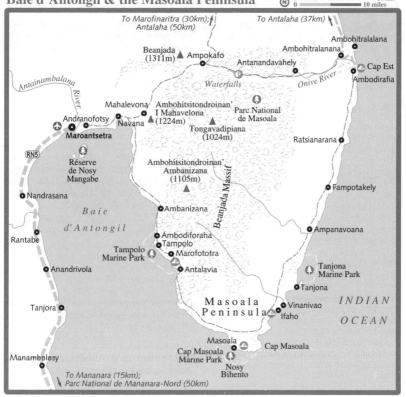

two full days and covers both land and sea. For any trip in the park, you'll need to be self-sufficient with food and water, and, if hiking, in good shape. Camping is Ar5000 per tent. A limited amount of camping equipment is available for hire at the park office.

Mananara-Nord sees very few tourists. This region is not only difficult to reach, but the park itself is not great value. The two-hour terrestrial circuit requires four hours of hiking to get there and back. The marine circuit is a quick 15 minutes to Nosy Atafana, but the circuit is only an hour – not long for the price.

If you are coming from Maroantsetra, the large, mountainous and lush Nosy Mangabe (7 sq km) offers a lot more than the small and flat Nosy Atafana (0.23 sq km).

Aye-Aye Island   WILDLIFE WATCHING
(night tour Ar20,000) The patron of local hotel Chez Roger also owns this small island in the middle of the Mananara River and

offers night tours including transport (car and pirogue) and guide. The prize: an aye-aye lemur, caught in the beam of a torch, sitting up in the leaves of a palm tree. Watch as it digs out the meat from a coconut with its bizarre bony finger. Call Chez Roger to book ahead.

🛏 Sleeping & Eating

Chez Roger   BUNGALOW €
(☑ 033 14 265 33, 032 52 329 87; d Ar20,000) This is the best place to stay if you want to visit Aye-Aye Island. The big and comfortable bungalows out back have bathrooms (bucket showers), there are reasonable rooms available and the restaurant does decent meals.

Sahasoa Bungalows   BUNGALOW €
(☑ 033 19 671 81; d Ar15,000, set menu Ar5000) These clean bungalows on a tropical-paradise beach in Sahasoa are close to the

Parc National de Mananara-Nord office, and dirt cheap.

Hôtel Aye-Aye BUNGALOW €
(☏032 95 883 96; d Ar25,000; ⛱) This hotel near the airport is a good budget option, with basic en-suite bungalows among the palm trees, a small pool and a restaurant. Cold water only.

☆ Entertainment

Mananara is, surprisingly, a bit of a party town. For that Madagascan beat, try Volume 5 near the Boutique Orange.

❶ Getting There & Around

BOAT
The **Melissa Express** (☏ 032 44 743 03, 033 17 732 72; melissaexpress1@gmail.com) passenger boat offers a weekly service between Mananara and both Maroantsetra (Ar80,000) and Soanierana-Ivongo (Ar120,000). This is the only service of its kind on this coast, and inexpensive, but is subject to interruptions, particularly from June to September.

Cargo boats sail occasionally between Mananara, Île Sainte Marie, Maroantsetra and Tamatave. There are usually several departures weekly, although there are no set schedules. This journey is only really safe between September and March, due to sea conditions. Inquire at the small port in Mananara. Boats often come in and leave again fairly quickly, so you'll have to return often. Fares between Mananara and Île Sainte Marie or Maroantsetra average about Ar50,000; the trip takes at least eight hours, often sailing through the night. Occasional cargo boats go as far as Antalaha, Sambava or even Diego Suarez (Antsiranana) in the north. There are no facilities of any kind on the boats, so bring sun protection (an umbrella is handy), food and water.

PRIVATE 4WD
Taxi-brousse company **Kofifen** (☏ 033 11 640 95) rents private 4WDs. It quotes Ar1.6 million including driver and fuel to Maroantsetra, but in our experience hard bargaining can cut prices nearly in half.

TAXI-BROUSSE
Taxis-brousses heading south or north along the RN5 all stop here, so go to the station to inquire; it's on the main road near the town hall. You will definitely want to read up on the RN5 (p177) before you do.

Maroantsetra

If you were going to make a movie about old Madagascar, this would be the place to film it. Set at the apex of the Baie d'Antongil, near the mouth of the Antainambalana River, Maroantsetra is full of languid charm, and enjoys both river scenery and ocean views. Locals will tell you that very little has changed here in 30 years. And yet there is a lot for the visitor to do. This is the perfect base for exploring the entire bay, including the forests of Masoala, the island of Nosy Mangabe, and the humpback whales that visit and give birth from July to September. Just be aware that Maroantsetra's climate is one of the wettest in Madagascar, particularly from May to September.

☞ Tours

The local MNP has trained English-speaking guides with great local knowledge who can organise any itinerary you want to the Masoala Peninsula, Nosy Mangabe or Parc National de Mananara-Nord, for a reasonable price.

The Hippocampe hotel also offers a range of quality tours.

Mada Expeditions HIKING, KAYAKING
(☏032 77 266 42, 032 86 614 68; www.mada-expeditions.com) Offers extensive hiking and kayaking trips around Masoala; requires advance notice.

🛏 Sleeping

The properties on the canal benefit from a sea breeze, making them cooler than the inland options. Be careful of the hand-sized spiders that spin webs on hotel paths at night.

★ Le Coco Beach BUNGALOW €€
(☏032 04 807 58; cocobeachotelmaroantsetra @yahoo.fr; d Ar60,000, with air-con Ar91,000, without bathroom Ar20,000; ❄) This friendly midrange hotel has comfortable, well-maintained bungalows and an above-average restaurant (menu Ar30,000) set amid coconut palms. The atmospheric bungalows on the river are especially good value. Local tours organised.

Masoala Resort BUNGALOW €€
(☏032 11 075 51, 033 15 051 52; www.masoala resort.com; d garden/sea view Ar60,000/95,000; 🛜❄) This hotel occupies a fine location,

with a grand view of Nosy Mangabe, but the Versailles fountain, the water tower in the shape of a tea cup, the enormous decorative boat on the lawn, the garish amateur murals and the large water hazard (aka a swimming pool) make it look more like a minigolf course than a hotel. Driver, please.

Hippocampe GUESTHOUSE €€€
(☑ 032 64 418 99; www.madahippocampe.com; r Ar127,050, bungalow incl breakfast Ar163,350; ☒) This interesting *chambre d'hôte* (B&B) occupies a beautiful home on the canal, with six rooms, three bungalows and lovely views of Nosy Mangabe. The range of activities on offer are a big plus here, particularly as there is a sister lodge in the Masoala park. The unfiltered natural swimming pool, replete with fish, may not be to everyone's liking. The set menu is Ar36,300.

Hippocampe offers quality 4WD tours, boat trips and walking in the parks, personally run by the French owner (no English). Its two boats can be hired to visit Mananara (maximum seven people, Ar2.2 million), and Antalaha or Île Sainte Marie (maximum 16 people, Ar7 million). If the boat waits overnight for you, it costs another Ar50,000.

Hotel Ebène BUNGALOW €€€
(☑ 032 49 971 16, 033 14 908 73; mahafenokathy@yahoo.fr; d Ar75,000) A basic choice, but not bad for the price. There are two locations: the bungalows near the river are a better option than the rooms in town.

✗ Eating

Coco Beach provides some hearty meals that are good value, though service can be slow. For budget eating, locals praise the Chinese food at Florida Snack, on the main road near the Bank of Africa, along with Chez Tantine and La Vivanette.

☕ Drinking & Nightlife

There are two discos that comprise Maroantsetra nightlife: Zanzibar I in town and Zanzibar II on the road to the airport. Both attract a young and amiable crowd that dances into the wee hours. As you'll be going at night, a taxi is the only way to find these places.

ⓘ Information

Bank of Africa has a branch here for changing cash and travellers cheques, and there's an ATM.

ⓘ DON'T FORGET THE PROPRIETOR

The Madagascar travel scene is fascinating because hotels are rarely owned by large corporations. Due to the country's political and economic instability, there are no motel chains dotting the RN7, while in the cities the big international chains are noticeably absent. Instead, when not Malagasy-owned, hotels in this stretch of the globe are run by the most interesting expats you will ever meet, from the wizened French folks running end-of-the-earth bungalows to the impressive family-run resorts, such as La Relais de la Reine (p78) in Isalo (French), Princesse Bora (p183) in Île Sainte Marie (Swiss), 293 (p136) on Komba (South African) and La Pirogue (p175) in Mahambo (French-American).

Each proprietor stamps his or her own personality upon a place, turning it, for better or worse, into a work of hospitality art. And oh, the stories they can tell! So when you do meet the proprietors, be sure to lift the lid on their treasuries of tales. A trip to Madagascar is not complete until you do.

MNP Office (☑ 032 41 944 46) Located near the market.
Orange (per hr Ar3000; ☉7.30am-noon & 2.30-6pm Mon-Fri, to noon Sat) Internet access.

ⓘ Getting There & Away

AIR
➤ Air Madagascar flights connect Maroantsetra twice a week with Antananarivo (€260, 2½ hours) via Tamatave (€216, 1¼ hours). The Air Madagascar office is a few kilometres from town on the road to the airport.
➤ Flights to/from Maroantsetra are often full, especially between June and November – be sure to reconfirm your ticket. Weather may affect plane schedules, particularly during the rainiest months (July to September).

BOAT
➤ The **Melissa Express** (☑ Tamatave 033 18 732 72, Tamatave 032 44 743 03) passenger boat offers weekly service between Maroantsetra and both Mananara (Ar80,000) and Soanierana-Ivongo (Ar100,000). This is the only service of its kind on this coast, and inexpensive, but is subject to interruptions, particularly from July to September.

CAP EST

Remote and beautiful Cap Est is Madagascar's easternmost point. You can get here by hiring a car or taking a four-hour *taxi-brousse* ride south from Antalaha. Hotels here are routinely destroyed by cyclones, but in late 2015 the basic **Hotel du Voyageur** (✆ 033 32 256 41) was still standing. The nearby town of Ambodirafia has an MNP office that can provide you with all the necessary information and support (guides, porters) for hikes down the Masoala Peninsula's east coast. The walk from here to the very tip of the peninsula, Cap Masoala, takes about four days, camping along the way, with numerous rivers that must be crossed by pirogue. From there you have to either return, or continue around the peninsula to Maroantsetra, a hard but adventurous slog that could take another four to six days. Cargo boats also leave intermittently from Cap Masoala for Maroantsetra.

➡ Hippocampe (p189), in Maroantsetra, has two boats that can be hired to reach Mananara, Antalaha and Île Sainte Marie.

➡ There are also unscheduled but regular cargo boats sailing between Maroantsetra and Île Sainte Marie (10 hours), Tamatave (two days), Antalaha (12 to 15 hours) and Mananara (nine hours). Enquire at the port in Maroantsetra, and then be prepared for inevitable delays. The boats that take passengers are sometimes extremely overloaded, and some do capsize, so if the boat looks too full, don't get on. Good boats to look out for to Mananara are *La Baleine* and *Ambotosoa*. To Île Sainte Marie or Tamatave, look out for *Savannah, Red Rose* or *Rosita*.

PRIVATE 4WD

Taxi-brousse company **Kofifen** (✆ 033 11 640 95) also rents private 4WDs. It quotes Ar1.6 million including driver and fuel to Mananara and Ar2.2 million to Tamatave, but in our experience hard bargaining can cut these prices nearly in half.

TAXI-BROUSSE

Maroantsetra lies 112km north of Mananara at the end of the infamous RN5. *Taxis-brousses* depart for Mananara around 6am Tuesday, Thursday and Saturday (Ar40,000) and carry on to Tamatave (Ar90,000). There are no roads anywhere else.

🛈 Getting Around

The airport is about 7km southwest of town. The taxi fare is Ar15,000.

Réserve de Nosy Mangabe

The island of Nosy Mangabe (entry permit per day Ar45,000, compulsory guide per group per day Ar15,000-35,000), easily visible 5km offshore from Maroantsetra, is a must-visit for anyone with a smidgen of romance in their blood. This is a thickly forested and mountainous tropical island, with huge soaring canarium trees arising from flying buttress roots, a rusty shipwreck piercing one side, waterfalls, a spyglass hill, a yellow sickle beach, elusive animals, foreign inscriptions, and the omnipresent sound of the jungle. Whew! If that doesn't bring out the Robinson Crusoe in you, check your pulse. It rains a lot, though, so be prepared.

You have the option of taking a day trip here, or staying overnight. MNP runs a very well-equipped beachside **campground** (camping per tent Ar5000) with shelters, picnic tables, a kitchen and flush toilets, and some rental camping equipment. There are also a few basic bungalows if you don't have a tent. It's an idyllic spot, with a waterfall for a shower, and beckoning trailheads. A popular option takes you to the summit of the island, affording great views. Another leads to **Plage des Hollandais**, a beach with rocks bearing the scratched names of some 17th-century Dutch sailors. From July to September, you can see whales offshore.

The forest here is full of reptiles and amphibians, including the leaf-tailed gecko, one of nature's most accomplished camouflage artists; several species of chameleons; many frogs; and several harmless species of snake, including the Madagascar tree boa. It is also home to various lemurs, including the elusive aye-aye, which was introduced here in 1967 to protect the species from extinction. A sighting is by no means guaranteed.

🛈 Information

➡ Entry permits can be obtained at the MNP office (p189) in Maroantsetra, or on the island itself. The permits do not include the nearby Parc National de Masoala.

➡ Compulsory guides vary in cost: those with experience and wildlife knowledge are up to Ar35,000 per group per day, while trainee trail guides are Ar15,000 per day. Night walks (recommended) cost Ar10,000 for groups of up to four, plus Ar2000 for the guide's evening meal. Some guides will cook in the evenings for an extra fee.

ℹ Getting There & Away

Boat transfers can be arranged through the MNP office (p189). Rates per person for a return day trip are Ar100,000/60,000/ 40,000/35,000 for one/two/three/four people. The trip takes 30 to 45 minutes, but is weather dependent, so it is best not to wait until your last day.

Parc National de Masoala

The magical Masoala (mash-wala) Peninsula is the site of a 2100-sq-km **national park** (entry permit per day 45,000, compulsory guide per group per day Ar15,000-35,000) containing one of the best primary rainforests in the country. It also encompasses three protected marine areas: **Tampolo Marine Park** on the peninsula's southwestern coast, **Cap Masoala Marine Park** at the tip of the peninsula and **Tanjona Marine Park** on the southeastern coast. Most of the park is spread across the central part of the peninsula, extending southwest to Tampolo Marine Park. There are several small discrete parcels *(parcs détachés)* elsewhere on the peninsula as well. At the peninsula's southernmost tip is the beautiful Cap Masoala, which can be reached on foot or by bicycle from Cap Est.

The peninsula is famous for its vegetation, which includes primary forest, rainforest and coastal forest, as well as a variety of palm and orchid species. Ten lemur species are found here, along with several tenrec and mongoose species, 14 bat species, 60 reptile species and about 85 bird species. The marine national parks protect mangrove ecosystems, coral reefs, dolphins, dugong and turtles.

There are excellent opportunities here for sea kayaking, snorkelling and swimming. The entire peninsula is exceptionally wet, however, particularly during June and July, when river levels are highest. The months between October and December are somewhat drier and best for hiking.

The reserve is only accessible by boat, or on foot if you are hiking. Check at the MNP office or at hotels in Maroantsetra for boats to hire and guides. All the accommo-

dation options in the reserve provide boat transfers.

🏃 Activities

This is a hiker's paradise. If you are staying in the ecolodges on the west coast, there are many short trails that you can take. There are also three main long-distance trails for serious hiking. The **Maroantsetra to Antalaha direct trip** passes through rice paddies and gentler terrain. It is the easiest but also the least interesting. A guide for five days is Ar185,000.

For forest lovers, the **Maroantsetra to Antalaha via Cap Est route** (up to eight days) is more interesting, particularly the spectacular Cascade (waterfall) Bevontsira, but also more challenging, with river crossings and mountains. A guide is Ar275,000 and porters (you'll need two) are Ar12,000 each per day. Most nights are spent in villages, where it is customary to pay a few thousand ariary per person to the village chief. Carry a tent, however, as there are no villages in the forest, where you will spend three nights.

Finally, one can walk the entire rim of the peninsula, from **Maroantsetra to Antalaha via Cap Masoala and Cap Est**. This journey takes up to 15 days. A guide is Ar400,000. The hiking time can be cut by taking a boat from Maroantsetra to Cap Masoala (Ar400,000). A tent is required.

ℹ PARC NATIONAL DE MASOALA

Best time to visit August (for whales) to January.

Key highlight Seeing humpback whales and red-ruffed lemurs in the same day.

Wildlife Gold dust gecko, fork-marked lemurs, helmeted vanga shrike, serpent eagle, dugong.

Habitat Low, middle and highland rainforest, mangrove, littoral forest, reefs and rivers.

Gateway towns Maroantsetra and Antalaha.

Transport options Boat or walk in.

Things you should know Bring a raincoat. The sea can be rough in the afternoon.

Food, including for the guides and porters, and park entry permits are not included in these rates and are paid by the client.

All long-distance hikes are fairly demanding and involve muddy stretches. At certain times of the year you may be wading up to chest height over slippery rocks. Inquire at the MNP office (p189) about trail conditions.

🛏️ Sleeping & Eating

There are designated campsites (camping per person Ar5000 to Ar7000) all the way around the peninsula, including at Marofototra, Antalavia, Ambodilaitry, Ifaho and Cap Est. Grounds have wells and shelters for tents, but you'll need to bring in all other equipment. Bottled water and basic supplies are usually available in bigger villages such as Mahalevona, Ampokafo and Antanandavahely, but you will need to be self-sufficient with most food and water (bring a purifier).

In addition to basic village accommodation, there are several upmarket lodges along the coast near Tampolo on the southwestern side of the peninsula. Access is generally by boat. Expect higher prices for their packages in the wake of the National Park permit fee increases in November 2015. We recommend purifying your water, even at upmarket accommodation.

★ **Masoala Forest Lodge**　LODGE €€€
(☏ 032 05 415 86; www.masoalaforestlodge.com; per person 3 nights, all-inclusive €1365) Staying here is akin to going on a high-end safari, including the luxury tents (with hot water). Located on a 100,000-sq-m forest reserve, there are just seven palm-thatched tents up in the trees. The minimum program is €1365 per person for a three-night stay, all inclusive (transfers, park permits, meals and activities).

★ **Dounia Forest Lodge**　LODGE €€€
(☏ 034 00 200 00, 032 40 213 81; www.dounia group.com; d per person full board Ar477,000) This, the northernmost lodge at Tampolo, is now under new ownership. Set in 80,000 sq m of primary forest bordering the beach, the spacious bungalows contain two double beds and tea- and coffee-making facilities, and have large balconies. The restaurant caters for vegetarian, vegan and gluten-free diets. A three-night package for two including full board and transfers is Ar1.88 million per person.

Other packages and various excursions are available.

Ecolodge Chez Arol　LODGE €€€
(☏ 033 12 902 77, 032 40 889 02; http://arol lodge.free.fr; per person full board €171) ⌁ The most basic option in the park, with simple thatched-hut bungalows with hot water. The cheapest package of two days all inclusive (taxi and boat transfer, guide fees, entrance permits and full board) is €342 per person for two. The lodge offers camping and tree climbing in the canopy to see red-ruffed lemurs. In the Tampolo region of the park, south of Ambanizana.

There are some cheaper bungalows with shared facilities (per person for two days €286) and some with just cold water (per person for two days €316). Prices are based on two people sharing and are all-inclusive.

Part of the proceeds goes to support the local community.

Masoala Lodge　BUNGALOW €€€
(☏ 032 64 418 99; www.madahippocampe.com; per person full board Ar271,800) Sister to the Hippocampe (p189) in Maroantsetra, this lodge is on a splendid stretch of beach at Tampolo. Transfers are included in the price.

Tampolodge　LODGE €€€
(☏ 032 67 305 02, 032 42 713 37; www.tampo lodge-masoala.com; d bungalow full board per person €60) This lodge has a great location, on a fantastic arc of beach split by the alluring S-bend of a jungle river. Accommodation is in basic bungalows with cold water, but with large bathrooms. A double bungalow with bathroom is €60 per person with full board, although this doesn't include any transfers or activities.

❶ Information

➡ The main park headquarters is located at the MNP office (p189) in Maroantsetra. The guides here are well organised, and many speak English.

➡ Treks can also be arranged at the MNP office in Antalaha or in Ambodirafia, near Cap Est, although the staff and guides there don't speak English.

➡ Guides are mandatory in both terrestrial and marine parks. Those with experience and wildlife knowledge are Ar35,000 per day. Trail guides are Ar15,000 per day, porters Ar10,000 to Ar15,000 per day. There is an additional fee of Ar30,000 if the boat has to wait overnight.

Understand
Madagascar

Madagascar Today

Despite the return to political legitimacy following the 2013 legislative and presidential elections, Madagascar has struggled to regain the development oomph it had garnered in the mid-naughties. Political instability remains high, reforms are lagging, donors and investors are keeping their distance and Madagascar's fabulous potential remains mostly untapped. Malagasies are incredibly weary of their country's underperformance, but the mood is one of wilful optimism, not defeat.

Best on Film

Madagascar (2011) A three-part series by the BBC, narrated by Sir David Attenborough, showcasing the island's wildlife.

Madagascar (2005) With a stellar cast of voice-overs, this cartoon raised Madagascar's profile.

Best in Print

The Eighth Continent: Life, Death and Discovery in the Lost World of Madagascar (2013) by Peter Tyson

The Aye-Aye and I (1992) by Gerald Durrell

A History of Madagascar (2001) by Mervyn Brown

Etiquette

Respect local *fady* (taboos), which are cultural and social dictates that relate to food, behaviour and certain times of the week or year. Guides will explain.

Don't point, bend your finger or indicate with your palm.

Bring rice or a bottle of rum if you're invited to a Malagasy home.

Don't attend cultural celebrations such as exhumation or circumcision ceremonies unless you have been invited.

No Panacea

The 2013 presidential elections were a necessary first step for Madagascar to turn the page of the transition, but they have proved insufficient to solve the country's chronic political instability. President Hery Rajaonarimampianina was elected with little popular support and no party and he has struggled to get a majority in parliament and pass reforms.

Hery, as he is popularly known, has found himself stuck between a rock and a hard place with mostly hostile opposition parties (coup leader Andry Rajoelina's MAPAR and ousted president Marc Ravalomanana's TIM) and a large group of flip-flopping independent members of parliament.

The tempestuous relationship between the executive and legislative came to a head in May 2015 when, sensing that attack was its best defence, the national assembly impeached the president before he could dissolve it.

Hery was saved by the Constitutional Court, which threw out the impeachment procedure, but a month later the assembly put forward a motion of no-confidence against Prime Minister Jean Ravelonarivo. The motion failed, but only just.

International Wariness

These political quarrels have slowed Madagascar's return to 'business as usual'. It's taken 18 months for the National Development Plan to be approved and the municipal elections to take place, and two years for the senate to be installed.

Vital economic reforms are lagging. Madagascar notably needs to crack down on corruption, fraud and tax evasion, clean up its enormous civil-service payroll and radically reform loss-making state companies Jirama (the national water and electricity utility) and Air Madagascar (a month-long strike in June 2015 brought the country to a standstill and severely affected the tourism season). These reforms are not only essential for the economy, they're key to securing foreign aid: after the 2013 elections, donors had announced they were ready to resume their support, but unimpressed with the pace of reforms, many had yet to make firm commitments at the time of writing.

Foreign investors are shunning Madagascar, too. Despite the return to political legitimacy and the country's reintegration into the African Growth Opportunity Act (a trade agreement facilitating access to the US market), many are wary of the ongoing political instability and baulk at the numerous obstacles to doing business there (crippling lack of energy, widespread corruption, poor infrastructure etc).

International observers also bemoan the scale of wildlife trafficking, which carries on unabated. Containers of precious rosewood have been exported continuously and in complete impunity since the elections, and animal poaching has become so bad that conservationists have had to resort to desperate measures, including defacing the shell of every remaining ploughshare tortoise.

Tremendous Potential

This state of affairs is all the more damning since Madagascar has, at least on paper, so much going for it. The economy has grown just 3% in 2014 and 2015, whereas most economists agree it could easily reach 5% or 6% given its wealth.

It has large coal, uranium, bauxite and rare-earth mineral deposits, as well as potential gas and oil reserves (exploration is ongoing). Around 70% of its land is arable and productivity gains could be easily achieved with simple measures such as the use of (organic) fertilisers, modern agricultural techniques and better land tenure.

Madagascar's wonderful natural heritage also forms the backbone of the tourism industry, which is begging to get back to its pre-coup heyday (365,000 visitors came to the island in 2008, but only 220,000 in 2014). Tourism holds an important place in Madagascar because it is seen as a good way to combine sustainable economic growth with environmental conservation. The Malagasy are anxious to see the proceeds of their mineral wealth trickle through for instance, but they are concerned about the social and environmental impacts of such projects.

What is certain is that in a country where half the population is under the age of 15, the sense of expectation and the desire for change is palpable.

POPULATION: **23.8 MILLION**

AREA: **587,041 SQ KM**

GDP: **US$10.6 BILLION**

POVERTY (<US$2 A DAY): **92%**

LIFE EXPECTANCY: **65.5 YEARS**

LITERACY: **64.7%**

if Madagascar were 100 people

65 would live in a rural area
35 would live in an urban area

belief systems
(% of population)

Indigenous   Christian   Muslim

population per sq km

MADAGASCAR   SOUTH AFRICA   UK

≈ 33 people

History

In the grand scheme of history, Madagascar is a baby. Although the country has existed in its current form for nearly 100 million years, humans only set foot on the island about 2000 years ago.

Madagascar's first settlers came from Southeast Asia and were soon joined by migrants from neighbouring Africa and the Arabian Peninsula. This melting pot of Indian Ocean populations evolved in distinct kingdoms, which were only brought together as a unified people in the 18th century, and after much resistance.

This newfound unity proved too weak to sustain the repeated onslaught of European imperialists, however. The French eventually claimed Madagascar as their own in 1896, and they retained it until 1960. The independence movement had started during the 1930s and, after a brief interruption during WWII, regained momentum in the 1950s.

It took another decade or so to shake off colonialism's long shadow, and in 1975 President Didier Ratsiraka took Madagascar on a radically different path to socialism. The experiment came to an unhappy end in 1993, following elections brought about by two years of violent protests.

Since then Madagascar has bumped from one violently ousted leader to the next. In 1996 Albert Zafy was impeached for abuse of power and Ratsiraka made a brief comeback. He was eventually forced into exile in France after contesting the victory of Marc Ravalomanana in the 2001–02 presidential elections. In 2009 it was Ravalomanana's turn to be given the boot, after popular uprisings brought Andry Rajoelina to power.

In December 2013 Malagasies finally got the chance to elect a new president, Hery Rajaonarimampianina. The polls were peaceful but, two years on, Madagascar had yet to come out of its economic doldrums.

The word for zebu cattle in Malagasy is *hen'omby*, which is of Bantu origin. Linguists have established that all Malagasy words used for domestic animals have African roots, confirming the fact that African migrants who settled on the island brought with them the prized animals.

Arrivals from Asia & Europe

Considering that human beings evolved on the African continent just across the Mozambique Channel, their arrival in Madagascar was comparatively late (around AD 400) and by a rather circuitous route. Anthropological and ethnographical clues indicate that Indo-Malayan seafarers may have colonised the island after migrating in a single voyage, stopping en route at various points in the Indian Ocean. Their coastal craft possibly worked their way along the shores of India, Ara-

TIMELINE	5th century BC	5th century AD	15th century
	Although hard evidence has yet to be found, some scholars believe humans may have arrived in Madagascar as early as the 5th century BC.	Madagascar is settled by Indo-Malayans who migrate by sea from the distant shores of Indonesia and Malaysia. They bring with them agricultural, linguistic and cultural traditions.	Arabic script brought by Muslim immigrants is adapted to Malagasy language. Sorabe ('Great Writings') is the preserve of a selected few and used only for high-profile documents.

bia and East Africa, trading as they went, before finally arriving in Madagascar. Linguistic clues also support this theory, as elements of Sanskrit have been identified in the Malagasy language.

These first settlers brought with them the food crops of their homelands, such as rice. This Asian influence was tempered over the years by contact with Arab and African traders, who plied the seas of the region with their cargoes of silk, spices and slaves. Gradually the Asian culture of the new settlers was subsumed into a series of geographically defined kingdoms, which in turn gave rise to many different Malagasy tribes.

Marco Polo was the first European to report the existence of a 'great red island', which he named Madagascar, after possibly having confused it with Mogadishu in Somalia. But Arab cartographers had long known the island as Gezirat Al-Komor, meaning 'island of the moon' (a name later transferred to the Comoros). It wasn't until 1500 that the first Europeans set foot on Madagascar, when a fleet of Portuguese vessels arrived. The Dutch and British tried to establish permanent bases at various points around the coast, only to be defeated by disease and less-than-friendly locals.

More successful were the efforts of buccaneers from Britain, France and elsewhere, who, from the end of the 17th century onwards, made Madagascar a base from which they attacked merchant ships sailing between India and Europe.

Criminal suspects under Queen Ranavalona I were forced to drink a strong poison called *tanguin*. If they vomited profusely enough, they were declared innocent. Most died.

HISTORY 'NO FRONTIER BUT THE SEA'

'No Frontier but the Sea'

As Malagasy trade with Europe grew during the 18th century, several rival kingdoms began to vie for dominance. The Menabe people under Andriamisara I founded a capital on the banks of the Sakalava River, from which the modern-day Sakalava tribe took its name. Meanwhile on the east coast, Ratsimilaho – the son of an English pirate and a Malagasy

SORABE

Sorabe ('Great Writings'; from the Arabic word *sora*, 'to write', and the Malagasy *be*, meaning 'big') is an early written form of Malagasy using Arabic script. The earliest Sorabe manuscripts were written sometime after the 15th century under the influence of Muslim traders (academics disagree on whether they were from the Arabian Peninsula or what is now Indonesia) who wanted to reproduce pages of the Koran. Sorabe was later used to write histories and genealogies, astrologers' predictions and various works on traditional medicine. Knowledge of the script was primarily the preserve of specially trained scribes known as *katibo*. Most Sorabe manuscripts are in the possession of the Antaimoro and Antambohoaka tribes in southeast Madagascar, although the oldest surviving example is conserved in a library in Paris.

1500	1600	Late 18th century	1817
Portuguese sailors under the command of Diego Dias become the first Europeans to set foot on Madagascar; Dias names the island Ilha de São Lourenço.	Malagasy kings do a brisk trade in slaves with African, European and Arab traders. It is estimated that up to 150,000 slaves were exported during the 17th century.	Merina chief Ramboasalama assumes the throne at Ambohimanga and unifies the various Merina peoples into a powerful kingdom.	Radama I enters into diplomatic relations with Great Britain, beginning a period of British influence that carries on well into the 19th century. Missionaries convert the Merina court to Christianity.

princess – succeeded in unifying rival tribes into a people that became known as the Betsimisaraka. In central Madagascar a certain Chief Ramboasalama took the snappy name Andrianampoinimerinandriantsimitoviaminandriampanjaka (Andrianampoinimerina for short), meaning 'Hope of Imerina', and unified the Merina into a powerful kingdom that soon came to dominate much of Madagascar.

In 1810 Andrianampoinimerina was succeeded by his equally ambitious son Radama I, who organised a highly trained army that conquered Boina (the main Sakalava kingdom in northwestern Madagascar), the Betsimisaraka peoples to the east, the Betsileo to the south and the kingdom of Antakàrana in the far north, whose warrior princes preferred suicide or exile to surrender. Unable to take the Sakalava kingdom of Menabe by force, Radama prudently married Princess Rasalimo, daughter of the Menabe king, thereby fulfilling a vow made by his father that the Merina kingdom would have 'no frontier but the sea'.

His empire building complete, Radama I set about courting European powers, especially Great Britain. The London Missionary Society (LMS) soon arrived with a contingent of Welsh missionaries who began converting the Merina court and educating children in schools.

In 1828 Radama died at the tender age of 36. His successor was his widow Ranavalona I, who promptly set about reversing Radama's policies. Ties with European powers were almost severed, and those who refused to abandon Christianity (a European import) were hurled over the cliffs outside the Rova in Antananarivo (Tana). During her 33 years in power, Ranavalona elevated torture and execution to new plateaus of inventiveness. She was said to be sexually insatiable and had a stream of lovers.

French Conquest & Colonialism

Ranavalona died in 1861, understandably unlamented by what remained of her subjects. Her son Radama II succeeded her. He was a reformer and he rescinded most of his mother's policies and welcomed back the Europeans.

In May 1862, however, Radama II was assassinated. Rainilaiarivony, the king's assassin, took the post of prime minister and married Radama's widow, who took the title Rasoherina I. He quickly issued an edict stating that the queen could act only with the consent of her ministers – effectively leaving the real power to him, her husband.

Rasoherina survived until 1868 and was succeeded by Ranavalona II, who died in 1883 and was succeeded by Ranavalona III. Prime Minister Rainilaiarivony had married both queens and became the principal power behind the throne, building a magnificent residence in Antananarivo.

When Rainilaiarivony assassinated Radama II, he strangled him with a silken cord to avoid the *fady* (taboo) over the shedding of royal blood.

Merina Sights in Antananarivo

Ambohimanga

Rova

Musée Andafivaratra

Ilafy

1828	1835	1840s	1861
Ranavalona I becomes queen, commencing a 33-year reign. She declares Christianity illegal and denounces European influence, with the exception of French industrialist and engineer Jean Laborde.	The Bible is published in Malagasy, following the London Missionary Society's transliteration of the language in Roman alphabet. Until then, Malagasy had been written in the Arabic script Sorabe.	Jean Laborde kickstarts Madagascar's industrial revolution by building an industrial complex in Mantasoa complete with brickworks, blast furnaces, an arms and munitions factory and textile mills.	Ranavalona dies and Radama II becomes king, abolishing forced labour and reinstating freedom of religion. Missionary activity begins to expand and Christianity becomes the predominant religion of Madagascar.

By the late 19th century, British interest in Madagascar had begun to wane, and French influence had increased. That influence turned into outright aggression in 1883, when French warships occupied major ports and forced the Malagasy government to sign a treaty declaring the island a French protectorate. Further demands ensued, and in 1894 the French accused the Merina government of tyranny and demanded the capitulation of Queen Ranavalona III. When she rejected their demands, a French army marched on Antananarivo, taking the capital in September 1895.

On 6 August 1896 Madagascar was officially declared a French colony. A year later Queen Ranavalona III was sent into exile in Algeria and the Merina monarchy was abolished.

Malagasy Nationalism & Independence

In the early 20th century Madagascar's new rulers abolished slavery, although it was replaced with an almost equally exploitative system of taxes. Land was expropriated by foreign settlers and a coffee-based import and export economy developed. With economic growth and an expanding education system, a new Malagasy elite began to emerge, and resentment of the colonial presence grew in all levels of society. Several nationalist movements evolved among the Merina and Betsileo tribes, and strikes and demonstrations became more frequent.

Nationalist leader Jean Ralaimongo began the Malagasy independence movement in the 1930s, but his campaign was cut short by the outbreak of WWII. During the first half of WWII the French in Madagascar came under the authority of the pro-Nazi Vichy government. But the Allies, fearing the Japanese could use Madagascar as a base to attack shipping, launched a seaborne attack and captured the town of Diego Suarez. Antananarivo and other major towns also fell to the British after months of fighting, but were handed back to the Free French (those who fought on the side of the Allies in WWII) of General de Gaulle in 1943.

Postwar Madagascar experienced a nationalist backlash, with resentment towards the French culminating in a rebellion in March 1947. The rebellion was eventually subdued after an estimated 90,000 Malagasy were killed. During the 1950s nationalist political parties were formed, the most notable being the Parti Social Démocrate (PSD) of Philibert Tsiranana, and reforms paved the way to independence.

On 14 October 1958 the Malagasy Republic was proclaimed, becoming an autonomous state within the French Community. After a period of provisional government, a constitution was adopted in 1959 and full independence was achieved on 26 June 1960, with Tsiranana the country's first president.

Nationalist leader Jean Ralaimongo became a slave at the age of seven. He was freed in 1898, when the colonial government abolished slavery. After serving with the French during WWI, he stayed in France and met the young Ho Chi Minh, from whom he got many of his communist ideologies.

1862	1896	1930s	WWII
Radama II is assassinated by Rainilaiarivony, who becomes prime minister and marries Radama's widow, Rasoherina I. He will also marry the next two queens, Ranavalona II and Ranavalona III.	Madagascar becomes a French colony. Governor-General Joseph Gallieni declares French the official language and sets about destroying the power of the Merina and removing all British influence.	A Malagasy independence movement begins to gather momentum, fuelled by resentment of the French colonials by a growing, educated middle class and led by nationalist leader Jean Ralaimongo.	Madagascar is under the authority of the pro-Nazi Vichy French government. Fearing the Japanese could use the island as a base, the Allies attack and capture several towns.

After the euphoria, however, discontent with the country's ongoing ties with France and its poor economic performance grew. Following uprisings in 1971 and 1972, Tsiranana was forced to resign and hand over power to his army commander, General Gabriel Ramanantsoa.

The Third Republic

In February 1975, after several coup attempts, General Ramanantsoa stepped down and was replaced by Colonel Richard Ratsimandrava, who was assassinated within a week of taking office. The rebel army officers who had announced the military takeover were quickly routed by officers loyal to Ramanantsoa, and a new government headed by Admiral Didier Ratsiraka, a former foreign minister, came to power.

Ratsiraka attempted radical political and social reforms in the late 1970s, severing all ties with France and courting favour with former Soviet-bloc nations.

In March 1989 Ratsiraka was returned for a third seven-year term in an election that some regarded as questionable. It sparked riots, and 1991

At the World Park Conference in Durban in 2003, then-president Marc Ravalomanana announced his intention to triple Madagascar's protected areas, a commitment that remains on the agenda.

JEAN LABORDE

One of the few Europeans Queen Ranavalona tolerated was a French engineer, Jean Laborde (he was in fact her lover). Laborde was shipwrecked on the east coast of Madagascar in 1831, at a time when Ranavalona was busy sending Europeans packing. Laborde's engineering skills didn't go unnoticed, however, and Ranavalona, ever the cunning ruler, sensed an opportunity. She granted Laborde large tracts of land and access to unlimited forced labour if he could provide her with weapons that would, in turn, expedite the job of getting rid of foreigners.

Laborde set to work and within a few years he had not only built an arms and munitions factory in Mantasoa (about 60km east of Antananarivo), but a complete industrial complex, too, with blast furnaces to produce cast iron, puddling mills to produce wrought iron, a steel plant, glassworks, brickworks, a cement plant and textile mills. He also built a summer palace for Ranavalona in Ambohimanga and contributed to a host of engineering projects, from roads to bridges.

As Ranavalona became more and more tyrannical, Laborde decided to take part in a plot to overthrow her in 1857. The coup failed and Laborde was banned from the island. The 1200-or-so labourers who had slaved on the Mantasoa industrial complex took the opportunity to rebel and torched the place – the few buildings left standing can still be viewed in Mantasoa.

Laborde was invited back in 1861 by Radama II, Ranavalona's son, and was made France's first consul to the Merina court by Napoleon III. Laborde died in 1878 in Madagascar and is buried in Mantasoa, on a hill overlooking what was once the engine of Madagascar's industrial revolution.

1947	26 June 1960	1975	Late 1970s
A rebellion led by Joseph Raseta and Joseph Ravoahangy is brutally suppressed by the French. Thousands of Malagasy are killed and the rebellion's leaders are sent into exile.	Madagascar gains full independence from France in a peaceful transition. Philibert Tsiranana is elected president, though in effect the French still run the country and maintain military bases.	General Gabriel Ramanantsoa steps down after coup attempts; his followers appoint Admiral Didier Ratsiraka as leader. Ratsiraka adopts Soviet-style ideology and cuts ties with France, leading to economic decline.	Ratsiraka pushes his nationalist agenda. French is no longer taught in primary schools and he decrees that towns must be known by their Malagasy names.

was marked by widespread demonstrations demanding the president's resignation. The country ground to a halt as a result of general strikes and riots, and protests left dozens dead.

In late October 1991 an agreement was signed with opposition politicians in preparation for popular elections and the birth of the so-called 'Third Republic'. However, Ratsiraka still refused to step down. In July 1992 there was an attempted civilian coup, but the rebels failed to gain popular support and were forced to surrender.

Elections were finally held in 1993 and resulted in victory for opposition candidate Professor Albert Zafy, ending Ratsiraka's first 17 years in power. After trying to sack his prime minister, Zafy was unexpectedly impeached by his parliament in July 1996 for abuse of authority. New presidential elections were called in November 1996 and, to the surprise of everyone, including international monitors, Ratsiraka (who had been in exile in France for the previous 19 months) won.

Reform & New Optimism

Self-made millionaire Marc Ravalomanana began his path to success by pedalling around his home town on a bicycle selling pots of homemade yoghurt. By the time he became mayor of Antananarivo in 1999, his company, Tiko, was the biggest producer of dairy products in Madagascar.

Ravalomanana announced his candidacy for the presidency of Madagascar, under the banner of his TIM party (which stands in Malagasy for 'I Love Madagascar'), in December 2001 and went head to head with Didier Ratsiraka. Upon hearing the results, both men insisted they had won, and a bitter six-month struggle for power ensued. As Ravalomanana swore himself in as president, Ratsiraka declared a state of emergency and imposed martial law.

The military eventually swung towards Ravalomanana, tipping the balance of power, and in April 2002 the Malagasy High Constitutional Court declared Ravalomanana the outright winner. By August Ravalomanana's administration had received endorsement from the UN, then won a convincing majority in elections for the National Assembly. Ratsiraka refused to accept that the game was over, but left for exile in France anyway.

Ravalomanana quickly set about his reform agenda, introducing a new currency (the ariary). Foreign investors were cheered by a major hike in economic growth and wooed by laws that provided tax breaks and allowed foreigners to own land.

Ravalomanana comfortably won a second term in office in 2006. On the back of his electoral success, he organised a referendum to change the constitution, with many of the amendments conferring on him more power (notably the option of standing for two more terms). The

In 2015 underwater explorers pulled an ingot from a shipwreck off the coast of Île Sainte Marie, claiming it was part of the long-lost treasure of infamous Scottish pirate Captain William Kidd. UN investigators quickly dismissed the claim, however: the ingot was a mere block of lead, not silver.

1991	1996	2001	2006
Economic decline ignites widespread strikes and protests. The 'Third Republic' calls for elections but Ratsiraka refuses to step down. Opposition leader Albert Zafy is eventually elected president in 1993.	Among widespread accusations of criminal activities, President Zafy is impeached for abuse of power and general elections are called. Ratsiraka is returned to power and becomes president again in 1997.	Former yoghurt peddler Marc Ravalomanana swears himself in as president. Ratsiraka declares martial law, and violent protests ensue. Ravalomanana is declared the winner after a six-month showdown.	Marc Ravalomanana is swept to office for a second term as president. Encouraging economic growth leads the World Bank to wipe US$20 billion from Madagascar's national debt.

referendum scraped by, but the opposition was outraged by what they saw as an increasingly autocratic government.

The Coup & the Long Transition

In 2008 Ravalomanana made three decisions that antagonised the last of his supporters. In July he signed a lease with Korean company Daewoo Logistics for 13,000 sq km of arable land for commercial farming, a sacrilege in a country where land is generally perceived as belonging to ancestors.

In October he bought a second presidential plane. Not only was this perceived as outlandish in a poor country such as Madagascar, but the source of the financing was obscure, which led a number of international donors to withhold their funding in protest.

And finally, in December, Ravalomanana closed the TV and radio station Viva, owned by the ambitious mayor of Antananarivo, Andry Rajoelina. Rajoelina rallied opponents under his new TGV party and mass demonstrations took place in December and January. On 7 February 2009 the army opened fire on protesters gathered in front of the presidential palace, killing 37 and injuring around 200. With international pressure mounting, Ravalomanana finally handed his resignation to the army on 17 March 2009 and fled to South Africa. Within a few hours the army had swiftly passed all powers to Rajoelina, who was sworn in as president of the High Transitional Authority (Haute Autorité de Transition; HAT).

The events were widely condemned by the international community as a coup. They refused to recognise Rajoelina as Madagascar's legitimate leader and turned off whatever international-aid taps were left.

This had devastating consequences for Madagascar: international aid represented 75% of public expenditure, so public services dwindled to the bare minimum. The expulsion of Madagascar from the US-sponsored African Growth Opportunity Act (AGOA) also led to the collapse of the textile and other export-oriented industries, with the loss of 100,000 jobs. Between 2009 and 2014, the proportion of people living on less than US$2 a day went from 60% to 90% of the population.

The HAT had initially promised elections within 24 months, but it took more than two years to just draft the road map meant to get Madagascar out of the crisis. At the centre of the disagreement was who would be able to run for president (Rajoelina was keen, the international community wasn't) and the return of Ravalomanana from exile.

It took another two years to organise the polls (during which Rajoelina successively renounced, revived and finally withdrew his candidacy) and in December 2013, Hery Rajaonarimampianina was finally elected president.

Best History Books

....

A History of Madagascar by Mervyn Brown

....

Madagascar: A Short History by Solofo Randrianja and Stephen Ellis

March 2009	September 2011	October 2013	June 2015
Antananarivo mayor Andry Rajoelina overthrows Ravalomanana in an army-backed coup. The UN and the EU refuse to recognise the new government, and international donors withhold all aid.	A road map negotiated under the auspices of the international community lays out the way out of the crisis: elections without the main protagonists and return of political exiles.	First round of the long-awaited presidential elections. There are 33 candidates. President Hery Rajaonarimampianina is elected in the second round on 20 December.	President Hery Rajaonarimampianina narrowly escapes impeachment by parliament after the Constitutional Court rules in his favour.

Malagasy Life

Traditions and beliefs hold an important place in Malagasy life, influencing everything from the orientation of houses to who you should vote for. This isn't to say Malagasy society is static: economic development, population growth and globalisation are changing the country, although more slowly than many would like.

Behaviour & Etiquette

On arrival in Madagascar your first impression is likely to be of a polite but rather reserved people. This apparent timidity is a reflection of *fihavanana*, which means 'conciliation' or 'brotherhood'. It stresses avoidance of confrontation and achievement of compromise in all walks of life. It is unseemly to discuss some subjects, such as personal problems, even with close friends. Likewise, searching or indiscreet questions are avoided at all costs.

Politeness in general is very important to the Malagasy, and impatience or pushy behaviour is regarded as shocking. Passengers queuing for a flight, for instance, will place their tickets in a neat row on the check-in desk or put their luggage in an orderly line before patiently awaiting their turn.

The welcoming of strangers and the traditions of hospitality are held sacred throughout Madagascar. It is considered a household duty to offer food and water to a guest, no matter how poor the inhabitants are themselves. In return, travellers should always honour this hospitality by accepting what has been offered to them.

Population & Language

Malagasy people are divided into 19 tribes, whose boundaries are roughly based on old kingdoms. Tribal divisions are still evident between ancient enemies such as the Merina and the Antakàrana. Also important is the distinction between Merina highlanders, who have more prominent Asian origins and are associated with the country's aristocracy, and so-called *côtiers* (literally, 'those from the coast'), whose African influences are more pronounced and who are often looked down on by the Merina. In Antananarivo, well-off *côtières* (women from the coast) often straighten their hair to avoid discrimination against their coastal origins.

The main tribal groups are Merina, who make up 27% of the population, Betsimisaraka (15%), Betsileo (12%), Tsimihety (7%), Sakalava (6%), Antaisaka (5%) and Antandroy (5%). There are also small groups of Indian, Chinese, Comorian and French living on the island.

This ethnic patchwork is matched by a hotchpotch of dialects. The official Malagasy language of newspapers and schools is based on the Malagasy of the Merina people, but each region has its own dialect. Vocabulary and accents vary to the extent that people from different provinces struggle to understand one another.

Religion & Beliefs

About half of Madagascar's population adheres to traditional beliefs, while the efforts of proselytising Europeans during the 19th century have resulted in the other half worshipping at Catholic and Protestant churches. A small proportion is Muslim. In recent years evangelical churches have become popular, too, with charismatic preachers, inspirational singing and dancing and unusual venues (from stadiums to town halls).

The church and politics have gone hand in hand for many years, too. Former president Marc Ravalomanana is the vice-president of the

BANK ACCOUNTS

Only 6% of Malagasies have a bank account, one of the lowest rates in the world.

Malagasy Tribal Groups

0 ————— 180 km
0 ————— 80 miles

Diego Suarez
(Antsiranana)

Antakàrana

Tsimihety   Betsimisaraka

Majunga
(Mahajanga)

Sihanaka

Sakalava

Bezanozano

Betsimiraka

Merina   Tamatave
(Toamasina)

ANTANANARIVO

Betsileo

Antambahoaka

Zafimaniry

Tanala

Fianarantsoa   Antaimoro

Antaifasy

Bara

Antaisaka

Tuléar
(Toliara)

Mahafaly   Antanosy

Antandroy

FJKM, the largest Protestant church in Madagascar, while the Catholic church officially endorsed coup leader Andry Rajoelina when he took power in 2009 (a decision it has since regretted). Religious leaders have also been involved in reconciliation efforts to turn the page on the transition years.

Christian Malagasies often retain great respect for traditional beliefs, which are rooted in reverence for one's ancestors and their spir-

FAMADIHANA

On the crest of a hill, a grove of pine trees whispers gently. In the shade, trestle tables are spread with sticky sweetmeats and bowls of steaming rice. A band plays a rollicking, upbeat tune as the stone door of a family tomb is opened. Old ladies wait at the entrance, faces dignified under their straw hats. Middle-aged men indulge in lethal homemade rum, dancing jerkily to the rhythms of the band.

One by one the corpses are brought out of the tomb, wrapped in straw mats and danced above the heads of a joyful throng. The bodies are rewrapped in pristine white burial *lambas* (scarves), sprayed with perfume and meticulously labelled by name with felt-tip pens. Everyone wants to touch the ancestors and talk to them. A period of quiet follows, with family members sitting by the head of the dead in silent communication, weeping but happy at the same time. The air is charged with emotion.

Then it's time to feast, celebrate and gossip with all the relatives, all the while checking in on the ancestors, filling them in on the action, making sure they are part of the festivities.

Then the bodies are danced one more time around the tomb, a few traditional verses are read out and the stone is sealed with mud for another seven years.

Famadihana ceremonies take place between July and September in the *hauts plateaux* (highlands) region from Antananarivo south to Ambositra. These days it's generally OK to attend one, as long as your visit is arranged through a hotel or local tour company. On no account should you visit without an invitation and never take photos unless specific permission has been granted.

its. Among most tribes, this is manifested in a complex system of *fady* (taboos) and burial rites, the best known of which is the ceremonial exhumation and reburial known as *famadihana* (literally, 'the turning of the bones').

Malagasies invoke spirits for protection, fertility or good health at sacred sites, be it a baobab tree, a forest waterfall or a royal tomb. You'll recognise these sites from the offerings (zebu horns, *lamba* scarves, small denominations, blood, honey, sweets etc). Praying and offering ceremonies are popular Sunday family outings and are often accompanied by a picnic.

> If you see a young Malagasy man wearing a comb in his hair, he's advertising his search for a wife.

Concepts of time and date also have a great influence. Malagasies strongly believe in *vintana* (destiny), which determines the most auspicious date for activities (building a house, planting a new crop etc) or events such as circumcisions, weddings and funerals. Each day of the week has its connotations: Wednesday and Friday are good for funerals; Saturday, which is associated with nobility, is considered good for celebrations. To make sure they choose the most favourable date for an occasion, Malagasies will consult a *mpanandro* (astrologer) for guidance on *vintana*.

Every ceremony is invariably accompanied by the slaughter of a zebu, more than one if the family is wealthy or influential in the community. The blood and the horns are valuable offerings and the meat is shared by those attending.

The complex set of beliefs of the Malagasy has been constructed through the assimilation of diverse influences. The funeral rites of many tribes, for example, have Austronesian roots, while the status of cattle is thought to have African roots. Belief in *vintana*, on the other hand, is thought to originate from Islamic cosmology.

Family Life & Home

The family is the central tenet of Malagasy life and includes not only distant cousins, but also departed ancestors. Even urban, modern Malagasies, who reject the belief that ancestors have magic powers, regard those who are no longer alive as full members of the family. *Famadihanas* are an opportunity to communicate with ancestors. Families spend

> Many Malagasy surnames start with the honorary prefix 'Ra', the equivalent of 'Mr'. Similarly, many kings' names started with 'Andriana', a term that roughly translates as 'noble'.

> ### FADY
> ....
> *Fady* is the name given to local taboos designed to respect the ancestors. *Fady* can take innumerable forms and vary widely from village to village. It may be *fady* to whistle on a particular stretch of beach, to walk past a sacred tree, to eat pork, or to swim in a certain river.
>
> Although foreigners will be excused for breaking *fady*, travellers should make every effort to respect these taboos. The best thing to do is to ask locals for information, and be particularly careful on sacred sites and in the vicinity of tombs or burial sites.

a great deal of time and money on family reunions, and *taxis-brousses* (bush taxis) are often full of individuals visiting relatives.

Malagasy homes are arranged according to astrological principles: the northeast corner is the noble and auspicious part of the house, and doors always face west. Many Malagasies think life on earth is temporary, whereas life after death is permanent, so families will favour lavish tombs and keep a modest house.

Marriage is a pretty relaxed institution and divorce is common. Children are seen as the primary purpose of marriage and essential to happiness and security. The idea that some people might choose not to have children is greeted with disbelief.

Women

Women are a dynamic force in Malagasy society. They are very active in the workplace and are represented at every echelon of society, from street vendor to politician, school teacher to entrepreneur. Women are also regarded as the head of the domestic sphere, even if they also go out to work.

Women tend to marry and have children young: 16 or younger is typical in rural areas, while 20 is about average in urban areas, where women are more likely to go through secondary and superior education. A woman will generally move to her husband's village. Polygamy exists but is not commonplace.

Sexually, Malagasy society is fairly liberated. Women can dress quite provocatively, and they can be quite forward with sexual advances to men, including foreigners. Prostitution is rampant in a number of areas, and travellers should be aware that sex tourism is heavily punished.

Economy

Most Malagasies bemoan the fact that their country, despite having so much going for it, has failed to develop economically. Political instability and economic mismanagement are primarily to blame. Madagascar therefore remains one of the world's poorest countries. It ranked 155 out of 187 countries in the 2014 Human Development Index of the UN Development Programme (UNDP). Its GDP in 2014 was US$10.6 billion (138 out of 194 countries on the World Bank's ranking), lower than that of Afghanistan, Chad and Yemen.

Madagascar's economy is mainly subsistence agriculture, with rice, cassava, bananas and maize as the main food crops. The principal cash crops are coffee, vanilla, lychee, cloves and cocoa, with coffee and vanilla earning a substantial percentage of foreign exchange. Madagascar also exports nickel, cobalt and ilmenite (titanium ore) from two large-scale mining projects (one in Fort Dauphin in the south, the other in Ambatovy near Moramanga). The manufacturing industry represents about 14% of GDP, with food, drink and textiles the main sectors.

The EU is Madagascar's most important trading partner: it generates 80% of its tourism earnings, receives 50% of Malagasy exports

A common ritual after the death of a family member is for the entire family to go down to a local river and wash all their clothes, an event you'll often see from the roadside, with clothes drying along the riverbanks.

and represents about 15% of foreign direct investment (FDI) in the country. As in many parts of Africa, China is becoming an increasingly important trading partner – in a 2015 survey by Afrobarometer, 27% of Malagasies said China was the country with the greatest influence over Madagascar, second only to France (42%).

Urban & Rural Life

Any visitor to Madagascar will notice the huge disparities in development between rural and urban areas. This is due to several factors: physical isolation (road density in Madagascar is just nine kilometres per 1000 sq km, against an average of 35 kilometres per 1000 sq km in sub-Saharan Africa, and the roads that do exist are in poor condition); climate (the southern half of the country is arid and the east coast is prone to cyclones and floods, both of which affect agricultural productivity); and access to electricity (57.6% in urban areas, but just 4.7% in rural areas), which is essential for business activity. All in all, rural areas represent two-thirds of the population, but only contribute 26% of GDP.

On virtually every indicator (schooling, access to water and sanitation, malnutrition etc) rural populations fare worse than their urban counterparts. Surveys have found that poverty is not only more generalised in rural areas, it's also deeper, with people facing chronic and severe malnutrition. Child labour is also more prevalent, with nearly a quarter of children aged five to 17 classed as economically active in rural areas.

Sport

Malagasies love watching international football (soccer; the English Premier League, in particular) and rugby (the French and European leagues, notably). For all this enthusiasm, however, the national football and rugby teams have yet to make a splash on the international stage.

Where Malagasies punch above their weight is in the rather niche sport of pétanque, a form of boule (played with metal balls on dirt ground). A French import, it's become a case of the student outdoing (or certainly equalling) the master: Madagascar won the Pétanque World Championship in 1999, it was vice-world champion in 2010 and 2012 and Africa champion in 2011. Madagascar has also won numerous international opens, so don't be surprised to see the game played up and down the country, on the beach, in village squares, or wherever there is a flat enough bit of ground.

MALAGASY LIFE URBAN & RURAL LIFE

Household Facts

Households with access to improved sanitation: 50.1%

Households that have drinking water: 38.9%

Children who go to primary school: 69.4%

Students who carry on to university: 1%

VANILLA

Vanilla was introduced to Madagascar from Mexico by French plantation owners during the 19th century, naming it *vanille* (*lavanila* in Malagasy), from the Spanish *vainilla* or 'little pod'. It is a type of climbing orchid, *Vanila planifolia*, that attaches itself to trees. Each flower must be hand-pollinated, making vanilla production extremely labour intensive. The vanilla seeds grow inside long pods hanging from the plant that are collected and cured in factories.

Madagascar produces about 80% of the world's vanilla. The plant grows most abundantly in northeastern parts of the country, particularly the SAVA region (comprising Sambava, Andapa, Vohémar and Antalaha), where the hot and wet climate of the coast is ideally suited for its cultivation.

Cyclone Hudah destroyed more than 20% of Madagascar's vanilla crop in 2000, causing a shortage of supply and a huge escalation in price. Combined with the political instability of the 2002 elections and more bad weather in 2003, vanilla prices spiked at US$500 per kilogram in 2004. Since this historic high, however, vanilla prices bottomed at US$25 a kilo, and are now around US$50 a kilo.

Arts

Madagascar has a rich and diverse artistic tradition that goes far beyond the wonderful craftsmanship displayed in popular souvenirs – music, literature, poetry and storytelling are especially prolific genres. Discovering and appreciating it can be tough for those who speak neither French nor Malagasy, so make a point of asking your guide, or enthusiastic anglophone locals, to introduce you to their favourites.

Literature

The earliest Malagasy literature dates from historical records produced in the mid-19th century. Modern poetry and literature began to flourish in the 1930s and 1940s. The best-known figure was the poet Jean-Joseph Rabearivelo, who committed suicide in 1947 at the age of 36, reputedly after the colonial administration decided to send a group of basket weavers to France to represent the colony instead of him.

Modern-day literary figures include Michèle Rakotoson, Johary Ravaloson, David Jaomanoro, Elie Rajaonarison and Jean-Luc Raharimanana. Most of their works are published in French, and some have been translated into English.

Oral Traditions

Hira gasy are popular music, dancing and storytelling spectacles held in the central highlands of Madagascar. Brightly clad troupes of 25 performers compete for prizes for the best costumes or the most exciting spectacle. An important part of *hira gasy* is *kabary,* in which a performer delivers an oratory using allegory, double entendre, metaphor and simile. *Hira gasy* has long been used to deliver important information, or raise awareness of certain topics (health, politics, environmental issues, respecting family values etc). Unfortunately, unless you are fluent in Malagasy, you're unlikely to agree with the proverb that says, 'While listening to a *kabary* well spoken, one fails to notice the fleas that bite one'. All the same, it is a cultural event well worth seeing.

More accessible are the songs and dances after the *kabary*. Dancers are dressed in bright gowns called *malabary*, and women also wear the traditional *lamba* (scarf). The competition winner is decided by audience members, who throw small denominations at their favourite troupe.

Music

Most traditional Malagasy music revolves around favourite dance rhythms: the *salegy* of the Sakalava tribe, with both Indonesian and Kenyan influences; *watsa watsa* from Mozambique and the Congo; the *tsapika*, originating in the south; and the *sigaoma*, similar to South African music.

The most widely played traditional wind instrument is the *kiloloka*, a whistle-like length of bamboo capable of only one note. Melodies are played by a group of musicians, in a manner similar to a bell ensemble.

Two excellent collections of Malagasy writing are *Voices from Madagascar: An Anthology of Contemporary Francophone Literature*, edited by Jacques Bourgeacq and Liliane Ramarosoa, which contains Malagasy writing in French and English; and *Hainteny: The Traditional Poetry of Madagascar* by Leonard Fox, with translations of beautiful Merina poems charting love, revenge and sexuality.

The tubular instrument you'll see on sale at tourist shops and craft markets is a *valiha*, which has 28 strings of varying lengths stretched around a tubular wooden sound box (generally made of bamboo). It resembles a bassoon, but is played more like a harp and originates from Southeast Asia. The most famous performer of *valiha* is Justin Vali, a household name in world-music circles.

Apart from at special events such as the Donia festival in Nosy Be, traditional Malagasy music can be hard to find and it is often restricted to rural areas.

Malagasy pop music is usually a cheesy blend of guitar rock, rough-and-ready rap and hip hop, and soulful ballads, a genre best represented by national treasure Poopy (yes, that's her real name). For more traditional sounds, Jerry Marcos, a master of *salegy*, is guaranteed to have you shaking your stuff like there's no tomorrow.

A number of musicians have artfully mixed pop and traditional influences, including the wonderful singer-songwriter Nogabe Randriaharimalala (www.nogabe.com), Njava (www.myspace.com/njava), Tarika, Samoela or the more jazz-influenced Nicolas Vatomanga.

Contemporary Malagasy artists are relatively easy to see, especially in Antananarivo, where there are numerous venues (look in the newspapers on Friday for event details, or the free listings available in hotels and restaurants).

Architecture

Each region of Madagascar has its own architectural style and building materials. The Merina and Betsileo of the *hauts plateaux* (highlands) live in distinctive red-brick houses. The typical Merina home is a tall, narrow affair with small windows and brick pillars in the front that support open verandahs. The Betsileo dispense with the pillars and trim their houses with elaborately carved wood.

Coastal homes are generally constructed of lighter local materials, including *ravinala* (literally, 'forest leaves'; also known as travellers' palm) and raffia palm. Houses in humid areas are generally raised to promote ventilation and avoid insects.

Death being considered the passage to eternal life, tombs are often more elaborate than everyday dwellings. In the highlands, tombs are grand affairs: rectangular brick pavilions, often whitewashed, decorated with colourful geometric shapes. In the west the Sakalava decorate their tombs with erotic sculptures (increasingly rare because of looting), whilst in the south Antandroy and Mahafaly people decorate theirs with *aloalo*, ornate carved wooden steles topped with zebu horns. The carvings can be figurative or abstract.

Textiles

Textiles have always played a huge part in Malagasy society, with some types of cloth even being imbued, it is believed, with supernatural powers. The Merina used cocoons collected from wild silkworms to make highly valued textiles called *lamba mena* (red silk). The silks were woven in many colours and pattern combinations and, in the past, had strong links with royal prestige, expressed by the colour red. Worn by the aristocracy in life and death, *lamba mena* were also used in burial and reburial ceremonies.

Lamba are still used in funeral rites and you'll see red-and-white cloths tied to sacred trees across the country as tokens of gratitude to ancestors for fulfilled prayers.

ARTS ARCHITECTURE

The interesting film *Quand les Étoiles Rencontrent la Mer* (When the Stars Meet the Sea), directed by the Malagasy Raymond Rajaonarivelo, is the story of a young boy born during a solar eclipse.

Madagascar's endemic silkworm, *Borocera Madagascariensis*, feeds on tapia trees. Like its Chinese cousin *Bombyx Mori*, it produces silk in its cocoon. There is no sericulture of *Borocera* however: cocoons are collected in the wild.

Malagasy Cuisine

Food is taken seriously in Madagascar, where French, Chinese and Indian influences have blended with local eating traditions into an exciting and often mouth-watering cuisine. Regional variations are many, with a variety of fruit, vegetables and seafood dictating local tastes and recipes.

Malagasy Classics

Eating rice three times a day is so ingrained in Malagasy culture that people sometimes claim they can't sleep if they haven't eaten rice that day. In fact, the verb 'to eat' in Malagasy, *mihinam-vary*, literally means 'to eat rice'.

Rice is eaten in a broth for breakfast (*vary amin' anana*); for lunch and dinner it is generally accompanied by a helping of meat, such as *hen'omby* (boiled zebu), *hen'ankisoa* (pork), *hen'akoho* (chicken) or *hen'andrano* (fish). Common preparations include *ravitoto* (stew – usually beef or pork – with manioc greens and coconut), *sauce coco* (a delicious coconut curry, usually with chicken, fish or seafood) and the nondescript *sauce* or *ritra* (generally a tomato-based affair; served with anything from chicken to fish).

To keep things interesting, the Malagasies have developed an arsenal of aromatic condiments, such as *sakay* (a red-hot pepper paste with ginger and garlic), *pimente verde* (a fiery green chilli) and *achards* (hot pickled fruit, such as tomato, lemon, carrot or mango, used as relish – you'll see bottles of the stuff sold by the roadside).

Rice Alternatives

The most common alternative to rice is a steaming bowl of *mi sao* (fried noodles with vegetables or meat), or a satisfying *soupe chinoise* (clear noodle soup with fish, chicken or vegetables), dishes that show the Asian origins of the Malagasy. Poorer rural communities supplement their rice diet with starchy roots such as manioc or corn.

Best Madagascan Restaurants

Chez Mariette (Antananarivo)

Sharon (central Madagascar)

Chez Maman (northern Madagascar)

La Terrasse du Voyageur (northern Madagascar)

Les Bougainvilliers (western Madagascar)

WHERE TO EAT

What you eat in Madagascar will largely depend on *where* you eat. *Hotelys* or *gargottes* are small, informal restaurants found in every city and town. They are cheap and serve no-frills, typical Malagasy fare such as *romazava* (beef and vegetable stew), *poulet sauce* (chicken in tomato sauce) or grilled fish, with a mountain of rice for bulk. The quality ranges from rough to delicious. The tastier Malagasy food is often served in private homes, and what better excuse to make friends with the locals!

Restaurants, which range from modest to top-end establishments, serve various types of cuisines, including fancier versions of Malagasy standards. Quality is invariably good, sometimes outstanding. Many restaurants offer a *menu du jour* (three-course set menu), or a *plat du jour* (daily special), which are generally good value. Prices for these are usually around Ar15,000 to Ar25,000. For à la carte menus, the average price of a main course is Ar10,000 to Ar15,000.

NATIONAL FAVOURITES

Romazava A beef stew in a ginger-flavoured broth. It contains *brêdes mafana*, a green leaf reminiscent of Indian *saag* in taste that will make your tongue and lips tingle thanks to its anaesthetic properties!

Ravitoto Another well-loved Malagasy dish, it is a mix of fried beef or pork with shredded cassava leaves and coconut milk; truly delicious.

Pizza Just like Europeans and Americans, Malagasies have succumbed to pizzas! They are a popular treat among middle-class families and you'll find an inordinate number of pizza joints (often with takeaway) in every large town and city.

Seafood

Given that Madagascar is an island, it's hardly surprising that seafood features prominently on the menu. Prices are so low that all but those on the tightest budgets can gorge themselves at whim on fish, freshwater crayfish, prawns, lobster and even tiny oysters (from Morondava). Adhering to the motto that less is more, seafood is often cooked simply, grilled or fried, or in *sauce coco*.

> The African Cookbook by Bea Sandler has some good recipes from Madagascar.

Vegetarians & Vegans

The Malagasy don't find vegetarianism difficult to understand, and they are often more than happy to cater for special diets if you give them enough notice. If you eat eggs, you will have no problem as any restaurant can whip up an omelette. If you don't, getting enough protein could be a problem, as beans and lentils are not widely available.

Snacks & Munchies

One of the first things you'll notice on arriving in Madagascar is the dizzying variety of snacks available at street stalls. Savoury snacks include meat samosas (called *sambos*), small doughnuts called *mofo menakely* and *masikita* (tiny zebu kebabs).

The log-like cake you'll see sold on roadsides is *koba*, a concoction of ground peanuts or pistachios, rice flour and sugar, wrapped tightly in banana leaves, baked and sold in slices. *Hotelys* also make delicious sweet doughnuts, which they serve with a cup of black coffee.

In towns and cities you'll also find plenty of patisseries selling cakes, croissants, pastries and meringues. Baguettes can be bought from every street corner, although the quality is often poor.

> A number of Madagascar's signature dishes, such as *romazava* or *ravitoto*, used to be the preserve of the nobility. They were served in *tatao* or *hanim-pitoloha*, a banquet of seven dishes prepared to celebrate the royal bath on the Malagasy New Year.

Gourmet Cuisine

Madagascar has developed a unique strand of haute cuisine that blends Malagasy and French influences and makes the best of local ingredients. Among our favourites are zebu steak with green pepper sauce and *frites* (fries), roast chicken with vanilla mashed potatoes, and grouper in pink peppercorn sauce with sautéed potatoes. Desserts are equally exciting, with chocolate cakes and vanilla custard, crêpes and local fruit jams, exotic sorbets and ice cream.

Gourmet cuisine is served up and down the country in better restaurants and is an absolute highlight of any trip to the red island.

Hot Drinks & Soft Drinks

Most Malagasies like to accompany a rice meal with a drink of rice water. This brown, smoky concoction, known as *ranovola* or *ranon'apango*, is made from boiling water in the pot containing the burnt rice residue – definitely an acquired taste. That said, it is the safest water to drink in *hotelys* since it has been boiled.

> The growth of a rice plant is described in Malagasy using the same words as those for a woman becoming pregnant and giving birth.

THE MIGHTY ZEBU

Zebu cattle not only provide status and transport, they are also well known for their excellent meat. Zebu beef is prepared in much the same way as European cattle beef – in stews, kebabs (known locally as *masikita*, often tiny in size) and as succulent steak.

Zebus are synonymous with status and wealth (a zebu costs €500 to €800, a huge amount of money for a Malagasy family); zebu meat is therefore the festive food par excellence. Zebus will be slaughtered for weddings, *famadihanas* (exhumation and reburial ceremonies), circumcisions and other important festivals or events.

The hump, which is brown fat, is a delicacy (it used to be the preserve of the nobility). It is seldom served in restaurants, but it is a must at Malagasy celebrations, where it is served grilled or in kebabs.

Despite the fact that coffee is grown in Madagascar, only the most upmarket establishments offer espresso or good filter coffee. Elsewhere you'll have to content yourself with weak black coffee and learn to love condensed milk. Tea is better; TAF-brand teabags are excellent and the vanilla-flavoured black tea is highly recommended.

Soft drinks (Coke, Pepsi, Fanta) are sold at every bar under the Malagasy sun. Madagascar also produces its own sodas, including the synthetic-tasting Bonbon Anglais ('English sweet'), a lemonade.

Far and away the best sweet drinks, however, are the *jus naturels* (freshly squeezed fruit juices). Local wonders include *corossol* (soursop), *grenadelle* (passionfruit), papaya, mango and whatever is in season. In coastal areas, street vendors sell green coconuts, which they will split open so that you can drink the vitamin-packed juice.

If you're invited to a Malagasy celebration, bring a present (a small amount of money or a bottle of rum). Hold your wrist with the opposite hand when passing food or drinks.

Boozie Delights

The most popular Malagasy beer is Three Horses Beer (universally known as THB). Up a notch in the alcoholic stakes is the island's rum. Most bars and restaurants offer *rhum arrangé* – rum in which a variety of fruits and spices have been left to soak. Common flavours include lemon, ginger, cinnamon, lychee and vanilla, and these alcoholic concoctions generally line the back of the bar in an array of demijohns worthy of an apothecary. *Rhum arrangé* is drunk neat as an aperitif or an after-dinner liqueur.

Although illegal, moonshine (generally known as *toaka gasy*) is widely available. Its alcohol content will blow your socks off, so go easy on the shots. In eastern Madagascar the local tipple of choice is *betsa-betsa* (fermented sugar-cane juice), while in the north, *trembo* (palm wine) is popular.

Madagascar's small wine industry is centred on Fianarantsoa. You'll probably want to try a glass out of curiosity, but it's definitely not the island's forte. Imported French and South African wine is served in better restaurants throughout the country.

When you order a beer, you'll generally be asked 'PM *ou* GM?' Moderately thirsty travellers will opt for PM or *petit modèle* (small model, 33mL); parched visitors will quench their thirst with a GM or *grand modèle* (big model, 66mL).

Celebrations & Customs

A Malagasy proverb says 'the food which is prepared has no master'. In other words, celebrating in Madagascar means eating big. Weddings, funerals, circumcisions and reburials are preceded by days of preparations. Extended family, friends and often passers-by, too, are invited to share the food, usually a combination of meat dishes (note that turkey is considered a meat for special occasions), vegetables and, of course, a mountain of rice. At Malagasy parties, copious quantities of home-brewed rum are consumed and helpless drunkenness is entirely expected.

Environment

Madagascar is the world's fourth-largest island, after Greenland, Papua New Guinea and Borneo. Its incredibly diverse landscapes and unique wildlife are a product of history: cast adrift from Africa about 165 million years ago, Madagascar took with it a cargo of animals and plants that have been evolving in isolation ever since.

The Land

In the Beginning

What is now the island of Madagascar was once sandwiched between Africa and India as part of the supercontinent Gondwana, a vast ancient land mass that also included Antarctica, South America and Australasia.

Gondwana began to break apart about 180 million years ago, but Madagascar remained joined to Africa for another 20 million years. About 88 million years ago the eastern half of Madagascar broke off, moving northward to eventually become India, by which time modern Madagascar had drifted to its present position. Since then, Madagascar has remained at its present size and shape, geographically isolated.

The Natural History of Madagascar by Steven Goodman and Jonathan Benstead provides the most comprehensive overview of the island's precious natural heritage.

The Eighth Continent

Madagascar measures 1600km on its longest axis, aligned roughly northeast to southwest, and 570km from east to west at its widest point. Almost the entire island is in the tropics, albeit well south of the equator, with only the southern tip protruding below the Tropic of Capricorn. The 5000km-long coastline features many long, sweeping sandy beaches, with coral reefs and atolls offshore in some areas, and is dotted with around 250 islands, of which Nosy Be and Île Sainte Marie are the largest. It is such epic numbers that have earned Madagascar the nickname 'the eighth continent'.

A chain of mountains runs down the eastern seaboard, forming a steep escarpment and trapping moisture that helps create the island's rainforests, which are rich in biodiversity. There is no modern volcanic activity on the island, although volcanoes previously erupted in the central highlands.

The island's highest point is 2876m Maromokotro, an extinct volcanic peak on the Tsaratanana massif, followed by the 2658m Pic Imarivolanitra (formerly known as Pic Boby) in Parc National d'Andringitra.

The Eighth Continent: Life, Death and the Discovery in the Lost World of Madagascar by Peter Tyson is a scientific travelogue that guides readers through the island's unique natural history and biodiversity.

Mineral Beauty

Going east from the western coastline, limestone is replaced by sandstone, which rises into majestic formations in places such as Parc National de

---

LOST GIANTS

When humans first arrived, Madagascar supported many animals much bigger than contemporary species: hippopotamuses, aardvarks, gorilla-size lemurs and giant flightless birds, similar to modern African birds such as the ostrich, roamed the island. With the arrival of humans, many of the larger animals, which no doubt provided a ready supply of protein, were wiped out. During the past 1000 years, scientists estimate that 16 species of lemurs, plus tortoises, the hippopotamuses, giant aardvarks, the world's largest bird (the 3m-high elephant bird *Aepyornis*) and two species of eagle have become extinct.

The BBC's seminal three-part series *Madagascar*, narrated by Sir David Attenborough, makes for an inspirational introduction to the great island. It features the island's iconic fauna and flora, as well as its more obscure specimens, in fascinating detail and stunning images.

In 1994 there were 50 known species of lemur. By 2006, thanks to extensive research, the number had gone up to 71. Today there are 103 and primatologists say that new species are still being discovered.

l'Isalo. Northern and western Madagascar host impressive limestone karst formations – jagged, eroded rocks that contain caves, potholes, underground rivers and forested canyons rich in wildlife such as crocodiles, lemurs, birds and bats. Karst is known locally as *tsingy* and is protected within one of Madagascar's three Unesco World Heritage Sites, Parc National des Tsingy de Bemaraha, as well as in the Réserve Spéciale Ankarana and Parc National des Tsingy de Namoroka.

Wildlife

Madagascar's 80-million-year isolation has allowed its wildlife to take a remarkable evolutionary turn. Undisturbed by outside influences and human beings (who 'only' arrived 2000 years ago), the various fauna and flora followed their own interpretation of the evolution manual. The result is that 70% of animals and 90% of plants found in Madagascar are endemic.

As well as being completely unique, their sheer variety is staggering: Madagascar hosts 5% of all known animal and plant species. Habitat degradation threatens much of this incredible natural wealth, and habitat conservation is now a worldwide priority.

Fauna

Lemurs

Madagascar's best-known mammals are the lemurs, of which there are 103 species. As well as being entertaining to watch (they are primates after all, and therefore distant cousins of ours), it's hard to overrate how unique they are: Madagascar's lemurs are found nowhere else on earth, which also explains why primatologists class Madagascar in a category of its own, the other three being Africa, Southeast Asia and the Americas.

Lemurs are divided into five families: the beautifully marked *sifakas* and *indris* (of which only one species is extant), all known for their leaping abilities; a family of small, nocturnal mouse lemurs that includes the world's smallest primates; the 'true' lemurs, such as the ring-tailed and ruffed lemurs; the sportive lemurs; and, most remarkable of all, the bizarre, nocturnal aye-aye, which extracts grubs from under bark with its long, bony middle finger.

WILD EXPECTATIONS

Many first-time visitors naturally associate Madagascar with two things – Africa and wildlife – leading to visions either of East African game parks, or of zoo-like rainforests. The reality is quite different. First, there are no plains full of roaming beasts here. In fact, there are no wild animals larger than a small dog.

Outside the parks the most common impression is of the *absence* of wildlife. You can drive for days through the spiny forest in the south, for example, and see virtually nothing but a few domesticated zebu. Likewise, along the lush wetlands of the Canal des Pangalanes there are hardly any birds. There are many reasons for this, beginning with the impact of hunting and deforestation, which has decimated animal populations. But even the great biological diversity in the forests is not always obvious. Some animals are nocturnal, or shy of humans, or simply rare. The broad-nosed gentle lemur, for example, was thought to be extinct until it was rediscovered in Ranomafana in 1972. It was observed again in the late 1980s and is only occasionally seen today. Many fascinating animals, such as the world's smallest chameleon, are simply tiny. And rainforest is, by its very nature, a fairly effective shield for its inhabitants.

So when seeking out this country's wildlife, it is best to adjust your focus to a smaller scale, look carefully around you, be patient and hire a good guide. It can be challenging to spot that bamboo lemur in the canopy, but that's what makes it so rewarding when you do.

GOING, GOING...BACK AGAIN!

The last century saw several Malagasy bird species pushed close to the brink of extinction. Waterbirds have fared particularly badly: the Alaotra grebe was last seen in the 1980s and was declared extinct in 2010. All three of the country's endemic duck species are rare. One, the Madagascar pochard, had last been observed in 1994, when a female was rescued by a conservation worker from a fisherman's net on Lac Alaotra. The rescuer kept the bird alive in a bath in the hope that a mate would be found, but it succumbed and the Madagascar pochard was presumed extinct. But in 2006 the unthinkable happened: nine adult Madagascar pochards were discovered with young on a remote lake in the Alaotra basin in northern Madagascar.

In a desperate effort to save the species from extinction, the Durrell Wildlife Conservation Trust, the Wildfowl and Wetlands Trust (WWT), the Peregrine Trust and the government of Madagascar recovered eggs about to hatch and set up an emergency captive-breeding program, with the long-term aim of reintroducing the rare duck to its habitat. Only 25 pochards are currently left in the wild but the captive-breeding program has managed to rear more than 50 birds, giving conservationists hope.

ENVIRONMENT WILDLIFE

Other Mammals

Madagascar has many species of small mammals, such as bats, rodents and tenrecs. Tenrecs are related to shrews and fill a similar niche as tiny hunters of the leaf litter. Among their diverse forms are shrew tenrecs, the hedgehog-like spiny tenrecs and even an otter-like aquatic species.

There are six species of carnivores – all mongooses and civets – including the ring-tailed mongoose, fanaloka and the puma-like, lemur-eating fossa.

Madagascar's waters harbour rich marine life – dolphins, dugongs and humpback whales. Whales come to Madagascar to give birth and mate during winter months.

Best Whale Watching

Baie d'Antongil

Île Sainte Marie

Anakao

Nosy Be

Ifaty

Birds

Madagascar's birdlife has the highest proportion of endemic birds of any country on earth: of the 209 breeding species, 51% are endemic. A large percentage of birds are forest-dwelling and therefore under pressure from land clearing.

Among Madagascar's unique bird families are the mesites – skulking, babbler-like birds thought to be related to rails; the spectacular ground-rollers,including a roadrunner-like species unique to the spiny forests; the tiny, iridescent asities, similar to sunbirds and filling a similar niche; and the vangas, which have taken several strange twists as they evolved to fill forest niches. There are a number of predators, including the highly endangered Madagascar serpent eagle and fish eagle, and nocturnal species as well.

Most species are resident (ie nonmigratory), although a few are seasonal migrants to East Africa. Waterbirds are rather poorly represented in Madagascar because there are comparatively few large bodies of water. Some of the best concentrations are in the Mahavy-Kinkony Wetland Complex on the west coast. The richest habitat by far for birds (and all other terrestrial life forms) is the rainforest of the eastern seaboard, although many of these species are rare and poorly known.

Handy Field Guides

Madagascar Wildlife (Daniel Austin, Nick Garbutt)

Lemurs of Madagascar (Russell Mittermeier et al)

Reptiles & Amphibians

There are 346 reptile species on Madagascar, including most of the world's chameleons, ranging from the largest – Parson's chameleon, which grows to around 60cm – to the smallest, the dwarf chameleons of the genus *Brookesia*, which fits on your thumbnail! You might also spot the king of camouflage, the leaf-tailed gecko, and the amazingly colourful Labord's

Common tenrec mothers can give birth to 25 infants at one time, the most of any mammal in the world.

Between 1999 and 2010 an incredible 615 species were discovered in Madagascar, including 41 mammals, 61 reptiles, 42 invertebrates, 17 fish, 69 amphibians and 385 plants.

chameleon. Equally attractive are some of Madagascar's 300 species of amphibians, including spectacularly coloured frogs such as the bright-red tomato frog and iridescent Malagasy poison frogs.

Amazingly the verdant forests support not a single snake species harmful to people. Among the many beautiful snakes are the Madagascar boa and leaf-nosed snake. In contrast the Nile crocodile is just as dangerous here as it is in Africa and it kills people every year.

Five of the world's seven species of marine turtle can be found in Madagascar (all endangered, some critically). The country is also home to several species of tortoise, many of which are endangered. With its distinctive and ornate shell, the ploughshare tortoise is the most threatened because of poaching (a shell can fetch US$40,000): there are just 500 individuals left in the wild. In a desperate attempt to stem the illegal trade in ploughshare shells, the Durrell Wildlife Conservation Trust (which runs a captive breeding program at Parc National d'Ankarafantsika) and the government decided in 2015 to deliberately deface all remaining animals' shells in order to make them less attractive to poachers.

Invertebrates

As you might expect from somewhere that has such thriving wildlife, the bugs in Madagascar are out in force. It is thought there are some 100,000 species of insects on the island. Among the most charming specimens are hissing cockroaches, scorpions, giraffe-necked weevils, tarantulas, giant millipedes, stick insects and the incredible flatid bug, which looks more like a giant bit of paper confetti than an insect.

Fish

Freshwater fish are one of the most endangered groups of animal on Madagascar, owing to silting of rivers through erosion. A survey by the International Union for Conservation of Nature (IUCN) of 98 endemic species of freshwater fish found that 54% of the fish in Madagascar were either critically endangered, endangered or vulnerable.

Marine life is incredibly diverse, but similarly vulnerable to erosion run-off, notably the country's beautiful coral. Madagascar has the world's fifth-largest coral reef, but overfishing, pollution, climate change and sediment from soil erosion have greatly impacted its health.

Madagascar harbours a number of sharks, which, depending on your point of view, is either great (conservationists, fishers, some divers) or scary (swimmers, surfers, the other divers). Risks of attacks are particularly high on the east coast, less so in areas where fringing corals

LEMURS IN PERIL

Few people realise quite how endangered lemurs are. According to the International Union for Conservation of Nature (IUCN), they are now the most threatened mammal group on earth, with 94% of all species threatened with extinction (up from 64% in 2005).

This sorry state of affairs is down to several factors: deforestation, which has squeezed their natural habitat; poaching (for wildlife trade) and hunting (from impoverished local communities); and the 2009–13 political crisis, which not only saw a complete breakdown of the rule of law in protected areas, but also led a number of donors to suspend their funding for environmental conservation.

Lemurs are also at risk of climate change, which could shrink their habitat even further, and shift it by hundreds of kilometres in some cases.

Thankfully, the situation is now well documented and an internationally supported strategy is in place to protect lemurs. At its heart is the involvement of local communities and greater financial support for conservation efforts.

ICONIC TREES

Madagascar is home to seven of the world's eight baobab species, of which six are native and endemic (the seventh species is that found on mainland Africa, the eighth in Australia).

The trees stand out for their size (up to 30m high), huge trunks (one of the largest in the country is in Majunga, with a circumference of 21m), old age (many are thought to be several centuries old) and signature scraggly branches, which are in full view over the winter months, when baobabs have lost their foliage. The trees store water in their trunks and are therefore well adapted to dry environments.

Another of Madagascar's iconic plants – it is, technically, not a tree – is the *ravinala*, or travellers' palm, named so after the large quantities of rainwater it can store at the base of its leaves. *Ravinala*, which is native to the island, has many uses in Madagascar. The leaves are dried and used for building roofs in traditional houses, and bundles of dried leaves are sold by the roadside everywhere in northern and eastern Madagascar. Done well, a *ravinala* roof can last 10 years. The tough stems are often used to make beautiful ceiling or wall panels. The wood from the trunk is also used for various building purposes.

protect the shores. Their numbers have dwindled dramatically, however, especially in the southwest, because of demand for shark fins.

Flora

Madagascar's plants are no less interesting than its animals and its flora is incredibly diverse. About 12,000 species are known to science, including the bizarre octopus trees, several species of baobab and a pretty flower that is used to treat leukaemia.

The island's vegetation can be divided into three parallel north–south zones, each supporting unique communities of plants and animals: the hot, arid west consists of dry spiny desert or deciduous forest; the central plateau *(hauts plateaux)* has now been mostly deforested; and the wettest part of the country, the eastern seaboard, supports extensive tracts of rainforest. Mangrove forests grow in sites along the coast, particularly near large estuaries. All of these habitats have suffered extensive disturbance.

Arid Landscapes

The spiny desert is truly extraordinary. Dense tangles of cactus-like octopus trees festooned with needle-sharp spines are interspersed with baobabs whose bulbous trunks store water, allowing them to survive the dry season. The baobabs' large, bright flowers are filled with copious amounts of nectar, often sipped by fork-marked lemurs. About 60 species of aloe occur in Madagascar, and many dot the spiny desert landscape.

Dry deciduous forests are a feature of the western half of the country, although they do not look quite as bare as their northern-hemisphere counterparts in the depths of winter. The thinner winter foliage does make it prime bird- and lemur-watching time, however.

The Highlands

The vast areas of blond grassland of the *hauts plateaux* are actually the result of extensive felling by humans. The boundary of the sole remaining patch of natural forest, at Parc National Zombitse-Vohibasia, stands in forlorn contrast to the degraded countryside surrounding it.

Growing among the crags and crevices of Parc National de l'Isalo are nine species of *Pachypodia*, including a tall species with large, fragrant yellow-white blossoms, and the diminutive elephant-foot species that nestle in cliff crevices on the sandstone massif.

PERIWINKLE

The rosy periwinkle, a flower endemic to Madagascar, has been a source of alkaloids that are 99% effective in the treatment of some forms of leukaemia.

Rainforest

Madagascar's eastern rainforests once covered the entire eastern seaboard and still support the island's highest biodiversity, most of which is found nowhere else on earth. Giant forest trees are festooned with vines, orchids and bird's-nest ferns (home to tree frogs and geckos).

There are 1000 species of orchid in Madagascar, more than in all of Africa, and more than 60 species of pitcher plants are found in swampy parts of rainforests. Insects are attracted to the nectar of these carnivorous plants, but are trapped by downward-pointing spines along the inside of the 'pitcher' and are eventually dissolved and absorbed by the plant.

Madagascar is the only country outside of the UK where the prestigious Royal Botanic Gardens, Kew keeps a permanent presence. It has notably worked on the island's palms, documenting around 200 species.

Environmental Issues

Madagascar faces tremendous environmental challenges, none greater than deforestation. Like every other country, Madagascar is also going to have to contend with the effects of climate change on its unique biodiversity.

Deforestation

Around 96% of Malagasy households rely on firewood and charcoal for their domestic energy needs. This reliance has put immense pressure on Madagascar's forests, as has the need for agricultural and grazing land (slash-and-burn, or *tavy* in Malagasy, is widespread). Between 2005 and 2010 Madagascar experienced a deforestation rate of 0.4%. This rate is likely to have increased during the political crisis (2009–13), but even at 0.4%, conservation organisation WWF concluded that unless something was done, it would mean a 14% reduction in forest cover by 2050. Considering Madagascar has already lost around 80% of its forests since humans arrived, this is a damning prospect.

The impact of deforestation on such a large scale is catastrophic for Madagascar's wildlife. A 2015 report from IUCN found that 114 of the country's mammal species were threatened – the second-highest number for any country in the world.

Deforestation has also led to an increase in soil erosion. During the rainy season, Madagascar's laterite soils 'bleed' into the country's streams and rivers. The red earth saturates coastal waters, threatening fragile marine ecosystems, including precious coral reefs. Landslides have also become more common during the rainy season, damaging roads, rail tracks and people's homes.

In March 2014 scientists made a very unhappy discovery in Tamatave: Asian common toads. The venomous amphibians are thought to have arrived on a shipping container and conservationists are extremely concerned about the impact they could have on Madagascar's endemic fauna.

Natural Resource Exploitation

Madagascar has immense natural wealth: minerals, rare earth metals, coal, gemstones and precious woods. There are already a couple of large-scale mines in operation – one exploiting nickel and cobalt in Ambatovy near Moramanga, and another one mining ilmenite (titanium ore) and zircon (a gemstone) near Fort Dauphin (Taolagnaro).

WHAT YOU CAN DO

➡ Offset your air miles with carbon credits from Madagascar (www.standfortrees.org).

➡ Carefully consider your purchase of precious wood items.

➡ Never buy lemurs, tortoises or other protected species, no matter how sorry they look. Instead, report any mistreatment of animals to the police or the nearest MNP office.

➡ If you buy gemstones, buy from an established dealer and get an export permit.

ILLEGAL ROSEWOOD LOGGING

In April 2000 Cyclone Hudah tore through the Masoala Peninsula in northeast Madagascar. The storm left a trail of devastation in its wake: satellite images revealed that around 3% of the forest was severely damaged. Although rosewood (known locally as *bola bola*) exploitation had been banned, then president Marc Ravalomanana exceptionally allowed fallen trees to be sold as timber, which would open the floodgates of illegal logging.

In 2009 the transitional authorities decided to make rosewood export legal in a bid to generate new revenue streams (foreign donors had withheld their funding because of the unconstitutional change of power), driven by demand for luxury furniture and musical instruments from China and the US (a rosewood bed sells for US$1 million in China). The worst-affected areas were the northeastern national parks of Marojejy and Masoala and the adjoining Makira forest (now a protected area).

In 2009 an investigation by Madagascar National Parks, the environmental NGO Global Witness and the US Environmental Investigation Agency uncovered the scale of the pillaging. The report revealed that 100 to 200 trees were being taken down every day, a bounty worth US$80,000 to US$460,000. It also found that the police and officials at every level of the forestry sector had colluded with traffickers.

The Malagasy authorities reacted by forbidding all precious wood exports in April 2010. Its implementation has remained symbolic, however, with *bola bola* traffic continuing. Even the addition of rosewood and ebony to the Convention on International Trade in Endangered Species (CITES) and an international embargo since 2013 did little to stem the flow. As of 2015, logs of rosewood continue to find their way to China via Zanzibar, Tanzania, Kenya and Hong Kong.

The trade is devastating because of the deforestation it causes, and also because of the accompanying trafficking it brings (animal poaching, gold prospecting etc). Rosewood trees are now critically endangered: there are no seed-bearing trees left outside of national parks (rosewood grows slowly and takes 40 to 50 years to reach this stage).

Madagascar may also have large deposits of oil and gas – its proximity to Mozambique and Tanzania, where large reserves were discovered over the past few years, suggest this is likely, although prospecting is still at an early stage. Only one on-shore block has so far been confirmed as being commercially viable (a heavy oil deposit in western Madagascar).

Prospecting in the extractive sector virtually ground to a halt during the transition years (2009-13), but with the return to political stability in 2014, many are keeping a watchful eye on developments. The Malagasies are understandably keen to make the best of their natural wealth, but with this expectation comes great anxiety about the environmental impact of such projects. Madagascar was suspended from the Extractive Industries Transparency Initiative (EITI) during the transition but was reintegrated in June 2014 and is striving to become fully compliant.

Madagascar's seas also suffer from overfishing. Human population growth and lack of food and employment alternatives in the south have pushed marine ecosystems to the brink. A number of NGOs are currently working with coastal communities to improve their sustainability and have developed successful Locally Managed Marine Protected Areas.

The government of Madagascar is also working to move its shrimp industry towards Marine Stewardship Certification (MSC). The sector has gone through hard times since the early 2000s with the dwindling of stocks. Sustainable fishing practices would not only protect marine resources, but also guarantee long-term employment for those depending on this activity for their livelihood.

The Malagasy have nicknamed baobabs 'roots of the sky', after their scraggly branches. Legend has it that God made the baobab the most beautiful tree on earth. The devil was so jealous that he decided to plant baobabs upside down so that he could view them from hell!

ENVIRONMENT ENVIRONMENTAL ISSUES

Parks & Reserves

Many visitors come to Madagascar for its amazing parks and reserves, and rightly so: they often are the highlight of a trip. Madagascar's efforts to set aside so much of its land for protection deserve to be saluted and supported: poaching, financing and sustainable management remain challenges, although the government seems determined to tackle them.

A Brief History

Best Protected Areas for Lemurs

Réserve d'Anja

Réserve de Nahampoana

Parc National de Ranomafana

Réserve Spéciale d'Analamazaotra

Although protected areas in Madagascar have existed since the 1950s, the environmental movement began in earnest in 1985 with an international conference of scientists, funding organisations and Malagasy government officials. Biologists had long known that the country was an oasis of amazing creatures and plants, but the clear felling and burning of forests all over the island was threatening these treasures. Concerned international donors and the Malagasy government joined together to plan a major conservation program.

By 1989 Madagascar had a national Environmental Action Plan, which offered a blueprint for biodiversity action for the next 15 years. The first step was to create a national park system, called the Association Nationale pour la Gestion des Aires Protégées (Angap; National Association for the Management of Protected Areas), and then set Angap to work on creating new parks and training staff. The last phase of the program, which started in earnest in the naughts, aimed to develop sustainable tourism in the country's protected areas.

Although not perfect, great strides have been achieved in the country's protected areas since 1985. Angap changed its name to **Madagascar National Parks** (MNP; www.parcs-madagascar.com) in 2009 and it now manages 51 protected areas covering around 20,000 sq km. In total Madagascar now has more than 60,000 sq km of land (and sea) under protection.

WORLD HERITAGE SITE IN DANGER

In 2007 Unesco declared the eastern-seaboard Rainforests of the Atsinanana a World Heritage Site. The site includes six rainforest national parks: Parc National de Marojejy, Parc National de Masoala, Parc National de Zahamena, Parc National de Ranomafana, Parc National d'Andringitra and Parc National d'Andohahela. Unesco acknowledged the importance of these forests in maintaining Madagascar's high levels of biodiversity.

But in July 2010 the World Heritage committee decided to move the Rainforests of the Atsinanana to its List of World Heritage in Danger because of illegal logging and hunting of endangered species. The committee noted that 'despite a decree outlawing the exploitation and export of rosewood and ebony, Madagascar continues to provide export permits for illegally logged timber'.

Unesco urged Madagascar to respect the legislation, but as of 2015 there was still no sign that the rainforests of Atsinanana would be moved off the red list any time soon.

CARBON FOR SALE

The Parc Naturel de Makira in eastern Madagascar is the country's largest protected area and home to 1% of the world's biodiversity. In an effort to make the park financially sustainable, the government of Madagascar and the Wildlife Conservation Society (www. wcs.org) set up a REDD+ carbon credit scheme (REDD+ stands for Reducing Emissions from Deforestation and Forest Degradation Plus Conservation).

The idea is to assign financial value to the carbon stored in trees and to compensate the institution or community (in developing countries only) protecting the forested areas. Deforestation is thought to contribute around 20% of greenhouse gas emissions, so finding incentives to avoid it is an important climate-control mechanism. It's also a good way to 'make conservation pay', with 50% of carbon revenues used to benefit communities directly.

In September 2013 the government announced that more than 700,000 credits had been approved for sale, which would save 32 million tonnes of CO_2 from reaching the atmosphere.

Fragile Gains

At the World Parks Congress in Durban in 2003 (an event organised every 10 years by the International Union for Conservation of Nature), then president Marc Ravalomanana announced a bold plan to triple the extent of Madagascar's protected areas. Amazingly the country achieved its goal, a feat that president Hery Rajaonarimampianina proudly announced in November 2014 at the World Parks Congress in Sydney.

Despite this achievement, the picture inside Madagascar's protected areas isn't all rosy. National parks in the northeast of the country such as Marojejy and Masoala have been subject to severe illegal logging of precious hardwoods (rosewood in particular) during the transition (2009–13), and despite the return to constitutional rule in 2014, the illegal trafficking has continued. Poaching of rare tortoises, lemurs and birds has also increased substantially since 2009.

The government faces two more challenges: the sustainable management of protected areas (notably their financing, which is largely supported by international donors) and how to translate conservation efforts into economic development. Although local communities receive 50% of park admission fees, the government is keen to see conservation play a wider role in Madagascar's economic growth.

Undaunted, the president called on the international community at the Sydney conference to help Madagascar meet these challenges and set his country another goal: to triple the extent of marine protected areas by the next World Parks Congress.

Sustainable Conservation

Enlightened conservationists know that for conservation programs to succeed in poor developing nations, local people must be involved.

From the beginning, the needs of the people living in and around the parks were incorporated into park management plans. Money from park admission fees is used to build wells, buy vegetable seeds, help with tree nurseries, rebuild schools and build small dams to facilitate paddy, rather than hillside, rice cultivation.

Tourism has also fostered employment opportunities in villages around major national parks, with rangers, guides, porters and those working in guesthouses and restaurants all benefiting.

Every organisation involved in conservation has dedicated funding and projects to raise awareness about the importance of biodiversity

LORDS AND LEMURS

Lords and Lemurs by Alison Jolly is a history of the Réserve Privée de Berenty that skilfully weaves together the stories of the spiny desert Tandroy people, three generations of French plantation owners, lemurs and lemur-watchers.

and improve the livelihoods of communities living on the edge of protected areas. Activities include income-generating projects, training for park rangers and field assistants, school outreach programs, reforestation etc.

But the most successful examples are those where local communities are directly involved in the management of the protected area. The Réserve d'Anja is a great example. It is run and managed by village association Anja Miray, whose 250 members are local residents, and it attracts around 14,000 visitors a year, more than many national parks.

The many Locally Managed Marine Areas (LMMA) are another shining example of protected areas where local communities own, manage and enforce the protection of their coastline and seabed. A 2015 study of LMMAs in southwest Madagascar found that, over a period of eight years, short-term bans on octopus fishing had helped stocks recover and doubled fishers' incomes during the fishing season thanks to bigger catches – a win-win situation.

MADAGASCAR'S NATIONAL PARKS & RESERVES

PARK	FEATURES
Parc National Andasibe Mantadia p222	Pristine forest, excellent local guides, well-marked trails
Parc National d'Andohahela p222	Three types of forest: humid, transition and dry
Parc National d'Andringitra p222	Rugged granite peaks, fantastic trails and scenery
Parc National d'Ankarafantsika p222	Diverse landscapes, from dry forest to canyon and lakes
Réserve Spéciale Ankarana p222	*Tsingy* (limestone pinnacles), caves, dry forest
Parc National de l'Isalo p222	Sandstone mountains, gorges with natural swimming pools
Parc National de Kirindy-Mitea p222	Sand dunes, dry forest, brackish lakes, mangroves
Parc National de Marojejy p222	Remote peaks, lush rainforest, canyons
Parc National de Masoala p222	Primary rainforest, mangroves and protected marine areas
Parc National Montagne d'Ambre p222	Humid forest, old French botanical gardens, waterfalls
Parc National de Ranomafana p58	Secondary rainforest, forested slopes, waterfalls
Parc National des Tsingy de Bemaraha p222	Spectacular limestone pinnacles, Unesco World Heritage Site
Réserve d'Anja p222	The mountain-size 'three sisters' boulders; forest
Réserve Forestière de Kirindy p222	Dense, dry deciduous forest
Réserve Naturelle Intégrale de Lokobe p222	Primary forest on an isolated peninsula
Réserve de Nosy Mangabe p222	Rainforest-covered island
Réserve Spéciale de Cap Sainte Marie p222	Stark, windswept cape, Madagascar's southernmost point
Parc National Zombitse-Vohibasia p222	Southwestern Madagascar's last island of dense, dry forest

Scientific Research & Parks

The biodiversity that Madagascar's parks and reserves protect is of great interest to scientists, and many of the country's protected areas host research programs in primates, biodiversity, endemicity, the effects of climate change, deforestation and much more.

The Institute for the Conservation of Tropical Environments set up the ValBio research centre next to Parc National de Ranomafana. The Wildlife Conservation Society is highly involved in the management and protection of Parc National de Masoala, Baie d'Antongil and its new shark sanctuary and the Parc Naturel de Makira. The Durrell Wildlife Conservation Trust has had a captive tortoise breeding centre at Parc National d'Ankarafantsika for nearly 25 years. The German Primate Centre has been researching Réserve Forestière de Kirindy's lemurs since 1993. WWF is working on wildlife corridors between protected areas, and Conservation International is monitoring biodiversity and climate change in Parc National de Ranomafana as part of its Tropical Ecology Assessment

Gerald Durrell's hilarious book *The Aye-Aye and I* is an account of the Durrell Wildlife Conservation Trust's expedition to capture aye-ayes, gentle lemurs, giant jumping rats and other endangered species in a bid to set up captive breeding programs.

ACTIVITIES	WILDLIFE	BEST TIME TO VISIT
Hiking, lemur-watching, birdwatching	Lemurs (including the *indri*), abundant birdlife, reptiles, orchids	Oct-Nov
Hiking, camping, birdwatching	Spiny iguanas, birds, including harrier hawks	Apr-Dec
Trekking, climbing	Ring-tailed lemurs, orchids	Oct-Nov
Hiking, birdwatching, lemur-watching, boat trips	129 species of birds, eight species of lemur	Year-round
Hiking, caving, birdwatching, night walks	Bats, 11 species of lemur, birds (including flycatchers)	Jun-Dec
Hiking, swimming	*Sifakas*, ring-tailed lemurs, *Pachypodium*	May-Oct
Hiking, birdwatching, pirogue trips	Birds, including flamingos	May-Nov
Trekking on the Marojejy Massif, lemur-watching	Silky *sifakas*, reptiles, amphibians, millipedes	Aug-Nov
Trekking, sea kayaking	Red-ruffed lemurs, humpback whales, dugongs, turtles, orchids	Aug-Jan
Hiking, birdwatching, lemur-watching	Brookesia chameleons, amphibians, lemurs	Year-round
Hiking, lemur-watching, birdwatching	Lemurs, birds, insects, orchids	Sep-Dec
Climbing, hiking, pirogue trips	Lemurs, birds, reptiles	Apr-Oct
Hiking, climbing, lemur-watching	Ring-tailed lemurs	Year-round
Hiking, night walks, lemur-watching	Fossas, giant jumping rats, lemurs	Year-round
Hiking, lemur-watching, pirogue trips	Black lemurs, boa constrictors, birds, including owls	Year-round
Hiking, camping, night walks	Aye-ayes, whales, reptiles and amphibians	Jul-Sep
Hiking, camping, searching for elephant bird eggshells	Radiated tortoises, spider tortoises, whales offshore	May-Oct
Hiking, birdwatching	85 species of birds, lemurs	May-Oct

and Monitoring (TEAM) initiative, which seeks to assess the health of tropical ecosystems worldwide.

These are just a handful of projects taking place in the country's protected areas, but they highlight their importance to the scientific community, a fact that is, sadly, not always well explained to visitors.

Visiting Protected Areas

Admission Fees

In 1986 scientists 'rediscovered' the greater bamboo lemur (previously thought extinct) in what is now Parc National de Ranomafana. They also discovered a new species, the golden bamboo lemur. So extraordinary were these findings that they led to the creation of the park.

National park admission prices for foreign nationals depend on the park's category. The fee is per day. Children pay Ar25,000 per day in all parks.

Admission to other protected areas varies between Ar10,000 and Ar60,000 per day for an adult. Children generally pay a nominal fee.

Guides

Guides are compulsory in all MNP protected areas (national parks, special reserves and strict nature reserves), but not always in other protected areas. You don't need to book a guide in advance: just turn up at the MNP office on the day (or the day before if you'd like to discuss itineraries) and you will be assigned a guide who matches your request (guides work in rotation).

Unfortunately, there can be big variations in the level of knowledge about fauna and flora from one guide to another. All MNP guides speak French, and an increasing number now speak English.

Fees vary depending on the park and the length of walks, but in any case they are generally clearly displayed at the reserve or park entrance. A charge of Ar40,000 for half a day's walk is about average.

Camping

Almost all national parks have designated camping areas. The locations are invariably atmospheric, but facilities vary from pretty good to really basic.

Don't be put off if you haven't come equipped for camping: all you really need is a warm sleeping bag and some toilet roll. Some parks rent tents, cooking utensils etc and if they don't, they will usually know a local outfit that does. You can also hire porters and cooks (who can sometimes sort out supplies for you). Just drop by the MNP office the day before you need to set off to reserve everything.

NATIONAL PARK ADMISSION FEE

	PROTECTED AREAS	ADMISSION (AR/DAY)
King Parks	Ankarana, Isalo	65,000
Main Parks	Andohahela, Ankarafantsika, Bemaraha, Lokobe, Montagne d'Ambre, Nosy Hara, Ranomafana	55,000
Other Parks	Ambohitantely, Analamazaotra, Analamerana, Andasibe Mantadia, Andringitra, Baie de Baly, Beza Mahafaly, Cap Sainte Marie, Kirindy-Mitea, Mananara Nord, Manombo, Manongarivo, Marojejy, Masoala, Mikea, Nosy Mangabe, Sahamalaza, Tsimanampesotse, Tsingy de Namoroka, Zahamena, Zombitse-Vohibasia	45,000

Wildlife

When Madagascar broke away from Africa some 160 million years ago, its cargo of primitive animals evolved in some novel directions, free from the pressures felt on other land masses, such as human hunters. The result is one of the most important biodiversity hot spots in the world, and thanks to a great network of reserves and excellent local naturalist guides, Madagascar is also one of the world's great ecotourism destinations. Lemurs are the main attraction for most nature lovers, but the island also offers superb birdwatching and there is a host of smaller animals that could keep you occupied for several trips.

Suraka silk moth, Parc National de l'Isalo (p75)

KARL LEHMANN/GETTY IMAGES ©

Colourful Typical Lemurs

Lemurs are an extraordinarily diverse group of prosimians (primate ancestors) found only in Madagascar. 'Typical' lemurs are long-tailed, monkey-like animals with catlike faces, prominent ears and prehensile hands with separate fingers and toes.

Ring-Tailed Lemur

1 These sociable lemurs forage on the ground in groups of 13 to 15, searching for fruit, flowers, leaves and other vegetation in spiny and dry deciduous forest. Habituated troops live at Réserve d'Anja (p68). *Length 95–110cm; weight 2.3–3.5kg.*

Black & White Ruffed Lemur

2 This species' social behaviour is complex: males and females may occupy separate territories, or live in mixed social groups. They are easily seen at the Andasibe area parks (p162). *Length 110–120cm; weight 3.1–3.6kg.*

Red Ruffed Lemur

3 Like other ruffed lemurs, this species primarily eats fruit, is highly vocal and sometimes hangs by its hind feet while feeding. It is found only in lowland primary rainforest on the Masoala Peninsula (p186). *Length 100–120cm; weight 3.3–3.6kg.*

Mongoose Lemur

4 Recognisable by their piercing orange eyes and strongly marked bibs, mongoose lemurs live in pairs with their offspring. They tend to be more secretive than other 'typical' lemurs, but can be readily seen at Parc National d'Ankarafantsika (p108). *Length 75–83cm; weight 1.1–1.6kg.*

Plain Typical Lemurs

Many lemurs are plainly marked with mousy brown or grey colours that make them inconspicuous in the shaded forests where they live. Lemurs don't need strong social markings because they rely on scent to mark territories and signal their readiness to breed.

Crowned Lemur

1 Male and female (pictured) crowned lemurs have different colourations. They live in dry deciduous forest and rainforest in northern Madagascar. Habituated troops can be seen at Réserve Spéciale Ankarana (p150). *Length 75–85cm; weight 1.1–1.3kg.*

Common Brown Lemur

2 Living in groups of three to 12, these lemurs are active during the day but may be partly nocturnal in the dry season. Common at the Andasibe area parks (p162). *Length 100cm; weight 2–3kg.*

Black Lemur

3 Males (pictured) are dark brown or black, while females vary from golden brown to rich chestnut with flamboyant white ear and cheek tufts. They're easily seen in Réserve Naturelle Intégrale de Lokobe (p133). *Length 90–110cm; weight 2–2.9kg.*

Red Bellied Lemur

4 You can tell male red bellied lemurs from females by the white 'teardrops' of bare skin under their eyes. See them at Parc National de Ranomafana (p58), especially from May to June. *Length 78–93cm; weight 1.6–2.4kg.*

Eastern Lesser Bamboo Lemur

5 The most common of the bamboo lemurs is widespread in eastern rainforests at Parc National de Ranomafana (p58) and the Andasibe area parks (p162). *Length 56–70cm; weight 0.7–1kg.*

1

3

Sifakas & Indris

KARL LEMANN/GETTY IMAGES ©

Also known as simponas, *sifakas* are prodigious leapers that move rapidly by propelling themselves from tree to tree with their elongated back legs. Many are attractively marked and easily seen at national parks where troops have been habituated. *Indris* and *sifakas* are members of the same family.

Verreaux's Sifaka

1 This beautiful lemur is famous for balletic bounds across clearings, leaping sideways on its strong back legs. The species is restricted to dry deciduous forest in the south and is easily seen at Parc National de l'Isalo (p75). *Length 90–110cm; weight 3–3.5kg.*

Coquerel's Sifaka

2 These attractive *sifakas* commonly travel in groups. They're restricted to dry deciduous forest in Madagascar's northwest, such as Parc National d'Ankarafantsika (p108). *Length 93–110cm; weight 3.7–4.3kg.*

Diademed Sifaka

3 Arguably the most beautiful of all lemurs, this species is almost the same size as the *indri*. It's widely distributed on the eastern seaboard but is best seen at the Andasibe area parks (p162). *Length 94–105cm; weight 6–8.5kg.*

Decken's Sifaka

4 Protected by a strong local *fady* (taboo), these little-known *sifakas* sometimes live in towns in western Madagascar. They're common in Parc National des Tsingy de Bemaraha (p111). *Length 92–110cm; weight 3–4.5kg.*

Indri

5 Known locally as *babakoto*, the *indri* is the largest lemur and has the strongest voice, which can travel 3km through the forest. *Indris* can leap up to 10m between tree trunks, and they travel in family groups of two to six while foraging, mostly for leaves. See them at the Andasibe area parks (p162). *Length 69–77cm; weight 6–9.5kg.*

Common Nocturnal Lemurs

Approximately half of all lemur species are nocturnal. The nocturnal species are the smallest lemurs, and include mouse lemurs (the smallest of all primates), dwarf lemurs and sportive lemurs. The aye-aye is classified in its own family and even among lemurs stands out as unique.

Gray Mouse Lemur

1 Like most mouse lemurs, this species can be very common in suitable habitats, which include deciduous dry forest, spiny forest and secondary forest. It is typically active in the lower tree layers, although it moves very quickly and often retires from torchlight soon after being spotted. Mouse lemurs eat insects, fruit, flowers and other small animals, and are preyed upon by forest owls. *Length 25–28cm; weight 58–67g.*

Aye-Aye

2 With its shaggy, grizzled coat, bright orange eyes, leathery bat-like ears and long, dexterous fingers, the aye-aye is a strange-looking animal and the subject of much superstition. The middle digit of each forehand is elongated, and is used to probe crevices for insect larvae and other morsels. Aye-ayes are difficult to see but widely distributed in rainforests and dry deciduous forests. See them on Aye-Aye Island (p187). *Length 74–90cm; weight 2.5–2.6kg.*

Weasel Sportive Lemur

3 Found in rainforests of east-central Madagascar, these lemurs have dense woolly fur and spend the night munching on leaves, often staying for hours in the same tree. Males are solitary and highly territorial, while females remain with their offspring. *Length 30–35cm; weight 0.5–1kg.*

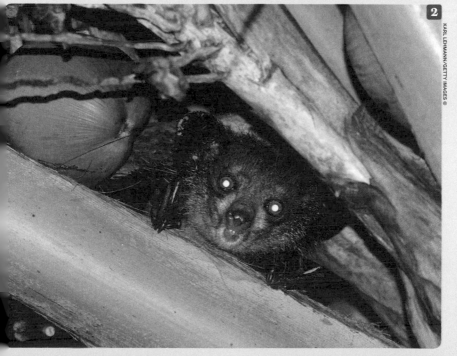

KARL LEHMANN/GETTY IMAGES ©

Rare Nocturnal Lemurs

Nocturnal lemurs are hard to find and may require the assistance of expert guides to spot. Some are thought to be highly endangered, while so little is known about others that their numbers and distribution have not been accurately determined.

Milne-Edwards' Sportive Lemur

1 Long, powerful back legs enable the eight species of sportive lemur to leap from tree to tree, balanced by their long tails. They sleep during the day in holes in trees and emerge after dark to feed. This species lives in dry deciduous forest in the west and northwest and can generally be seen at Parc National d'Ankarafantsika (p108). *Length 54–58cm; weight 1kg.*

Western Avahi

2 The two species of avahi have dense fur that gives them a woolly appearance, hence their alternative name of 'woolly lemurs'. Their diet consists of a large variety of leaves and buds, and families huddle together during the day in dense foliage in the forest canopy. Avahis are restricted to dry deciduous forest in west and northwest Madagascar. They're commonly seen at night at Parc National d'Ankarafantsika (p108) *Length 59–68cm; weight 0.9–1.3kg.*

Pygmy Mouse Lemur

3 Owing to its size and nocturnal habits, this very small lemur went undetected for more than 100 years until it was rediscovered in 1993. It has been found in dry forests at Parc National des Tsingy de Bemaraha (p111), but almost nothing is known of its history, whether it's threatened or if new populations will be found. *Length 12–13cm; weight 43–55g.*

PREMAPHOTOS/ALAMY STOCK PHOTO ©

Carnivorous Mammals

Although lemurs are the undoubted highlight, Madagascar has many other types of native land mammal, including eight predators, dozens of bats and rodents, and tenrecs (primitive, shrew-like animals that have evolved into at least two-dozen forms, including spiny and aquatic species). A few of the island's unique carnivores are highlighted here.

Fossa

1 The legendary fossa is a solitary and elusive predator of lemurs and other animals. It is extremely agile and catlike, even descending trees head first. It is reputed to follow troops of lemurs for days, climbing trees to pick them off as they sleep at night. Fossas were the villains in the animated film *Madagascar*. They are regularly spotted at Réserve Forestière de Kirindy (p114). *Length 140–170cm; weight 5–10kg.*

Fanaloka

2 Also known as the Malagasy or striped civet, the nocturnal, fox-like fanaloka is found in eastern and northern rainforests. It hunts mostly on the ground but can climb well, eating rodents, birds and other animals. During the day it sleeps in tree hollows and under logs. It can be found at Parc National de Ranomafana (p58). *Length 61–70cm; weight 1.5–2kg.*

Ring-Tailed Mongoose

3 This attractive mongoose is widespread and active by day, and is therefore probably the easiest carnivore to spot. Family parties communicate with high-pitched whistles as they forage for small animals, including reptiles, birds and eggs, insects, rodents and even small lemurs. Generally seen at Parc National de Ranomafana (p58) and Réserve Spéciale Ankarana (p150). *Length 60–70cm; weight 0.7–1kg.*

RHONDA GUTENBERG/GETTY IMAGES ©

Omnivorous Mammals

Many of Madagascar's mammals are omnivorous, which means they eat a little bit of everything they come across, including insects, berries, fruit and seeds. Some specialise in fruit; others vary their diets according to which foods are available at different times of the year.

Hedgehog Tenrec

1 Nocturnal hedgehog tenrecs forage by sniffing out insects and their larvae and fallen fruit among leaf litter. During the day they shelter in tunnels under logs or tree roots. They are found in many habitats, including forests near Antananarivo, and are usually seen on nocturnal walks in Parc National Montagne d'Ambre (p148). *Length 16–22cm; weight 180–270g.*

Madagascar Flying Fox

2 Flying foxes roost upside down in big, noisy colonies, like most bats, but use trees rather than caves as roosting sites. Colonies can number up to a thousand individuals and great flocks take to the wing at dusk, fanning out across the countryside to feed on fruit. A colony of this species is a permanent fixture at Réserve Privée de Berenty (p94). *Length 23–27cm; wingspan 1–1.2m; weight 500–750g.*

Giant Jumping Rat

3 Madagascar's largest rodent is strictly nocturnal. Pairs live in burrows with their offspring, foraging for seeds and fallen fruit after dark. They generally move on all fours but also hop on their hind legs. They were formerly more widespread but now live in a relatively small area of dry deciduous forest in western Madagascar and are regularly encountered at Réserve Forestière de Kirindy (p114). *Length 54–58cm; weight 1.1–1.3kg.*

2

DEA/DANI-JESKE/GETTY IMAGES ©

Birds of Open Country

Madagascar's birds are unusual: many evolved in isolation and 80% of the country's species are found nowhere else in the world. Sadly, many of these are now rare or endangered and others have become extinct within the last 100 years or so.

Madagascar Bee-Eater

1 Best seen in full sunlight, loose flocks of these graceful birds forage for flying insects over open country. They nest in hollows in river banks and road cuttings. *Length 23–31cm.*

Madagascar Kingfisher

2 A flash of orange usually gives this bird away when it dives into water for small fish and tadpoles. Otherwise, it sits still for long periods and could be overlooked. It is common everywhere near fresh water. *Length 15cm.*

Madagascar Kestrel

3 Madagascar has comparatively few birds of prey but this is a common species. It is often seen hovering over grasslands near highways before swooping down to catch small animals. *Length 25–30cm.*

Madagascar Hoopoe

4 In flight this extraordinary bird shows off its stripes and looks like a huge butterfly. Its crest can be fanned but normally lies flat. It is common across the island, especially in dry deciduous forest. *Length 32cm.*

Sickle-Billed Vanga

5 This crow-sized bird lives in noisy flocks that move through forests making nasal *waa waa waa* calls, and probes for food under bark and crevices with a long, down-curved bill. It's common at Parc National d'Ankarafantsika (p108). *Length 32cm.*

Rainforest Birds

Madagascar's rainforests support the island's highest bird diversity; birdwatching in this environment can be both challenging and extremely rewarding. Long, quiet spells can be suddenly broken by a frenetic 'wave' of feeding birds composed of a dozen or more different species that will have you flipping through your field guide trying to identify them before they disappear into the foliage.

Madagascar Paradise-Flycatcher

1 Females of this large, active rainforest flycatcher are rufous with a black head, while males sport 12cm tail streamers and may be rufous, white or black, or a combination of all three. They're common at Parc National de Ranomafana (p58). *Length 18–30cm.*

Helmet Vanga

2 The helmet vanga looks like no other bird – its extraordinary, bright-blue bill is incongruously large, almost toucan-like, and thought to act as a resonator when it calls in the forest. Restricted to intact rainforests of the Masoala Peninsula (p186). *Length 29cm.*

Blue Vanga

3 The stunning vanga is unmistakable and common in a variety of forest types across the island. Vangas can be conspicuous birds that travel in pairs or small groups, often in the company of other forest birds. *Length 16cm.*

Nelicourvi Weaver

4 Most weavers are found in grasslands, but this rainforest species often associates with flocks of greenbuls while foraging in the forest. Both sexes have yellow heads but females lack the striking black mask of males. *Length 15cm.*

PAUL SOUDERS/GETTY IMAGES ©

Reptiles & Amphibians

Reptiles are usually overlooked, but chameleons are among Madagascar's most famous animals – for good reason. They have a fantastic ability to change their colours, and have eyes that swivel independently of each other on raised cones, and sticky tongues that shoot out to catch prey.

Nile Crocodile

1 Crocodiles are found in freshwater habitats, including the Pangalanes Lakes (p165), and in the cave system of Réserve Spéciale Ankarana (p150). *Length up to 5m.*

Parson's Chameleon

2 The world's largest chameleon prefers rainforests and lives in the forest canopy. Males have a massive casque (helmet-like structure) and two blunt 'horns'. *Length up to 40cm, in rare cases up to 69cm (males); females are smaller.*

Radiated Tortoise

3 Confined to dry forests in southern Madagascar, this striking tortoise is endangered due to hunting. It is the subject of an intensive conservation program and is being bred in captivity at Arboretum d'Antsokay (p82). *Length 40cm; weight 15kg.*

Pygmy Leaf Chameleon

4 This chameleon is one of the world's smallest vertebrates. It can be found on Nosy Be (p123), where it hunts among leaf litter and on low branches. *Length 28mm (males), up to 33mm (females).*

Tomato Frog

5 This bizarre frog is restricted to north-western Madagascar and endangered because of the pet trade. Females are larger and brighter than males, and both sexes exude sticky mucus when threatened by a predator. *Length 6cm (males), up to 10.5cm (females).*

OLIVIER CIRENDINI/GETTY IMAGES ©

Fish & Coral-Reef Animals

Coral reefs and marine environments are among Madagascar's most overlooked and relatively unstudied treasures. The island's southwest coast alone has the fifth-largest coral-reef system in the world. While reefs in the southwest have suffered massive damage from coral bleaching, scientists were stunned to discover on a recent survey that the reefs of the northeast coast are remarkably healthy and have the highest coral diversity in the western Indian Ocean.

Hawksbill Sea Turtle

1 These attractive coral-reef sea turtles were once abundant in the waters around Madagascar but are now critically endangered because their shells are made into colourful trinkets. *Length 1m.*

Humpback Whale

2 Whale-watching is a popular activity at the Baie d'Antongil (p186) and Île Sainte Marie (p177) when several hundred humpbacks arrive from Antarctica in June and linger with their calves until September. *Length 12–16m.*

Clown Triggerfish

3 This exceptionally colourful reef fish has a stout orange-lipped mouth adapted for crushing sea urchins and clams. When threatened they wedge themselves among rocks with their rigid fins. *Length 25–50cm.*

Bicolour Parrotfish

4 The parrotfish is a blast of fluorescent orange, blue and purple. The fish plays a major role in reef ecosystems by ingesting coral and breaking it down into sand with the special teeth in its throat. *Length 50–80cm.*

Insects & Other Invertebrates

Madagascar's forests support thousands of fascinating and unusual invertebrates. Most are inconspicuous and easily missed, but you will also encounter clouds of brilliant butterflies, huge moths and bizarre beetles unlike anything you've ever seen.

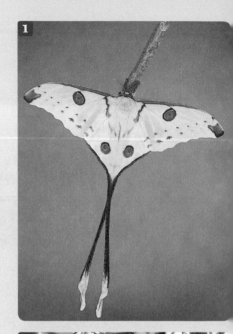

Comet Moth

1 These stunning yellow moths with long dangling tails are bigger than your hand. Their habitat is threatened but fortunately the legendary moths are being successfully bred in captivity. *Wingspan up to 22.5cm; tail length 20cm.*

Flatid Leaf Bug

2 Looking at first glance like clusters of tiny fuchsia flowers, colonies of adult leaf bugs have evolved in this way as protection against predators. Their young, known as nymphs, look like pieces of lace or lichen attached to branches. *Length 5mm.*

Giraffe-Necked Weevil

3 This bizarre little beetle with an outrageously long neck is found only on the small tree *Dichaetanthera cordifolia*. They are quite common in Parc National de Ranomafana (p58) and the Andasibe area parks (p162). 'Necks' on males are much longer than on females. *Length 2.5cm.*

Madagascar Hissing Cockroach

4 Strangely, this flightless cockroach has become a popular pet outside its native Madagascar. In the wild it lives in rotting logs, where females give birth to live young. Females are gregarious but males are solitary. When disturbed, both sexes can emit a hissing sound by forcing air through their spiracles (breathing pores) as a defence mechanism, although rival males also hiss to assert dominance. *Length 12.5cm.*

Survival Guide

Directory A–Z

Accommodation

Accommodation in Madagascar is cheap compared to Europe or North America, but not as cheap as you might perhaps expect.

Madagascar's winter months (July to September) are the busiest. It's a good idea to book ahead at this time of year, particularly in popular destinations such as Nosy Be, Île Sainte Marie or Parc National des Tsingy de Bemaraha.

Few hotels have official low-/high-season prices, although many offer discounts at quiet periods, notably during the rainy season.

Top-end places are the most heterogeneous, with some luxury resorts costing as much as €500 (Ar1.5 million) per night for a double room with full board.

Because of the depreciation of the ariary, an increasing number of hotels (even midrange) are quoting their prices in euros. You then settle in ariarys, at the day's exchange rate (some places will accept euros).

Full-board accommodation rates includes three meals a day, and half-board includes breakfast and dinner.

In late 2015 the *vignette* (tourist tax) of Ar600 to Ar3000 per night, which was included in prices, was abolished and replaced with a one-off €10 charge at the airport upon arrival in Madagascar.

Camping

Camping is possible, mostly in national parks. Facilities vary, from showers, toilets and well-equipped cooking areas, to nothing more than a cleared area of bush and a long-drop toilet.

Some national parks rent camping equipment, as do local tour agencies (often the same companies organising packages in the parks).

A few budget hotels offer tent pitches on their premises (and use of the shared bathrooms), although you will need to have your own equipment.

Homestays

In rural areas you can sometimes arrange a homestay by politely asking around a village for a place to sleep. Pay a fair fee – about Ar20,000 to Ar30,000 per couple is appropriate.

If you can, bring some rice (the main staple) too – you can generally buy it by the measure (about 300g) in markets and village shops.

Hotels & Bungalows

Hotels in Madagascar come in many guises, from simple pensions to luxury resorts.

Bungalows are stand-alone structures. They are often wooden and popular in seaside locations and scenic areas. Bungalows can be anything from very basic to plush and elegant.

Hot water is rare in budget accommodation, hit and miss in midrange places, but reliable in top-end places (and in all categories in the highlands, where winter nights are freezing). Central heating is unheard of, however, so you'll have to make do with extra blankets to keep warm.

Air-con is only really necessary in summer months (December to March); on the coast, the night sea breezes are often enough.

SLEEPING PRICE RANGES

€ less than Ar35,000 Simple room, often with shared facilities, normally with fan and mosquito net, where needed.

€€ Ar35,000 to Ar80,000 A notch above budget in decor, rooms are generally en suite, though hot water does not always work. Air-con may be available.

€€€ more than Ar80,000 All mod cons, good hotel facilities – pool, wi-fi etc. Prices quoted in euros in most upmarket establishments.

RESPONSIBLE DIVING & SNORKELLING

Consider the following tips when diving and help preserve the ecology and beauty of reefs.

➡ Don't touch living marine organisms or drag equipment across the reef. If you must hold onto the reef, only touch exposed rock or dead coral.

➡ Be conscious of your fins. Even without contact, the surge from fin strokes near the reef can damage delicate organisms.

➡ Take great care in underwater caves. Spend as little time within them as possible as your air bubbles may be caught within the roof and thereby leave organisms high and dry.

➡ Resist the temptation to collect or buy corals or shells.

➡ Do not feed fish, even if operators offer it.

All but the most basic hotels provide mosquito nets in coastal areas. They are not commonplace in Antananarivo (Tana) or the highlands however, despite the fact that mosquitoes are becoming more prevalent.

Activities

Madagascar is an excellent destination for sporting activities. Climbing, diving, hiking and canoeing/kayaking are all in plentiful supply.

Multiday hikes (three to 10 days, such as Maroantsetra to Antalaha, Ambalavao to Manakara, the Razafimaniry villages, Isalo and Makay etc) are becoming more popular and are often the highlight of a trip, but they require advance planning (for reservations and equipment to bring).

Whatever activity you embark on, pick a reliable operator, especially with high-risk activities such as diving, kitesurfing and rock climbing. Check the operator's affiliations, the instructors' qualifications and inspect your gear.

Divers, note that there is no hyperbaric chamber in Madagascar, so should you have a mishap underwater, you will have to go to Réunion to be depressurised.

Children

There are few dedicated children's facilities in Madagascar. That said, Malagasies love children and will always do their best to accommodate families.

Many hotels provide *chambres familiales* or double rooms with an extra bed (single or double) geared for use by parents and children.

Disposable nappies and infant milk formula are available in Antananarivo and other large cities, but are hard to find elsewhere.

Some midrange and top-end hotels/restaurants have high chairs and games or play areas for children. Some also have dedicated children's menus.

For more information, check out Lonely Planet's *Travel with Children*.

Customs Regulations

Travellers are allowed to leave the country with the following:

➡ 2kg of vanilla (dried)

➡ 1kg of hallmarked jewellery with receipts

➡ 1kg peppercorns

➡ 1kg coffee

Precious stones and woods must come with an export certificate. If the retailer doesn't provide it to you, enquire at the customs desk at the airport.

For a full list of regulations, check **Douanes Malgaches** (Malagasy Customs; www. douanes.gov.mg).

Electricity

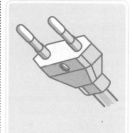

220V/50Hz

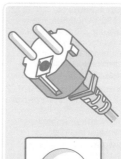

220V/50Hz

FAIR TRADE TOURISM

In 2014 Madagascar got its first six hotels certified under the **Fair Trade Tourism** (www.fairtrade.travel) label. Accredited hotels must:

➡ Comply with all existing legislation (including labour and tax requirements) and follow governance best practice (training for staff, HIV awareness etc)

➡ Respect the local natural and cultural heritage

➡ Make meaningful community engagement

➡ Monitor their environmental impact (renewable energy, carbon and water footprint etc)

The certified hotels are: Salary Bay (p89), Mantasoa Lodge, on the shores of Lac Mantasoa; Tsara Camp (p72); Bush House (p168); Hôtel Le Paradisier (p88) and Iharana Bush Camp (p151).

Embassies & Consulates

Australian High Commission (☏+230 202 0160; www.mauritius.embassy.gov. au; Mauritius) The Australian High Commission in Mauritius has consular responsibility for Madagascar.

Canadian Consulate (☏020 22 397 37; consulat.canada@ gmail.com; Immeuble Fitaratra, Ankorondrano) Consulate under the responsibility of the High Commission of Canada in Pretoria, South Africa.

French Embassy (☏020 22 398 98; www.ambafrance-mada.org; 3 Rue Jean Jaurès, Ambatomena) There are also representatives in Diego Suarez (Antsiranana), Majunga (Mahajanga) and Tamatave (Toamasina).

German Embassy (☏020 22 238 02; www.antananarivo.diplo. de; 101 Rue Pasteur Rabeony, Ambodiroatra) German representation in Madagascar.

Netherlands Consulate (☏020 23 682 31; nl.mg@ moov.mg; Villa Christina No 88, Lotissement Bonnet, Ivandry) Consulate under the responsibility of the Dutch Embassy in Dar Es Salaam, Tanzania.

South African Embassy (☏020 22 433 50; antana narivo.consular@dirco.gov. za; Rue Ravoninahitriniarivo, Ankorondrano) South African representation in Madagascar.

UK Embassy (☏020 22 330 53; http://ukinmadagascar.fco. gov.uk; 9th fl, Tour Zital, Rue Ravoninahitriniarivo, Akorondrano) The embassy reopened in 2013 after an eight-year hiatus.

US Embassy (☏020 23 480 00; www.antananarivo.us embassy.gov; Point Liberty, Andranoro, Antehiroka) Located about 15km north of Antananarivo, on the road to Ivato airport.

Food

Eating in Madagascar is a treat: food is generally good and excellent value.

The majority of restaurants in Madagascar fall in the midrange category and standards are often excellent.

Meal times are as follows:

➡ Breakfast 6am to 9am

➡ Lunch 11.30am to 2.30pm

➡ Dinner 6.30pm to 9.30pm

For more information about the culinary delights Madagascar has in store, see p210.

Gay & Lesbian Travellers

Homosexuality is legal in Madagascar, but not openly practised. The age of consent is 21.

Overt displays of affection (whether the couple is of the same or opposite sex) are considered to be culturally inappropriate.

Insurance

A travel-insurance policy to cover theft, loss and medical problems is essential. Some policies specifically exclude dangerous activities, which can include diving, motorcycling or even hiking.

Check that the policy covers an emergency flight home. This is an important consideration for Madagascar, given the cost of air tickets to most destinations.

Worldwide travel insurance is available at www.lonely planet.com/travel-insurance. You can buy, extend and claim online anytime – even if you're already on the road.

Internet Access

Virtually every hotel (even budget ones) now offers complimentary wi-fi, even if only in the reception area. The same is true for midrange and top-end restaurants. The connection is generally good enough for emails, but can struggle with more demanding applications such as Skype/FaceTime or downloads.

Internet cafes can be found in all major towns and cities. Connection speeds vary from pretty good to woefully slow. Prices range from Ar30 to Ar50 per minute.

If you have a smartphone, an excellent alternative is to buy a local SIM card and a 3G package: Ar25,000 will buy you 1GB of data. The mobile coverage is excellent, so you should be connected reliably, except in very remote areas.

Legal Matters

Malagasy authorities take sex tourism very seriously – offenders risk five to 10 years in jail and forced labour. Sentences are particularly severe when minors are affected.

The use and possession of marijuana and other recreational drugs is illegal in Madagascar, including the stimulant *khat* (even though the latter is widely and openly consumed in the north).

If you are arrested, ask to see a representative of your country.

Maps

Regional maps and street maps of provincial capitals are produced by Foiben Taosarintanin'i Madagasikara (FTM). FTM maps can be fairly dated but are generally accurate, although they can be hard to find (normally in bookshops for around Ar20,000).

Carambole publishes detailed maps of Antananarivo, which are widely available at bookshops and cost about Ar15,000. Topographical maps are hard to find in Madagascar, so buy one before you leave home.

Money

Madagascar changed its currency from the Malagasy franc (FMG) to the ariary (Ar) in 2005. But despite having had several years to get used to the new currency, many Malagasies still count in FMG (one ariary is worth five FMG), so it is essential you clarify which currency a price is being quoted in, particularly in rural areas.

Inflation is high in Madagascar, and the denominations are struggling to keep up. The biggest bank note currently available is Ar10,000, but with a main course at a restaurant costing Ar10,000 to Ar15,000, many agree it won't be long until larger denominations are printed.

For travellers it means that changing just €300 will produce a wad some 90 notes thick...

Some hotels (often at the higher end of the range) will accept payments in foreign currency.

ATMs

➡ You'll find ATMs in all major towns and cities.

➡ Withdrawals from ATMs are capped at Ar300,000.

➡ All ATMs accept Visa.

➡ BNI Madagascar and Société Générale (BFV-SG) ATMs also accept MasterCard.

Credit Cards

Visa credit cards are accepted at some upmarket hotels and shops, Air Madagascar and a number of travel agencies.

MasterCard can be used at some ATMs, but only a small number of outfits will accept payments with it.

Some places levy a commission of about 5% to 8% for credit-card payments.

Visa and MasterCard can be used at most banks to obtain cash advances of up to Ar10 million; commission rates go as high as 5%, depending on the bank.

Moneychangers

The main banks:

➡ Bank of Africa (BOA)

➡ BNI Madagascar

➡ Banky Fampandrosoana'ny Varotra-Société Générale (BFV-SG)

➡ Banque Malgache de l'Océan Indien (BMOI)

All banks will readily exchange euros; US dollars are generally accepted, too. Other currencies will be harder to exchange outside major cities.

Most banks will refuse €100 or US$100 notes (for fear of counterfeit), so bring small denominations only. The opposite is true on the black market.

Upmarket hotels often have currency-exchange facilities, but check how competitive their rates are.

The bureaux de change at Ivato airport will change Malagasy currency back into euros or dollars, but require a minimum of €50.

Tipping

The following is just a guide, especially when it comes to tipping guides (be they guides in national parks or your driver), where it all comes down to how pleased you are with their services. To put things in perspective, the minimum wage (for those lucky enough to be employed) is Ar133,000 a

---

EATING PRICE RANGES

€ less than Ar10,000 Food stalls, *hotelys* or *gargottes* (informal Malagasy eateries). Rice dishes are the staple, and there is also a huge variety of fritters.

€€ Ar10,000 to Ar17,000 Restaurants, some of which are very fancy. A small increase in price, but a big jump in quality: zebu steaks, grilled seafood and vegies, which are often delicious.

€€€ more than Ar17,000 Expect haute cuisine, elaborate presentation, decadent wine or rum selections and elegant surroundings.

month. A teacher would earn about Ar200,000 a month.

Taxis, bars	Not expected
Porters	Small note (Ar200 or Ar500)
Restaurants	5% of the bill
National park/local guides	10% of the fee
Driver guide	Ar5000 to Ar20,000 a day

Travellers Cheques

All banks in Antananarivo exchange travellers cheques. Outside of the capital, the BFV-SG is your best bet.

As with cash, prefer euros and stick to small denominations (banks need the approval of their headquarters to exchange denominations of €100 or more).

Opening Hours

Businesses (Antananarivo) 8am to 4pm Monday to Friday

Businesses (rest of the country) 7.30am to 11.30am and 2pm to 4.30pm Monday to Friday

Restaurants 11.30am to 2.30pm (lunch) and 6.30pm to 9.30pm (dinner)

Bars 5pm to 11pm

Shops 9am to noon and 2.30pm to 6pm Monday to Friday, 9am to noon Saturday

Post

There are post offices located in every town and city. The postal service is slow, but generally OK for postcards and letters. Parcels, however, seem to be regularly stolen and Malagasies never send valuables through the post. Instead, use an international courier such as **DHL** (☏020 22 428 39; www.dhl.com), which has offices in Tana, Diego Suarez, Antsirabe and Tamatave.

The cost for a postcard is Ar1600 to Europe and Ar1900 to North America or Australia, and for a letter it's Ar2700 to Europe and Ar2900 to North America or Australia.

Public Holidays

Accommodation and flights can be harder to find during French school holidays, when residents from neighbouring French territories Mayotte and Réunion travel in the region. To find out when these holidays are, visit www.ac-reunion.fr/outils/infos-pratiques/calendrier-scolaire.html.

Government offices and private companies close on the following public holidays. Banks are generally also closed the afternoon before a public holiday.

New Year's Day 1 January

Insurrection Day 29 March; celebrates the rebellion against the French in 1947

Easter Monday March/April

Labour Day 1 May

Ascension Thursday May/June; occurs 40 days after Easter

Pentecost Monday May/June; occurs 51 days after Easter

National Day 26 June; Independence Day

Assumption 15 August

All Saints' Day 1 November

Christmas Day 25 December

Safe Travel

Crime

Insecurity has increased in Antananarivo since the 2009 coup, so always travel by taxi at night and watch out for pickpockets, especially around Ave de l'Indépendance.

Batterie Beach near Tuléar is also to be avoided following a series of attacks on foreigners.

Natural Disasters

Cyclone season runs from December to March. The east coast is the most affected but cyclones can also hit the west coast. Heed local warnings and seek advice at the time for transport and activities.

Robbery

Vehicles travelling at night have been subject to attacks over the past few years. *Taxis-brousses* are now therefore required to travel in convoy at night, but private vehicles should avoid being on the road after dark (many drivers will, in fact, refuse to drive at night).

The area between Ihosy and Ambovombe should also be avoided because of banditry.

Telephone

The country code for Madagascar is ☏+261. Phone numbers have 10 digits.

Landline numbers start with ☏020; mobile numbers start with☏ 032, 033 or 034.

MADAGASCAR'S CULTURAL CALENDAR

Alahamady Be (March) The low-key Malagasy New Year.

Santabary (April/May) The first rice harvest.

Fisemana (June) A ritual purification ceremony of the Antakàrana people.

Sambatra (June to December) Circumcision festivals held by most tribes between June and September, and in November and December in the southwest.

Famadihana (July to September) The 'turning of the bones'.

To call out of Madagascar, dial 🔲+00 before the country code.

If you don't have a mobile phone, *télécartes* (phone cards) are sold at post offices and in some shops. Phone services (including fax) are offered at some post offices, upmarket hotels and internet cafes.

Mobile Phones

Mobile phone coverage is excellent in Madagascar. The main networks are **Telma** (www.telma.mg), which is government owned, **Airtel** (www.africa.airtel.com/madagascar) and **Orange** (www.orange.mg). Some remote areas only have coverage from one network.

SIM cards are very cheap (Ar500 to Ar2000) and can be bought from the mobile networks' offices.

You can buy credit at literally every street corner in towns and cities and in grocery shops in the form of electronic credit or scratch cards (Ar1000 to Ar100,000).

A national/international SMS costs around Ar120/340. National calls cost around Ar720 per minute.

International calls from mobile phones cost Ar870 to Ar4500 per minute.

Tourist Information

Madagascar's **tourist offices** (www.madagascar-tourisme.com) range from useless to incredibly helpful. They will generally be able to provide listings of hotels and restaurants in the area and, in the best cases, help you organise excursions or find a guide.

MNP (www.parcs-madagascar.com) offices are generally excellent (with a couple of exceptions) when it comes to logistics and practical advice, but they often have little in the way of maps or literature.

Travellers with Disabilities

Madagascar has few facilities for travellers with disabilities. This, combined with a weak infrastructure in many areas of the country, may make travel here difficult.

Wheelchair users will struggle with the lack of surfaced paths; visually impaired travellers should be especially careful of open drains and irregular pavements.

Public transport is very crowded and unable to accommodate a wheelchair unless it is folded up. Private vehicle rental with a driver is commonplace, however, and would offer a good alternative. Make sure you talk through any special requirements with the agency at the time of booking.

In Antananarivo and most of the provincial capitals there are hotels with either elevators or accommodation on the ground floor. While most bungalow accommodation – a common type of lodging in Madagascar – is generally on the ground floor, there are often steps up to the entrance, and inner doorways can be too narrow for a wheel-chair. Few bathrooms are large enough to manoeuvre a wheelchair in, and almost none have any sort of handles or holds.

The good news, however, is that one organisation in France has been working to develop accessible tourism in Madagascar and plans to offer a fully accessible circuit along the RN7 from 2016. All the hotels on the circuit have built dedicated accessible bungalows or rooms, travel will be in a specially equipped vehicle and circuits in national parks will be offered in *Joëlette* (a one-wheeled, all-terrain chair held by two people). Contact **Dominique Dumas** (🔲+33 6 63 76 57 91 or +33 4 73 90 88 69, d.dum2@wanadoo.fr) for more information.

Organisations that provide information on world travel for the mobility impaired include the following:

➡ **Independent Traveler** (www.independenttraveler.com)

➡ **Mobility International USA** (www.miusa.org)

➡ **Society for Accessible Travel & Hospitality** (www.sath.org)

Visas

All visitors must have a visa to enter Madagascar. Travellers will need to provide a return plane ticket, have a passport valid for at least six months after the intended date of return, and one free page in the passport for the visa stamps.

Visas of up to 90 days can be purchased at the airport upon arrival.

➡ 30-day visas cost Ar60,000 (free 30-day visas were abolished in late 2015)

➡ 60-day visas cost Ar100,000

➡ 90-day visas cost Ar140,000

Longer or different types of visas must be arranged before travel – note that applications can be long.

ETHICAL SHOPPING

Madagascar is a lovely destination for shopping. The arts and crafts are varied, unusual and often of high quality, making for wonderful souvenirs and gifts. If possible, try to buy directly from the producer, or from a local association, to ensure your money goes where it's most needed.

The purchase of some souvenirs, however, should be weighed carefully. Many gemstones and gold, for instance, are illegally mined, in dreadful health and safety conditions, often by children, and with no environmental safeguards, so try to buy from a well-established business that can guarantee the provenance of the minerals and obtain an export certificate.

The same note of caution goes for souvenirs made of precious hardwoods such as palisander, rosewood and ebony. All three species are seriously threatened by large-scale deforestation and illegal logging and are listed by CITES (the Convention on International Trade in Endangered Species of Wild Fauna and Flora). It's not the few sculptures and carvings in souvenir shops that are driving deforestation (and these activities do support livelihoods), but they are part of the big picture. Whatever you choose to do, you will need an export certificate.

Always check with your nearest representation on the latest conditions and fees.

Volunteering

More people are showing interest in volunteering for community-enhancement and scientific-research projects in Madagascar. The following organisations regularly take on volunteers, although most placements require payment.

Access Madagascar Initiative (☎+44 20 8699 1301; www.accessmadagascar.org) This British charity organises placements in villages in central Madagascar. Most placements involve teaching of some kind – languages or skills – but activities are varied, including tree planting, working on the local radio program, running the English club etc. Individuals as well as families are welcome. Placements cost £695/1505 for three/12 weeks.

Akany Avoko (☎034 22 441 58; www.akanyavoko.com) An Antananarivo-based children's home that cares for around 120 orphans, street kids and youngsters with little or no family support. Akany Avoko has been around for 50 years and is sustained by charitable donations and income-generating projects.

It welcomes volunteers, whether they have half a day or a year to spare. Inexpensive accommodation can be provided.

Azafady (☎+44 20 8960 6629; www.madagascar.co.uk) Based in the Anosy region in southeastern Madagascar, British charity Azafady works on poverty alleviation and environmental conservation through sustainable development initiatives. Volunteering opportunities include conservation fieldwork, English teaching, and community and construction work. The minimum donation required for a 10-week placement is £1995.

Blue Ventures (☎+44 20 7697 8598; www.blueventures.org) Based in London, with a field site in Andavadoaka, this hugely impressive organisation coordinates teams of volunteer divers to work with local NGOs and biologists in marine-conservation programs that are spreading throughout the length of the reef, helping staunch its decline. Volunteering stints range from three to 12 weeks (£1900 to £4075) and include PADI scuba-diving certification.

Volunteering must be organised in advance through the London office.

Hope for Madagascar (www.hopeformadagascar.org) Poverty alleviation is the remit

of this US charity, which runs projects as diverse as building schools, organising cultural exchanges between Malagasy schools from different parts of the country and providing clean water in rural villages. It welcomes volunteers to teach English and art in local schools.

Peace Corps (www.peacecorps.gov) The US government's volunteering program (whose mission is 'to promote world peace and friendship') is very active in Madagascar, where it has around 140 members. Placements are usually two years and volunteers usually end up speaking fluent Malagasy by the end of their stint. The scheme is open to American nationals over 18.

Women Travellers

Most women do not feel threatened or insecure in any way when travelling in Madagascar. The most you can expect is some mild curiosity about your situation, especially if you are single and/or don't have children (Malagasy women marry and have children young).

A limited selection of tampons is available in Antananarivo and some of the larger towns, but it's best to bring your own supply.

Transport

GETTING THERE & AWAY

Entering Madagascar

If you are coming from a yellow-fever-infected country, you will be asked for a yellow fever vaccination certificate.

Air

International flights come into **Ivato airport** (www. antananarivoairport.com), 20km north of Antananarivo (Tana). The airports in Majunga (Mahajanga), Diego Suarez (Antsiranana) and Tamatave (Toamasina) also handle flights from Réunion, Mauritius and the Comoros.

Air Austral (☑020 22 303 31; www.air-austral.com; 23 Ave de l'Indépendance – Analakely, Antananarivo) Airline serving France and Indian Ocean islands, including Madagascar, Réunion and Mauritius.

Air France (☑020 23 230 23; www.airfrance.com; Tour Zital, Route des Hydrocarbures, Ankorondrano) French carrier with five flights a week between Paris and Antananarivo.

Air Madagascar (☑020 22 222 22; www.airmadagascar. com; 31 Ave de l'Indépendance, Antananarivo) The embattled national carrier has direct flights from France, South Africa, Kenya, Thailand, Guangzhou (China) and neighbouring Indian Ocean islands. The airline has had financial difficulties for some years, however, and is plagued by delays and cancellations.

Air Mauritius (www.air mauritius.com) Flies between Mauritius and Tana four times a week.

Corsair (☑020 22 633 36; www.corsair.fr; Gare Soarano, 1 Ave de l'Indépendance – Analakely, Antananarivo) Up to three flights a week between Paris and Antananarivo.

Kenya Airways (www. kenya-airways.com) Two flights a day between Nairobi and Tana.

South African Airways (www.flysaa.com) Daily flights between Johannesburg and Tana. The airline was also due to start direct flights between Johannesburg and Nosy Be at the time of writing.

Tickets

Because there isn't much competition to fly to Madagascar, airfares can be expensive.

Expect to pay €800 to €1500 for a return ticket from Europe (where there are more options), and at least €1500 from North America or Australia.

Sea

Private Yacht

Yachts regularly sail to Madagascar to/from South Africa, Mozambique, Mayotte, Réunion and Mauritius,

---

CLIMATE CHANGE & TRAVEL

Every form of transport that relies on carbon-based fuel generates CO_2, the main cause of human-induced climate change. Modern travel is dependent on aeroplanes, which might use less fuel per kilometre per person than most cars but travel much greater distances. The altitude at which aircraft emit gases (including CO_2) and particles also contributes to their climate change impact. Many websites offer 'carbon calculators' that allow people to estimate the carbon emissions generated by their journey and, for those who wish to do so, to offset the impact of the greenhouse gases emitted with contributions to portfolios of climate-friendly initiatives throughout the world. Lonely Planet offsets the carbon footprint of all staff and author travel.

Major Domestic Air Routes

N

0   200 km
0   100 miles

Diego Suarez
(Antsiranana)

€166
25 min

€166
45 min

Nosy Be

Sambava

*Mozambique
Channel*

€242
1½ hr

€242
2 hr

Antalaha

Majunga
(Mahajanga)

€242
2 hr

Maroantsetra

€242
1¼ hr

€200
1½ hr

€242
1 hr

Ambodifotatra

€242
1 hr

€242
1 hr

Tamatave
(Toamasina)

ANTANANARIVO

€200
1 hr

€242
1 hr

Morondava

€242
1¼ hr

€242
1¾ hr

€242
1 hr

*INDIAN
OCEAN*

Tuléar
(Toliara)

€200
1 hr

Fort Dauphin
(Taolagnaro)

and travellers may be able to join the crossing as crew members. Your best options to find a boat are online forums, word of mouth and asking around at ports (Nosy Be in particular).

Tours

The following European, American and Australian tour operators offer all-inclusive trips to Madagascar, whether tailor-made or as part of a group.

Adventure Associates (www.adventureassociates. com; Australia) Runs two trips a year to Madagascar, some of them led by famous wildlife TV presenter Richard Morecroft.

Baobab Travel (www.baobab. nl; Netherlands) Offers a south and east circuit.

Comptoir de Madagascar (www.comptoirdemadagascar. com; France) Numerous circuits offered, from general discovery to activity-led (mountain biking) and beach-based (Nosy Be, Île Sainte Marie etc).

Cortez Travel & Expeditions (www.air-mad.com; USA) Well established operator with an agency in the USA and one in Madagascar. Offers organised tours as well as customised trips.

Madagaskar Travel (www. madagaskar-travel.de; Germany) General and specialist fauna-and-flora itineraries.

Priori (www.priori.ch; Madagascar) Cultural and wildlife tours, run by a Swiss national who is a long-time Madagascar resident.

Rainbow Tours (www.rainbowtours.co.uk; UK) Specialist and general-interest guided trips to Madagascar; highly recommended by travellers.

Reef & Rainforest Tours (www.reefandrainforest.co.uk; UK) Focuses on top-end wildlife holidays.

Terre Voyages (www. terre-voyages.com; France) A wide range of tours to Madagascar.

Wildlife Worldwide (www. wildlifeworldwide.com; UK) Wildlife-viewing tours.

Zingg Event Travel (www. zinggsafaris.com; Switzerland) Individual and group circuits.

GETTING AROUND

Air

Flying within Madagascar can be a huge time saver, considering the distances and state of the roads. Unfortunately most domestic routes are between Tana and the provinces, with few direct routes between provinces. Internal flights are also notoriously unreliable; you are therefore strongly advised to leave plenty of time if you need to catch an onward flight.

Airlines in Madagascar

Air Madagascar (☎020 22 222 22; www.airmadagascar. com; 31 Ave de l'Indépendance) is the main airline to provide domestic flights. Cancellations and delays are unamusingly frequent.

Tickets are expensive (around €200 for a one-way ticket), but generally exchangeable.

You can pay for tickets by credit card or in ariary, euros or US dollars at the head office in Antananarivo and Air Madagascar offices in larger towns. Smaller offices may only accept ariary or euros, however.

Certain routes, such as Morondava–Tuléar (Toliara) during the high season (May to September) and all flights to/from Sambava during the vanilla season (June to October), are often fully booked months in advance.

A new airline, **Madagasikara Airways** (www.madagasikaraairways.com), started flights in late 2015 between Antananarivo, Tamatave (Toamasina) and Île Sainte Marie.

Bicycle

A mountain bike is normally essential if cycling in Madagascar. Inner tubes and other basic parts are sometimes available in larger towns.

The terrain varies from very sandy to muddy or rough and rocky.

It's usually no problem to transport your bicycle on *taxis-brousses* or trains.

You'll find mountain bikes for hire (around Ar20,000 per day) in most large towns and tourist hot spots such as Île Sainte Marie (Nosy Boraha) and Nosy Be.

Boat

Cargo Boat

In parts of Madagascar, notably the northeast and southwest coasts and Canal des Pangalanes, cargo boats (sometimes called *boutres*)

AIR PENNY SAVER

Domestic flights are about 30% cheaper when bought in Madagascar compared to when purchased abroad. If your itinerary is flexible, this is a great way to save money. But bear in mind that flights on popular routes are booked far in advance and that it is difficult to get tickets at short notice.

Air Madagascar also offers a 50% discount on domestic flights to travellers who flew with the airline to Madagascar. The discount doesn't apply to taxes, so the final saving is about 30% of the final fare; still, not to be sniffed at.

are the primary means of transport. Cargo boats have no schedules and leave with the tides. There are no amenities, so passengers travel on deck, where they are exposed to the elements.

Capsizing occurs regularly, so don't get in if the seas are rough, or if the boat is overcrowded. Some precautions to keep in mind:

➡ Always check the forecast and ask local advice before setting off.

➡ Make sure there are life jackets on board.

➡ Bring plenty of water (and food) and sun protection (hat and cream).

➡ Don't travel at sea during the cyclone season between January and March.

Pirogue

Engineless pirogues or *lakanas* (dugout canoes), whether on rivers or the sea, are the primary means of local transport where roads disappear.

Pirogues can easily be hired, along with a boatman, but bear in mind that the ride can be quite rough.

Car & Motorcycle

Due to the often-difficult driving conditions, most rental agencies make hiring a driver compulsory with their vehicles.

Of Madagascar's approximately 50,000km of roads,

less than 20% are sealed, and many of those are riddled with potholes the size of an elephant. Routes in many areas are impassable or very difficult during the rainy season.

The designation *route nationale* (RN) is sadly no guarantee of quality.

Driving in Madagascar is on the right-hand side.

Police checkpoints are frequent (mind the traffic spikes on the ground) – always slow down and make sure you have your passport and the vehicle's documents handy.

If you see a zebu on the road, slow right down as it can panic; also, there may be another 20 in the bushes that haven't yet crossed.

Car Hire

If you insist on driving yourself, note the following rules:

➡ You must have an International Driving Licence.

➡ You must be age 23 or over and have had your licence for at least a year.

➡ Wearing a seatbelt is mandatory.

You'll find petrol stations of some kind in all cities and towns. Fuel shortages are frequent, even in Tana, so stock up. For longer trips and travel in remote areas, take extra fuel with you.

Spare parts and repairs of varying quality are available in most towns. Make sure to check the spare tyre (and

jack) of any car you rent before setting out.

Charter Taxi

An alternative to hiring a car and driver (difficult in areas where there is little tourism) is chartering a taxi or a *taxi-brousse*, whether for one or several days. Here are some tips to make the best of it:

➡ Enquire at the *taxi-brousse* stand, or ask your hotel for the going rate for your journey.

➡ Be sure to clarify such things as petrol and waiting time.

➡ Check that the vehicle is in decent shape before departing.

➡ For longer, multiday journeys, check that the driver has the vehicle's documents and a special charter permit (indicated by a diagonal green stripe).

➡ Prepare a contract that you and the driver will sign stipulating insurance issues, the agreed-upon fee (including whether or not petrol is included) and your itinerary.

Motorcycle

Motorcycles can be hired by the halfday or full day at various places in Madagascar, including Tuléar, Nosy Be and Île Sainte Marie.

Chinese motorbikes are increasingly replacing the well-known Japanese brands.

Wearing a helmet is compulsory; it should be provided in the rental.

Hitching

Hitching is never entirely safe in any country in the world, and we don't recommend it. Travellers who do decide to hitch should understand that they are taking a small but potentially serious risk. People who do choose to hitch will be safer if they travel in pairs and let someone know where they are planning to go.

ROAD SOLIDARITY

Public transport options are few and far between in remote areas – and sometimes nonexistent during the six months of the rainy season. If you've hired a 4WD to travel through remote areas, you'll see many locals hitching for a lift to the next town or village – you (and the driver) may be keen to help out, but some car-hire companies forbid drivers from accepting hitchhikers because of security concerns. Note, too, that villagers reuse water bottles to store chutneys and juices and will often ask whether you have any spare (to the cry of 'Eau Vive! Eau Vive!'), so don't throw them away.

CAR & DRIVER Q&A

In Madagascar the road-transport system is such that most rental cars come with a mandatory driver, making the choice of both a critical decision in your travel planning. Here are the key issues to consider.

Do I Need a 4WD?

It depends on your route. If you're sticking to the RN7 between Tana and Tuléar (Toliara), you don't need a 4WD. Two-wheel-drive vehicles are cheaper to rent and run, so this is an important cost consideration. Discuss your itinerary with the car-hire company.

How Do I Find a Good Driver?

Go through an agency (p263), your hotel or a word-of-mouth recommendation. Either way, it is essential you shop around. Talk to the driver ahead of time. Make sure you speak a common language and that the driver has experience in your region. If you're not hiring through a reputable agency, take a look at the car, particularly if you are going on a long journey. See how well the driver takes care of it. If you are out of the country, ask him to send you pictures.

How Much Does a Car and Driver Cost?

The car and driver are one package (this includes the driver's food and board allowance). Fuel is generally extra, although not always. Prices for a car are typically Ar100,000 to Ar150,000 per day. Prices for a 4WD are Ar150,000 to Ar250,000 per day. Some drivers will charge by the road surface – dirt or sealed – regardless of the car. Prices also decrease with long-term rentals of 10 days or so. This is negotiable, but a 10-day 4WD rental typically ranges from Ar130,000 to Ar200,000 per day. Also, the renter is responsible for paying to return the vehicle to where it began, which involves both a daily rental fee plus fuel. Finally, make sure you clarify whether or not extras, such as toll roads and ferry crossings, are included as they can add up quickly.

How Can I Pay?

If you go through an agency, you may be able to pay by card or bank transfer. Otherwise you'll have to go through Western Union or pay cash. Whatever method you opt for, it's customary to pay 30% to 50% at booking, and the rest at the end of the trip.

Traffic between towns and cities is thin and most passing vehicles are likely to be *taxis-brousses* or trucks, which are often full. If you do find a ride, you will likely have to pay the equivalent of the *taxi-brousse* fare.

Along well-travelled routes, or around popular tourist destinations, you can sometimes find lifts with privately rented 4WDs.

Local Transport

Charette

In rural parts of Madagascar, the *charette*, a wooden cart drawn by a pair of zebu cattle, is the most common form of transport. Fares are entirely negotiable.

Pousse-Pousse & Cyclo-Pousse

The colourful pousse-pousse (rickshaw) is a popular way to get around in some cities. Fares vary between Ar500 and Ar2000 for a ride, depending on distance. When it's raining and at night, prices increase. Some travellers may feel uncomfortable being towed around by someone in this fashion, but remember that this is the driver's living, and your patronage will be most welcome to them.

Another variation of the pousse-pousse is the cyclo-pousse, in which the cab is attached to a bicycle. They're quicker than pousse-pousse, so fares tend to be slightly more expensive.

Taxi-Brousse

The good news is that *taxis-brousses* are cheap and go everywhere. The bad news is that they are slow, uncomfortable, erratic and sometimes unsafe.

Despite the general appearance of anarchy, the *taxi-brousse* system is actually relatively well organised. Drivers and vehicles belong to transport companies called *coopératives* (cooperatives). *Coopératives* generally have a booth or an agent at the *taxi-brousse* station (called *gare routière* or *parcage*), where you can book your ticket.

TAXI-BROUSSE GLOSSARY

The term *taxi-brousse* (literally 'bush taxi') is used generically in Madagascar to refer to any vehicle providing public transport. When you buy your *taxi-brousse* ticket, therefore, you could be about to climb into anything from a pick-up truck to a rumbling juggernaut with entire suites of furniture tied to its roof.

The most common guise of the *taxi-brousse* is the 14-seater Japanese minibus (Mazda especially). On longer routes (eg Tana–Morondava or Tana–Tuléar), Mercedes Sprinter minibuses are increasingly popular: they seat 18 people and are the most spacious and comfortable of the lot (comparable to a low-cost European airline).

For shorter journeys (eg Diego Suarez to Joffreville) and in rural areas, ancient Peugeot 504s or 505s are the go. They are smaller and therefore fill quicker and also tend to fill more than their theoretical number of seats (three at the front and four or five at the back).

A *bâché* is a small, converted pick-up truck, which usually has some sort of covering over the back and benches down each side. *Bâchés* are used on shorter, rural routes and are hideously uncomfortable.

The *camion-brousse* is a huge 4WD army-style truck, fitted with a bench or seats down each side, although the majority of passengers wind up sitting on the floor, on top of whatever supplies the truck is carrying. They are used for particularly long or rough journeys. Small Tata trucks now ply long-distance off-road journeys such as Tana–Fort Dauphin – they're more comfortable than the army trucks but agonisingly slow.

Although the going can be slow, *taxis-brousses* stop regularly for toilet breaks, leg stretching and meals (at *hotelys* along the road).

There are national and regional services (called *ligne nationale* and *ligne régionale*). They can cover the same route, the difference being that on national services the *taxis-brousses* go from A to B without stopping and only squeeze three people to a row. On regional services, people hop on and off along the way, and there are four people per row, so tickets are cheaper. Make sure you stipulate which service you'd like when booking your ticket.

SEATS & LUGGAGE

➡ Most *taxis-brousses*, notably the Mercedes Sprinter minibuses used for long journeys, stick to the number of seats in the vehicle. This is less true of *bâchés* and *camions-brousses*.

➡ The two front seats beside the driver are usually the most spacious and most sought after. They are, however, the most dangerous in the event of an accident since there are no seatbelts.

➡ Seats at the back of the Mazda minibuses will be very uncomfortable for anyone taller than 1.65m and downright impossible for anyone taller than 1.85m (but they'll be fine in the much more spacious Sprinter vehicles).

➡ You can buy more than one seat.

➡ Specific seats can be booked, but you'll have to book at least the day before at the *taxi-brousse* station.

➡ Luggage goes on the roof under a tarpaulin and is tightly roped in.

➡ *Taxis-brousses* leave when full, which can take an hour or a day. If you'd like to speed up the process, buy the remaining seats.

➡ The choice of a *taxi-brousse* will often come down to joining the next vehicle to leave, which will be packed to the roof, or holding out for a decent seat in a later *taxi-brousse*.

COSTS

➡ Fares for all trips are set by the government and are based on distance, duration and route conditions. Ask to see the list of official fares: it is generally displayed in cooperative booths.

➡ *Never* buy your ticket from a tout – always get it from the cooperative booth at the *taxi-brousse* station, or from the driver if in doubt. In any case, get a receipt.

➡ Prices are the same for locals and foreigners. However, fares can vary between vehicle types and the service (regional/national).

➡ Children under five travel free (but must sit on a parent's lap).

SAFETY

Japanese and German minibus *taxis-brousses* are generally in pretty good condition (which can't be said of the ancient Peugeots or *bâchés* plying rural areas), but the one thing to watch out for is smooth tyres. General safety advice is not to travel after dark, but on longer routes it simply can't be helped. Note, however, that *taxis-brousses* are required to travel in convoys at night.

Tuk-Tuks

The ubiquitous yellow tuk-tuks (motorised rickshaws) are starting to overcome pousse-pousse in popularity. They fit three people in the cab and generally work on a flat-fare basis (Ar500 to Ar1000). You can charter them for longer journeys (to go to the airport or the port for instance).

Tours

Madagascar's many tour operators can organise anything from a three-week discovery trip to more specialist tours such as mountain-bike excursions, walking tours, wildlife-viewing trips, and cultural and historic tours. All have English-speaking guides and/or drivers.

Following is a nonexhaustive list of reliable companies that can arrange excursions throughout Madagascar. They can all arrange a car and driver too, if you want to organise your itinerary yourself.

Asisten Travel (☎020 22 577 55; www.asisten-travel. com) Excellent Malagasy-owned and run travel agency offering high-end, tailor-made trips to Madagascar. All staff and guides are fluent in English.

Boogie Pilgrim (☎020 22 248 47; www.boogiepilgrim-madagascar.com; Tana Water Front, Bâtiment Trio Property, Ambodivona; ☺8am-noon & 1-5pm Mon-Fri) Adventurous ecotours and camps in several places in Madagascar, including Parc National d'Andringitra and Canal des Pangalanes. English and German speaking.

Espace Mada (☎034 05 828 45; www.madagascar-circuits. com) Vehicles, guides and 4WD rental. Specialist for Tsiribihina River and Parc National des Tsingy de Bemaraha trips.

Mad Cameleon (☎020 22 630 86; www.madcameleon. com) Reliable operator offering anything from classic itineraries to more offbeat options such as combined sailing and hiking trips in the north, multiday hikes and activity-led tours.

Madamax (☎020 22 351 01; www.madamax.com) Specialist in adventure-packed holidays; rock-climbing and river trips are its forte.

Malagasy Tours (☎020 22 356 07; www.malagasy-tours. com) A reliable, upmarket operator offering tours in all areas of the country. It is particularly well known for its hikes.

Mikaia Rasolofoma-nana (☎034 02 693 27; mikaiasamoel@gmail.com) A small Malagasy operator offering good vehicles and excellent driver-guides, including English-speaking ones. Great value and reliable.

Ortour (☎032 07 704 64; www.ortour.com) All manner of trips, including excellent hiking options. All tours offered as midrange or top end.

Ramartour (☎020 22 487 23; www.ramartour. com) Malagasy-Dutch travel agency offering classic circuits across Madagascar as well as homestays and day trips around Antananarivo.

Tany Mena Tours (☎020 22 326 27; www.tanymenatours. com) This agency specialises in sustainable tourism. As well as taking in the country's main sights, all circuits have an emphasis on cultural experiences, with village visits and specialised Malagasy guides.

Za Tours (☎020 22 424 22; www.zatours-madagascar.com) Well-regarded English-speaking tour company offering general interest as well as birdwatching tours.

Train

The Malagasy rail system, known as the Réseau National des Chemins de Fer Malgaches (RNCFM), is made up of over 1000km of tracks, but is used mostly by freight transport.

Madarail (www.madarail.mg) Operates lines from Moramanga.

FCE (Fianarantsoa-Côte Est) Operates trains between Fianarantsoa and Manakara.

TRAIN JOURNEYS

These are the only regular passenger train routes.

JOURNEY	DAY	DEPARTURE	ARRIVAL	FARE (AR)
Moramanga–Tamatave	Mon	7am	7pm	14,000
Tamatave–Moramanga	Tue	8am	8pm	14,000
Moramanga–Ambila	Thu	2pm	10.30pm	14,000
Ambila–Moramanga	Fri	8am	4pm	14,000
Fianarantsoa–Manakara	Tue & Sat	7am	7pm-2am	40,000
Manakara–Fianarantsoa	Wed & Sun	7am	7pm-2am	40,000

Health

As long as you stay up to date with your vaccinations and take some basic preventive measures, you'd have to be pretty unlucky to succumb to any serious health hazards while in Madagascar.

REQUIRED & RECOMMENDED VACCINATIONS

The **World Health Organization** (www.who.int) recommends the following vaccinations as routine (many are administered as part of standard childhood immunisation programs in developed countries, but adults may need a booster):

➡ BCG (tuberculosis)

➡ Diphtheria, tetanus and pertussis (DTP)

➡ Haemophilus influenzae type b (HIB) – this is the leading cause of bacterial meningitis

➡ Hepatitis B

➡ HPV

➡ Measles, mumps and rubella (MMR)

➡ Pneumococcal disease

➡ Polio

➡ Rotavirus

Vaccinations for the following are also recommended for Madagascar:

➡ Hepatitis A

➡ Typhoid

Rabies is endemic in Madagascar, but vaccination is only recommended for visitors who will be spending extensive periods of time in remote areas.

Many vaccines don't ensure immunity until two weeks after they are given, so visit a doctor four to eight weeks before departure.

Ask your doctor for an International Certificate of Vaccination or Prophylaxis (otherwise known as ICVP or 'the yellow card'), listing all the vaccinations you've received.

BEFORE YOU GO

Get a check-up with your dentist and your doctor six to eight weeks before coming to Madagascar to ensure you are up to date with immunisations, to discuss malaria prophylaxis, and to make sure tooth decay won't turn into an abscess while you're away.

Insurance

Find out in advance whether your insurance plan will make payments directly to providers or will reimburse you later for overseas health expenditures (most medical facilities and doctors in Madagascar expect payment upfront).

It's vital to ensure that your travel insurance will cover the emergency transport required to get you to a good hospital – in South Africa or Réunion, or all the way home – by air and with a medical attendant if necessary. Not all insurance plans cover this, so check the contract carefully.

Medical Checklist

It's a good idea to carry a medical and first-aid kit with you. Following is a list of items you should consider packing. Contact-lens wearers should also make sure they have spares and plenty of lens solution.

➡ Adhesive or paper tape

➡ Antibacterial ointment for cuts and abrasions

➡ Antibiotics (if travelling off the beaten track)

➡ Antidiarrhoeal drugs (eg loperamide)

➡ Antihistamines (for hay fever and allergic reactions)

➡ Anti-inflammatory drugs (eg ibuprofen)

➡ Antimalaria pills

➡ Bandages, gauze and gauze rolls

➡ Insect repellent for the skin

➡ Insect spray for clothing, tents and bed nets

➡ Iodine tablets (for water purification)

➡ Oral rehydration salts

➡ Paracetamol (acetaminophen) or aspirin

➡ Scissors, tweezers and safety pins

➡ Steroid cream or hydrocortisone cream (for rashes)

➡ Sunblock (very difficult to find in Madagascar)

➡ Syringes and sterile needles (if travelling off the beaten track)

➡ Thermometer

Websites

It's a good idea to consult your government's travel health website before departure, if one is available. The following websites can help:

Australia (www.smartraveller. gov.au)

Canada (www.phac-aspc.gc.ca)

United Kingdom (www.fitfor travel.nhs.uk)

United States (www.cdc.gov/ travel)

World Health Organisation (WHO; www.who.int)

IN MADAGASCAR

Availability & Cost of Health Care

Getting Treated

Pharmacies For minor problems such as cuts, bites, upset stomachs or colds, pharmacies should be your first port of call in Madagascar. Pharmacists are, on the whole, well trained, the pharmacies are clean and well stocked, and there is an efficient on-call rotation in most towns and cities (generally displayed in the window). Most drugs and bandages cost the same or a little less than in developed countries (generic drugs are used more widely).

Medical centres & hospitals For more serious conditions, you will need to go to a medical centre or a hospital. Public hospitals are, on the whole, poorly equipped and underfunded, but they are sometimes the only option available (note that patients often have to buy medicine, sterile dressings, intravenous fluids etc from the local pharmacy). There are good medical centres in touristy areas such as Nosy Be, and good private facilities in Antananarivo. For anything serious, however, you will need to be evacuated to Réunion (a French territory) or South Africa.

Dentists There are dentists across Madagascar, and their standard of care varies from excellent to bad.

Standards

Health care standards vary a lot from one practitioner to another and from one hospital to the next: standards are pretty good in Antananarivo, but patchy outside the capital. If you find yourself in need of medical assistance, contact your embassy or consulate for a list of recommended practitioners or establishments in your area.

Your insurance company may also have advice.

Infectious Diseases

Despite the intimidating list of infectious diseases in Madagascar, most are extremely rare among travellers. However, if you do experience unusual symptoms for more than three days, seek medical advice.

Cholera

Spread through Contaminated drinking water.

Symptoms & effects Profuse watery diarrhoea, which causes debilitation if fluids are not replaced quickly.

Prevention Cholera is usually only a problem during natural or artificial disasters, eg cyclones, war, floods or earthquakes. An oral cholera vaccine is available, but it is not particularly effective. Boil drinking water, or drink bottled water.

Dengue Fever

Spread through Mosquito bites.

Symptoms & effects Feverish illness with headache and muscle pains similar to those experienced with a bad, prolonged attack of influenza.

Prevention Avoid mosquito bites by covering up and wearing repellent during outbreaks. Seek medical advice if flulike symptoms persist.

Diphtheria

Spread through Close respiratory contact with an infected person.

Symptoms & effects A temperature and a severe sore throat. Sometimes a membrane forms across the throat, and a tracheotomy may be needed to prevent suffocation.

Prevention Vaccination (DTP) is recommended and lasts 10 years.

Hepatitis A

Spread through Contaminated food (particularly shellfish) and water.

Symptoms & effects Jaundice and prolonged lethargy. First symptoms include dark urine and a yellow colour to the whites of the eyes. Sometimes a fever and abdominal pain might be present.

Prevention Vaccination is available and recommended.

Hepatitis B

Spread through Infected blood, contaminated needles and sexual intercourse.

Symptoms & effects Jaundice and occasionally liver failure.

Prevention Vaccination is available and recommended.

HIV

Spread through Infected blood, contaminated needles and sexual intercourse.

Symptoms & effects Attacks the body's immune system.

Prevention HIV prevalence in Madagascar is low (0.5%, similar to North America), so risk to travellers is minimal, but the same precautions apply here as at home: never have unprotected sex and make sure all hospital equipment is sterile.

Malaria

Spread through Bite of the female *Anopheles* mosquito.

Symptoms & effects The early stages of malaria include headaches, fever, generalised aches and pains, and malaise, which could be mistaken for flu. Other symptoms can include abdominal pain, diarrhoea and a cough. If not treated, the disease can progress to jaundice, re-duced consciousness and coma, followed by death.

Prevention Malaria is present throughout Madagascar, although the risks of contracting the disease are higher on the coast (particularly in the east) than in the highlands. It is recommended that all travellers take prophylaxis: there is a variety of drugs available nowadays, ranging in price, regime and secondary effects. Atovaquone/proguanil (Malarone), doxycycline and mefloquine (Lariam) seem to be the most commonly prescribed – discuss your options with a medical professional. It is essential you seek medical help if you suffer from a persistent high fever during your stay or in the six weeks afterwards, as hospital treatment is essential.

Plague

Spread through Bite from infected fleas carried by rodents, handling infected animals (rodents, rabbits and cats in particular), or inhaling droplets from coughs of infected individuals.

Symptoms & effects Pneumonic plague is the most common type of plague in Madagascar. Sufferers will experience shortness of breath, blood-stained sputum and, in the worst cases, septicaemia (blood poisoning) and respiratory failure.

Prevention Plague occurs in small but regular outbreaks in remote areas of Madagascar. There is no vaccine. Travellers are very unlikely to be affected, but as a precaution, never handle animals and use insect sprays to avoid flea bites.

Poliomyelitis

Spread through Contaminated food and water.

Symptoms & effects Polio can be carried asymptomatically (ie showing no symptoms) and can cause a transient fever. In rare cases it causes weakness or paralysis of one or more muscles.

Prevention The vaccine is given in childhood and should be boosted every 10 years.

Rabies

Spread through Bite or lick on broken skin by an infected animal.

Symptoms & effects Rabies causes acute encephalitis (inflammation of the brain). It is always fatal once the clinical symptoms start, which might be up to several months after an infected bite.

Prevention A preventive vaccine of three injections exists, which gives a person bitten by an infected animal more time to seek medical help. If you have not been vaccinated you will need a course of five injections within 24 hours of being bitten.

Schistosomiasis (Bilharzia)

Spread through Flukes (minute worms) that are carried by a species of freshwater snail; the snails shed the flukes in slow-moving or still water. The parasites penetrate human skin during paddling or swimming and migrate to the bladder/bowel.

Symptoms & effects Transient fever and rash, and blood in stools or urine. In chronic cases, schistosomiasis can cause bladder cancer or damage to the intestines.

Prevention Avoid paddling or swimming in suspect freshwater lakes and slow-running rivers. A blood test can detect antibodies if you suspect you have been exposed, and treatment back home is then possible in specialist travel or infectious-disease clinics.

TAP WATER

Madagascar's water is not safe to drink from the taps anywhere in the country – including the most expensive hotels. Bottled water (Ar1800 to Ar4000) is available throughout the country. If you can get clear water from a tap or well, water-purifying tablets are a good option.

If you're planning to get off the beaten track, consider investing in a portable water filter/steriliser such as SteriPen (about US$100) or LifeStraw (about US$30).

Avoid ice in drinks without first asking if it's been made from filtered water.

TRAVELLER'S DIARRHOEA

Although it's not inevitable that you will get diarrhoea while travelling in Madagascar, it's certainly very likely. Diarrhoea is the most common travel-related illness: figures suggest that at least half of all travellers to Africa will get diarrhoea at some stage. Sometimes dietary changes, such as increased spices or oils, are the cause. To avoid diarrhoea, eat fresh fruits and vegetables only if they have been cooked or peeled, and be wary of dairy products that might contain unpasteurised milk. Although freshly cooked food can often be a safe option, plates or serving utensils might be dirty, so you should be highly selective when eating food from street vendors (and make sure that cooked food is piping hot all the way through).

If you develop diarrhoea, drink plenty of fluids, preferably an oral rehydration solution containing lots of salt and sugar. A few loose stools don't require treatment, but if you start having more than four or five loose stools a day for more than a couple of days, you could start taking an antibiotic (usually a quinoline drug, such as ciprofloxacin or norfloxacin). If diarrhoea is bloody, persists for more than 72 hours or is accompanied by fever, shaking chills or severe abdominal pain, you should seek medical attention.

TUBERCULOSIS (TB)

Spread through Close respiratory contact and, occasionally, infected milk or milk products.

Symptoms & effects TB can be asymptomatic, only being picked up on a routine chest X-ray. Alternatively, it can cause a cough, weight loss or fever, sometimes months or even years after exposure.

Prevention The BCG vaccination is recommended for those mixing closely with locals, although it gives only moderate protection.

Typhoid

Spread through Food or water contaminated by infected human faeces.

Symptoms & effects Usually a fever or a pink rash on the abdomen. Sometimes septicaemia can occur.

Prevention A vaccine is available and gives protection for three years.

Environmental Hazards

Heat Exhaustion

Causes Heavy sweating and excessive fluid loss with inadequate replacement of fluids and salt.

Symptoms & effects Headache, dizziness and tiredness.

Prevention & treatment Aim to drink sufficient water to produce pale, diluted urine. To replace salt loss, drink oral rehydration fluids or plenty of savoury and sweet liquids (soup, fruit juice etc).

Heatstroke

Causes Occurs when the body's heat-regulating mechanism breaks down because of extreme heat, high humidity, dehydration and physical exertion.

Symptoms & effects An excessive rise in body temperature, irrational and hyperactive behaviour and, in the most serious cases, loss of consciousness.

Prevention & treatment Acclimatisation to different climate conditions is the best way to prevent heatstroke. Cool the person down with water and keep them in a cool, dark place. Treatment is similar to that for heat exhaustion, but emergency fluids (intravenous) may be needed for extreme cases.

Insect Bites & Stings

Causes Mosquitoes, fleas, scorpions, bedbugs and spiders.

Symptoms & effects Aside from the fact that some bugs can transmit diseases, insect bites or stings can cause irritation, infections and pain. Scorpion stings can be very nasty (fever is common), and sometimes fatal in people with heart conditions, so seek medical help if you're stung.

Prevention & treatment Avoiding getting bitten or stung is obviously the best way to go: wear trousers and long sleeves in the evenings as well as insect repellent. In Ankarana, where scorpions are rife, don't sit on large rocks or logs, and if you camp, check your shoes in the morning and take great care when folding your tent. Antihistamine or steroid creams can help relieve itching from the more benign bites. Painkillers can be effective in dealing with painful bites. If you have a severe allergy (anaphylaxis) to bee or wasp stings, carry an adrenaline injection or similar with you as you won't find any outside of major cities.

Traditional Medicine

Although Western medicine is available in larger cities and towns, *fanafody* (traditional medicine or herbal healing) plays an important role in Madagascar, particularly in rural areas where there are few alternatives. *Ombiasy* (healers) hold considerable social status.

Language

Madagascar has two official languages: Malagasy and French. Malagasy is the everyday spoken language while French is often used for business and administrative purposes, and in the more upmarket sectors of the tourism industry. Unless you travel on an organised tour, stick to big hotels in major towns or speak Malagasy, some basic French will help you get by comfortably in the cities. In rural areas, where knowledge of French is less widespread, you may need to learn a bit of Malagasy too.

FRENCH

The sounds used in French can almost all be found in English. There are a couple of exceptions: nasal vowels (represented in our pronunciation guides by o or u followed by an almost inaudible nasal consonant sound m, n or ng), the 'funny' *u* (ew in our guides) and the deep-in-the-throat *r*. Bearing this in mind and reading our pronunciation guides as if they were English, you'll be understood just fine.

Note that French has two words for 'you' – use the polite form *vous* unless you're talking to close friends or children, in which case you'd use the informal *tu*. Of course, you can also use *tu* when a person invites you to do so.

All nouns in French are either masculine or feminine, and so are the adjectives and articles *le/la* (the) and *un/une* (a) that go with the nouns. We've included masculine and feminine forms where necessary, separated by a slash and indicated with 'm/f'.

WANT MORE?

For in-depth language information and handy phrases, check out Lonely Planet's *French Phrasebook*. You'll find it at **shop.lonelyplanet.com**, or you can buy Lonely Planet's iPhone phrasebooks at the Apple App Store.

Basics

Hello.	Bonjour.	bon·zhoor
Goodbye.	Au revoir.	o·rer·vwa
Excuse me.	Excusez-moi.	ek·skew·zay·mwa
Sorry.	Pardon.	par·don
Yes.	Oui.	wee
No.	Non.	non
Please.	S'il vous plaît.	seel voo play
Thank you.	Merci.	mair·see

How are you?
Comment allez-vous?   ko·mon ta·lay·voo

Fine, and you?
Bien, merci. Et vous?   byun mair·see ay voo

You're welcome.
De rien.   der ree·en

My name is ...
Je m'appelle ...   zher ma·pel ...

What's your name?
Comment vous   ko·mon voo·
appelez-vous?   za·play voo

Do you speak English?
Parlez-vous anglais?   par·lay·voo ong·glay

I don't understand.
Je ne comprends pas.   zher ner kom·pron pa

Accommodation

Do you have any rooms available?
Est-ce que vous avez   es·ker voo za·vay
des chambres libres?   day shom·brer lee·brer

How much is it per night/person?
Quel est le prix   kel ay ler pree
par nuit/personne?   par nwee/per·son

Is breakfast included?
Est-ce que le petit   es·ker ler per·tee
déjeuner est inclus?   day·zher·nay ayt en·klew

campsite	un camping	un kom·peeng
dorm	un dortoir	un dor·twar
guesthouse	une pension	ewn pon·syon

hotel	*un hôtel*	un o·tel
youth hostel	*une auberge de jeunesse*	ewn o·berzh der zher·nes

a ... room	*une chambre ...*	ewn shom·brer ...
single	*à un lit*	a un lee
double	*avec un grand lit*	a·vek un gron lee

with (a)...	*avec ...*	a·vek ...
air-con	*climatiseur*	klee·ma·tee·zer
bathroom	*une salle de bains*	ewn sal der bun
window	*fenêtre*	fer·nay·trer

Directions

Where's ...?
Où est ...? oo ay ...

What's the address?
Quelle est l'adresse? kel ay la·dres

Could you write it down, please?
Pourriez-vous l'écrire, s'il vous plaît? poo·ryay·voo lay·kreer seel voo play

Can you show me (on the map)?
Pouvez-vous m'indiquer (sur la carte)? poo·vay·voo mun·dee·kay (sewr la kart)

at the corner	*au coin*	o kwun
at the traffic lights	*aux feux*	o fer
behind	*derrière*	dair·ryair
in front of	*devant*	der·von
far (from)	*loin (de)*	lwun (der)
left	*gauche*	gosh
near (to)	*près (de)*	pray (der)
next to ...	*à côté de ...*	a ko·tay der...
opposite ...	*en face de ...*	on fas der ...
right	*droite*	drwat
straight ahead	*tout droit*	too drwa

Eating & Drinking

What would you recommend?
Qu'est-ce que vous conseillez? kes·ker voo kon·say·yay

What's in that dish?
Quels sont les ingrédients? kel son lay zun·gray·dyon

KEY PATTERNS

To get by in French, mix and match these simple patterns with words of your choice:

Where's (the entry)?
Où est (l'entrée)? oo ay (lon·tray)

Where can I (buy a ticket)?
Où est-ce que je peux (acheter un billet)? oo es·ker zher per (ash·tay un bee·yay)

When's (the next train)?
Quand est (le prochain train)? kon ay (ler pro·shun trun)

How much is (a room)?
C'est combien pour (une chambre)? say kom·buyn poor (ewn shom·brer)

Do you have (a map)?
Avez-vous (une carte)? a·vay voo (ewn kart)

Is there (a toilet)?
Y a-t-il (des toilettes)? ee a teel (day twa·let)

I'd like (to book a room).
Je voudrais (réserver une chambre). zher voo·dray (ray·ser·vay ewn shom·brer)

Can I (enter)?
Puis-je (entrer)? pweezh (on·tray)

Could you please (help)?
Pouvez-vous (m'aidor), s'il vous plaît? poo·vay voo (may·day) seel voo play

Do I have to (book a seat)?
Faut-il (réserver une place)? fo·teel (ray·ser·vay ewn plas)

I'm a vegetarian.
Je suis végétarien/ végétarienne. zher swee vay·zhay·ta·ryun/ vay·zhay·ta·ryen (m/f)

I don't eat ...
Je ne mange pas ... zher ner monzh pa ...

Cheers!
Santé! son·tay

That was delicious.
C'était délicieux! say·tay day·lee·syer

Please bring the bill.
Apportez-moi l'addition, s'il vous plaît. a·por·tay·mwa la·dee·syon seel voo play

I'd like to reserve a table for ...	*Je voudrais réserver une table pour ...*	zher voo·dray ray·zair·vay ewn ta·bler poor ...
(eight) o'clock	*(vingt) heures*	(vungt) er
(two) people	*(deux) personnes*	(der) pair·son

Signs

Entrée	Entrance
Femmes	Women
Fermé	Closed
Hommes	Men
Interdit	Prohibited
Ouvert	Open
Renseignements	Information
Sortie	Exit
Toilettes/WC	Toilets

Key Words

appetiser	entrée	on·tray
bottle	bouteille	boo·tay
breakfast	petit déjeuner	per·tee day·zher·nay
children's menu	menu pour enfants	mer·new poor on·fon
cold	froid	frwa
delicatessen	traiteur	tray·ter
dinner	dîner	dee·nay
dish	plat	pla
food	nourriture	noo·ree·tewr
fork	fourchette	foor·shet
glass	verre	vair
grocery store	épicerie	ay·pee·sree
highchair	chaise haute	dewn shay zot
hot	chaud	sho
knife	couteau	koo·to
local speciality	spécialité locale	spay·sya·lee·tay lo·kal
lunch	déjeuner	day·zher·nay
main course	plat principal	pla prun·see·pal
market	marché	mar·shay
menu (in English)	carte (en anglais)	kart (on ong·glay)
plate	assiette	a·syet
spoon	cuillère	kwee·yair
wine list	carte des vins	kart day vun
with	avec	a·vek
without	sans	son

Meat & Fish

beef	bœuf	berf
chicken	poulet	poo·lay
cod	morue	mo·rew
herring	hareng	a·rung
lamb	agneau	a·nyo
mackerel	maquereau	ma·kro
mussel	moule	mool
oyster	huître	wee·trer
pork	porc	por
salmon	saumon	so·mon
seafood	fruit de mer	frwee der mair
shellfish	crustacé	krew·sta·say
squid	calmar	kal·mar
trout	truite	trweet
turkey	dinde	dund
veal	veau	vo

Fruit & Vegetables

apple	pomme	pom
apricot	abricot	ab·ree·ko
asparagus	asperge	a·spairzh
beans	haricots	a·ree·ko
beetroot	betterave	be·trav
cabbage	chou	shoo
cherry	cerise	ser·reez
corn	maïs	ma·ees
cucumber	concombre	kong·kom·brer
grape	raisin	ray·zun
lemon	citron	see·tron
lettuce	laitue	lay·tew
mushroom	champignon	shom·pee·nyon
peach	pêche	pesh
peas	petit pois	per·tee pwa
(red/green) pepper	poivron (rouge/vert)	pwa·vron (roozh/vair)
pineapple	ananas	a·na·nas
plum	prune	prewn
potato	pomme de terre	pom der tair
pumpkin	citrouille	see·troo·yer
spinach	épinards	eh·pee·nar
strawberry	fraise	frez
tomato	tomate	to·mat
vegetable	légume	lay·gewm

Other

bread	pain	pun
butter	beurre	ber
cheese	fromage	fro·mazh
egg	œuf	erf
honey	miel	myel
jam	confiture	kon·fee·tewr
oil	huile	weel
pasta	pâtes	pat
pepper	poivre	pwa·vrer

rice	riz	ree
salt	sel	sel
sugar	sucre	sew·krer
vinegar	vinaigre	vee·nay·grer

Drinks

beer	bière	bee·yair
coffee	café	ka·fay
(orange) juice	jus (d'orange)	zhew (do·ronzh)
milk	lait	lay
red wine	vin rouge	vun roozh
tea	thé	tay
(mineral) water	eau (minérale)	o (mee·nay·ral)
white wine	vin blanc	vun blong

Emergencies

Help!
Au secours! o skoor

I'm lost.
Je suis perdu/perdue. zhe swee·pair·dew (m/f)

Leave me alone!
Fichez-moi la paix! fee·shay·mwa la pay

There's been an accident.
Il y a eu un accident. eel ya ew un ak·see·don

Call a doctor.
Appelez un médecin. a·play un mayd·sun

Call the police.
Appelez la police. a·play la po·lees

I'm ill.
Je suis malade. zher swee ma·lad

It hurts here.
J'ai une douleur ici. zhay ewn doo·ler ee·see

I'm allergic to ...
Je suis allergique ... zher swee za·lair·zheek ...

Shopping & Services

I'd like to buy ...
Je voudrais acheter ... zher voo·dray ash·tay ...

Can I look at it?
Est-ce que je peux le voir? es·ker zher per ler vwar

I'm just looking.
Je regarde. zher rer·gard

I don't like it.
Cela ne me plaît pas. ser·la ner mer play pa

How much is it?
C'est combien? say kom·byun

It's too expensive.
C'est trop cher. say tro shair

Can you lower the price?
Vous pouvez baisser le prix? voo poo·vay bay·say ler pree

There's a mistake in the bill.
Il y a une erreur dans la note. eel ya ewn ay·rer don la not

ATM	guichet automatique de banque	gee·shay o·to·ma·teek der bonk
credit card	carte de crédit	kart der kray·dee
internet cafe	cybercafé	see·bair·ka·fay
post office	bureau de poste	bew·ro der post
tourist office	office de tourisme	o·fees der too·rees·mer

Time & Dates

What time is it?
Quelle heure est-il? kel er ay til

It's (eight) o'clock.
Il est (huit) heures. il ay (weet) er

It's half past (10).
Il est (dix) heures et demie. il ay (deez) er ay day·mee

morning	matin	ma·tun
afternoon	après-midi	a·pray·mee·dee
evening	soir	swar
yesterday	hier	yair
today	aujourd'hui	o·zhoor·dwee
tomorrow	demain	der·mun

Monday	lundi	lun·dee
Tuesday	mardi	mar·dee
Wednesday	mercredi	mair·krer·dee
Thursday	jeudi	zher·dee
Friday	vendredi	von·drer·dee
Saturday	samedi	sam·dee
Sunday	dimanche	dee·monsh

Transport

boat	bateau	ba·to
bus	bus	bews
plane	avion	a·vyon
train	train	trun

Question Words

How?	Comment?	ko·mon
What?	Quoi?	kwa
When?	Quand?	kon
Where?	Où?	oo
Who?	Qui?	kee
Why?	Pourquoi?	poor·kwa

Numbers		
1	un	un
2	deux	der
3	trois	trwa
4	quatre	ka·trer
5	cinq	sungk
6	six	sees
7	sept	set
8	huit	weet
9	neuf	nerf
10	dix	dees
20	vingt	vung
30	trente	tront
40	quarante	ka·ront
50	cinquante	sung·kont
60	soixante	swa·sont
70	soixante-dix	swa·son·dees
80	quatre-vingts	ka·trer·vung
90	quatre-vingt-dix	ka·trer·vung·dees
100	cent	son
1000	mille	meel

I want to go to ...
Je voudrais aller à ...   zher voo·dray a·lay a ...

Does it stop at (Amboise)?
Est-ce qu'il s'arrête à   es·kil sa·ret a
(Amboise)?   (om·bwaz)

At what time does it leave/arrive?
À quelle heure est-ce   a kel er es
qu'il part/arrive?   kil par/a·reev

Can you tell me when we get to ...?
Pouvez-vous me   poo·vay·voo mer
dire quand   deer kon
nous arrivons à ...?   noo za·ree·von a ...

I want to get off here.
Je veux descendre   zher ver day·son·drer
ici.   ee·see

first	premier	prer·myay
last	dernier	dair·nyay
next	prochain	pro·shun

a ... ticket	un billet ...	un bee·yay ...
1st-class	de première classe	der prem·yair klas
2nd-class	de deuxième classe	der der·zyem las
one-way	simple	sum·pler
return	aller et retour	a·lay ay rer·toor

aisle seat	côté couloir	ko·tay kool·war
delayed	en retard	on rer·tar
cancelled	annulé	a·new·lay
platform	quai	kay
ticket office	le guichet	ler gee·shay
timetable	l'horaire	lo·rair
train station	la gare	la gar
window seat	côté fenêtre	ko·tay fe·ne·trer

I'd like to hire a ...	Je voudrais louer ...	zher voo·dray loo·way ...
4WD	un quatre-quatre	un kat·kat
car	une voiture	ewn vwa·tewr
bicycle	un vélo	un vay·lo
motorcycle	une moto	ewn mo·to

child seat	siège-enfant	syezh·on·fon
diesel	diesel	dyay·zel
helmet	casque	kask
mechanic	mécanicien	may·ka·nee·syun
petrol/gas	essence	ay·sons
service station	station-service	sta·syon·ser·vees

Is this the road to ...?
C'est la route pour ...?   say la root poor ...

(How long) Can I park here?
(Combien de temps)   (kom·byun der tom)
Est-ce que je peux   es·ker zher per
stationner ici?   sta·syo·nay ee·see

The car/motorbike has broken down (at ...).
La voiture/moto est   la vwa·tewr/mo·to ay
tombée en panne (à ...).   tom·bay on pan (a ...)

I have had an accident.
J'ai eu un accident.   zhay ew un ak·see·don

I have a flat tyre.
Mon pneu est à plat.   mom pner ay ta pla

I've run out of petrol.
Je suis en panne   zher swee zon pan
d'essence.   day·sons

I've lost my car keys.
J'ai perdu les clés de   zhay per·dew lay klay der
ma voiture.   ma vwa·tewr

MALAGASY

Malagasy has around 18 million speakers. It belongs to the Malayo-Polynesian branch of the Austronesian language family and is unrelated to other African languages – its closest relative is a language from southern Borneo. Over the centuries Malagasy has incorporated influences from Bantu (particularly in some of the west coast dialects) and Arabic. It has also been influenced by English and French – first in the 19th century by British and French missionaries, and later as a result of colonisation by the French in the first half of the 20th century. Malagasy was first written using a form of Arabic script. Its modern Latin-based alphabet was developed in the early 19th century.

The pronunciation of Malagasy words is not always obvious from their written form. Unstressed syllables can be dropped and words pronounced in different ways depending on where they fall in a sentence. If you read our pronunciation guides as if they were English, you'll be understood. Note that dz is pronounced as the 'ds' in 'adds'. The stressed syllables are indicated with italics.

Basics

Hello.	*Manao ahoana.*	maa·*now* aa·hon
Goodbye.	*Veloma.*	ve·*lum*
Good night.	*Tafandria mandry.*	taa·faan·*dri* maan·dri
Yes.	*Eny.*	e·ni
No.	*Tsia.*	tsi·aa
Please.	*Azafady.*	aa·zaa·faad
Thank you.	*Misaotra.*	mi·*sotr*
Sorry.	*Miala tsiny.*	mi·aa·laa tsin
Mr	*Ingahy*	in·*gaa*
Mrs	*Ramatoa*	raa·maa·*tu*
Miss	*Ramatoakely*	raa·maa·*tu*·kel

How are you?
Manao ahoana ianao? maa·*now* aa·ho·*ni*·aa·now

Fine, and you?
Tsara, ary ianao? tsaar aa·ri·*aa*·now

What's your name?
Iza no anaranao? i·zaa nu aa·*naa*·raa·now

My name is ...
... no anarako. ... nu aa·*naa*·raa·ku

Do you speak English?
Miteny angilisy ve ianao? mi·*ten* aan·gi·*lis* ve i·aa·now

I don't understand.
Tsy azoko. tsi aa·zuk

Accommodation

Where's a ...? *Aiza no misy ...?* ai·zaa nu mis ...

| **campsite** | *toerana* | tu·e·raan |
| | *filasiana* | fi·laa·*si*·naa |

guesthouse	*tranom-bahiny*	traa·num·baa·hin
hotel	*hôtely*	o·tel
youth hostel	*fandraisana Tanora*	faan·*drai*·saa·naa *taa*·nur

Do you have a ... room?	*Misy ... ve ato aminao efitra iray ...?*	mis ... ve aat·waa·*mi*·now e·fi·traa i·*rai* ...
single	*ho an' olon-tokana*	waan u·lun·to·*kaa*·naa
double	*misy fandriana lehibe*	mis faan·*dri*·naa le·hi·*be*
twin	*misy fandriana kely*	mis faan·*dri*·naa kel

How much is it per night/person?
Ohatrinona isan' alina/olona? o·trin i·saan aa·lin/*u*·lun

Can I camp here?
Mahazo milasy eto ve aho? maa·*haa*·zu mi·*laas* e·tu ve ow

Directions

Where's the ...?
Aiza ...? ai·zaa ...

What's the address?
Inona ny adiresy? i·nu·naa ni aa·di·*res*

Place Names
Although most people continue to use French place names in Madagascar, since the time of independence places have been known officially by their Malagasy names. The following list may help alleviate confusion.

Malagasy	*French*
Ambohitra	Joffreville
Anantsogno	St Augustin
Andasibe	Périnet
Andoany	Hell-Ville
Antananarivo	Tananarive
Antsiranana	Diego Suarez
Fenoarivo	Fénérive
Iharana	Vohémar
Mahajanga	Majunga
Mahavelona	Foulpointe
Nosy Boraha	Île Sainte Marie
Taolagnaro	Fort Dauphin
Toamasina	Tamatave
Toliara	Tuléar

DIALECTS

Despite the linguistic unity of Malagasy, regional differences do exist, and in some coastal areas, you'll hear little standard Malagasy. The three broad language groups are those of the highlands; the north and east; and the south and west. However, even within these areas there are local variations. The following list indicates a few of the lexical and phonetic differences between standard Malagasy and some of the regional dialects.

English	Highlands	North & East	South & West
Greetings.	*Manao ahoana.*	*Mbola tsara anarô.*	*Akore aby nareo.*
(in response)	*Tsara.*	*Mbola tsara.*	*Tsara./Soa.*
What's new?	*Inona no vaovao?*	*Ino vaovaonao?*	*Talilio?*
Nothing much.	*Tsy misy.*	*Ehe, tsisy fô manginginy.*	*Mbe soa.*
Where?	*Aiza?*	*Aia?*	*Aia?*
Who?	*Iza?*	*La?*	*La?*
spouse	*vady*	*vady*	*valy*
ancestor	*razana*	*raza*	*raza*

Can you write it down, please?
Mba afaka   mbaa *aa*-faak
soratanao ve   su-raa-*taa*-now ve
izany azafady?   i-zaan aa-zaa-*faad*

Can you show me (on the map)?
Afaka asehonao   aa-faak aa-se-u-*now*
ahy (eoamin'ny   waa (e-uaa-min-*ni*
sarintany) ve   saa-rin-*taan*) ve

How far is it?
Hafiriana avy eto?   haa-fi-*ri*-naa *aa*-vi et

How do I get there?
Ahoana no lalako   ow-o-naa nu *laa*-laa-ku
mankany?   maa-kaan

Turn left/right.
Mivilia ankavia/   mi-vi-*li* aan-kaa-*vi*/
ankavanana.   aan-kaa-*vaa*-naan

It's ...	... *ilay izy.*	... *i*-lai iz
behind ...	*Ao ambadiky ny ...*	ow aam-*baa*-di-ki ni ...
in front of ...	*Manoloana ny ...*	maa-nu-*lo*-naa ni ...
near	*Akaiky ny*	aa-*kai*-ki ni
next to ...	*Manaraka ny ...*	maa-naa-*raa*-kaa ni ...
on the corner	*Eo an-jorony*	e-waan-*dzu*-run
opposite ...	*Mifanatrika ...*	mi-*faa*-naa-trik ...
straight ahead	*Mandeha mahitsy*	maan-*de* maa-*hits*
there	*Eo*	e-u

Eating & Drinking

Can you recommend a ...?
Afaka manoro   aa-faa-kaa maa-*nur*
ahy... tsara   waa ... tsaar
ve ianao?   ve *i*-aa-now

bar	*bara*	baa-*raa*
dish	*sakafo*	saa-*kaaf*
place to eat	*toerana hisakafoanana*	tu-e-raan i-saa-kaa-fu-*aa*-naan

I'd like ..., please.
Mba mila ny ..., azafady.   mbaa *mi*-laa ni ... aa-zaa-*faad*

the bill	*fakitiora*	faak-ti-*ur*
the menu	*lisitra sakafo*	*lis*-traa saa-kaaf
a table for (two)	*latabatra ho an' (olon-droa)*	laa-*taa*-baa-traa waan (u-lun-*dru*)
that dish	*iny sakafo iny*	in saa-*kaa*-fu in

cup of coffee/tea ...	*kafe/dite iray kaopy ...*	kaa-*fe*/di-*te* i-*rai* kop ...
with milk	*misy ronono*	mis *ru*-nun
without sugar	*tsy misy siramamy*	tsi mis si-*raa*-maam

Could you prepare a meal without ...?
Mba afaka manao sakafo tsy misy ... ve ianareo?   mbaa aa-faak maa-now saa-kaaf tsi mis ... ve i-aa-*naa*-re-u

eggs	*atody*	aa-*tud*
meat stock	*hena*	he-naa

Do you have vegetarian food?
Manana sakafo tsy misy hena ve ianareo?   maa-naa-naa saa-kaaf tsi mis he-naa ve i-aa-naa-re-u

beer	*labiera*	laa-*bi*-er
bottle	*tavoahangy*	taa-vu-*haan*-gi
breakfast	*sakafo maraina*	saa-kaaf maa-*rai*-naa

coffee	kafe	kaa·*fe*
cold	mangatsiaka	maan·gaa·*tsik*
dairy products	ronono	ru·*nun*
dinner	sakafo hariva	saa·*kaa*·fu aa·*ri*·vaa
drink	zava-pisotro	zaa·vaa·*pi*·su·tru
eggs	atody	aa·*tud*
fish	trondro	*trun*·dru
food	sakafo	saa·*kaaf*
fork	forisety	fu·ri·se·ti
fruit	voankazo	vu·aan·*kaaz*
glass	vera	ve·raa
hot	mahamay	*maa*·mai
hungry	noana	*no*·naa
knife	antsy	*aant*·si
lunch	sakafo atoandro	saa·*kaaf* waa·tu·*aan*·dru
meat	hena	*he*·naa
milk	ronono	*ru*·nun
nuts	voanjo	vu·*aan*·dzu
plate	lovia	lu·*vi*
restaurant	hôtely fisakafoana	o·*te*·li fi·saa·kaa·*fu*·aa·naa
seafood	hazan drano	haa·*zaan*·draa·nu
spoon	sotro	*su*·tru
sugar	siramamy	si·*raa*·maam
tea	dite	di·*te*
thirsty	mangetaheta	maan·ge·taa·*he*·taa
vegetarian	tsy misy hena	tsi mis *he*·naa
waiter	mpandroso sakafo	paan·*dru*·su saa·kaaf
(boiled) water	rano (mangotraka)	raa·nu (maan·*gu*·traak)
wine	divay	di·vai
without ...	tsy misy ...	tsi mis ...

Emergencies

Help!
Vonjeo! vun·*dze*·u

I'm lost.
Very aho. ve·ri ow

Where are the toilets?
Aiza ny trano fivoahana? ai·zaa ni *traa*·nu fi·vu·*aa*·haan

Call the doctor/police.
Antsoy ny dokotera/ polisy. aant·*su*·i ni duk·*ter*/ po·*lis*

It hurts here.
Marary eto. maa·*raa*·ri e

I'm allergic to (penicillin).
Tys mahazaka (penisilina) aho. tsi maa·haa·*zaa*·kaa (pe·*ni*·si·lin) ow

Shopping & Services

I'm looking for ...
Mitady ... aho. mi·*taa*·di ... ow

How much is it?
Ohatrinona? o·*trin*

Can you write down the price?
Mba afaka soratanao ve ny vidiny? mbaa aa·*faa*·kaa su·raa·*taa*·now ve ni *vi*·din

What's your lowest price?
Ohatrinona ny vidiny farany? o·*trin*·naa ni *vi*·din faa·raan

There's a mistake in the bill.
Miso diso ny fakitiora. mis *di*·su ni faak·*tu*·raa

I'd like a receipt, please.
Mba mila resiò aho, azafady. mbaa *mi*·laa re·si·*u* ow aa·zaa·*faad*

It's faulty.
Tsy marina io. tsi maa·ri·*ni*·u

Can I have my ... repaired?
Afaka amboarina ve ny ... -ko? aa·faa·kaamb·*waa*·rin ve ni ... ·ku

When will it be ready?
Rahoviana no vita? row·*vi*·naa nu *vi*·taa

I'd like to change money.
Mba te hanakalo vola aho azafady. mbaa te haa·naa·*kaa*·lu vu·laa ow aa·zaa·*faad*

market	tsena	tsen
mobile phone	paoritabila	por·*taa*·bi·laa
internet cafe	sibera	si·ber
pharmacy	farimasia	faa·ri·*maa*·si
post office	paositra	po·si·traa
tourist office	biraon' ny vahiny	bi·row·ni *vaa*·hin

Time & Dates

What time is it?
Amin'ny firy izao? aa·min·*ni*·fi ri·zow

It's (two) o'clock.
Amin'ny (roa) izao. aa·min·*ni* (ru) *i*·zow

Half past (one).
(Iray) sy sasany. (rai) si *saa*·saan

Quarter past (one).
(Iray) sy fahefany. (rai) si faa·*he*·faan

Quarter to (eight).
(Valo) latsaka (vaal) *laat*·saa·kaa
fahefany. faa·*he*·faan

At what time ...?
Amin'ny firy ...? aa·min·*ni* fir ...

At ...
Amin'ny ... aa·min·*ni* ...

yesterday	*omaly*	*u*·maal
today	*androany*	aan·*dru*·aan
tomorrow	*rahampitso*	raa·haam·*pits*
Monday	*Alatsinainy*	aa·laat·*si*·nain
Tuesday	*Talata*	taa·laat
Wednesday	*Alarobia*	aa·laa·*ru*·bi
Thursday	*Alakamisy*	aa·laa·*kaa*·mis
Friday	*Zomà*	zu·*maa*
Saturday	*Asabotsy*	aa·saa·*buts*
Sunday	*Alahady*	aa·laa·*haad*

Transport

A ... ticket *Tapakila ...* taa·paa·*kil* ...
(to Toliary), *(mankany* (*maa*·kaan
please. *Toliary)* tu·*li*·aar)
 iray, azafady. *i*·rai aa·zaa·*faad*

   one-way *mandroso* *maan*·drus
   return *miverina* mi·*ve*·rin

Is this *Ity ve ny ...* i·*ti* ve ni ...
the ... to *mankany* *maa*·kaan
(Toamasina)? *(Toamasina)?* (to·*maa*·sin)

   boat *sambo* saamb
   bus *aotobisy* o·to·bis
   plane *roaplanina* ro·plaan
   train *lamasinina* laa·*maa*·sin

bus stop	*fijanonana*	fid·zaa·*nu*·naan
economy class	*kilasy faharoa*	ki·*laa*·si faa·haa·*ru*
first class	*kilasy voalohany*	ki·*laa*·si vu·aa·*lu*·haan
train station	*gara*	*gaa*·raa

Numbers

How long does the trip take?
Hafiriana ny dia? haa·fi·*ri*·naa ni di

Is it a direct route?
Tsy mijanojanona tsi mi·dzaa·nu·*dzaa*·nu·naa
ve? ve

How long will it be delayed?
Hafiriana ny haa·fi·*ri*·naa ni
fahatarany? faa·haa·*taa*·raan

How much is it to ...?
Ohatrinona ny ...? o·*trin*·naa ni ...

Please take me to (this address).
Mba ento any amin' mbaa *en*·tu aa·ni aa·min
(ityadiresy ity) aho (tiaa·di·*res* ti) ow
azafady. aa·zaa·*faad*

I'd like to hire a car/4WD.
Mba te hanarama mbaa te haa·naa·*raa*·maa
fiara/4x4 aho fi·*aar*/kaat·*kaat*·raa ow
azafady. aa·zaa·*faad*

Is this the road to (Antsirabe)?
Ity ve ny lalana i·*ti* ve ni laa·laan
mankany (Antsirabe)? *maa*·kaan (aan·tsi·raa·*be*)

bicycle	*bisikileta*	bis·ki·*le*·taa
highway	*lalambe*	laa·*laam*·be
motorcycle	*môtô*	mo·to
oil (engine)	*menaka*	me·naa·kaa
park (car)	*fijanonana*	fid·zaa·*nu*·naan
petrol	*lasantsy*	laa·*saant*·si
tyre	*kodiarana*	*ku*·di·aa·raan

GLOSSARY

andriana – noble

Antaimoro – east coast tribe from the region around Manakara; also the name given to a type of handmade paper

Antakarana – tribe from northern Madagascar

ariary – Madagascar's unit of currency

aye-aye – rare nocturnal lemur

bâché – small, converted pick-up truck

baie – bay

Basse-Ville – lower town

be – 'big' in Malagasy; denotes larger parts of a town

Betsileo – Madagascar's third-largest tribe after the Merina and the Betsimisaraka

Betsimisaraka – Madagascar's second-largest tribe

boutre – single-masted dhow used for cargo

camion-brousse – large truck used for passengers

cassava – root vegetable also known as manioc

Creole cuisine – a blend of African, Asian and European influences

fady – taboo, forbidden

famadihana – exhumation and reburial; literally 'the turning of the bones'

fossa – local name for the striped civet

gare routière – bus station

gargote – cheap restaurant

gasy – Malagasy (pronounced 'gash')

gîte – rustic shelter

Haute-Ville – upper town

hauts plateaux – highlands; the term is often used to refer to Madagascar's central plateau region

hira gasy – music, dancing and storytelling spectacles

hotely – small roadside place that serves basic meals

Imerina – region ruled by the Merina

indri – largest of Madagascar's lemur species

kely – 'small' in Malagasy; often used to denote a township or satellite town

lac – lake

lalana – street

lamba – white cotton or silk scarf

maki – Malagasy term for a lemur

Merina – Madagascar's largest tribe, centred in Antananarivo

MNP – Madagascar National Parks

mora mora – 'slowly, slowly' or 'wait a minute'; often used to mean the Malagasy pace of life

nosy – island

Nouvelle-Ville – new town

parc national – national park

parcage – *taxi-brousse* station

pic – peak

pirogue – dugout canoe

pousse-pousse – rickshaw

ravinala – literally 'forest leaves'; also known as travellers' palm, the most distinctive of Madagascar's palm trees

réserve spéciale – special reserve (often similar to a national park)

RN – route nationale; national road (often still no more than a track)

rova – palace

Sakalava – western tribe

sambatra – mass circumcision ceremony

SAVA – region comprising Sambava, Andapa, Vohémar (Iharana) and Antalaha

sifaka – a type of lemur, known in French as a 'propithèque'

taxi-be – literally 'big taxi'; also known as a 'familiale'

taxi-brousse – bush taxi; generic term for any kind of public passenger truck, car or minibus

tenrec – small mammal resembling a hedgehog or shrew

THB – Three Horses Beer; Madagascar's most popular beer

tilapia – freshwater perch (fish)

tsingy – limestone pinnacle formations; also known as karst

vazaha – foreigner or white person

Vezo – nomadic fishing subtribe of the Sakalava, found in the southwest

via ferrata – mountain route equipped with fixed cables, stemples, ladders and bridges.

ylang-ylang – bush with sweet-smelling white flowers used to make perfume

Zafimaniry – a subgroup of the Betsileo people who live in the area east of Ambositra, and are renowned for their woodcarving skills

zebu – a type of domesticated ox found throughout Madagascar; it has a prominent hump on its back and loose skin under its throat

Behind the Scenes

SEND US YOUR FEEDBACK

We love to hear from travellers – your comments keep us on our toes and help make our books better. Our well-travelled team reads every word on what you loved or loathed about this book. Although we cannot reply individually to postal submissions, we always guarantee that your feedback goes straight to the appropriate authors, in time for the next edition. Each person who sends us information is thanked in the next edition – the most useful submissions are rewarded with a selection of digital PDF chapters.

Visit **lonelyplanet.com/contact** to submit your updates and suggestions or to ask for help. Our award-winning website also features inspirational travel stories, news and discussions.

Note: We may edit, reproduce and incorporate your comments in Lonely Planet products such as guidebooks, websites and digital products, so let us know if you don't want your comments reproduced or your name acknowledged. For a copy of our privacy policy visit lonelyplanet.com/privacy.

OUR READERS

Many thanks to the travellers who used the last edition and wrote to us with helpful hints, useful advice and interesting anecdotes:

A Anneka Bunt **B** Benjamin Heinrich, Birgit Will, Britta Hillen **C** Chris Weseloh, Clemens Capek **E** Eduardo Fajer **F** Fanny Duffourg, Fika Perié **H** Hanna Pietrzak **I** Inez de Ligt **J** Jan Kaczmarczyk **K** Kara Lawrence, Kate Austen **L** Lesley Gowland, Louise Ysart **M** Machiel Crielaard, Marisa Abarca, Marja Nijboer, Mark Darter, Mike Dunphy **N** Nicole Angehrn **O** Orhan Dertsavar **P** Penelope Guillard, Per Bråmå **R** Richard Maurice, Robin Verwest, Rodger Ambrose **S** Samuel Merson, Susan Sharp **T** Tai Kuncio, Tajan Tober, Thomas Ming

AUTHOR THANKS

Emilie Filou

In Madagascar, big thanks to Patricia Rajeriarison for many useful introductions; to Mikaia Rasolofomanana for putting me in the good hands of driver extraordinaire Harrison Randrianandrasana, who was great company and full of judicious advice. Thanks also to fellow authors Anthony Ham and Helen Ranger for such a great partnership. Back home, immense thanks to Moon and Loli, who went beyond the call of grandmother duty, and most importantly, to Adolfo and Sasha for letting me do this.

Anthony Ham

Thanks to Matt Phillips for such a long and fruitful shared love of Africa, and to my expert co-authors Emilie Filou and Helen Ranger. In Madagascar, thanks to my indefatigable drivers, Mino and Rija, and to Mikaia Rasolofamana for making sure all went smoothly. Thanks also to David Andrew, Maxence Bigey, Toussaint, Dario and Valerio, and for the kindness shown to me and assistance given by numerous anything-but-ordinary local people. Thanks to Marina, Carlota, Valentina, Jan and Lisa for such love and support and for getting me home. My work on this book is dedicated to my father and faithful follower of my journeys, Ron Ham, who died soon after my return from Madagascar.

Helen Ranger

Thanks to Matt Phillips for the opportunity to return to this fascinating country, and to fellow authors Emilie and Anthony. On the road, Jules Randrianirina – with whom I saw much more of the country than anticipated – was unstintingly helpful and a superb driver over rough pistes and dubious bridges. Germain Raharison in Sambava, Patrick Randriamboavonjy in Tamatave, Marcine Cooper on Nosy Be and Orpheu Todivelou in Ambodifotatra shared their knowledge generously. Striking Air Madagascar crew get no cigars.

ACKNOWLEDGMENTS

Climate map data adapted from Peel MC, Finlayson BL & McMahon TA (2007) 'Updated World Map of the Köppen-Geiger Climate Classification', *Hydrology and Earth System Sciences*, 11, 163344.

Cover photograph: Gecko, Martin Harvey/ Alamy ©.

BEHIND THE SCENES

THIS BOOK

This 8th edition of Lonely Planet's *Madagascar* guidebook was researched and written by Emilie Filou, Anthony Ham and Helen Ranger. The previous edition was written by Emilie Filou and Paul Stiles, and the 6th edition was written by David Andrew, Aaron Anderson, Becca Blond and Tom Parkinson. This guidebook was produced by the following:

Destination Editor
Matt Phillips

Product Editors
Andi Jones, Amanda Williamson

Senior Cartographers
Corey Hutchison, Anthony Phelan

Book Designer Mazzy Prinsep

Assisting Editors Andrew Bain, Imogen Bannister, Michelle Bennett

Cover Researcher Naomi Parker

Thanks to Daniel Corbett, James Hardy, Catherine Naghten, Karyn Noble, Kirsten Rawlings, Kathryn Rowan, Angela Tinson, Lauren Wellicome, Tony Wheeler

Index

Map Legend

Sights

- Beach
- Bird Sanctuary
- Buddhist
- Castle/Palace
- Christian
- Confucian
- Hindu
- Islamic
- Jain
- Jewish
- Monument
- Museum/Gallery/Historic Building
- Ruin
- Shinto
- Sikh
- Taoist
- Winery/Vineyard
- Zoo/Wildlife Sanctuary
- Other Sight

Activities, Courses & Tours

- Bodysurfing
- Diving
- Canoeing/Kayaking
- Course/Tour
- Sento Hot Baths/Onsen
- Skiing
- Snorkelling
- Surfing
- Swimming/Pool
- Walking
- Windsurfing
- Other Activity

Sleeping

- Sleeping
- Camping

Eating

- Eating

Drinking & Nightlife

- Drinking & Nightlife
- Cafe

Entertainment

- Entertainment

Shopping

- Shopping

Information

- Bank
- Embassy/Consulate
- Hospital/Medical
- Internet
- Police
- Post Office
- Telephone
- Toilet
- Tourist Information
- Other Information

Geographic

- Beach
- Gate
- Hut/Shelter
- Lighthouse
- Lookout
- Mountain/Volcano
- Oasis
- Park
- Pass
- Picnic Area
- Waterfall

Population

- Capital (National)
- Capital (State/Province)
- City/Large Town
- Town/Village

Transport

- Airport
- Border crossing
- Bus
- Cable car/Funicular
- Cycling
- Ferry
- Metro station
- Monorail
- Parking
- Petrol station
- Subway station
- Taxi
- Train station/Railway
- Tram
- Underground station
- Other Transport

Note: Not all symbols displayed above appear on the maps in this book

Routes

- Tollway
- Freeway
- Primary
- Secondary
- Tertiary
- Lane
- Unsealed road
- Road under construction
- Plaza/Mall
- Steps
- Tunnel
- Pedestrian overpass
- Walking Tour
- Walking Tour detour
- Path/Walking Trail

Boundaries

- International
- State/Province
- Disputed
- Regional/Suburb
- Marine Park
- Cliff
- Wall

Hydrography

- River, Creek
- Intermittent River
- Canal
- Water
- Dry/Salt/Intermittent Lake
- Reef

Areas

- Airport/Runway
- Beach/Desert
- Cemetery (Christian)
- Cemetery (Other)
- Glacier
- Mudflat
- Park/Forest
- Sight (Building)
- Sportsground
- Swamp/Mangrove

OUR STORY

A beat-up old car, a few dollars in the pocket and a sense of adventure. In 1972 that's all Tony and Maureen Wheeler needed for the trip of a lifetime – across Europe and Asia overland to Australia. It took several months, and at the end – broke but inspired – they sat at their kitchen table writing and stapling together their first travel guide, *Across Asia on the Cheap*. Within a week they'd sold 1500 copies. Lonely Planet was born.

Today, Lonely Planet has offices in Franklin, London, Melbourne, Oakland, Beijing and Delhi, with more than 600 staff and writers. We share Tony's belief that 'a great guidebook should do three things: inform, educate and amuse'.

OUR WRITERS

Emilie Filou

Coordinating Writer, Antananarivo, Central Madagascar Emilie first travelled to Africa aged eight to visit her grandparents, who had taken up a late-career opportunity in Mali. Many trips and a geography degree later, Emilie now works as a freelance journalist focusing on development issues in Africa (read her work at www.emiliefilou.com). For this trip, Emilie loved discovering the central plateaux of Madagascar, especially taking the (very) slow train from Manakara to Fianarantsoa and buying wild silk in the remote village of Soatanana; her highlight was watching dawn break from the top of Pic Boby (Imarivolanitra) in Parc National d'Andringitra. Emilie also wrote the Plan, Understand and Survival Guide sections.

Read more about Emilie at:
http://auth.lonelyplanet.com/profiles/emiliefilou

Anthony Ham

Southern Madagascar, Western Madagascar Anthony (www.anthonyham. com) brings to Madagascar sixteen years of travelling through, writing about and photographing in Africa. His passion for the continent began in North and West Africa, and more recently he has travelled extensively through East and Southern Africa and Indian Ocean islands, writing about natural history and conservation issues, nomadic and indigenous peoples and countries in conflict, for newspapers and magazines around the world. When he's not in Africa, Anthony moves between Melbourne and Madrid with his wife and two daughters.

Read more about Anthony at:
http://auth.lonelyplanet.com/profiles/anthonyham

Helen Ranger

Northern Madagascar, Eastern Madagascar In three visits to Madagascar, Helen has researched rainforest essential oils, been woken by the eerie cries of *indris* in the Parc National Andasibe Mantadia, been marooned on a remote beach in the Masoala National Park, marvelled over a bright red giraffe-necked weevil, peered at ornate tombs and travelled by small plane, *taxi-brousse* and pousse-pousse. This time Air Madagascar's month-long strike meant travelling by pot-holed road and seeing much more of the country at ground level – a bone-rattling blessing in disguise. Find Helen at www.helenranger.com and on Twitter @helenranger.

Published by Lonely Planet Publications Pty Ltd
ABN 36 005 607 983
8th edition – June 2016
ISBN 978 1 74220 778 0
© Lonely Planet 2016 Photographs © as indicated 2016
10 9 8 7 6 5 4 3 2 1
Printed in China